THE CONTINUING CITY

I. *Jerusalem*, copy E, plate *28*

THE CONTINUING CITY

William Blake's *Jerusalem*

MORTON D. PALEY

CLARENDON PRESS · OXFORD
1983

Oxford University Press, Walton Street, Oxford OX2 6DP
London Glasgow New York Toronto
Delhi Bombay Calcutta Madras Karachi
Kuala Lumpur Singapore Hong Kong Tokyo
Nairobi Dar es Salaam Cape Town
Melbourne Auckland
and associated companies in
Beirut Berlin Ibadan Mexico City Nicosia

Oxford is a trade mark of Oxford University Press

Published in the United States by
Oxford University Press, New York

British Library Cataloguing in Publication Data
Paley, Morton D.
The continuing city.
1. Blake, William, 1757–1827. Jerusalem
I. Title
821'.7 PR4144.J/
ISBN 0-19-812803-7

Library of Congress Cataloging in Publication Data
Paley, Morton D.
The continuing city.
Includes index.
1. Blake, William, 1757–1827. Jerusalem. I. Title.
PR4144.J43P34 1983 821'.7 83-3940
ISBN 0-19-812803-7

Typeset by Joshua Associates, Oxford
Printed in Great Britain
at the University Press, Oxford
by Eric Buckley
Printer to the University

In Memory of
Lionel Trilling

'Dear Reader, forgive what you do not approve'

Prefatory Note

In writing this book, I have benefited from the assistance of fellow scholars whose friendship and generosity have helped to sustain me through years of research, composition, and revision. Drafts of chapters were read and criticized by David Bindman, Morris Eaves, Robert N. Essick, Suzanne R. Hoover, Tim Hoyer, Bo Ossian Lindberg, Josephine Miles, and Alicia Ostriker. To their suggestions I owe far more than I can adequately acknowledge. Martin Butlin generously answered many questions about Blake's art and allowed me to use proof pages of the *Jerusalem* section of his then-unpublished *catalogue raisonné* (*The Paintings and Drawings of William Blake* [New Haven and London, Yale University Press, 2 vols., 1981]). G. E. Bentley, Jr. kindly offered much-appreciated advice on some bibliographical matters. For information, stimulation, and encouragement I am deeply grateful to Frederic Amory, Anthony Bulloch, Frances Carey, David V. Erdman, Ruth Fine, Northrop Frye, Jean H. Hagstrum, Nelson Hilton, Jenijoy LaBelle, Anne K. Mellor, Patrick Noon, the late Mark Schorer, E. P. Thompson, the late Ruthven Todd, Deirdre Toomey, Aileen Ward, and Robert R. Wark. All these friends 'with whom to be connected is to be blessed' have brought to life for me what is so often a mere expression: the idea of a community of scholars.

Among libraries and museums, I am indebted to the British Library, the British Museum Department of Prints and Drawings, the Bancroft Library, the Beinecke Library, the Bodleian Library, the Cambridge University Library, the University of California Libraries, the Fitzwilliam Museum, the Houghton Library, the Henry E. Huntington Library and Art Gallery, the Library of Congress, the Manchester City Art Galleries, the Metropolitan Museum of Art, the National Gallery of Scotland, the New York Public Library, the Philadelphia Museum of Art, the Pierpont Morgan Library, the Tate Gallery, the Victoria and Albert Museum, the Widener Library, and the Witt Collection (Courtauld Institute of Art).

For their generosity in allowing me to study material in their private collections, I wish to thank Lord Cunliffe, George Goyder, the late Sir Geoffrey Keynes, Mr and Mrs Paul Mellon, the late Kerrison Preston, and the late Lessing J. Rosenwald.

This book could not have been written without the assistance of research fellowships granted by the John Simon Guggenheim Foundation and by the National Endowment for the Humanities. I am also grateful to the University of California and to the Royal Swedish Academy of Sciences for grants in aid of research. The inclusion of two colour plates was made possible by a subvention from the John Simon Guggenheim Foundation; transparencies for these were loaned by Mr Paul Mellon and the Yale Center for British Art.

I have tried to keep to a minimum the repetition of material from my previously published articles, but in a few instances passages ranging from a few sentences to several paragraphs have been included in the present text. In each case, I have referred the reader to the original publication for more extensive treatment of the subject. I am grateful to the original publishers of these articles, as indicated in the appropriate footnote citations, for allowing me to incorporate this limited amount of material. Grateful acknowledgement is also made to the owners of original Blake material reproduced in this book, as indicated in the List of Plates.

MORTON D. PALEY

Berkeley, California
June 1981.

Contents

List of Illustrations xi

A Note on Conventions xiii

INTRODUCTION 1

Chronology 1
Publishing History 7
Critical Interpretation 12

I POETRY 33

Intellectual Verse 33
A True Orator 42
The Sublime and the Pathos 57
Supplementary Note 78

II ART 83

Types and Symbols, or How to Read Blake's Pictures 89
25 99
31/35 104
41/46 107
46/32 111
76 113

III MILLENNIUM 120

History 121
City and Temple 136

IV THE MYTH OF HUMANITY 167

The Sexual Myth 167
The Anterior Myth 172
Jerusalem 178
Jerusalem Surrogates 184

Vala 189
Albion 196
Sons and Daughters 211
Albion Rose 230

V THE PROPHETIC MYTH 234
Los 234
Spectre and Emanation 244
'My Great Task' 261
Urthona 273

VI FORM 278
Critical Views 278
Models 283
The Form of *Jerusalem* 294

Index of Works by William Blake 315

General Index 319

List of Illustrations

MONOCHROME
between pp. 82–3

1. *Jerusalem*, copy F, plate *33/37*
The Pierpont Morgan Library

2. *Jerusalem*, copy F, plate *46/32*
The Pierpont Morgan Library

3. *Jerusalem*, copy F, plate *76*
The Pierpont Morgan Library

4. J. Matham, engraving after Tintoretto. *The Miracle of the Slave* (detail)
British Museum

5. *Jerusalem*, copy F, plate *31/35*
The Pierpont Morgan Library

6. *Biblia Pauperum*. Detail of the creation of Eve
British Museum

7. Hartman Schedel, *Liber Chronicorum* (Nuremberg, 1493, folio 6). Creation of Eve
Henry E. Huntington Library

8. *Jerusalem*, plate *28*. First proof state
The Pierpont Morgan Library

9. *Jerusalem*, plate *28*. Second (intermediate) proof state
The Pierpont Morgan Library

10. *Jerusalem*, copy I (posthumous), plate *28*
Library of Congress

11. *Jerusalem*, copy F, plate *51*
The Pierpont Morgan Library

12. *Jerusalem*, plate *51*. Separate plate
Sir Geoffrey Keynes

13. Pencil drawing related to *Jerusalem*, plate *51*
Hamburger Kunsthalle

14. *Jerusalem*, plate *1*. Proof state
Sir Geoffrey Keynes

15. Anonymous engraving, probably after Mantegna. *The Descent to Hell*
British Museum

16. Marcantonio Raimondi, engraving after an unknown artist. *Vulcan, Venus, and Cupid*
British Museum

17. The *[First] Book of Urizen*, copy G, plate 21
Library of Congress

18. *Jerusalem*, copy F, plate *100*
The Pierpont Morgan Library

COLOUR

I. *Jerusalem*, copy E, plate *28* — *frontispiece*
From the collection of Mr and Mrs Paul Mellon

II. *Jerusalem*, copy E, plate *100* — *facing* Figure 18
From the collection of Mr and Mrs Paul Mellon

HANDWRITING EXAMPLES

I. Comparison of Copperplate Hand with calligraphic script — p. 95
(*FZ* 25: 25: 40–4; *J* 7: 30–4)

II. Comparison of Modified Copperplate Hand with calligraphic script — p. 97
(*FZ* 18: 11–12; *J* *23*: 24–5)

A Note on Conventions

The edition of Blake's poetry and prose used for purposes of citation in this study is (with the exception of the letters) *The Poetry and Prose of William Blake*, ed. David V. Erdman with a Commentary by Harold Bloom (Garden City, NY: Doubleday & Co., 4th printing with revisions, 1970). This edition is cited as E., followed by page numbers where necessary. Illuminated books and the *Four Zoas* manuscript are cited as follows: plate or page number, line number, page reference. *The Four Zoas, Milton*, and *Jerusalem* are sometimes abbreviated as *FZ, M*, and *J*. Thus *M* 41: 1–10, E. 141 would refer to plate 41, lines 1–10 of *Milton*, on page 141 of the Erdman edition. For *Jerusalem* I have italicized the plate numbers. An italicized plate number always refers to *J*. For Chapter II I use the plate numbers of the majority order followed by the plate numbers of the minority order; *33/37*, for example, refers to plate *33* in copies A, C, and F but to plate *37* in copies D and E.

Blake's letters are cited from *The Letters of William Blake*, ed. Geoffrey Keynes (Cambridge, Mass.: Harvard University Press, 2nd edn., 1968), referred to as *Letters*.

The following frequently cited titles are abbreviated:

G. E. Bentley, Jr., *Blake Records* (Oxford: The Clarendon Press, 1969) = *BR*.

David V. Erdman, *The Illuminated Blake* (Garden City, NY: Anchor Press/Doubleday, 1974) = *Ill. Bl.*

Blake Newsletter, afterwards *Blake: an Illustrated Quarterly*, published by the University of New Mexico, Albuquerque, N.M. = *Blake*.

As various editors and bibliographers have employed different systems of foliation for Blake's illuminated books, there is sometimes a problem in making plate references. Fortunately, only ch. 2 of *J* is affected by this. In citing the texts of other illuminated books, I have followed the foliation as given in *Poetry and Prose*; but in referring to designs in these books, I use the plate numbers as given by G. E. Bentley, Jr. in *Blake Books* (Oxford: The Clarendon Press, 1977).

Introduction

It could be said that Blake's entire creative life up to *Jerusalem* was a prelude to that great work. Blake's habit of mind was to synthesize; one senses even in his earliest works the drive towards an inclusive myth. In 1790–3 Blake promised the world 'the Bible of Hell', which he set about producing in the form of the Lambeth books.[1] Then, discontinuing these, he began anew *c.* 1797, working on the manuscript at first called *Vala* and then *The Four Zoas*. Here the major beings of the prophecies of the earlier 1790s, now classified as Zoas and their emanations, were made constituent faculties of the Eternal Man, whom Blake named Albion. *The Four Zoas* could not, however, accommodate the weight of meaning Blake wished to place on it; he abandoned this epic but not before he had started on the material that became *Milton* and *Jerusalem*. Of these three long works, *Jerusalem* has a special status. Unlike *The Four Zoas*, it is a finished illuminated work, consisting of 100 plates arranged in four chapters. It is therefore twice the length of even a conflated copy of *Milton*, which forms a prelude to it.[2] It is, moreover, an encyclopaedic work. At once Blake's *Paradise Lost* and his *Divine Comedy, Jerusalem* presents both the mythic history and the visionary future of mankind, all devolving on the present moment. Of all Blake's works, it makes the highest claims upon its readers and presents the most demanding challenges.

Chronology

Blake etched the date 1804 on his title-page, which may

[1] See *The Marriage of Heaven and Hell*, E. 43. On Blake's several attempts at a unified myth, see my *Energy and the Imagination* (Oxford: The Clarendon Press, 1970).

[2] As Northrop Frye says, '*Milton* describes the attainment by the poet of the vision that Jerusalem expounds in terms of all humanity.' (*Fearful Symmetry*, Princeton: Princeton University Press, 1947, p. 356.) On *Milton* as a prelude poem, see Thomas A. Vogler, *Preludes to Vision* (Berkeley and Los Angeles: University of California Press, 1971), pp. 39–50.

indicate the year in which his idea for *Jerusalem* crystallized.[1] At one point he seems to have envisaged the book as comprising 28 chapters,[2] of which the first was to end at the end of plate 14.[3] Such a gigantic work might indeed have justified Blake's claim to have written more than 'six or seven epic poems as long as Homer'.[4] But as far as we know, *Jerusalem* was never longer than its present 100 plates, and that round number had to be made up by energetic exertion and ingenuity in the end. Blake appears to have worked on the book for at least sixteen years, according to the evidence of watermarks and contemporary records. Progress at first seems to have been rapid. On 6 June 1807 George Cumberland wrote excitedly in his notebook: 'Blake has eng[d] 60 Plates of a new Prophecy!'[5] A few years later Blake evidently felt confident enough to show parts of the work. 'He showed S.[outhey] a perfectly mad poem called Jerusalem', wrote Henry Crabb Robinson in his Diary entry for 24 July 1811. 'Oxford Street is in Jerusalem.'[6] (Evidently Robinson was referring to the magnificent passage about the Gate of Los on plate *38*.) In the following year, Blake exhibited four works at the Water Colour Society, including 'Detached Specimens of an original illuminated Poem, entitled "*Jerusalem, the Emanation of the Giant Albion*" '.[7] *Jerusalem* is not included in the list of works ready for sale which Blake sent to Dawson Turner on 9 June 1818,[8] but Blake may have begun to print Chapter 1 later in that year, and it may have been then that he produced coloured copy B, consisting of twenty-five plates, three of them watermarked 1818.[9] Chapter 2 was finished by the end of the following year, for on 30 December 1819 Blake wrote John Linnell a receipt for 'Fourteen Shillings for Jerusalem

[1] Erdman (p. 727) suggests that it may be the date at which a larger work was divided into the books which became *Milton* and *Jerusalem*.

[2] 'In XXVIII Chapters' was deleted from the title-page according to Erdman, p. 731.

[3] 'End of the / 1st Chap:' was deleted from the bottom of the text of *14*; see Erdman, p. 731; Bentley, I. 445.

[4] Recorded from conversation with Henry Crabb Robinson in 1826; see *BR*, p. 547.

[5] *BR*, p. 187. Although the title is not given by Cumberland, Bentley points out that the only illuminated work by Blake of over 50 plates is *Jerusalem*.

[6] *BR*, p. 229. [7] *BR*, p. 231. [8] *Letters*, p. 139.

[9] See Geoffrey Keynes, 'New Lines from *Jerusalem*', and Bentley, *Blake Studies* (Oxford: The Clarendon Press, 2nd edn., 1971), p. 117; *BB*, p. 226.

Chap 2'.[1] Apparently eighty-eight plates had been etched by 18 August 1820, when Thomas Griffiths Wainewright, writing in *The London Magazine*, puffed Blake's work as '*an eighty-eight pounder*! which he proposeth to fire off in your next'.[2] The complete work had been etched by 24 February 1821, when Linnell's account book recorded the payment of 15*s*. to Blake for 'Balance of Jerusalem'.[3] Finally, writing of *Jerusalem* to George Cumberland on 12 April 1827, Blake says 'One I have Finish'd'[4]—evidently meaning coloured. He was correct in predicting that it was unlikely that he would find a customer for it.[5]

The documentary evidence thus points to rapid progress during the years 1804–7 and much slower or interrupted progress from 1808 to 1821. Both periods can be narrowed somewhat further. When the Blakes returned to London from Felpham at the end of September 1803, they brought with them a large quantity of manuscript material. This included *The Four Zoas* and probably at least parts of *Milton* and *Jerusalem*. Blake was to continue working on the *FZ* manuscript until perhaps 1807,[6] at last abandoning his efforts to finish it. The other manuscript material is referred to in rather similar terms in 1803 and in 1809. The first of these references is in Blake's letter to Thomas Butts dated 25 April 1803.

> But none can know the Spiritual Acts of my three years' Slumber on the banks of the Ocean, unless he has seen them in the Spirit, or unless he should read My long Poem descriptive of those Acts; for I have in these three years composed an immense number of verses on One Grand Theme, Similar to Homer's Iliad or Milton's Paradise Lost, the Persons & Machinery intirely new to the Inhabitants of Earth (Some of the Persons Excepted).[7]

This Grand Poem must be *Milton* or the hypothetical ur-*Milton* of '12 Books' originally referred to on the *M* title-page,[8] but a close link with *Jerusalem* as well is indicated in

[1] *BR*, p. 581. [2] *BR*, pp. 265–6. [3] *BR*, p. 585.

[4] *Letters*, p. 163. Blake implies that he considered the monochrome copies unfinished (which may account for their dirty inking, which would have been largely obscured by colouration).

[5] Copy E passed from Catherine Blake to Frederick Tatham. *BB*, p. 259.

[6] See Bentley, *Writings*, II. 1722–4.

[7] Keynes, *Letters*, p. 67.

[8] Altered to '2 Books' in copies B and D. See *BB*, p. 311.

the very first sentence of the latter: 'After my three years slumber on the banks of the Ocean, I again display my Giant forms to the Public . . .' (E. 143). This long poem is again described as unpublished in Blake's letter to Thomas Butts dated 6 July 1803: 'Thus I hope that all our three years' trouble Ends in Good Luck at last . . . to speak to future generations by a Sublime Allegory, which is now perfectly completed into a Grand Poem. . . . This Poem shall, by Divine Assistance be progressively Printed & Ornamented with Prints & given to the Public.'[1] An unpublished poem is described in Blake's *Descriptive Catalogue* of 1809, but this time its tenor seems more like that of *Jerusalem*:

> How he [the fourfold man] became divided is a subject of great sublimity and pathos. The Artist has written it under inspiration, and will, if God please, publish it; it is voluminous, and contains the ancient history of Britain, and the world of Satan and of Adam.[2]

On the other hand, it once more seems to be *Milton* to which Blake refers in his *Public Address* of 1810: 'The manner in which I have routed out the nest of villains will be seen in a Poem concerning my Three years ⟨Herculean⟩ Labours at Felpham which I will soon publish.'[3] The 'nest of villains' refers to 'Hand', the monster which Blake introduced into *Milton* (19: 58 and 23: 15) after the attacks upon him by *The Examiner*, whose editorial siglum, representing the three brothers Hunt, was a pointing hand.[4] (Hand figures more prominently in *Jerusalem*, but that work cannot properly be said to concern Blake's Herculean labours, at Felpham, as *Milton* can.) The evidence seems to indicate that Blake divided his manuscript material, separating *Milton* and *Jerusalem*, in 1804; that he continued to add to and to etch plates for both until 1810, when he completed the first two copies of *Milton* and printed them.[5] The periods of most intense activity on these projects were probably from mid-January 1804 to September 1805, and again from February 1806 to the summer of 1807. We may imagine that work on

[1] *Letters*, p. 69. [2] E. 533–4. [3] E. 561.

[4] See David V. Erdman, 'Blake's "Nest of Villains" ', *Keats–Shelley Journal*, II (1953), 60–1.

[5] As copies A, B, and C exhibit no watermarks other than 1808, they could have been issued as early as that year, which is indeed Bentley's view (*BB*, p. 308).

the illustrations to Blair's *Grave*, resulting in the production of at least twenty water-colours and one white-line etching from September 1805 to January 1806,[1] would have taken up most of his energies during those five months. Cumberland's journal entry marks the end of the second part of this very fertile period. After that, the building of *Jerusalem* went on at a slower pace.

In December 1808, Blake, replying to George Cumberland's enquiry on the behalf of a possible buyer of illuminated books, wrote:

> I . . . should immediately Engage in reviving[2] my former pursuits of printing . . . if I had not now so long been turned out of the old channel into a new one, that it is impossible for me to return to it without destroying my present course.[3]

What had turned Blake out of his old channel? He informs Cumberland that 'my time . . . in future must alone be devoted to Designing & Painting . . .'.[4] He had been producing Bible pictures for Thomas Butts, but this kind of activity seems to have peacefully coexisted with his work on illuminated books at other times. By the end of 1808 Blake was preparing for his ill-fated exhibition, and his energies had probably been directed towards that end for many months. In the few years preceding the exhibition of 1809–10 Blake produced some of his greatest and most ambitious pictures: *The spiritual form of Nelson* (*c.*1805–9), *The spiritual form of Pitt* (*c.*1805–9), *The Fall of Man* (1807), the Petworth *Last Judgment* (1808), and *Sir Geoffrey Chaucer and the nine and twenty Pilgrims* (1808), among others. When we consider that Blake was also producing major works unrelated to his exhibition at this period, including the two sets of water-colours illustrating *Paradise Lost* (one *c.*1807 and the other 1808), we can see why he had little time for his former pursuits of printing. But

[1] See Robert N. Essick and Morton D. Paley, *Robert Blair's* The Grave *Illustrated by William Blake* (London: the Scolar Press, 1982).

[2] Keynes (p. 134) reads 'revising' here and Bentley 'reviewing' (*BR*, p. 212 and *Writings*, II. 1644), but the context seems to demand 'reviving' as in E. 706.

[3] *Letters*, p. 134. Had Blake had a copy of *Milton* ready for sale in December 1808, it seems unlikely that he would have fobbed off Cumberland and his prospective buyer.

[4] Ibid.

he did not intend to abandon them—as we have seen, Blake expressed the hope of publishing his inspired poem. After the failure of his exhibition and the dashing of his hopes of attracting new buyers and new commissions, Blake returned to his illuminated books.

He chose to print *Milton* first because, we may infer, it was written or virtually so by 1810. *Jerusalem* may then have begun to assume the dimensions of a valedictory work. In other words, Blake may initially have conceived *Jerusalem* as only one of a number of longer illuminated books—longer, that is, than any of the Lambeth books—which he would produce, starting with what became *Milton*, in the years after his return to London. It may, then, have been only in the years following 1807 that he decided to make *Jerusalem* unique in scope and breadth among his illuminated books. From, we assume, 1810 to perhaps 1818 or even 1821 Blake added forty plates, if we accept Cumberland's figure of sixty plates in 1807; this corresponds closely to Bentley's conclusion on bibliographical evidence 'that some thirty-seven plates were etched later than their immediate neighbours'.[1] In the circumstances of his life from 1810 to 1818, years which Gilchrist rightly termed 'Years of Deepening Neglect',[2] it must have been difficult for Blake to soldier on with a work which no one might ever buy or even read. Yet he did; Cumberland's son George reported on 21 April 1815 'his time is now intirely taken up with Etching & Engraving'.[3] At one point, though, Blake appears to have lost heart and literally attacked the copperplate (*3*) of his address 'To the Public', gouging out words expressing confidence in his relationship to his reader. Thanks to the editorial labours of Geoffrey Keynes and of David V. Erdman,[4] we can now read some of the deleted passages. Blake had confidently etched 'My former Giants & Fairies have reciev'd the highest reward possible: the love and

[1] *BB*, p. 228.

[2] This is Gilchrist's title for his Chapter XXVII, covering 'the half-dozen years of Blake's life succeeding the exhibition in Broad Street' (*Life of William Blake*, ed. Ruthven Todd, London and New York: J. M. Dent and E. P. Dutton, rev. edn., 1945, pp. 256, 258).

[3] *BR*, pp. 235–6. Young Cumberland appears not to realize that the fact that the Blakes were 'durtyer than ever' was a result of their work.

[4] As recorded in their respective editions and in Erdman, 'The Suppressed and Altered Passages in Blake's *Jerusalem*', *Studies in Bibliography*, XVII (1964), 1–54.

friendship of those with whom to be connected, is to be blessed'—but he deleted the words 'love', 'friendship', and 'blessed'.[1] Among the other deletions on this page are Blake's expression of confidence that the reader will not think him presumptuous or arrogant (E 144): 'Therefore Dear Reader, forgive what you do not approve, & love me for this energetic exertion of my talent' was emended so as to omit the words 'Dear', 'forgive', and 'love'. And in the first line of verse on this page, 'Reader! lover of books! lover of heaven', the word 'lover' was removed both times. It is a touching fact that when he came to complete *Jerusalem*, Blake did not restore the words he had destroyed, although the lines could have been mended with a few strokes of the pen in each copy. Evidently he wished his retraction to stand, and some words have been irretrievably lost.

Blake's relationship with John Linnell appears to be the factor that enabled him to complete *Jerusalem*, or that spurred him on to conclude the work and print it. Blake had met Linnell, 'who [as Gilchrist puts it] was to become the kindest friend and stay of the neglected man's declining years',[2] by June 1818.[3] The only dated watermarks in copy B of *Jerusalem* are 1818, and 1818 watermarks are among those that occur in copies A and C as well. Copy C was issued in parts and bought by Linnell himself; copy A was later sold through Linnell to William Young Ottley. Once moved to finish his greatest illuminated work, Blake worked comparatively swiftly, producing one finished copy, four monochrome copies, and one coloured copy of Chapter 1 between 1818 and his death in 1827.

Publishing History

Jerusalem is the rarest finished masterpiece of the Romantic era. In Blake's own terms, only one copy was ever 'finished': copy E, which, wrote Allan Cunningham in 1830, 'he wrought incessantly upon . . . tinting and adorning it, with the hope

[1] These three restorations are common to the editions of Erdman (p. 144) and of Bentley (p. 419), but Bentley expresses reservations toward some of the further restorations (which are, however, accepted by Keynes, *Complete Writings*, pp. 620–1); see *Writings*, pp. 419–20 and notes.

[2] *Life*, p. 258.

[3] See *BR*, p. 256.

that his favorite would find a purchaser'.[1] The others are either incomplete (coloured copy B, comprising 25 coloured plates) or uncoloured (copies A, C, D, and F). These 5¼ original copies have been described in bibliographical detail elsewhere,[2] and the descriptions need not be repeated here. There are also a considerable number of separate plates of *J*. Some of these are manifestly trial proofs, a number of which are printed on the versos of pages of early illuminated books. At least three bear an 1802 watermark,[3] and while it is unlikely that they were printed in that year, the watermark does suggest that plates *28, 45*, and *56* may belong to a relatively early phase of composition. Others are clearly not trial proofs at all, but separate works intended for exhibition and sale. Among these are the beautiful examples of designs, mostly without text—plates *25, 46/32, 37/41*, and *47*—which may have been among those 'Detached Specimens' that Blake exhibited in 1812.[4] At least two separate leaves must have been printed by Tatham, as their 1831 watermarks testify. If we exclude these and assume that the remaining proofs were published by Blake, we have a total of 39 examples from 30 plates. Interestingly, we know of only 8 examples from 8 plates of Chapters 3 and 4, which suggests that Blake was working at greater speed when he printed the pages of the second half of the book.

After Blake's death at least three more copies of *Jerusalem* were printed by Frederick Tatham from the original plates: H (Fitzwilliam Museum), I (Library of Congress), and J (Yale).[5] These copies are on the whole well printed; while some pages have been inked more lightly than they ought to be, many others are more clearly inked than Blake's originals. Although they lack independent authority, the posthumous

[1] *BR*, p. 501, from *Lives of the Most Eminent British Painters, Sculptors and Architects*.

[2] See *BB*, pp. 224–60; notes to *Writings*, II. 416–641. The most detailed account of visual variants is that of *Ill. Bl.*, pp. 283–379.

[3] In the Pierpont Morgan Library. For these and other details, see the table in *BB*, pp. 226–7.

[4] In addition there are, as noted by Bentley (*BB*, p. 229 n. 3), six other coloured pages which might also have been shown. It should be noted that Bentley's foliation of *Jerusalem* follows the minority order for Chapter 2.

[5] The supposed copy G, which once belonged to Felix Isman of New York, is untraced.

copies are invaluable in one respect: the etched pages bear no additions in indian ink or water-colour, so that here we may see what was actually on the copperplate and no more. Certain details can thus be seen to have been added by pen or brush after printing, while others emerge more clearly. For example, in plate 99, the small object in the right hand of the father figure[1] can be seen most distinctly in the posthumous copies. On the other hand, the face of the dove-like creature in *24* is featureless in the posthumous copies; the features that appear in copies B and E were an afterthought. In such details the posthumous copies help us to understand both Blake's intentions and his methods. The copperplates themselves are not known to have survived, and so all subsequent editions of *Jerusalem* as a whole have depended on reproductive processes.

One of the best facsimiles of *Jerusalem* ever produced was also the first: John Pearson's photolithographic reproduction of copy D. The original was purchased from Pearson by the Boston collector E. W. Hooper, who then found fault with the facsimile on rather curious grounds. In a handwritten note now included with the Harvard copy, Hooper wrote: 'In the reproduction the process has made the length of the printed page greater in proportion to the width than in the original, and all the half tints are lost (which is a great injury to the artistic effect) but the reproduction is valuable in giving a good idea of the nature of the book.' However, measurement shows the Pearson pages to be exactly the same size as Blake's originals, each varying as the other does from a norm of approximately 12.5 × 23.5 cm. And 'tints' is not an appropriate word for the black indian ink work in copy D. Pearson's reproduction is still valuable today; the same is not true of the next facsimile of *Jerusalem*: that in *The Works of William Blake, Poetic, Symbolic, and Critical*, ed. E. J. Ellis and W. B. Yeats (London: Bernard Quaritch, 1893). All that can be said in favour of this botched hand-drawn lithographic reproduction is that the editors recognized the need to present

[1] In 'A Book To Eat', *Blake*, XV (1982), 170–5, David V. Erdman suggests that this object is the book which John is commanded by the Lord to eat in Revelation 10, following Ezekiel 2 and 3. Observers tend to disagree as to whether this object can be seen in Blake's original copies—it is suggested most clearly in A and C.

Blake's works in the form in which they were originally produced, although they did not know how to achieve the desired result. More than half a century passed before the next facsimile reproduction—the magnificent colour facsimile of copy E sponsored by the William Blake Trust (London, 1951),[1] produced by painting in water-colours through stencils over a collotype outline base. This was followed by the Blake Trust's heliogravure facsimile of copy C (London, 1952)[2] and then by its superb colour facsimile of the 25-plate copy B (London, 1974), produced by the same processes as the copy E facsimile. Copies A and F have never been reproduced in their entirety.

The rest of the publishing history of *Jerusalem* concerns editions printed from set type. *Jerusalem* has been edited six times from Blake's original text. It was first published in a scrupulously edited form by E. R. D. Maclagen and A. G. B. Russell in 1904.[3] A much less accurate text appeared in Edwin J. Ellis's *The Poetical Works of William Blake*[4] two years later. In 1925 Geoffrey Keynes published his monumental *The Writings of William Blake*, the text of which was the basis for his subsequent *The Complete Writings of William Blake.*[5] Keynes's edition of *Jerusalem* is probably the one known to most readers and retains considerable importance. Yet another independently executed edition, by D. J. Sloss and J. P. R. Wallis, appeared in 1925:[6] *The Prophetic Writings of William Blake* contained more elaborate and extensive

[1] Published for the Blake Trust by the Trianon Press (Paris), this book as well as the Blake Trust's other productions was produced by the late Arnold Fawcus, to whom all lovers of Blake are permanently indebted.

[2] Also published by the Beechurst Press, New York, 1955. A collotype reproduction of the unique proof of plate 1 is included. This facsimile is accompanied by a letterpress text based on that of Maclagen and Russell (see below) but 'again edited from the original' by Geoffrey Keynes. See Keynes's 'Foreword', n.p.

[3] London: A. H. Bullen.

[4] London: Chatto and Windus, 2 vols., 1906. According to Keynes, 'The text contains most of the same inaccuracies as EY [Ellis & Yeats].' See *Bibliography of William Blake* (New York: Grolier Club, 1921), pp. 282–3.

[5] London: The Nonesuch Press, 3 vols. This was the first text to print all the (then known) variant readings. It has been followed by a series of revised editions (see *BB*, pp. 495, 502), the most recent of which is *The Complete Writings of William Blake* (London: Oxford University Press, 1972).

[6] Oxford: The Clarendon Press, 2 vols. Vol. II is mostly devoted to critical and interpretive discussion of Blake's writings, in the form of an introduction and an index of symbols.

bibliographical apparatus (as well as critical and interpretive material) for *Jerusalem* than had hitherto been produced. Thus in a period of twenty-two years, four entirely independent texts of *Jerusalem* were published, three of which were of very high quality. All three supply editorial punctuation.

The case for editorial punctuation was put succinctly by Maclagen and Russell:

> Much as we had desired to retain Blake's original punctuation unaltered, we have found it impossible to do so; for not only is it extremely unusual and inconsistent, but in the engraved pages it is very often impossible to distinguish the stops from one another and from the small smears and dots which have accidentally appeared on the page, or form part of the marginal decoration. While, therefore, the punctuation of the present edition represents that of the original (where it can be definitely ascertained) in the majority of cases, we have felt it necessary to make frequent alterations: these mainly consist in supplying stops at the ends of the lines, in modifying semi-colons and other stops in commas, and in inserting commas for clearness' sake.[1]

If one accepts their assumptions, one must conclude that Maclagen and Russell had no alternative but to supply editorial punctuation, and this would apply also to Keynes and to Sloss and Wallis. However, an alternative possibility would be to treat *Jerusalem* as a first edition rather than as a manuscript and to render the text as Blake etched it, or at least to provide as close an approximation as possible. One could also argue that the reader willing to face the difficulty of understanding *Jerusalem* might also welcome the problem of construing Blake's sentences. This opportunity was at last afforded in 1965 with the publication of *The Poetry and Prose of William Blake,*[2] edited by David V. Erdman. Erdman's edition, an outgrowth of work on the great Blake *Concordance,*[3] provides only occasional inserted punctuation, observing for the most part Blake's idiosyncrasies of pointing, and includes valuable textual notes. The most recent edition of *Jerusalem*

[1] p. 122.

[2] With a commentary by Harold Bloom. Garden City, New York: Doubleday & Co., 1965. The most recent revision is that of 1970 but a new revised and enlarged edition has been announced for 1982.

[3] *A Concordance to the Writings of William Blake*, ed. David V. Erdman with Thiesmeyer and Richard J. Wolfe, *et al.* (Ithaca, NY: Cornell University Press, 1967), 2 vols. The *Concordance* is cued to the one-volume Keynes edition.

provides both alternatives. In *William Blake's Writings*, edited by G. E. Bentley, Jr.,[1] editorial punctuation is rendered in square brackets, making the user aware of both Blake's original punctuation and the editorial construction given to it. Other books in which *Jerusalem* is available are based upon previously edited versions.[2]

The question of whether or not *Jerusalem* ought to be punctuated in a reading text is complex; strong arguments can be marshalled for either view, as well as for a composite of both. For the purposes of this study, however, it is appropriate to render Blake's text as closely as possible to the manner in which he presented it.[3] I have chosen to use the Erdman *Poetry and Prose* while paying due attention to any significant differences in the rendering of passages cited between this work and the Bentley *Writings*.

Critical Interpretation

Jerusalem received no critical notices during Blake's lifetime, and very few between his death and the publication of Gilchrist's *Life* in 1863.[4] In John Thomas Smith's sympathetic and interesting account of Blake, published in 1828, two passages of four lines each are quoted with approval 'as a convincing proof of how highly he reverenced the Almighty'.[5]

[1] Oxford: The Clarendon Press, 1978. 2 vols.

[2] Three deserve mention here for their annotation: *Jerusalem, Selected Poems, and Prose*, ed. Hazard Adams (New York: Holt, Rinehart, and Winston, 1970); *The Poems of William Blake*, ed. W. H. Stevenson (London: Longman/New York: Norton, 1971); and *William Blake/The Complete Poems*, ed. Alicia Ostriker (Harmondsworth, Middlesex: Penguin, 1977). Stevenson and Ostriker use the Erdman text as a base, Stevenson with editorial punctuation added throughout, Ostriker without editorial punctuation but with some differences in the interpretation of Blake's own punctuation. Adams states (p. xx) that he has 'chosen to punctuate Blake anew and to modernize, in most cases the spelling'; the edition used as a basis for the text is not, however, specified.

[3] As Ostriker puts it: 'As a rule, any punctuation mark may be taken simply as a sign for a greater or lesser *pause* in the flow of language, rather than as an indicator of grammatical relationships. . . . It may create a sense of freedom and buoyancy, and an openness of syntactic construction, which brings considerable aesthetic and intellectual pleasure.' (*Complete Poems*, p. 8.)

[4] On Blake's reputation during this period, see Suzanne R. Hoover, 'William Blake in the Wilderness: A Closer Look at His Reputation, 1827–1863', *William Blake: Essays in Honour of Sir Geoffrey Keynes*, ed. Morton D. Paley and Michael Phillips (Oxford: The Clarendon Press, 1973), pp. 310–48.

[5] *BR*, p. 458, from *Nollekens and His Times*, vol. II.

An anonymous writer in the *London University Magazine* in 1830 showed considerable understanding of some central ideas in *Jerusalem*—without, however, naming the work. The writer, who may have been Blake's Swedenborgian friend, Charles Augustus Tulk, asserted—surprisingly for the year 1830—that 'The figures surrounding and enclosing the poems, produce fresh delight', and he urged the reader to try to understand Blake's genius rather than dismiss him as a madman.

For instance, Albion, with which the world is very little acquainted, seems the embodying of Blake's ideas on the present state of England; he viewed it, not with the eyes of ordinary men, but contemplated it rather as a province of one grand man, in which diseases and crimes are continually engendered, and on this account he poured forth his poetical effusions somewhat in the style of Novalis, mourning over the crimes and errors of his dear country: and it is more extraordinary still that, like Novalis, he contemplated the natural world as the mere outbirth of the thought, and lived and existed in that world for which we are created. Horrid forms and visions pervade this Albion, for they were the only representatives, in his opinion, of the present state of mankind. No great genius wrote without having a plan, and so in this, a light is frequently thrown across the pictures, which partly discover the interior design of the Poet.[1]

The author does not, however, reveal what the plan of the work or the interior design of the poet are more specifically; the essay remains remarkable for its time in arguing that there is any plan at all.

The view of Allan Cunningham is more typical of this period: *Jerusalem* is 'an extensive and strange work', 'extravagantly wild', the meaning of its one hundred designs 'unexplained'.[2] Cunningham's remarks reflect the puzzlement that *Jerusalem* produced in an uninitiated reader—and in 1830 there were few initiated readers.

[1] *BR*, p. 383. Tulk's authorship was originally suggested in 1949 by Geoffrey Keynes; see 'Blake with Lamb and His Circle', *Blake Studies*, 2nd edn., p. 84. See also Deborah Dorfman, *Blake in the Nineteenth Century: His Reputation As a Poet from Gilchrist to Yeats* (New Haven: Yale University Press, 1969), pp. 42–3. On Tulk, see Ray H. Deck, Jr., 'New Light on C. A. Tulk, Blake's Nineteenth-Century Patron', *Studies in Romanticism*, XVI (1977), 217–36.

[2] *BR*, pp. 489–90, from *Lives of the Most Eminent British Painters, Sculptors, and Architects.*

It seems [writes Cunningham] of a religious, political, and spiritual kind, and wanders from hell to heaven, and from heaven to earth; now glancing into the distractions of our own days, and then making a transition to the antediluvians. The crowning defect is obscurity; meaning seems now and then about to dawn; you turn plate after plate, and read motto after motto, in the hope of escaping from darkness into light. But the first might as well be looked at last; the whole seems a riddle which no ingenuity can solve.[1]

Cunningham's actual critical method, though he does not say as much, is to divide Blake's works into those he thinks are simple (the *Songs, The Gates of Paradise, Job*) and those he knows are complex (*Urizen, Europe, America, Jerusalem*). He praises the first group and dismisses the second, explaining that Blake suffered from 'an overflow of imagination'.[2] Yet he does reserve some praise for the designs. 'If the work be looked at for form and effect rather than for meaning, many figures may be pronounced worthy of Michael Angelo.'[3] In this way Cunningham anticipates later nineteenth-century critics who could not follow the meaning of *Jerusalem* but who could appreciate its pictorial beauty.

Frederick Tatham's *Life of Blake* was not published until 1906[4] but was completed in manuscript in 1832. Apparently intended to help Tatham sell the Blake works, including copy E of *Jerusalem*, in his possession, Tatham's biography contains some astute remarks. Of Blake's Albion, Tatham writes:

He recounted his deeds, he exhausted the Incidents of his History & when he had accomplished this 'he then imagined new.' He made him a spiritual Essence—representing the Country of Brittain under this one personification he has made him the Hero of nearly all his Works—He has connected Albion with Jerusalem & Jerusalem with other mysterious Images of his own fancy, in such a manner, as will be difficult to unravel, but not entirely impossible, it is imagined, after reading the remainder of his writings, which will absorb time and pains.[5]

Thus Tatham affirmed the possibility of understanding *Jerusalem*, although, like the author of the 1830 review, he gave no advice on how to do so. Presumably, as a companion of

[1] *BR*, p. 490. [2] *BR*, p. 503. [3] *BR*, p. 490.

[4] The manuscript has remained with copy E, now in the collection of Mr and Mrs Paul Mellon. A printed text was first included in *The Letters of William Blake*, ed. A. G. B. Russell (London, 1906); my text is that of *BR*, pp. 507–35.

[5] *BR*, p. 513.

Blake's during Blake's old age, Tatham may have had access to information about the symbolism of the work that was denied the common reader, but no indication of such understanding appears in the *Life*. Instead, while defending Blake's intelligibility in *Jerusalem*, Tatham leaves the door open for an alternative possibility: that the work may be appreciated for the sublimity of its designs alone.

Again in reference to the authenticity of Blakes Visions, let any one contemplate the designs in this Book; are they not only new in their method & manner; but actually new in their class & origin. Do they look like the localities of common circumstances, or of lower Worlds? The combinations are chimerical, the forms unusual, the Inventions abstract, the poem not only abstruse but absolutely according to common rules of criticism as near ridiculous, as it is completely heterogeneous. With all that is incomprehensible in the poem, with all that might by some be termed ridiculous in the plan, the designs are possessed of some of the most sublime Ideas, some of the most lofty thoughts, some of the most noble conceptions possible to the mind of man. You may doubt however the means, & you may criticise the peculiarity of the notions, but you cannot but admire nay 'wonder at with great admiration' these Expressive, these sublime, these awful diagrams of an Etherial Phantasy. Michael Angelo, Julio Romano or any other great man never surpassed Plates 25, 35, 37, 46, 51, 76, 94, and many of the stupendous & awful scenes with which this laborious Work is so thickly ornamented.

'Visions of glory spare my aching sight
Ye unborn ages crowd not on my Soul.'

Even supposing the poetry to be the mere Vehicle or a mere alloy for the sake of producing or combining these wonderful thoughts it should at all events be looked upon with some respect.[1]

Tatham in effect reaches the same conclusion as the more negative Cunningham. Cunningham regards the text as unintelligible, but suggests that the designs may be appreciated for their visual effect alone. Tatham, while regarding the poem as accessible to those who trouble to work out its meaning, sees *Jerusalem* as being capable of being appreciated for the pictures alone. Since neither Cunningham nor Tatham ventures any interpretation of the designs, their critical standpoint is the same although they start from different premisses

[1] *BR*, p. 520. The quotation has not been identified.

—an effect that was to be reinforced by Blake's greatest nineteenth-century defence.

In subtitling his great *Life of William Blake*, *'Pictor Ignotus'*,[1] Alexander Gilchrist indicated one aspect of his view of Blake. Although Gilchrist tried to do justice to Blake as both poet and painter, he appreciated the latter far more than the former, at least as far as Blake's most ambitious works are concerned. Gilchrist died with the section on *Jerusalem* unwritten, even though it comes not near the end of the *Life* but (owing to an excessively literal interpretation of the title-page date of 1804) shortly after the mid-point. Part of this section was written by Dante Gabriel Rossetti;[2] some may have been written by Anne Gilchrist.[3] The fundamental incoherence of the poetry is assumed—'dark oracles, words empty of meaning to all but him who uttered them'.[4] 'Such a chaos of words, names, and images, that, as the eye wanders, hopeless and dispirited, up and down the large closely-written pages, the mind cannot choose but busy itself with the question, how a man of Blake's high gifts ever came to produce such; nay, to consider this, as he really did, his greatest work.'[5] Yet the Gilchrist *Life* is not entirely without insight into the larger meaning of the work. *Jerusalem*, we are told, 'is to be regarded as an allegory in which the lapse of the human race from a higher spiritual state, and its return to such, are the

[1] London: Macmillan, 1863. In discussing Gilchrist's *Life* for its historical importance, I cite the first edition. (An expanded edition was published in 1880, without the 'Pictor Ignotus' subtitle.) When reference is made to Gilchrist's *Life* for other reasons, Todd's edition (based on that of 1880) is used.

[2] Rossetti's part is reprinted in his *Collected Works*, ed. William Michael Rossetti (London, 1886), I. 473–7. Presumably he did not write the remainder, which is not printed here, as W. M. Rossetti attests that all his brother's contributions to the Gilchrist *Life* are printed on pp. 433–77 of the *Collected Works* (see notes to vol. I, p. 527).

[3] Dorfman, *Blake in the Nineteenth Century*, implies that Anne Gilchrist wrote the part that Rossetti did not (pp. 69n., 81). Mrs Gilchrist does say that she borrowed copies of illuminated books, including *Jerusalem*, from Monckton Milnes, copying out passages with the aid of William Haines. 'Then', she writes, 25 August 1862, 'there was to write the account of them and to keep the printer going. . . .' This, however, does not quite establish that it was she who wrote the account. In March or early April 1862 she had written to William Michael Rossetti to enlist the Rossettis' help with *Jerusalem*. D. G. Rossetti's contribution was in any event considerably more than the 'short descriptions of the illustrations' mentioned by Dorfman (p. 81). See H. H. Gilchrist, *Anne Gilchrist, Her Life and Writings*, with a Prefatory Notice by William Michael Rossetti (London, 1887), pp. 121–6.

[4] Gilchrist, *Life*, I. 184.

[5] Ibid., 192.

main topics'[1]—certainly a defensible generalization. Some passages are quoted in illustration of Blake's philosophy, and for his time Rossetti is remarkable in declaring, 'For his philosophy *had* cornerstone and foundation, and was not miraculously suspended in the air, as his readers might sometimes feel tempted to believe.'[2]

In discussing the *Jerusalem* designs, Rossetti shows himself to be almost innocent of any knowledge of Blake's iconography, but he describes the images in magnificent Carlylean prose, and his response to the purely visual quality of copy E is very fine indeed.

> It is printed in a warm, reddish brown, the exact colour of a very fine photograph; and the broken blending of the deeper tones with the more tender shadows—all sanded over with a sort of golden mist peculiar to Blake's mode of execution—makes still more striking the resemblance to the then undiscovered 'handling' of Nature herself. The extreme breadth of the forms throughout, when seen through the medium of this colour, shows sometimes, united with its grandeur, a suavity of line which is almost Venetian.[3]

Of course Rossetti knew what Blake thought of the Venetians, and the forceful independence of his observation here is characteristic of the best mode of his criticism. As for the Gilchrist *Life* in general, it contributed no new prejudices to the extant view of Blake, while it dispelled many old ones. The book retains a pungent evocativeness about Blake which no subsequent biography has approached. Yet the effect of its discussion of *Jerusalem* was to consolidate the view that the work was primarily a collection of beautiful, if often incomprehensible, pictures and that the poetry was seldom as beautiful, though as frequently incomprehensible, as the designs. As for overall form, it is sensed but not demonstrated. *Jerusalem* was still in quest of the kind of reader whom Blake had hopefully addressed in 'To the Public'.

Algernon Charles Swinburne might have been expected to be such a reader. Indeed, Swinburne's *William Blake: A Critical Essay*, published in 1868,[4] had the most extensive discussion

[1] Gilchrist, *Life*, I. 185. [2] Ibid., 191. [3] Ibid., 193–4.

[4] London: John Camden Hotten. On the circumstances leading to and surrounding the publication of this book, see my essay, 'John Camden Hotten, A. C. Swinburne, and the Blake Facsimiles of 1868', *Bulletin of the New York Public Library*, LXXIX (1976), 259–96.

of *Jerusalem* to that date—some six thousand words, very little of it quotation. In some ways Swinburne was highly perceptive in his understanding of Blake's ideas, and his critical essay is more daring than the Gilchrist *Life* in its exposition of the work's doctrinal content. Gone is Gilchrist's pious mystic; instead we have Blake the heretic, perhaps a more convincing figure. The possibility that, in theory, *Jerusalem* might be understandable to a future editor is held out—only to be controverted in practice. 'Seriously,' Swinburne writes, 'one cannot imagine that people will ever read through this vast poem with pleasure enough to warrant them in having patience with it.'[1]

Swinburne's difficulty is with Blake's myth. Some of the symbolic figures, including Albion, Jerusalem, and Golgonooza (but not Los and Vala) he understands in part; what he does not understand is the interrelatedness of the figures. He dismisses what he calls 'the external scheme or literal shell of the *Jerusalem*', including in this designation sons and daughters, spectres and emanations, and topographical and numerical symbolism. 'In earnest, the externals of this poem are too incredibly grotesque—the mythologic plan too incomparably tortuous—to be fit for any detailed coherence of remark.'[2] Lacking an apprehension of causality in *Jerusalem*, Swinburne says, 'The main symbols are even of a monotonous consistency; but no accurate sequence of symbolic detail is to be looked for in the doings and sayings of these contending giants and gods.'[3] Yet Swinburne was hardly alone in 1868 in dismissing Blake's myth as arbitrary and meaningless, and he did extend the discussion of the concepts of *Jerusalem* into areas previously unexplored. Only in the matter of the designs, to which he devoted a single paragraph of dithyrambic description, did Swinburne fail to go beyond previous work. Nevertheless, in rejecting Blake's myth as incoherent, Swinburne provided a discouraging example to other readers. Where Swinburne, so often accused of obscurity, feared to tread, who would rush in?

In 1870, just two years after its publication, Edwin John Ellis read Swinburne's *William Blake* and began pondering the

[1] *William Blake*, p. 276.
[2] Ibid., p. 282. [3] Ibid., p. 286.

meaning of Blake's symbolism.[1] Later, discovering a fellow enthusiast in the greatest poet of the age, Ellis began the collaboration with William Butler Yeats that was to result in their three-volume *The Works of William Blake* in 1893, consisting of two volumes of exposition and commentary and one of facsimiles and letterpress text.[2] I have already commented on the poor quality of the facsimile, but the criticism and commentary are another matter. Fortunately, the Yeats–Blake relationship is the subject of an admirable book by Hazard Adams;[3] and so I may confine my discussion to the question of what Ellis and Yeats's work contributed to the understanding of *Jerusalem*. As the section entitled 'The Symbolic System' takes the late symbolism of Blake as the norm for his *œuvre,* I must consider that essay as well as the commentary on *Jerusalem* in volume II. This mass of interpretive material constituted by far the most extensive discussion of *Jerusalem* in the nineteenth century, the commentary alone comprising eighty-four pages, and it also made larger and different claims for our subject than had been made before.

Ellis and Yeats begin by addressing what they see as the two neglected subjects that had kept the critics from understanding Blake: 'First . . . the solidity of the myth and its wonderful coherence. . . . Second . . . the variety of terms in which the sections of it are revealed.'[4] Criticizing Swinburne ('the one-eyed man of the proverb among the blind'), Gilchrist, and William and D. G. Rossetti for ignoring the substance of Blake's myth, Ellis and Yeats set themselves to remedy this omission. Their 'Symbolic System' may too easily be faulted by writers familiar with an ensuing eight decades of scholarship. In particular, Ellis and Yeats overstressed the

[1] See Ellis and Yeats, *The Works of William Blake, Poetic, Symbolic, and Critical*, I. viii–ix.

[2] The manuscript has been discussed in detail by Ian Fletcher, who gives an admirable account of its history and of the circumstances of its production; see 'The Ellis–Yeats–Blake Manuscript Cluster', in *To Geoffrey Keynes: Articles Contributed to the Book Collector to Commemorate His Eighty-Fifth Birthday* (London: The Book Collector, 1972), pp. 90–112. Fletcher distinguishes the contributions of each of the authors in the original drafts, but since the work is presented by both as a collaboration, I refer to it as their joint work.

[3] *Blake and Yeats: The Contrary Vision* (Ithaca, NY: Cornell University Press, 1955).

[4] *Works*, I. viii.

affinity of the 'perennial philosophy' to Blake's thought, as some later writers have also done, and they over-systematized the structure of the symbolism in what at times seems an almost Urizenic spirit. Yet they also correctly stressed the importance of the Swedenborgian and Behmenist traditions to an understanding of the 'System', and if they did not provide a magical key to the wonderful coherence of the myth, they did set goals which subsequent interpreters could attain with the help of their efforts. In a sense the very assumption that the myth was coherent and could be explicated in detail made the work of Damon and Frye possible.

In their approach to *Jerusalem* as a whole, Ellis and Yeats assume that the work has 'the arrangement of a scrap-book', and they even go so far as to reject Blake's order of pages,[1] yet they do see in the four chapters a progression of Creation, Redemption, Judgement, and Regeneration. In their exposition of events in the myth, personifications are taken to represent clear, rationally definable conceptions. The consequences can be seen in their exposition of the sexual myth of plates *20–4*:

> His [Albion's] bodily strength had loved Vala, his heart had held Jerusalem, for the senses love memory as the aspirations love prophecy. His exaltation had even rent the veil which makes of the past a regret, not a possession, and of the future a mystery, not an open experience. . . . Then as Jerusalem—inspired love—leaped from Albion's personal bosom, the divine bosom, also in Albion, the Lamb received her.[2]

Turning Blake's myth into allegory, Ellis and Yeats try to make up for the resulting simplification by providing further meanings. 'The Veil is morality. Rebellion breaks it. It is not permanently destroyed. It mends from this kind of hurt by its own coherence.'[3] This is indeed one aspect of the veil symbol, and Ellis and Yeats even perceive the sexual origin of Albion's conviction of guilt, equating Albion with Adam in this regard. 'Adam's sin was not the nakedness of which he was ashamed, but the following of beauty's act with misguided

[1] *Works*, II. 176, 179. Although Ellis and Yeats knew of the existence of two different paginations of Chapter 2, this only reinforced their discounting of Blake's final numeration.

[2] *Works*, II. 189–90.

[3] *Works*, II. 192.

opinion,—the belief that the state of innocence—an eternal state—was no more. The shame was then his disease, and the beginning of his punishment.'[1] So it is neither prudery nor lack of perception that leads Ellis and Yeats to skirt the essentially sexual meaning of the veil in this myth. It is rather that, despite their frequent use of the word 'symbol', Ellis and Yeats read *Jerusalem* as several allegories held in loose suspension. Their endeavour is in effect to translate Blake's symbols into a series of their own metaphors, for in their use of undefined terms they substitute their figurative language for Blake's. Consequently, their exposition of *Jerusalem* is fragmentary rather than unified, although in their rich and frequently profound study they demonstrate a far more extensive understanding of the work than their predecessors.[2]

During the early years of the twentieth century, D. J. Sloss and J. P. R. Wallis prepared their edition of and commentary on Blake's 'prophetic writings', sending their manuscript to press in 1912. Owing to the intervention of the war, their work was not published until 1926, but it belongs to an earlier epoch of Blake scholarship than that date would otherwise suggest.[3] In addition to their General Introduction and their Index of Symbols, Sloss and Wallis provide a preface to *Jerusalem* and a running commentary in the form of footnotes to the text. They subject *Jerusalem* to a detailed scrutiny, trace the development of central themes and symbols, and point out significant differences between this and Blake's previous works. Their approach is tough-minded and sensible: they put questions to Blake's text (without, however, concerning themselves with the designs), answer them if possible, and frankly declare their inability to solve some of the problems they encounter.

In a way, Sloss and Wallis's approach may show more respect for *Jerusalem* than do the apologies of those who find every line justified. But in the end they fail to engage Blake's great work fully. They dismiss Blake's large claims for it

[1] *Works*, II. 191.

[2] Ellis also includes a commentary on *Jerusalem* in his 1906 *Poetical Works of William Blake*, II. 469–92.

[3] Although Sloss and Wallis refer to Damon's work of 1924 (see below), they do not address the issues raised by Damon and they regard as insoluble dilemmas aspects of *Jerusalem* which Damon explained. See *Prophetic Writings*, I. 442.

outright, remarking of the passage on prosody in the Preface to Chapter 1: 'There is then no evading the fact that Blake not merely acknowledges but claims special merit for just the two features that his readers find least acceptable, the symbolism and the measure.'[1] The content of *Jerusalem* is seen as hopelessly obscure:

The relatively plain expositions of the earlier works are caught up and transformed in a bewildering variety of abstruse forms and combinations. Uncouth mythopoeia and terminology inhibit the native ease essential to poetry, and though there are passages of dramatic force, they are too remote from normal experience and association, and affect us as little more than strange violence and overwrought declamation.[2]

The problem here is not simply one of differing evaluation. Sloss and Wallis no doubt would present *Jerusalem*, on which they expended so much labour, as a masterpiece if they could. It is rather that they ask the wrong questions and so obtain no answers.

Throughout their work, Sloss and Wallis attempt to describe and evaluate Blake's *œuvre* as a vehicle for ideas; and one senses that for them these ideas are virtually textbook definitions of empiricism, idealism, and other philosophical views. Judged according to such presuppositions, *Jerusalem* must be a failure. It is a symbolic work, a vehicle of myth and not of paraphrasable philosophical positions. This does not, of course, mean that it is inaccessible to rational analysis and exposition—the present study would be in vain if it were. But the *kind* of clarity and the kind of consistency that Sloss and Wallis demand of *Jerusalem* are not what it offers. Perhaps not all good structure is in a winding stair, but the structure of *Jerusalem* simply cannot be elucidated by Sloss and Wallis's methods, as we can see again in the discussion of the sexual myth of plates *20–4*. This is one of numerous episodes in *Jerusalem* which Sloss and Wallis declare unintelligible. Saying that 'The mythical incident alluded to here and in p. 23. 5–6 cannot be related to anything else in Blake', Sloss and Wallis hesitantly offer the hypothesis that the veil may relate 'to the "allegorical and mental signification" which when man fell, was perverted into "corporeal command" ',

[1] I. 107. [2] I. 113–14.

and that 'Blake may intend by it an intermediate state between the "golden" and the fallen ages wherein communion with the truth of eternity is mediate, and accompanied by the consciousness of the symbol.'[1] This is ingenious but wrong, and it is not just a matter of being mistaken about one detail; it is the inability or unwillingness to study a literary myth as such. Although in many details Sloss and Wallis's commonsensical reading of *Jerusalem* produced glosses that are correct and helpful, what was still needed at this point was a critical frame of reference that would accommodate Blake's myth.

The modern criticism of Blake began in 1924 with S. Foster Damon's monumental *William Blake: His Philosophy and Symbols*,[2] a book that made even Blake's most difficult works accessible. The paths of Damon and Blake intersected at a propitious time, for the great works published by Yeats, Joyce, and Eliot during the preceding decade[3] had taught sympathetic young critics how to interpret symbolism of great complexity. Damon could call *Jerusalem* 'the obscurest of the three epics'[4] and still regard it as a masterpiece. He could discuss lucidly not only the main themes of the work but also such especially difficult features as its topographical symbolism, the analogy of the tribes of Israel with the counties of Britain and Ireland, the Cathedral Cities, and the identities of the Sons and Daughters of Albion. Some of these are regarded by Damon as defects, but none is considered unintelligible. The work as a whole is seen as grand but not as entirely unified. Damon describes *Jerusalem* as 'Blake's biggest storehouse (we dare not say "vehicle") of thought, decorated with splendid passages of poetry, austere, profound, and proudly beautiful'.[5] Of course much more is to be said on that subject, but as R. P. Blackmur, who

[1] I. 480–1. They add, 'Ethically the veil represents a state of untrammelled pity and love' (481)—which is, of course, even further from its meaning.

[2] Boston: Houghton Mifflin, repr. 1958 (Gloucester, Mass.: Peter Smith). Also indispensable to the study of *Jerusalem* is Damon's copious *A Blake Dictionary*, Providence: Brown University Press, 1965, repr. 1979 (Boulder, Col.: Shambhala Press) with an excellent index by Morris Eaves.

[3] *A Portrait of the Artist as a Young Man* was published in 1916, *Prufrock and Other Observations* in 1917, *The Wild Swans at Coole* (including 'The Phases of the Moon') in 1919, *Ulysses* and *The Waste Land* in 1922.

[4] p. 185.

[5] p. 195.

presents *William Blake* as an exemplary book of criticism, puts it:

> Mr. Damon made Blake exactly what he seemed least to be, perhaps the most intellectually consistent of the greater poets in English. . . . The picture Mr. Damon produced cannot be destroyed, even though later and other scholarship modifies it, re-arranges, or adds to it with different or other facts.[1]

Damon radically alters the understanding of *Jerusalem* in two further ways. First, he does not regard Blake's thought as static, but recognizes that new doctrines and attitudes appear in *Jerusalem*. Among these, he points out the identification of the Father–Creator and the Son–Redeemer, the synthesis of the two Testaments that previously (or at least until *Milton*) had been seen as opposed. He also observes that with the doctrine of Individuals and States as well as the creation of Woman by the Divine Mercy, an optimistic cast is given to Blake's interpretation of the created world—now seen largely as the creation of Los and not of Urizen. 'Blake', says Damon, 'had originally considered Creation as the lowest point of the Fall; now he insists that it is the first step upward from the nadir.'[2] The recognition of this change of perspective is of the greatest importance to an appreciation of *Jerusalem* (and, once more, of *Milton* as well). Damon was also the first to include a commentary on each design as part of his study of *Jerusalem*. By consistently relating the meaning of the designs to the symbolism established in the text, Damon inaugurated what we now take for granted: the study of the work as a manifestation of both arts. In reading the designs, however, as in reading the text, Damon generally finds a single, unambivalent meaning in the symbolic figures, where we might find a greater degree of complexity today.

More than half a century has passed since the first publication of Damon's work and, as one would expect, the considerable advances in our knowledge of Blake since 1924 have made *William Blake* appear dated in some respects. There is one particular way in which Damon's approach to Blake needs

[1] 'A Critic's Job of Work', in *The Double Agent* (New York: Arrow Editions, 1935), pp. 297–8.

[2] p. 194.

to be augmented. Like Ellis and Yeats, Damon reads the events of *Jerusalem* as allegorical. We can see this, for example, in his interpretation of the sexual myth of plates *21–4*.

Man is smitten. Over him Freedom and Nature (Jerusalem and Vala) sorrow, Freedom complaining of Nature's dominion over Man. He in turn accuses them both of polluting Love. In vain Freedom protests. . . . But Man mistakes Pity for Love; he tries to tear away the Veil of Moral Virtue (Vala's Veil); and sinks into the sleep of Beulah, after a last soliloquy of doubt and despair over his miserable shame.[1]

This is not wrong—as the Ellis-Yeats and Sloss-Wallis interpretations of the same passage are wrong—but it does indicate certain limitations in Damon's method. The symbols are taken as allegorical personifications which can be explained by single terms like Nature and Freedom. Jerusalem is indeed Freedom and Vala Nature, but they are more, much more, than that. The specifically sexual nature of Albion's rending of the veil is not perceived by Damon, and, as with Ellis and Yeats, the reason for this cannot be self-censorship, as Damon too recognizes explicitly sexual symbolism elsewhere. As the action is conceived as allegory and not as myth, the critic is obliged to come away with one level of the meaning, and this is true of his approach to the designs as well. Damon's book remains, after nearly six decades, a valuable guide to *Jerusalem*, but one which must be augmented by a reading of the myth as myth.

It was of course Northrop Frye who in *Fearful Symmetry*[2] provided the critical framework by which *Jerusalem*'s myths could be understood. In some ways Frye was anticipated by Milton O. Percival, whose *William Blake's Circle of Destiny*[3] explores Blake's mythology and demonstrates the wonderful coherence that Ellis and Yeats had only asserted. Frye's contribution, however, goes much further, so much so as to pass into general literary discourse as no other study of Blake has done. Frye presents Blake as a central rather than a peripheral figure in English literature, and he defends *Jerusalem* as Blake's supreme achievement. At a time when in an anthology

[1] p. 188.
[2] Princeton: Princeton University Press, 1947.
[3] New York: Columbia University Press, 1938.

of Blake's poetry *Jerusalem* could be called a 'fantastic jumble',[1] Frye writes:

The justification for Blake's kind of dehydrated epic is a simple matter of literary honesty. Poems must take their own forms, and these precipitates of meaning are the forms which poetry takes in Blake's crystallizing mind. An epic of such forms cannot be expanded. . . . The beauty of *Jerusalem* is the beauty of intense concentration, the beauty of the Sutra, of the aphorisms which are the form of so much of the greatest vision, of a figured bass indicating the harmonic progression of ideas too tremendous to be expressed by a single melody.[2]

Practising a kind of dehydrated statement himself, Frye asserts: 'In reading *Jerusalem* there are only two questions to consider: how Blake interpreted the Bible, and how he placed that interpretation in an English context.'[3] This is perhaps true in the sense that Coleridge regarded the Bible as 'The Statesman's Manual', a repository of archetypal situations which are repeated throughout history. Frye's enormous contribution to Blake studies lies partly in his relating of these symbols to one another and partly in relating them to a literary (rather than an occultist) tradition—a tradition that despite its challenges to interpretation is not obscurantist but part of our cultural history.

In his overall approach to *Jerusalem*, Frye, unlike all his predecessors, finds it a unified whole. Details of this and other such views are best considered in discussing the form of *Jerusalem* in Chapter VI; in general, Frye considers the four chapters as structural units, each appropriate to the audience to which it is addressed. So persuasive is Frye's exposition that it risks implying that *Jerusalem* is a seamless garment in which even what appear to be faults are part of an overarching unity.

The motive [writes Frye] that drives Blake on through his gloomy and tormented visions is the same motive that drove Goya through his recording of the disasters of war. In both cases the charge of ugliness is irrelevant, and intensity, honesty, and a grim resolve to portray experience as it is regardless of its horror, and a passionately sincere clairvoyance, are the prophetic qualities involved.[4]

[1] Alfred Kazin, in his Introduction to *The Portable Blake* (New York: Viking, 1946), p. 50.
[2] *Fearful Symmetry*, p. 359.
[3] Ibid., p. 357.
[4] Ibid., p. 356.

The point is well taken as far as 'ugliness' is concerned—one might compare Dante's *rima petrosa* in this respect—and the comparison with Blake's great contemporary is apt. Yet the problem that many readers encounter in *Jerusalem* is not so much an impression of ugliness as one of disjointedness. There is a difference between the coherence of the myth which Frye brilliantly demonstrates and the coherence of the work, which remains to be demonstrated. Also, Frye devotes little attention to the function of the designs or to the generic nature of what is now called 'composite art'. If subsequent critics were to add to Frye's extraordinary accomplishment, these were directions in which they could go.

One further level of *Jerusalem* that remained largely unexplored until 1954 comprises its social, political, and historical content. Indeed, it was often assumed that after Blake's period of sympathy with the French Revolution he lost interest in the broad realm of politics. Such a view was partially corrected by Mark Schorer, whose important book, *William Blake: The Politics of Vision*[1] places Blake in the culture of his own period. Schorer nevertheless believes that although Blake was still concerned with history in *Milton*, in *Jerusalem* he 'freed his system of direct temporal associations'.[2] However, the assumption that Schorer makes about Blake so productively for the rest of his book can be made for *Jerusalem* as well: 'He was a visionary poet deeply immersed in radical religious and political movements of the eighteenth century, aware of and keenly interested in the major currents of opinion of his time.'[3] That this was true of Blake in the nineteenth century as well is persuasively argued by David V. Erdman in a paper presented to the English Institute in 1950: '*Jerusalem* deals with the latter phase of the Napoleonic wars. . . . The poem's central prophetic theme is a plea to Albion and his Sons not to pursue the war with France to mutual ruin or to make a vengeful peace that would destroy the freedom and natural brotherhood of the two nations.'[4] Erdman's *Blake: Prophet Against Empire*,

[1] New York: Henry Holt and Co., 1946; repr. 1959 (New York: Vintage Books).

[2] 1959, p. 312.

[3] Ibid., p. vii.

[4] 'Blake: The Historical Approach', in *English Institute Essays 1950*, ed. Alan S. Downer (New York: Columbia University Press, 1951), p. 220.

subtitled *A Poet's Interpretation of the History of His Own Times,*[1] supports that thesis in rich detail. Not only the Napoleonic wars, but also domestic repression in Britain, the relations of England and Ireland, and even insurrection in Mexico, are here shown to be part of the fabric of Blake's grand poem. Although his beliefs were not entirely the same as those of the period of *America* and *Europe*, Blake is now understood to be as concerned with human events in *Jerusalem* as he was earlier, thanks largely to Erdman's work.

The only book-length study of *Jerusalem* to be published prior to *The Continuing City* is *William Blake's Jerusalem* by Joseph Wicksteed.[2] Although this work appeared in 1954, it makes no reference to any Blake scholarship later than Sloss and Wallis. Wicksteed offers many true perceptions about *Jerusalem*; his book is clearly the product of a lifetime of reflection on Blake;[3] yet because so many of Wicksteed's statements are unproven and even unprovable, his book has a curious status. At its best the work of a learned amateur in the highest sense of the word, at its worst it is arbitrary and quirky. No one other than Wicksteed has, to my knowledge, seen a barge entering a dark cavern in plate *11* or has observed Semitic features in the male figure on plate *28.*[4] Highly subjective interpretations like these are common in Wicksteed's discussion of the designs, and the same is true of his textual exegesis. For example, the idea that the important references to Bath on plate *40* can have anything to do with baths Blake may (or may not) have taken at Felpham[5] is in the unprovable category. To say that Wicksteed's study does not meet the standards of modern scholarship may be unfair, as it does not aspire to those standards. Belonging in essence to an earlier epoch in Blake scholarship, *William Blake's Jerusalem* can only be regarded as ancillary to the achievements of Damon, Frye, and Erdman.

[1] Princeton: Princeton University Press, 1954; rev. edn., 1969, 3rd edn., 1977. Subsequent citations are from the 3rd edn.

[2] London: Trianon Press, 1954; New York: Beechurst Press, 1955.

[3] Wicksteed was the author of the highly important *Blake's Vision of the Book of Job* (London and New York: J. M. Dent and E. P. Dutton, 1910) and of *Blake's Innocence and Experience: A Study of the Songs and Manuscripts* (London and Toronto: J. M. Dent & Sons, 1928).

[4] *William Blake's Jerusalem*, 1955, pp. 159, 130.

[5] Ibid., p. 180.

Jerusalem has also been the subject of chapters or sections in a number of more recent books about Blake. In *Blake's Apocalypse*, Harold Bloom disregards the designs as inadequate to the poetry, but gives considerable space to the latter. Regarding *Jerusalem* as 'the only rival to Wordsworth's *The Prelude* as the supreme long poem in English since Milton',[1] Bloom provides a detailed commentary which is heavily indebted to Frye. This approach Bloom has more recently repudiated as 'the received misreading of the earlier Bloom',[2] as yet Bloom has not provided an antithetical reading of *Jerusalem.*[3] Another extensive commentary on *Jerusalem* is that of John Beer, who in *Blake's Visionary Universe*[4] provides a more detailed exegesis than any to date save Wicksteed's. Beer sees *Jerusalem* as presenting problems of interpretation and of continuity but as both understandable and coherent. 'The poem as a whole', he writes, 'depicts struggles and contentions which are . . . part of a larger pattern, the travails of creation to define its true nature.'[5] In addition to these two commentaries should be mentioned those of Hazard Adams, W. H. Stevenson, and Alicia Ostriker, appended to their respective editions of Blake's poetry.[6] Despite many differences concerning details, Bloom, Beer, Adams, Stevenson, and Ostriker display a remarkable degree of agreement in their interpretations. Indeed, the period 1963–77 could be called an age of commentary in the study of *Jerusalem*, thanks to these five, to whom all subsequent critics must be indebted.

Blake's relation to literary and philosophical tradition has been the subject of three studies which give considerable attention to *Jerusalem*. In *The Valley of Vision,*[7] Peter F.

[1] Garden City, New York: Doubleday & Co., 1963, p. 365.

[2] *Poetry and Repression: Revisionism from Blake to Stevens* (New Haven and London: Yale University Press, 1976), p. 46. Of course 'misreading' as employed by Bloom can have an honorific meaning.

[3] The argument of Bloom's 'Blake's *Jerusalem*: The Bard of Sensibility and the Form of Prophecy' does not appear to me incompatible with that of *Blake's Apocalypse*. See Harold Bloom, *The Ringers in the Tower: Studies in Romantic Tradition* (Chicago and London: University of Chicago Press, 1971), pp. 65–80.

[4] Manchester: Manchester University Press, 1969. [5] p. 176.

[6] See p. 12 n. 2. Bloom's commentary appended to the Erdman *Poetry and Prose* is largely identical to that in *Blake's Apocalypse*.

[7] University of Toronto Department of English Studies and Texts, No. 9, 1961.

Fisher provides a philosophical view of Blake that is both lucid and complex. Although Fisher did not live to write his chapter on *Jerusalem*, his book is full of insights about its ideational structure, a structure that he regards as underlying all Blake's *œuvre*.

> Universal history [Fisher writes] becomes the analogy of individual biography, and goes through the same phases until, at last, the metaphorical likeness between the two is recognized as identical, and the separate experiences which form the events of history become one common human experience in the vision of the Giant Albion. Complete knowledge means the identity of the knower and the object of knowledge, and man can know neither history nor the world of objects except as one act of observation on the part of one observer. The epic form of history is still only the mythical representation of the dream of universal humanity expressed as a 'Divine Analogy,' because it can only be reproduced in an image or likeness until the awakening into the realization of a final unity actually takes place.[1]

Fisher's view extends to the philosophical aspects of Blake's 'system' the assumptions of comprehensibility and centrality that Frye so fruitfully made for Blake as a literary figure. A contrasting, esoteric view of Blake is provided by Kathleen Raine, whose *Blake and Tradition*, despite its massive learning, suffers from an over-literal application of supposed occult sources.[2] For example, Miss Raine posits sources in Agrippa or in Fludd for the Eyes of God in *55*: 33–4 but goes on to admit 'discrepancies' and to remark: 'Agrippa, moreover, says nothing about the successive fall of these potencies, which is the significant point of Blake's use of them, and neither does Fludd.'[3] However, what happens to the Eyes in *Jerusalem* is not a 'fall' of 'potencies' in any meaningful sense, and since their names all occur in the Bible,[4] it seems futile to speculate with Miss Raine 'That Blake had some other, unwritten source of cabalistic knowledge.'[5] In my own *Energy and the*

[1] pp. 28–9. In a footnote to 'Divine Analogy', Fisher cites *Jerusalem 85*: 7.

[2] 2 vols., Princeton: Princeton University Press, 1968. See my review in *English Language Notes*, VII (1970), 304–10.

[3] *Blake and Tradition*, II. 212–13.

[4] Lucifer is named in Isaiah; Molech (or Moloch) in I Kings and elsewhere; Elohim, Shaddai, Pahad, and Jehovah in Genesis. The seventh Eye is Jesus, and the Eighth is unnamed. See Damon, *A Blake Dictionary*, s.v.

[5] *Blake and Tradition*, I. 213.

Imagination[1] I have tried to trace the development of Blake's ideas in his work with due regard for his use of traditional sources, but without distorting Blake's relation to tradition. Blake was not a mere versifier of what others had thought but a powerful original thinker who synthesized his reading into a 'System'. How successful I have been in showing this is for the reader to judge, but I shall avoid repeating the content of *Energy and the Imagination* in this book, making reference when appropriate to the earlier one.

The designs of *Jerusalem* have been subjected to a closer scrutiny than ever before by David V. Erdman, whose *The Illuminated Blake*[2] presents a detailed commentary on every plate. These analyses are, as they should be, highly individual: I, for example, do not see any reason to identify the naked marginal figures of plate *36/40* as either Los or Enitharmon or William and Catherine Blake.[3] It would be misdirected, however, to go through *The Illuminated Blake* pointing out disagreements, for the desideratum of such a book cannot be universal agreement. Erdman's fecundity of conception, his cross-referencing of themes from one part of *Jerusalem* to another, and his due regard for variants from one copy to another all make *The Illuminated Blake* a book which must be consulted frequently in any discussion of the *Jerusalem*'s designs. It does not, however, aim at developing an overall view of the work. One such view is presented by Anne K. Mellor in *Blake's Human Form Divine.*[4] Taking as her points of reference Heinrich Wöfflin's conception of closed and open form and the perceptual approaches to art of E. H. Gombrich and of Rudolph Arnheim, Professor Mellor places Blake's use of the human form at the centre of her exposition. 'The visual world of *Jerusalem*', she argues, '. . . is the human form: here the human body creates its own compositional relationships.'[5] Mellor explores these relationships in both the poetry and the designs of *Jerusalem*, and I shall have occasion to refer to her views as well as to those of Erdman and others in relation to specific interpretations.

[1] Oxford: The Clarendon Press, 1970.
[2] Garden City, New York: Anchor Press, 1974; hereafter cited as *Ill. Bl.*
[3] *Ill. Bl.*, p. 315.
[4] Berkeley, Los Angeles, London: University of California Press, 1974.
[5] *Blake's Human Form Divine*, pp. 286–7.

The relationship of the two constituent elements of Blake's illuminated books is the chief concern of *Blake's Composite Art* by W. J. T. Mitchell.[1] In his ambitious chapter on *Jerusalem*, Mitchell advances the discussion of this generic aspect of the work much further than it had gone before, providing stimulating and sometimes provocative readings of texts and designs. Whether or not one agrees with Mitchell about the interpretation of certain designs (which I shall consider in Chapter 2), the importance of his critical stance lies in his fertile assumption that '*Jerusalem* is no longer treated as a quarry for Blakean "philosophy," but is being investigated as a poetic structure whose generic elements are now coming into focus.'[2] At this point we do not need yet another recension of the beliefs of an idealized Blake. *Jerusalem* will always be a difficult work, but it has been made accessible to willing readers; further work on it must, as Mitchell's has done, assimilate the accomplishments of past scholarship without replicating them.

With the growing acceptance of *Jerusalem*'s importance and comprehensibility, there has been a remarkable increase in the number of articles about it published in journals and in collections of essays by various hands. Only a critical bibliography could do justice to these: for my purposes it is best to refer to some of them later, at appropriate points in the discussion. As, even at such points, it is obviously not possible to consider all published views, my principle is to select—whether in agreement or disagreement—strong and interesting interpretations as representative. It may be that a critical edition of *Jerusalem* on the model of the Shakespeare variorum is now in order—but that would be another book.

[1] Princeton: Princeton University Press, 1978.

[2] *Blake's Composite Art*, pp. 38–9.

Chapter I

Poetry

'What Blake hath joined together let no man dare to sunder' might be a good motto for critics if we but had a mode for talking about both poetry and art at the same time. Perhaps such an exposition could only be written on a Möbius strip, whose image of four-dimensionality would be an apt medium for conveying Blake's fourfold structure. However, no such external representation could substitute for the coming-together of Blake's composite art in the reader–viewer's mind. To support Blake's claim to know himself both Poet and Painter, I intend to provide the reader with 'Ideas to build on',[1] ideas about Blake's transformations of tradition in his practice of both arts. And since Blake refers to *Jerusalem* as a Poem,[2] it is with Blake's mature theory and practice of poetry that I begin.

Intellectual Verse

Addressing the Public at the beginning of *Jerusalem*, Blake dismissed 'a Monotonous Cadence like that used by Milton & Shakspeare & all writers of English Blank Verse, derived from the modern bondage of Rhyming'.[3] He proposed instead to unfetter poetry as part of his programme of freeing art and nation.

> I therefore have produced a variety in every line, both of cadences & number of syllables. Every word and every letter is studied and put into its fit place: the terrific numbers are reserved for the terrific parts—the mild & gentle, for the mild & gentle parts, and the prosaic, for inferior parts: all are necessary to each other.[4]

[1] *The Marriage of Heaven and Hell*, E. 35.

[2] *3*, E. 144.

[3] Ibid. As Damon (*William Blake*, p. 435) points out, Blake here alludes to the note on the verse prefaced to *Paradise Lost*. Cf. Milton, *Complete Poems and Major Prose*, ed. Merritt Y. Hughes (New York: Odyssey Press, 1957), p. 210. The relation of Blake's verse to Milton's is discussed below.

[4] *3*, E. 144.

This declaration was dismissed by Blake's earlier critics, even the most avowedly sympathetic ones. According to Gilchrist's *Life*: 'The poem, since poem we are to call it, is mostly written in prose; occasionally in metrical prose; more rarely still it breaks forth into verse.'[1] Swinburne's view is: 'For metrical oratory, the plea that follows against ordinary metre may be allowed to have some effective significance; however futile if applied to purer and more essential poetry.'[2] And Sloss and Wallis describe the pattern of the earlier prophecies as 'unrhymed measures, a seven stressed iambic line with free substitutions', but say 'it soon passes into the avowed lawlessness of the *Milton* and *Jerusalem* verse'.[3] More recent studies by Josephine Miles[4] and by Alicia Ostriker[5] suggest that the poetry of *Jerusalem* displays far greater artistry than this. What Blake meant in his preface and how successfully he carried out his purpose are questions that demand our attention here. Was Blake justified in his large claims for the verse of *Jerusalem*? Does it display the unity in variety that he claims for it? How is Blake's statement that 'this Verse was first dictated to me' compatible with 'I therefore have produced' one sentence later? As this last question has often been answered in such a way as to imply that this Verse cannot be poetry at all, I begin with the matter of Blake's inspiration.

Blake claimed to have written *Jerusalem* 'under inspiration' (*Descriptive Catalogue*, E. 533), a statement that has been used by some scholars to account for the work's supposed weaknesses. 'What mattered to Blake was obviously the vision that possessed him at the moment: and his unwillingness to do more than merely transcribe it produces frequently the effect of inconsistency.'[6] This idea of the poet as a mere transcriber

[1] Ed. Todd, p. 200. [2] *William Blake*, p. 285. [3] I. 1.

[4] 'The Sublimity of William Blake', in *Eras and Modes in English Poetry* (Berkeley and Los Angeles: University of California Press, 1964), pp. 78–99; and 'Blake's Frame of Language', in *Poetry and Change* (Berkeley and Los Angeles: University of California Press, 1974), pp. 91–105. Several passages from *Jerusalem* are discussed in the latter.

[5] *Vision and Verse in William Blake* (Madison and Milwaukee: University of Wisconsin Press, 1965). Still more recently, William Kumbier has achieved some interesting results by scanning Blake's lines according to musical notation. See 'Blake's Epic Meter', *Studies in Romanticism*, XVII (1978), 163–92.

[6] Sloss and Wallis, I. 439.

—an idea which admittedly does have support in Blake's statements—reduces him to the status of the rhapsodist in Plato's *Ion*. Against such a view we may set our knowledge of Blake's manner of composition as indicated by his manuscripts. None, unfortunately, exists for *Jerusalem*, but the Notebook and *The Four Zoas* supply ample evidence to show that Blake's visions were frequently subject to revision. As *The Four Zoas* contains a number of passages that appear, mostly in revised form, in *Jerusalem*, I shall examine some of these.[1] The works will be cited in the abbreviated forms *FZ* and *J*, followed by plate or page numbers and then by line numbers. Such a comparison ought to give us some insight into the practice of a poet who claims to have put every word into its fit place.

Some changes involve an attempt to find the most appropriate wording. Albion is 'all exiled' in *FZ* 120: 2 but more penetratingly 'self-exiled' in *J 19*: 13 'from the face of light & shine of morning'. The 'Exalted Senses' of the Council of God in *FZ* 21: 2 become the more doctrinal 'infinite senses' of the Divine Family in a parallel passage in *J 34*: 17. A longer passage, *FZ* 22: 22–6, was revised for reasons of both style and substance. The manuscript reads:

And Tharmas took her in pitying Then Enion in jealous fear
Murderd her & hid her in her bosom embalming her for fear
She should arise again to life Embalmd in Enions bosom
Enitharmon remains a corse such thing was never known
In Eden that one died a death never to be revivd

These lines serve as a basis for *J 80*: 23–4, 27–9, where Blake changed the characters from Tharmas, Enitharmon, and Enion to Albion, Vala, and Luvah, rewriting the passage as follows:

. . . . & Luvah gave
The Knife into his daughters hand! such thing was never known

[1] It is difficult to number the lines precisely because some of them involve conceptual adaptations and others a phrase rather than a whole line. Bentley counts the lines of the parallel passages as 174 in number. See *Vala or the Four Zoas* (Oxford: The Clarendon Press, 1963), p. 216.

Before in Albions land, that one should die a death never to be reviv'd!
For in our battles we the Slain men view with pity and love:
We soon revive them in the secrets of our tabernacles
But I Vala, Luvahs daughter, keep his body embalmd in moral laws
With spices of sweet odours of lovely jealous stupefaction.
Within my bosom, lest he arise to life & slay my Luvah
Pity me then O Lamb of God! O Jesus pity me!
Come into Luvahs Tents, and seek not to revive the Dead!

In addition to changing the characters here, Blake has also changed the symbolic significance of the action. Albion is embalmed like Jesus so that the dead letter of the law may, in the power of what Blake calls Natural Religion, triumph. Blake rearranges the lines, adds two lines referring to the prelapsarian state, and adds two ironical lines at the end (ironical because Vala does not know that Luvah's functions are subsumed in Jesus, who has come precisely to revive the dead). The evocatively double-edged 'spices of sweet odours of lovely jealous stupefaction' is an especially fine elaboration, bringing in an almost Keatsian sensuosity and then tingeing it with the ironically negative 'jealous', thus making 'lovely' and 'sweet' suspect. Such revision is in the direction of a style richer in nuance, more powerfully compressed.

We can see this process again in Blake's use of *FZ* 9: 9–18 as the basis of *J 48*: 27–40. Here the central conception is the creation of Time as part of the process that makes redemption possible. The abstract version in *The Four Zoas* is transformed in *J* into a concretely visualized myth.

FZ 9: 9–18:

Then Eno a daughter of Beulah took a Moment of Time
And drew it out to Seven thousand years with much care & affliction
And many tears & in Every year made windows into Eden
She also took an atom of space & opend its center
Into Infinitude & ornamented it with wondrous art
Astonishd sat her Sisters of Beulah to see her soft affections

To Enion & her children & they pondered these things wondring
And they Alternate kept watch over the Youthful terrors
They saw not yet the Hand Divine for it was not yet reveald
But they went on in Silent Hope & Feminine repose

J 48: 27–40:

The Emanations of the grievously afflicted Friends of Albion
Concenter in one Female form an Aged pensive Woman.
Astonish'd! lovely! embracing the sublime shade: the Daughters of Beulah
Beheld her with wonder! With awful hands she took
A Moment of Time, drawing it out with many tears & afflictions
And many sorrows: oblique across the Atlantic Vale
Which is the Vale of Rephaim dreadful from East to West,
Where the Human Harvest waves abundant in the beams of Eden
Into a Rainbow of jewels and gold, a mild Reflection from
Albions dread Tomb. Eight thousand and five hundred years
In its extension. Every two hundred years has a door to Eden
She also took an Atom of Space, with dire pain opening it a Center
Into Beulah: trembling the Daughters of Beulah dried
Her tears. she ardent embrac'd her sorrows. occupied in labours

In *J* the 'Aged pensive Woman', soon to be identified as Erin, is graphically depicted in relation to the Daughters of Beulah instead of being a merely abstract name observed by them. The verse becomes pliant: the lines in the *FZ* passage tend to terminate in pauses: of the ten lines, eight end in nouns, every one of which is the object either of a verb or of a preposition. In the *J* passage there is enjambement after the verbs 'took' and 'dried' and after the preposition 'from', all followed by their objects in the line following. The strongly metrical *FZ* lines are relatively unimpeded by breath pauses, with ampersands connecting the word groupings; while in the *J* lines there are unpredictable cesurae creating an impetuous, rushing feeling. Compare:

> She also took an atom of space & opend its center
> Into Infinitude & ornamented it with wondrous art

and

> She also took an Atom of Space, with dire pain opening
> it a Center
> Into Beulah: trembling the daughters of Beulah dried Her
> tears.

(In *FZ* the daughters merely 'Astonishd sat . . . to see her soft affections'.) The *J* passage has four present participles extending its processes, the *FZ* lines only one. Such examples of technique show that Blake rewrote the original lines with as delicate an ear as he ever employed in the *Songs*. Of course there is an aspect of the revision that goes beyond technique, that is a powerful new creation: Erin drawing out the Moment 'oblique across the Atlantic Vale . . . Where the Human Harvest waves abundant in the beams of Eden . . .'. These magnificent lines do much to justify Blake's high claims to inspiration, yet, as we have seen, they are embedded in a passage which is a highly successful reworking of an earlier one.

There are, of course, no guarantees of success in revision, and some passages were altered with mixed results. An example of this is the incorporation in *J 65* of a long *FZ* passage comprising 92: 11–37 and 93: 1–19. Some of the changes introduce names significant in Blake's later symbolism: 'Albion' (four times), 'Lambeth', 'Bath', 'Britain', 'Cheviot', 'Annandale', 'Malden', 'Canterbury'. This was done simply by adding prepositional phrases to existing structures with the result that, as Ostriker puts it, 'Blake has broken the back of his general movement, changing a flowing narrative to something much heavier.'[1] For example, the beautiful *FZ* line 'And all the arts of life they changed into the arts of death' (92: 21) is merely impeded by the addition of 'in Albion' (*J 65*: 16). Blake also tinkered with some other parts of the original passage without necessarily improving them. For example, 'that

[1] *Vision and Verse*, p. 193.

they may grind / And polish brass and iron' (*J 65*: 23–4) is actually less clear in its significance than 'that they might file / And polish brass & iron' (*FZ* 92: 28–9), since brass and iron normally would be filed but not ground. In line 51 of the *J* passage, 'shadows of the oak' substitutes a Blakean formula for the more general 'clarions of war'; the result is really no better. 'Bound to the chariot of Love' in *FZ* 93: 11 becomes 'compelld to the chariot of love' in *J 65*: 51 for no other reason than anaphora, 'Compelld to leave the plow' occurring in the next line. There are nevertheless some very successful revisions in this segment, as in Blake's new description of the sacrifice of Luvah. In *FZ* 'They piercd him with a spear & laid him in a sepulcher / To die a death of Six thousand years bound round with desolation' (92: 14–15). An entirely new conception is introduced in *J 65*: 9–10: 'They staind him with poisonous blue, they inwove him in cruel roots / To die a death of Six thousand years bound round in vegetation.' Here Luvah retains his parallel with Christ but also becomes a victim of 'Druid' sacrifice, the poisonous blue referring to the woad. Blake's myth of the weaving of the body of man connects the 'cruel roots' of the first line with the 'vegetation' of the second, while 'bound round with desolation' is merely hollow rhetoric. Another, two-stage, example of successful revision can be seen in what Blake did to 'And bowels hidden in darkness are ripped forth upon the Ground' (93: 17). First he changed the manuscript reading from 'in darkness are' to 'in hammerd Steel'—still formularized perhaps, but far more graphic. Then, in writing the line in 65: 53, he made the line even more horribly visual: 'And bowels hid in hammerd steel rip'd quivering on the ground'. The introduction of a spondee—*ríp̀p'd quívering*—in a line iambic up to that point gives added force to the image. In addition, there is a magnificent added sequence of four new, deeply moving lines (33–6), where a chorus of impressed seamen turns the previously generalized descriptions of battle into a terribly concrete reality. Here the place-names 'London', 'Westminster', and 'Marybone' are not superadded but locations of all too literal events.

Another extensive parallel passage occurs from *J 67*: 44 to *68*: 9, consisting of twenty-eight lines in all. The counterpart text in Night VIII of *FZ* (105: 31–54) is so very late that it has been suggested that it derives from *J* and not the other way around.[1] This is not implausible, since this part of Night VIII could have been written as late as 1807,[2] when more than half of *J* had already been etched. Furthermore, the mysterious line 'To see the boy spring into heaven ['heavens' in *J*] sounding from my sight' appears in both texts but has been deleted from *FZ*, suggesting at least that Blake was actively working on page 105 of *FZ* after he had etched plate *67* of *J*. On the other hand, 3½ lines of the *J* passage (*67*: 61–2, *68*: 1–2) do not appear in *FZ*. The latter breaks off after 'Shriek not so my only love', while *J* continues:

I refuse thy joys: I drink
Thy shrieks because Hand & Hyle are cruel & obdurate to me
O Skofield why art thou cruel? Lo Joseph is thine! to make
You One: to weave you both in the same mantle of skin

Whichever way the revision went, we see here an example of Blake's tendency to adapt his poetry to new purposes. In *FZ* VIII the situation involves the torture and crucifixion of the Lamb of God; the related situation in *J* concerns a 'Victim' who is the Luvah of *J 65*. I have already discussed the adaptation of *FZ* 92–3 from Night VIIa for *65*, and on the whole it seems more likely that Blake drew on two different Nights of *FZ* in writing a sustained section of *J* than vice versa. Most of the other variants between the two passages are relatively unimportant,[3] but one other also suggests traffic from *FZ* to *J*. *FZ* 105: 40–1 reads

In channels thro my fiery limbs O love O pity O pain
O the pangs the bitter pangs of love forsaken

In comparison we have in *J 67*: 54–5:

In channels thro my fiery limbs: O love! O pity! O fear!
O pain! O the pangs, the bitter pangs of love forsaken

[1] Stevenson, *The Poems of William Blake*, p. 773n.; Bentley, *Writings*, II. 235n.

[2] For dating, see Bentley, *Writings*, II. 1722–5.

[3] *J 67*: 47 has 'these Rocks', *FZ* 105: 33 'the rocks'. In the next line of each, 'thine eyes that used to beam' in *J* 'used to wander' in *FZ*. The lead in Rahab/Tirzah's furnaces is 'melted' in *J 67*: 53 but 'molten' in *FZ*: 105: 39.

It is more likely that Blake would have filled out the second line to seven feet, the basic foot pattern being the septenary in the *J* passage, than that he would have reduced it to six for no apparent reason. The rushing on created by one further 'O' phrase, the furthering of the alliterative effect in the second line, and the pairing of the two Aristotelian emotions in the first all point to the passage in *Jerusalem*'s being the product of further thought. The deleted line on page 105 of *FZ* could have been deleted after the passage was adapted for *Jerusalem*, as Blake seems to have continued to work on some pages of *FZ* sporadically before abandoning the work. Such a hypothesis would account for the absence from *FZ* of the last line of *J 67* and the first two of *68*. The lines first bring in the two chief Sons of Albion and then ironically posit an equivalence—we must remember that Rahab/Tirzah is speaking—between Skofield, the man of war, and Joseph, the parallel to Christ as victim. The content expands that of the passage at large, and it seems likelier that this reflects addition to *J* than pruning in *FZ*.

A comparison of the parallel passages of *FZ* and *J*[1] suggests that Blake revised his material as much as any other poet. At times he merely tinkered, making minor improvements in wording and adapting passages to new contexts; he revised at other times in order to introduce new material. In some instances revision produced passages of extraordinary beauty and power. The fact that Blake blotted some of his lines does not mean that his claim to inspiration is not to be taken seriously:

> This theme calls me in sleep night after night, & ev'ry morn
> Awakes me at sun-rise, then I see the Saviour over me
> Spreading his beams of love, & dictating the words of this mild song. (*4*: 3–5)

This statement puts Blake in this, as in so many other respects, in the tradition of Milton, who wrote

> Of my Celestial Patroness, who deigns
> Her nightly visitation unimplor'd,

[1] For a discussion of some of the less important revisions, see the Supplementary Note.

And dictates to me slumb'ring, or inspires
Easy my unpremeditated Verse:[1]

The very difference in the two passages (Saviour/Urania, dawn/night) point up the underlying similarity of conception. Such statements as these attempt to describe that process by which the imagination attains a seeming autonomy—the poetic discipline which Coleridge calls 'method'. We may well apply to Blake in this regard Coleridge's magnificent characterization of Shakespeare: 'No mere child of nature; no automaton of genius; no passive vehicle of inspiration possessed by the spirit, not possessing it; [he] first studied patiently, meditated deeply, understood minutely, till knowledge, become habitual and intuitive, wedded itself to his habitual feelings, and at length gave birth to that stupendous power, by which he stands alone. . . .'[2]

A True Orator

'The terrific numbers', Blake says in his statement 'To the Public', 'are reserved for the terrific parts—the mild & gentle, for the mild & gentle parts, and the prosaic for inferior parts . . .' (*3*). 'Numbers' can refer to metrical feet, lines of poetry, or both. Milton says that 'musical delight . . . consists only in apt Numbers, fit quantity of syllables, and the sense variously drawn out from one Verse into another'.[3] Blake's statement, then, refers to prosody and to sound values, since 'numbers' comes to poetry from the language of musical notation.[4] *Jerusalem* presents a variegated prosodic display that is the culmination of Blake's lifelong interest in the technique of verse, richly displayed from *Poetical Sketches* on. There are passages in couplets, in quatrains rhyming abxb, in quatrains rhyming aabb, and in blank verse, in addition to the long line which is the metrical base of the poem. Blake's long lines, varying from five to seven and sometimes even more feet, are capable of great rhythmical variation in accordance with different artistic purposes.

[1] *Paradise Lost*, IX. 21–5 (p. 379).

[2] *Biographia Literaria*, ed. J. Shawcross (London: Oxford University Press, 1958), vol. II, pp. 13–14.

[3] 'The Verse', *Paradise Lost*, p. 210.

[4] See Kumbier, 'Blake's Epic Meter'.

Superficially, the long lines of *Jerusalem* appear similar to the fourteeners of Chapman's translation of Homer, a book which Blake is thought to have owned.[1] There is indeed some resemblance, but Chapman's feet are overwhelmingly disyllabic, and they scan perfectly as iambic septenaries if we allow for variation in up to three feet.

> This said, he left her there, and forth did to his bellows go,
> Apposde them to the fire again, commanding them to blow
> Through twenty holes made to his harth at once blew twenty paire,
> That fir'd his coles, sometimes with soft, sometimes with vehement ayre
> As he will'd and his work requir'd. Amids the flame he cast
> Tin, Silver, precious Gold and Brasse, and in the stocke he plac't
> A mighty anvile; his right hand a weightie hammer held,
> His left the tongs . . .[2]

Blake also takes the seven-foot rising line as his basis, but he allows himself far more freedom than Chapman or any other observer of strict metre:

> Los saw the envious blight above his Seventh Furnace
> On Londons Tower on the Thames: he drew Cambel in wrath,

[1] In 1829 John Linnell purchased from Blake's widow a copy of Homer which was later identified by A. T. Story as *The Whole Works of Homer; prince of Poets . . . translated according to the Greeke, by Geo. Chapman. London, [1616]*. See *BR*, p. 584, citing Story's *Life of John Linnell* (London, 1892), I. 78.

[2] *Chapman's Homer*, ed. Allardyce Nicoll. Vol. I, *The Iliad* (Princeton: Princeton University Press, 2nd edn., 1967), p. 384.

Into his thundering Bellows, heaving it for a loud blast!
And with the blast of his Furnace upon fishy Billingsgate
(*82*: 56–9)

As John Hollander says, the verse of *Jerusalem* does not involve a rejection of what Hollander calls 'the metrical contract': 'What he . . . does in *Jerusalem* is to extend the loosening of the fourteener in several directions from regular to loose, from syllabic fourteeners with only five or six major stresses to cluttered ones of eight.'[1] Rather than being 'rhythmed prose-verse' anticipatory of Whitman's free verse,[2] the long lines of *Jerusalem* may be characterized as irregular verse departing from and returning to a seven-foot base, the dominant feet being iambic and anapaestic. This poetry sets up complex metrical expectations which it sometimes fulfils, sometimes frustrates.

I have already quoted Frye's view that 'In reading *Jerusalem* there are only two questions to consider: how Blake interpreted the Bible, and how he placed that interpretation in an English context.'[3] This provocative statement is true of the style of the work in the same sense that it is true of the content: Blake's adaptation of biblical style is the single most important contributing factor to the poetry of *Jerusalem*. This subject has two aspects. One is broad and general: how Blake reshaped the language of the Bible for his own purposes. The other is more restricted, concerned with the understanding of biblical poetry in Blake's own time. It is of course impossible to erect a firm division between these two aspects of the subject, yet a discussion of the second may sharpen our apprehension of the first. The Bible obviously had an enormous direct impact upon Blake's poetic sensibility; at the same time, his understanding of biblical poetry must necessarily have been affected by advances in the study of the subject made during the later eighteenth century.

In *Energy and the Imagination* I suggested that Blake's ideas about what he calls 'the Sublime of the Bible' were

[1] John Hollander, *Vision and Resonance: Two Senses of Poetic Form* (New York: Oxford University Press), p. 208.

[2] The view of George Saintsbury, *A Manual of English Prosody* (London: Macmillan, 1914), pp. 33n., 298.

[3] *Fearful Symmetry*, pp. 356–7.

influenced by Bishop Robert Lowth's *Lectures on the Sacred Poetry of the Hebrews.*[1] It has since been argued that Lowth's theories about Hebrew poetry also influenced Blake's practice in his early prophecies;[2] and this plausible notion is worth considering in relation to *Jerusalem* as well. In the 'Preliminary Dissertation' to his new translation of Isaiah, Lowth notices 'a manifest conformity between the Prophetical Style, and that of the Books supposed to be Metrical', which leads him to conclude 'that the Poetical and Prophetical character of style and composition, though generally supposed to be different, are really one and the same'.[3] Lowth declares that rhyming is not an essential part of Hebrew verse; its harmony rather arises from its rhythm, although the laws governing its metre are now irrecoverable. There are two types of verse, long and short, the latter being 'elegiac'.[4] Verses are distinguished by parallelism, which is classified according to three types: 'Parallels Synonymous, Parallels Antithetic, and Parallels Synthetic'.[5] The effect of the whole is described as follows: 'This peculiar conformation of Sentences; short, concise, with frequent pauses, and regular intervals, divided into pairs, for the most part, of corresponding lines, is the most evident characteristic of poetry remaining among the Hebrews.'[6] It is also strikingly characteristic of some parts, though by no means all, of *Jerusalem*.

It is of course difficult to say what particular lines in *Jerusalem* may reflect Lowth's speculations about Hebrew prosody or the example of his own translation of Isaiah as distinguished from the direct stylistic influence of the Authorized Version. Yet there are parts of the poem which seem particularly good examples of Lowth's ideas:

> What is a Wife & what is a Harlot? What is a Church & What
> Is a Theatre? are they Two & not One? can they Exist Separate?

[1] pp. 20–1, 46–7, 50. Lowth's book, originally published in Latin, was published in English translation by Joseph Johnson in 1787.

[2] By Leslie Tannenbaum, in *Biblical Tradition in Blake's Early Prophecies: The Great Code of Art* (Princeton: Princeton University Press, 1982).

[3] *Isaiah: A New Translation, with a Preliminary Dissertation, and Notes Critical, Philological, and Explanatory* (London: Dodsley and Cadell, 1778), p. iii.

[4] Ibid., p. 32. [5] Ibid., pp. x–xi. [6] Ibid., p. *l*.

Are not Religion & Politics the Same Thing? Brotherhood
is Religion
O Demonstrations of Reason Dividing Families in Cruelty
& Pride!

(*57*: 8–10)

Here we have two groups of Parallels Synonymous, consisting first of two questions and then of three, culminating in a powerful declaration. A good example of Parallel Antithetic is the famous

I must Create a System, or be enslav'd by another Mans
I will not Reason & Compare: my business is to Create

(*10*: 20–1)

Parallel Synthetic—'the correspondence and equality between different propositions in respect of the shape and turn of the whole sentence, and of the constructive parts'[1]—may occur as a form of Blakean logic, as in *61*: 50–2, where the two-part question is balanced by an affirmation which is in turn expanded in a parallelism:

Wilt thou make Rome thy Patriarch Druid & the Kings
of Europe his
Horsemen? Man in the Resurrection changes his Sexual
Garments at will
Every Harlot was once a Virgin: every Criminal an Infant
Love![2]

In other instances whole passages are built up of groupings of parallels, parallels which are not merely reiterative but which create a sense of complex interplay:

What may Man be? who can tell! but what may Woman
be?
To have power over Man from Cradle to corruptible Grave.

[1] Lowth, *Isaiah*, p. xxi.

[2] The highly compressed meaning moves from the conjunction of ecclesiastical hierarchy and feudalism to the regenerate state of humanity which, with its free-flowing libidinal energy, breaks through such stratification; the third line points to the attainability of such freedom by calling upon our knowledge of Individuals and States.

There is a Throne in every Man, it is the Throne of God
This Woman has claimd as her own & Man is no more!
Albion is the Tabernacle of Vala & her Temple
And not the Tabernacle & Temple of the Most High
(*30/34*: 25–30)

As the thoughts balance, augment, or contradict each other, we sense the parallelism as integral to the content, not imposed on it. Sometimes, as in the example immediately above, the parallel elements are confined to single lines or pairs of lines; at other times, as we have seen, they overflow the boundaries of the line, and in so doing become more fluid than Lowth's theory would allow. Of course our supposition here is not that Blake tried to write Hebrew verse in English according to a set prosodic plan, but rather that he could have found support in Lowth's ideas for what he wanted to do. Most important would have been the notions that various kinds of parallelism were the structural elements of Hebrew verse and of the harmony as proceeding from 'accents, tones, and musical modulations'.[1] If that is indeed so, then Blake shared the influence of Lowth's prosodic ideas with another visionary poet, Christopher Smart, and a brief comparison of the two will be of interest, whether or not Blake had an opportunity to see *Jubilate Agno* in manuscript.[2]

Christopher Smart not only read the Latin edition of Lowth's *De Sacra Poesi Hebrorum* (1753) but also reviewed the book, calling it 'one of the best performances that have been published for a century'.[3] *Jubilate Agno*, strikingly different in method from Smart's other poems, is characterized by unrhymed verse, parallelism of different types, and short

[1] Lowth, *Isaiah*, p. xlii.

[2] The manuscript was for some time in the possession of William Hayley. Hayley gave it to his friend the Revd. Thomas Carwardine at a time prior to Hayley's association with Blake, when Hayley and Carwardine were trying to help William Cowper in his madness. Apparently they hoped to gain some understanding of Cowper's state through the poem Smart had written while insane. (See *Jubilate Agno*, ed. William Force Stead. London: Jonathan Cape, 1939, p. 15.) Hayley could, of course, have taken a copy of some part of the manuscript and might even have recited some of it to Blake, as he did other poetry. However, my interest here is not in a hypothetical direct influence of Smart upon Blake but rather in how Lowth's theories of Hebrew prosody may be reflected in both.

[3] Quoted by Stead, p. 297. Smart's review appeared in *The Universal Visiter* in 1756.

concise sentences often arranged in pairs. Sometimes these structural arrangements are fairly loose:

For St. Paul was caught up into the third heavens.

For there he heard certain words which it was not
possible for him to understand.
For they were constructed by uncommunicated letters.

For they are signs of speech too precious to be communicated for ever.[1]

In other passages there is a stronger consciousness of the internal relationships of phrases according to parallelism and antithesis, emphasized by caesuras:

For the Glory of God is always in the East, but cannot
be seen for the cloud of the crucifixion.
For due East is the way to Paradise, which man knoweth
not by reason of his fall.[2]

A characteristic structure of Smart's is the two-part parallelism followed by a summary statement:

For the SUN is an intelligence and an angel of the human
form.
For the MOON is an intelligence and an angel in shape like
a woman.
For they are together in the spirit every night like man
and wife.[3]

Blake's practice presents striking parallels. Consider, for example, *83*: 16–22:

I woo to Amalek to protect my fugitives[.] Amalek
trembles:
I call to Canaan & Moab in my night watches, they mourn:
They listen not to my cry, they rejo[i]ce among their
warriors
Woden and Thor and Friga wholly consume my Saxons:
On their enormous Altars built in the terrible north:

[1] *Jubilate Agno*, ed. W. H. Bond (London: Rupert Hart-Davis, 1954), p. 127.
[2] Ibid., p. 69.
[3] Ibid., p. 93.

From Irelands rocks to Scandinavia Persia and Tartary:
From the Atlantic Sea to the universal Erythrean.

Like Smart, Blake constructs his passages according to parallelism and antithesis, thinking in terms of relatively short units (one need only contrast one of Milton's blank verse paragraphs—as I shall—to become fully aware of this). What Stead says of Smart may be applied to Blake as well. 'We are not to suppose that he set out to imitate the English Bible or Prayer Book versions of the Psalms and other religious poetry of ancient Israel; the point is, rather, that he was writing in a form which he had reason to believe resembled the original compositions of the sacred poets.'[1]

Of course Blake's imitation of the Bible as mediated by eighteenth-century theory cannot be fully distinguished from his direct use of the Authorized Version as a model, and much that has been said above could apply to either or both. Blake's method in *Jerusalem* is to inweave biblical references tightly with biblical stylistic devices. The interchange of Jesus and Jerusalem in *62* will serve as a particularly rich example. In this passage Jerusalem envisages the Maternal Line in a list of twelve names that presents the maternal ancestry of Jesus as comprising outsiders and transgressors.[2] She then asks rhetorically 'Shall Albion arise?' and answers: 'I know he shall arise at the Last Day! / I know that in my flesh I shall see God . . .' (15–16). In these lines are incorporated references to John 11: 23 and to Job 20: 25; the speech then goes on to develop John 11: 25 into a statement of Blakean doctrine:

Jesus said unto her, I am the resurrection and the life: he that believeth in me, though he were dead, yet shall he live.

Jesus replied. I am the Resurrection & the Life.
I Die & pass the limits of possibility, as it appears
To individual perception. (18–20)

In passages like these, the biblical language is deeply embedded in Blake's own, and Blake freely imbues the biblical terms with

[1] Stead, pp. 296–7.

[2] On the Maternal Line, see Damon, *Blake Dictionary*, pp. 265–6.

his own meanings and uses them as vehicles for his mythology. So Albion is at once Lazarus and Job, and the eternal life promised by Jesus becomes an expansion of human perception. Jesus's further words to Jerusalem allude to the journey of the Hebrews through the wilderness, yoking this with a reworking of Matt. 28: 20.[1] The journey described in Exodus[2] is rewritten so as to constitute a wandering in error to be redeemed through the realization of an indwelling Christ:

> I will command the cloud to give thee food & the hard
> rock
> To flow with milk & wine, tho thou seest me not a season
> Even a long season & a hard journey & a howling wilder-
> ness!
> The Valas cloud hide thee & Luvahs fires follow thee!
> Only believe & trust in me, Lo. I am always with thee!
> (25-9)

The appropriation of the language of the Bible in parts of *Jerusalem* goes far beyond mere imitation; it is the product of a remarkable assimilation of biblical texts that can then be recast into new forms of utterance.

Next to the Bible, the greatest exemplar for Blake's poetry is of course Milton's. From Milton Blake learned the powerful long line of prophetic authority, a line gathering force through the accumulation of phrases interspersed by caesuras. The pauses do not typically create a balanced tension, as often in Augustan poetry, but rather appear to resist the onrush of the verse and then to yield to it. Participial constructions extend spatial imagery to the furthest imaginable limits; noun-adjective inversion creates a sense of vatic archaism; enjambement transfers energy from one line to another and creates a sense that statements (not always sentences) are structural units.

> A Concave Earth wondrous, Chasmal, Abyssal, Inco-
> herent!

[1] 'Lo, I am always with you, even unto the end of the world.'

[2] The specific allusions are to Exodus 16, 17, and 13, as noted by Stevenson (p. 757).

Forming the Mundane Shell: above; beneath: on all sides surrounding
Golgonooza: Los walks round the walls night and day.
(*13*: 53–5)

Like Milton, Blake can employ Latinate diction and syntax and then, as above, suddenly break from it into a simple Anglo-Saxon statement that gains enormous dramatic force by the contrast.

In their use of larger units, on the other hand, Milton and Blake may appear to be more similar than they are. The text of *Jerusalem* is spatially arranged on the page so as to look like verse paragraphs. But Blake, unlike Milton, does not *think* in terms of a unit of many lines. Characteristically, the verse of *Jerusalem* is structured in units seldom more than two or three lines long, and these do not develop into the extended, complex, contrapuntal sentences of the Miltonic verse paragraph. Consider the difference between the six opening lines of *Paradise Lost*, Book III, and *Jerusalem 15*: 6-13:

Hail, holy Light, offspring of Heav'n first-born,
Or of th'Eternal Coeternal beam
May I express thee unblam'd? since God is Light,
And never but in unapproached Light
Dwelt from Eternity, dwelt then in thee,
Bright effluence of bright essence increate.

I see the Four-fold Man. The Humanity in deadly sleep
And its fallen Emanation. The Spectre & its cruel Shadow.
I see the Past, Present & Future, existing all at once
Before me; O Divine Spirit sustain me on thy wings!
That I may awake Albion from his long & cold repose.
For Bacon & Newton sheathd in dismal steel, their terrors hang
Like iron scourges over Albion, Reasonings like vast Serpents
Infold around my limbs, bruising my minute articulations

Rather than flowing on in the Miltonic manner, Blake's statement employs short rhythmic units which are balanced with, opposed to, or set in parallel motion against one another. The passage as a whole, which is set off spatially as if it were a verse paragraph, has an anaphoric relation to the three following it; these begin respectively 'I turn my eyes' (14), 'I see in deadly fear' (21), and 'I see Albion' (30), resulting in a statement of enormous cumulative power. Eschewing the expressive possibilities of the Miltonic verse paragraph, Blake finds structures like these appropriate to his own habit of thought.

In his quest for the poetic latitude necessary for a True Orator, Blake also turned to British models that were believed to be primitive. His early prose poems had been influenced by the diction and rhetoric of Ossian, and this was also true of early prophecies such as *The French Revolution*. As his poetic art developed, the Ossianic bluster diminished, being reserved at last for blusterers like Urizen and Hand and Hyle. Blake's admiration for Ossian persisted, as can be seen in a comment he wrote in the margin of a copy of Wordsworth's *Poems*, lent to him by Henry Crabb Robinson in 1825 or 1826: 'I own myself an admirer of Ossian equally with any other poet whatever Rowley and Chatterton also.'[1] This admiration of the archaic (or the pseudo-archaic) is parallel to Blake's attitude towards primitivism in painting, as we shall see in Chapter 2. Blake's view of Ossian may have been strengthened by the *Reports of the Committee of the Highland Society* published in 1805, in which many supposed Erse sources of James Macpherson's forgeries were cited.[2] In the verse of *Jerusalem* Blake continued to emulate the archaic style of Ossian, but with greater discrimination. Damon points out that

> Although 'Ossian's' poems were printed as prose, they were really written in rough septenaries and alexandrines, with a great variety of unaccented syllables; but though the accents and caesuras are strong, the lines are insensitive, short-breathed, and monotonous. Blake's free septenaries in the Prophetic Books were evidently derived from Ossian's; but Blake's rhythms vary according to the sense, from *Tiriel* and the limpid *Thel* to the choral thunders of *Jerusalem*.[3]

[1] E. 655. For dating, see *Blake Books*, p. 701.

[2] Edinburgh: Constable. The compiler was Henry Mackenzie, Chairman of the Committee. In his edition, *The Poems of Ossian* (Edinburgh: Constable, 1805), Malcolm Laing remarks: 'The Committee of the Highland Society has been very laudably employed in collating one forgery with another.' (Vol. I, p. xlvii.)

[3] *Blake Dictionary*, pp. 312–13. See also Ostriker, *Vision and Verse*, pp. 124–5.

Blake had a basis for unrhymed verse in John Milton's example, and a rationale for it in Milton's declaration prefaced to *Paradise Lost*: 'This neglect then of Rime is so little to be taken for a defect, that it is rather to be esteem'd as an example set, the first in *English*, of ancient liberty recover'd to the Heroic poem from the troublesom and modern bondage of *Rimeing*.'[1] Milton's reform being insufficient for what Blake calls 'a true Orator', Ossian could provide a model for the irregular verse that Blake wanted to write.

To what extent Ossian was in Blake's ear in *Jerusalem* can be demonstrated by arranging a passage from *Carthon*, chosen almost at random, into lines of verse and scanning them.

> When shalt / thou rise, / Balclu/tha's joy! / When,
> Car/thon, shalt / thou arise? /
> Who comes / so dark / from o/cean's roar, / like au/tumn's
> sha/dowy cloud? /
> Such were the / words of the / bards, in the / day of their
> / mourning; /
> Ossian / often / joined / their voice; / and ad/ded to /
> their song.[2]

As I scan these lines, three of the four are septenaries, the exception being the third, which consists of four dactyls plus one trochee. The first line can be scanned as six iambs followed by an anapaest unless one chooses to accentuate 'when' both times, in which case there are two spondees and an anapaest varying a basically iambic line. The second line is iambic with the exception of the first foot, a spondee, and the last, an anapaest. The fourth line, assuming 'Ossian' to be trisyllabic, has only three iambs varied by an initial dactyl, two trochees, and a pyrrhic. The third line creates a dramatic reversal from rising to falling rhythm, but this is only possible because the ear is led to expect less radical departures from the iambic septenary base of the preceding two lines. In the fourth line the falling cadence continues for the first

[1] See Damon (*William Blake*, p. 435).
[2] *The Poems of Ossian*, I. 341.

three feet, then reverses once more into the dominant rising pattern. Compare the cadences of

> Ĭ rĕdóun/dĕd frŏm Álb/iŏns bós/ŏm ĭn / mў vír/gĭn
>   lóve/lĭnéss.
> Thĕ Lámb / ŏf Gód / rĕciév'd / mĕ ĭn / hĭs árms / hĕ
>   smíl'd / ŭpón ús (˘):
> Hĕ máde / mé hĭs / Bríde &̆ / Wífe: hĕ / gáve thée / tŏ
>   Ál/bĭŏn.
> Thén wăs / ă tíme / ŏf lóve / : Ó whý / ĭs ĭt páss/ĕd ăwáy!
> (*20*: 37–40)

The first three lines are septenaries, the fourth a hexameter. The first gives a smooth rising effect, although it will not quite scan perfectly, with its three anapaests followed by a pyrrhic and then by three iambs. This effect is continued in the second line,[1] but the third is irregular. The fourth is varied, containing an initial trochee and a spondee, but rising feet—two iambs and two anapaests—are in the majority. Of the twenty-seven feet, thirteen are iambs—not quite enough to establish an iambic meter, but enough to give us a sense of dominant pattern, especially as there are also five anapaests. Like most of *Jerusalem*, this passage consists principally of septenaries departing freely from an iambic base.

Another primitive influence on Blake's verse in *Jerusalem*, and a more authentic one than *The Poems of Ossian*, was medieval Welsh poetry. Blake's interest in Welsh antiquities, as indicated by the Welsh place-names introduced in some late passages of *The Four Zoas* and in *Jerusalem*, is likely to have been stimulated by his friend William Owen, who called himself Owen Pugh. Robert Southey had information about this from the Blakes themselves, and reported on the passages 'from the Welsh Triades' printed in Blake's exhibition advertisement of 1809–10:

> It [Blake's description of his painting *The Ancient Britons*] begins with a translation from the Welsh supplied to him no doubt by that good,

[1] I do not count the glides in 'reciev'd' and 'smil'd' as syllables to be scanned, since Blake evidently wanted to distinguish these from the syllabic -ed of 'passed'.

simple-hearted, Welsh-headed man William Owen, whose memory is the great storehouse of all Cymric tradition and lore of every kind.[1]

Blake's interest in Bardism as described by Pugh is more appropriately discussed in relation to the myth of the Poet (see Chapter VI); here we are concerned with the effect of Pugh's translations upon Blake's poetry. We can see this most obviously in the two three-line stanzas published in Blake's Advertisement of 1809.[2] The first stanza has been identified as an adaptation from the *Myrvian Archailogy,*[3] a Welsh compilation published in parts by Pugh and others from 1801 to 1807. The second stanza is apparently Blake's own, as no source has been found for it.

> The most Beautiful, the Roman Warriors trembled before
>   and worshipped
> The most Strong they melted before him and dissolved
>   in his presence:
> The most Ugly they fled with outcries and contortion
>   of their Limbs.

These three lines (like the preceding three) are septenaries. Iambs and anapaests dominate, but not so much so as to make the lines scan regularly. There are an extraordinary number of unstressed syllables. These, with the irregular foot pattern, create a rough, prose-like effect; at the same time metrical expectations are kept up by the seven-foot lines and the preponderance of rising feet. This passage would not seem out of place in *Jerusalem*.

In Owen Pugh's published translations the language is too stiff for poetry, but it is possible to see how Blake could have imitated these poems for his own purposes. Consider, for example, Pugh's rendering of Taliesin:

> Into a dark receptacle I was thrown,
> In the laving ocean I was overwhelmed;

[1] *BR*, p. 226, from *The Doctor*, VI. 116–17.

[2] 'Exhibition of *Paintings in Fresco*, Poetical and Historical Inventions, by Wm. Blake', E. 517.

[3] See Damon, *Blake Dictionary*, p. 443.

It was to me tidings of gladness when I was happily
suffocated,
God the Lord from confinement set me free.[1]

Blake's description of the fallen Albion strikes a similar note of elegiac sadness in evoking the buried life:

In the dark world a narrow house! he wanders up and
down,
Seeking for rest and finding none! and hidden far within,
His Eon weeping in the cold and desolated Earth.
(*19*: 14–16)

The similarity of cadence can be seen more clearly if we imagine a line break after the caesura in the first line above, making a passage of four lines instead of three. It is of course not so much a matter of specific source passages as of similar effects attained through the use of long lines, freely varied foot patterns, and frequent caesuras, giving a rough effect which is like prose and yet still poetry.

Let me be guided onward, thou fierce ashen spear; bitter
And sullen as the maddening sea was the hoarse shouting
of the war,
Where the fiery soul of Urien raged.
(*Heroic Elegies*, p. 23.)

Brightly glitters the top of the hard holly, that opens its
golden leaves;
When all are asleep on the surrounding walls,
God slumbers not when he means to give deliverance.

. . . .

Glittering are the tops of the brakes, birds are their fair
jewels;
The long day is the gift of the radiant light,
Mercy was formed by God, the most beneficent.
(*Heroic Elegies*, p. 19.)

There are of course significant differences, too, between this versification and Blake's. Seldom is the thrust of a line carried beyond a single verse in Owen Pugh's translations, while the sense units of *Jerusalem* typically flow over the line endings.

[1] *The Heroic Elegies and Other Pieces of Llywarc Hen* (London, 1792), p. xxxi.

Nor does Blake try to follow the canons of versification laid down by Owen Pugh. Welsh poetry, like *Ossian*, serves as a model in some respects, while in others Blake's ear is tuned to a different drummer.

The Sublime and the Pathos

In his preface 'To the Public' Blake instructs us to look for three types of poetry in *J*: 'terrific', 'mild & gentle', and 'prosaic', each type fitted to corresponding subject-matter. The first two of these modes correspond to the eighteenth-century notions of the sublime and the pathetic and can be most usefully discussed in relation to each other, while the third may be considered separately. If we read *J* keeping in mind the distinctions Blake himself establishes, we can see that the diction, rhetoric, and imagery of the poem are governed by a sense of decorum—alien as this notion may seem to some readers of Blake—similar in some respects to that of *The Prelude*. It has been persuasively argued by Klaus Dockhorn and later by Herbert Lindenberger that Wordsworth's long poem observes traditional rhetorical distinctions;[1] these are not precisely those followed by Blake in *Jerusalem*, but what the two have in common in this respect is the decorum that results from observing certain definable relationships between style and subject-matter. Of course these relationships, as Lindenberger points out with respect to *The Prelude*, do not constitute 'a rigid formula which Wordsworth used to determine the form and meaning of his work in advance'.[2] They are nevertheless of the greatest functional importance; as Blake says, 'all are necessary to each other' (*3*).

Blake drew upon the eighteenth-century notion of the sublime with sophisticated awareness,[3] and in so doing he developed a type of sublimity which, whatever its debts to tradition may be, is characteristic of Blake alone. The Blakean

[1] Dockhorn, 'Wordsworth und die rhetorische Tradition in England', *Nachrichten der Akademie der Wissenschaften in Gottingen*, Phil.-Hist. Kl. (1944), 255–92, and 'Die Rhetorik als Quelle des vorromantischen Irrationalismus in der Literatur- und Geistesgeschichte', ibid. (1959), pp. 109–50. Lindenberger, *On Wordsworth's* Prelude (Princeton, NJ: Princeton University Press, 1963), pp. 15–39.

[2] *On Wordsworth's* Prelude, p. 38.

[3] See *Energy and the Imagination*, pp. 1–60, 200–60.

sublime emanates from the productive resources of mind and body, as manifested in prophetic vision, in artistic creation and in the act of love; its visual epitome is the naked, dancing Albion preparing to give himself for the nations. The role of the pathetic in Blake's thought and work has been less extensively discussed, but scattered references to it in Blake's writings show that it is less inclusive a conception there than it is in Quintilian's *Institutiones Oratoriae*. For Quintilian '*pathos* is almost entirely concerned with anger, dislike, fear, hatred, and pity'[1]—with intense and momentary emotions which are to be distinguished from those continuous affections which come under the head of ethos. But eighteenth-century aestheticians and rhetoricians, drawing upon the tradition of Longinus and other later writers, distinguish between the sublime and the pathetic, reserving the sublime for 'high' and intense manifestations of Quintilian's pathos and making the latter term mean very much what Quintilian calls ethos. Thus, for example, Dr Johnson's famous statement that 'there is in the *Paradise Lost* little opportunity for the pathetick; but what little there is has not been lost. . . . But the passions are moved only on one occasion; sublimity is the general and prevailing quality in this poem.'[2] Jean H. Hagstrum distinguishes two kinds of antithesis made by Johnson between the sublime and the pathetic: a distinction between the grander aspects of external nature and the passions of human life, and 'an aesthetic contrast of mood and feeling between that which arouses terror and awe (the sublime) and that which arouses sympathy and tenderness (the pathetic)'.[3] It is the latter distinction which bears most closely on Blake, though as usual Blake makes his distinction with a difference.

From the scattered references in Blake's writings we may construe his idea of pathos. Certain paintings of Romney's, for example, are assigned this characteristic. Writing to Hayley

[1] Quintilian, *Institutiones Oratoriae*, VI. ii. 21 (Loeb Classical Library, p. 429). But Quintilian admits a mid-point between pathos and ethos: 'The emotions of love and longing for our friends and connexions is perhaps of an intermediate character, being stronger than *ethos* and weaker than *pathos*' (VI. ii. 17, p. 427). This type of feeling would be categorized as pathos by most critics in Blake's time.

[2] *Lives of the English Poets*, ed. George Birkbeck Hill (Oxford: The Clarendon Press, 1905), I. 180.

[3] *Samuel Johnson's Literary Criticism* (Minneapolis: University of Minnesota Press, 1952), p. 139.

of his engraving of Romney's *Shipwreck*, Blake says 'I hope you will be able to judge of the Pathos of the Picture.'[1] Another writer might well have seen *The Shipwreck*, with its catastrophic waves enveloping men and horse alike as an example of Burke's sublime of terror, but for Blake natural disaster was not a source of the sublime; it was, however, productive of pathos in the suffering of its victims. Again, of Romney's *Lear and Cordelia* Blake says, perhaps thinking of his own early rendering of the same subject (Tate Gallery), '[it is] exquisite for expression; indeed, it is most pathetic'.[2] As Blake specifies that the Romney represents the moment 'when he awakes and knows her',[3] we can see precisely what constitutes the pathos of the scene. As for the pathetic in language, we know that Blake considered the Psalms examples of this;[4] and in his *Descriptive Catalogue* Blake refers to 'that most pathetic passage in the book of Ruth . . . "Whither thou goest I will go; and where thou lodgest I will lodge, thy people shall be my people, and thy God my God: where thou diest I will die, and there will I be buried; God do so to me and more also, if ought but death part thee and me." '[5] The Blakean pathos employs a language of affect which describes the emotional relations between human beings and between the human and the divine. Although perhaps less conspicuous than the sublime in *Jerusalem*, the pathos is of nearly equal importance. In the bright sculptures of Los's halls are carved 'every pathetic story possible to happen from Hate or / Wayward Love & every sorrow & distress . . . / Every Affinity of Parents Marriages & Friendships' (*16*: 63–5).

Literary critics before and during Blake's time often spoke of sublimity and pathos as combined, though, as we have

[1] 28 September 1804, *Letters*, p. 104.

[2] 4 May 1804, *Letters*, p. 96. The connection between the pathetic and the expressive, here and elsewhere, should be noted. In a letter to Hayley, 28 September 1804, Blake proposes to execute an engraving after Romney's *Tobit and Tobias*: 'The Expression of those truly Pathetic heads would thus be transmitted to the Public', *Letters*, p. 105.

[3] *Letters*, p. 96.

[4] 'It was this [Poetic Genius] that our great poet King David desired so fervently & invokes so patheticly', says Ezekiel in *The Marriage of Heaven and Hell*, 12 (E. 38). Stevenson notes: 'The reference is not to a particular passage, though B. may have had II *Samuel* xxii (i.e., *Psalm* xviii), or *Psalm* lx in mind' (p. 113).

[5] E. 539–40; the passage quoted is from Ruth 1: 16.

seen, that was not Johnson's view. Thomas Warton, for example, wrote of Chaucer: 'He abounds not only in strokes of humour, which is commonly supposed to be his sole talent, but of pathos, and sublimity, not unworthy a more refined age.'[1] The Scottish Parliamentary report on Ossian found in the poems 'Some strokes of the sublime and pathetic.'[2] Such conjoinings of pathos and sublimity go back to Longinus, who, as Samuel H. Monk says, 'habitually associates the two'.[3] Blake too views the sublime and the pathetic as originally combined: this is in fact part of his myth, according to which the disjunction of the two is a result of the fall. Writing in 1809 of the now lost *Ancient Britons*, Blake says:

The Strong Man represents the human sublime. The Beautiful man represents the human pathetic, which was in the wars of Eden divided into male and female. The Ugly man represents the human reason. They were originally one man, who was fourfold; he was self-divided, and his real humanity slain on the stems of generation, and the form of the fourth was like the Son of God. How he became divided is a subject of great sublimity and pathos. (*Descriptive Catalogue*, E. 533.)

Blake goes on to promise to publish this story in a poem, which, as we have seen, is almost certainly *Jerusalem*. Indeed, on the very frontispiece of the poem, in lines that were printed in the unique trial proof and later deleted,[4] this separation takes place in Albion: 'His Sublime & Pathos become Two Rocks fixd in the Earth' (*1*: 4). The consequence is a terrible sexual agony where

no more the Masculine mingles
With the Feminine. but the Sublime is shut out from the Pathos
In howling torment, to build stone walls of separation, compelling
The Pathos, to weave curtains of hiding secresy from the torment. (*90*: 10–14)

[1] *Observations on the Fairy Queen of Spenser*, 2nd edn., 1762, I. 197.

[2] *Report on the Poems of Ossian* (1805), p. 33.

[3] *The Sublime* (Ann Arbor: University of Michigan Press, 1960 [1935]), p. 14.

[4] The deletion was probably made not for any doctrinal reason but simply because these lines had a busy effect on a powerfully simple full-page design. The lines were not deleted from the plate itself; a posthumous proof of *1*, probably printed by Tatham and bearing an 1831 watermark, shows much of the text.

Thus the sublime and the pathetic are seen as rooted in indwelling human characteristics; their separation necessitates poetic styles appropriate to each.

The sublime passages of *J* are not difficult to locate, constituting as they do some of the most powerful and memorable portions of the work—indeed, some identify themselves as such.

> . . . for Cities
> Are Men, fathers of multitudes, and Rivers & Mountains
> Are also Men; every thing is Human, mighty! sublime!
> (*34/38*: 45–7)

> But the revolving Sun and Moon pass thro its porticoes,
> Day & night, in sublime majesty & silence they revolve
> And shine glorious within! (*58*: 27–9)

Here too is the increased 'emphasis on cumulative size and mass' which Josephine Miles has seen as a characteristic of *Jerusalem.*[1] Other sublime passages bear the identifying characteristics of wonder—in its most heightened form astonishment—and terror.

> Terrified at the sublime Wonder, Los stood before his Furnaces.
> And they stood around, terrified with admiration at Erins Spaces (*12*: 22–3)

Many such passages could be cited to show how, despite Blake's 'Contempt & Abhorrence'[2] for Burke, the sublime moments of *Jerusalem* often manifest the characteristics of the Burkeian sublime. Likewise the stylistic characteristics of the sublime—notably simplicity and power—of the kind that Hugh Blair adduces in the Old Testament, in Ossian, and in *Paradise Lost*[3] are also manifest in *Jerusalem*. (It is also worth noting that Blair regards rhyme as an impediment to the sublime and that all the examples of the sublime in Blair's fourth lecture, 'The Sublime in Writing', are unrhymed.)

[1] *Eras and Modes*, p. 98.

[2] See Annotations to Reynolds, E. 650. On Blake and Burke, see *Energy and the Imagination*, pp. 18–19, 45, 228–9.

[3] *Lectures on Rhetoric and Belles Lettres* (London: T. Allman, 1841 [1782]).

Useful as it is, however, to define Blake's poetry in relation to the literary culture of his period, there is a further point to be made. In some respects, Blake's sublimity affects us as a profound experience beyond the realm of eighteenth- and early nineteenth-century definitions. As in the greatest poetry of Wordsworth and of Keats, Blake's 'terrific numbers' are related to the earlier conception of the sublime but far transcend it.

A. C. Bradley, in his Oxford lecture, 'The Sublime', observes

> In 'beauty' that which appears in a sensuous form seems to rest in it, to be perfectly embodied in it, and to have no tendency to pass beyond it. In the sublime, even where no such tendency is felt and sublimity is nearest to 'beauty', we still feel the presence of a power held in reserve, which could with ease exceed its present expression. In *some* forms of sublimity again, the sensuous embodiment seems threatening to break in its effort to express what appears in it.[1]

It is in that quality of threatening to break through the forms of expression, through myth, through language itself, that Blake's most characteristic sublimity consists. We find it most often associated with Los, for it is typically Los who embodies the elemental energies of life in *Jerusalem*.

> I saw terrified; I took the sighs & tears, & bitter groans:
> I lifted them into my Furnaces; to form the spiritual
> sword.
> That lays open the hidden heart: I drew forth the pang
> Of sorrow red hot: I workd it on my resolute anvil:
> (*9*: 17–20)

Here the treatment of the insubstantial as if it were material —the pang of sorrow that can be worked like a piece of hot metal and the unforgettable image of the sword formed out of human suffering—make us uneasily aware of how (just barely) the imagery of the smithy accommodates the tenor. The tension may be contrasted with that which Geoffrey Hartman has described in Wordsworth as Wordsworth's attempt to naturalize the imagination.[2] One could never argue

[1] *Oxford Lectures on Poetry* (London: Macmillan, 1934), p. 58.

[2] *Wordsworth's Poetry 1787–1814* (New Haven and London: Yale University Press, 1964).

of Blake's sublime-apocalyptic passages, as Hartman does of the vision from Snowdon in *The Prelude* V, that 'the poet comes face to face with his Imagination yet calls it Nature'.[1] Blake's imagination is by definition apocalyptic, and in his most sublime passages one glimpses, like Ahab on the quarter-deck but to far different effect, the stirring of elemental forces behind the thin partitions of nature. We see this in the great passages of the climactic vision in *97–9*.

The image of the bow and arrows which begins this long passage is familiar from other contexts, particularly the lyric prefixed to *Milton* which adumbrates *Jerusalem* itself. At first it may seem as if this powerful image, or rather complex of images, uniting sexual potency and intellectual energy, will be one of a series intended as a vehicle for 'an Eternal Death & Resurrection' (*98*: 20) which humanity now must undergo. But the work of the bow is soon done—'the Druid Spectre was Annihilate' in *98*: 6, just as the actual combat of Demogorgon and Jupiter takes but a few lines in *Prometheus Unbound*. The predominant imagery is drawn from Revelation:

> And every Man stood Fourfold. each Four Faces had.
> One to the West
> One toward the East One to the South One to the North.
> the Horses Fourfold
> And the dim Chaos brightend beneath, above, around!
> Eyed as the Peacock
> According to the Human Nerves of Sensation, the Four
> Rivers of the Water of Life (*98*: 12–15)

Even this archetypal imagery, however, becomes less important as *98* continues. The weight of apocalyptic meaning is borne by long discursive lines, marked by repetition and reiteration and by the accumulation of adjectives.

> And they conversed together in Visionary forms dramatic
> which bright
> Redounded from their Tongues in thunderous majesty,
> in Visions
> In new Expanses, creating exemplars of Memory and of
> Intellect

[1] Hartman, *Wordsworth's Poetry*, p. 226.

Creating Space, Creating Time according to the wonders Divine
Of Human Imagination, throughout all the Three Regions immense
Of Childhood, Manhood & Old Age[;] & the all tremendous unfathomable Non Ens
Of Death was seen in regenerations terrific or complacent varying
According to the subject of discourse & every Word & Every Character
Was Human according to the Expansion or Contraction, the Translucence or
Opakeness of Nervous fibres such was the variation of Time & Space
Which vary according as the Organs of Perception vary & they walked
To & fro in Eternity as One Man reflecting each in each & clearly seen
And seeing: according to fitness & order. (28–40)

It cannot be said that this passage is without imagery, but the imagery and the technical vocabulary have become, as Frye puts it, 'a kind of ideographic alphabet'.[1] Thanks to more than half a century of exegesis, we can understand the conceptual meanings of the ideograms, but we are all the more aware that these words do not even try to constitute a landscape of the imagination whose features can then be read in Coleridgean fashion. Rather, we sense in these lines the effort of the language to abandon its function as mediator and to become meaning itself. As of course it cannot do this, the result is an effect of Titanic striving which is in itself a mode of the sublime. As Karl Kroeber remarks, in *99*, the last plate on which text appears, 'no word "stands for" or "represents" anything other than itself', and in the syntactic reversal of the seemingly prosaic last line 'the condition of true, Regenerated reality is attained, a condition in which time, activity and passivity, individuality and collectiveness, as we have known them in Generation, are transcended'.[2]

[1] *Fearful Symmetry*, p. 359.

[2] 'Delivering *Jerusalem*', *Blake's Sublime Allegory*, ed. S. Curran and J. A. Wittreich, Jr. (Madison, Wis.: University of Wisconsin Press), pp. 350, 351.

Thus several types of sublimity in *Jerusalem* may be distinguished. Certain passages exhibit a style recognizably sublime in an eighteenth-century sense; others exhibit a psychological and poetic intensity which we experience more directly and usually have in mind when we refer to 'Blakean' qualities; while the concluding plates of text strain after an ultimate meaning that cannot be fully realized. To these categories we should add one more: a kind of anti-sublimity or parody of sublimity that is assigned to demonic figures like the Spectre(s) and the giant Sons of Albion. Blake works by antitypes, and it is fitting that such figures speak in a parody of the sublime, as in the war speech of the Sons of Albion in *65* or the description of the Covering Cherub as

> majestic image
> Of Selfhood, Body put off, the Antichrist accursed
> Coverd with precious stones, a Human Dragon terrible
> And bright, stretchd over Europe & Asia gorgeous
> (*89*: 9–12)

When pushed far enough, such pseudo-sublimity becomes overtly grotesque:

> Derby Peak yawnd a horrid Chasm at the Cries of Gwendolen, & at
> The stamping feet of Ragan upon the flaming Treddles of her Loom
> That drop with crimson gore with the Loves of Albion & Canaan (*64*: 35–7)

The activity of Albion's terrible daughters is modelled on that of Gray's Fatal Sisters in one of the poems Blake illustrated in 1797–8: 'Shafts for shuttles, dipt in gore / Shoot the trembling cords along'.[1] Gray's poem (actually a translation from

[1] 'The Fatal Sisters', *The Complete Poems of Thomas Gray*, ed. H. W. Starr and J. R. Henderson (Oxford: The Clarendon Press, rev. edn., 1972), p. 29. On the importance of this poem for Blake, see Paul Miner, 'William Blake: Two Notes on Sources', *Bulletin of the New York Public Library*, LXII (1958), 203–7. For discussions of Blake's designs for this poem, see: Irene Tayler, *Blake's Illustrations to the Poems of Gray* (Princeton: Princeton University Press, 1971), pp. 110–16; and Geoffrey Keynes, *William Blake's Water-Colour Designs for the Poems of Thomas Gray* (London: The Trianon Press for the William Blake Trust, 1971), pp. 60–2. The designs are reproduced in both these volumes and also in facsimile by the William Blake Trust (1971); the originals are in the collection of Mr and Mrs Paul Mellon.

Old Norse) seeks to capture the sense of sublime terror, while Blake's lines—and his designs for the poem as well—parody it, turning it into the grotesque. Likewise some of the speeches of the Spectres of Los and of Albion have a hollow ranting quality, like Herod's in the Mysteries, as does at times the language of Albion:

> The Malvern and the Cheviot, the Wolds Plinlimmon & Snowdon
> Are mine. here will I build my Laws of Moral Virtue!
> Humanity shall be no more: but war & princedom & victory! (*4*: 30–2)

Such inversions of the sublime reinforce the strength of Blake's claim to be a true Orator.

The language of pathos in *Jerusalem* is a language of relationship, of connectedness—or of lament for their absence. It is the language of brotherhood, of marital affection, of parental love. 'I am in you and you in me,' says Jesus to Albion, 'mutual in love divine: / Fibres of love from man to man thro Albions pleasant land' (*4*: 7–8). These fibres are also the vehicle of sexual desire, as that of Los for Enitharmon:

> And Enitharmon like a faint rainbow waved before him
> Filling with Fibres from his loins which reddend with desire (*86*: 50–1)

Another term characterizing the Blakean pathos is 'mild'—as in 'mild & gentle parts'. 'What shall we do for thee O lovely mild Jerusalem?' ask Los's sons and daughters (*12*: 4), one of the seven references to Jerusalem as mild in *J*; the unfallen Albion was the 'mildest son of Eden' (*40/45*: 3); the poem itself, dictated by Jesus, is 'this mild song' (*4*: 5). Blake is probably the only English poet to promote the usually innocuous adjective *mild* to such an important status, and this fact shows us something of the importance of the pathetic in his work. Other adjectives associated with Blake's pathos are 'sweet', 'lovely', 'soft', 'gentle', and 'tender'. In the grouped frequency word-list appended to the *Concordance*, the first three of these rank among the first 100 frequencies, while the second two (and 'mild') are in the second 100.[1] The nouns 'tears', 'pity', 'mercy', and 'desire'—ranked 40th, 85th, 128th, and 147th respectively—and the verb 'to weep' ('weep', 'wept' are 137th and 143rd; 'weeping' is 85th) are all important elements in the diction of the mild and gentle parts. 'Love', the twelfth most frequent word in Blake's verse, is too inclusive to be limited to the pathetic but is of course of great importance there, and the same may be said of 'beauty' (98th). These individual examples are important, but even more important are their interrelationships.

The Blakean language of pathos is perhaps encountered most intensively in the speeches of Jerusalem herself:

> . . . but mercy is not a Sin
> Nor pity nor love nor kind forgiveness! O! if I have Sinned
> Forgive & pity me! O! unfold thy Veil in mercy & love! (*20*: 24–6)

> I walk weeping in pangs of a Mothers torment for her Children: (*80*: 2)

In passages such as these Jerusalem seeks corresponding feelings in others, and she finds them in Jesus, who says to her:

> Mild Shade of Man, pitiest thou these Visions of terror & woe!
> Give forth thy pity & love. fear not! lo I am with thee always. (*60*: 66–7)

The episode of Joseph and Mary (*61*) is a particularly moving example of interchange in this pathetic mode. At other points united voices of the human community—the Daughters of Beulah, the Friends of Albion—employ such diction, entreating reciprocity:

> As the Sons of Albion have done to Luvah: so they have in him
> Done to the Divine Lord & Saviour, who suffers with those that suffer:

[1] See *Concordance*, II. 2181–5. It should be noted that these are *verse* frequencies and that as words become less frequent more of them tend to be tied for their respective places. Nevertheless, the frequencies give a vivid indication of the importance of these elements of Blake's diction.

For not one sparrow can suffer, & the whole Universe
not suffer also,
In all its Regions, & its Father & Saviour not pity and
weep. (*25*: 6–9)

Demonic figures like Hand and Hyle, in contrast, can only employ the language of pathos by negation:

But father now no more!
Nor sons! nor hateful peace & love, nor soft complacen-
cies
With transgressors meeting in brotherhood around the
table,
Or in the porch or garden. No more the sinful delights
Of age and youth and boy and girl and animal and herb,
And river and mountain, and city & village, and house &
family. (*18*: 13–18)

Denying the pathetic, they deny all relationship except 'All bold asperities / Of Haters met in deadly strife' (21–2).

There is, furthermore, a language of the pseudo-pathetic as there is a language of the pseudo-sublime. The exaggerated styles of Spectres and Giant Sons are grotesque; the styles associated with Vala/Rahab/Tirzah and the daughters are often ironic, parodying the language of pathos:

On her white marble & even Neck, her Heart
Inorb'd and bonified: with locks of shadowing modesty,
shining
Over her beautiful Female features, soft flourishing in
beauty
Beams mild, all love and all perfection, that when the lips
Recieve a kiss from Gods or Men, a threefold kiss returns
From the pressd loveliness . . .[1] (*70*: 21–6)

[1] The passage also parodies Burke's idea of the beautiful: 'Observe that part of a beautiful woman where she is perhaps the most beautiful, about the neck and breasts; the smoothness; the softness; the easy and insensible swell; the variety of the surface, which is never for the smallest space the same; the deceitful maze, through which the unsteady eye slides giddily, without knowing where to fix, or whither it is carried.' (*A Philosophical Enquiry into the Origin of Our Ideas of the Sublime and Beautiful*, ed. J. T. Boulton, Notre Dame, Ind.: University of Notre Dame Press, 1968, p. 115.)

Only 'inorb'd and bonified' lead us to suspect 'beautiful', 'soft', 'mild', and 'love' until the passage shifts from the ironic to the literal:

> From the pressed loveliness: so her whole immortal form three-fold
> Three-fold embrace returns: consuming lives of Gods & Men
> In fires of beauty melting them as gold & silver in the furnace[.] (26–8)

Since the sublime and the pathos are associated by Blake with the masculine and the feminine, it is fitting that the perversions of each sexual identity find expression in parodies of each mode. Tirzah speaks the language of love to her victim, but the essential destructiveness of her motive is betrayed (as in the previous passage quoted) by the intrusion of metal-working imagery: 'my roaring furnaces / Of affliction; of love; of sweet despair; of torment unendurable' (*67*: 50–1). The true pathos establishes relations between human beings and between God and man; in its ironical inversion it becomes the language of other-ness in which the recipient of the message becomes a love object in the most literal sense.

As for the 'prosaic' numbers, these have perhaps given critics the most difficulty. It was one such passage that T. S. Eliot singled out for proof that 'Blake's occasional marriages of poetry and philosophy are not so felicitous':[1]

> He who would do good to another, must do it in Minute Particulars
> General Good is the plea of the scoundrel hypocrite & flatterer:
> For Art & Science cannot exist but in minutely organized Particulars (*55*: 60–2)

These are, as Blake says, 'inferior parts', but such doctrinal passages have their function, just as does Raphael's disquisition on angelic digestion in *Paradise Lost*. The expository, doctrinal passages constitute a sort of interstitial tissue which connects the dramatic passages, both sublime and pathetic,

[1] 'William Blake' (1920), in *Selected Essays* (New York: Harcourt, Brace and Co., 1950), p. 278.

and establishes a frame of reference for them. Some of these parts, 'inferior' though they may be, are crafted with great care:

To be their inferiors or superiors we equally abhor;
Superior, none we know: inferior none: all equal share
Divine Benevolence & joy . . . (*55*: 7–9)

This characterization of the society of 'those who disregard all Mortal Things' (1), with its parallelisms and reiterated 'none', seems almost a rewriting of Gonzalo's dream in *The Tempest* of the perfect commonwealth in which there should be 'no sovereignty':

Letters should not be known; riches, poverty,
And use of service, none; contract, succession,
Bourn, bound of land, tilth, vineyard, none[1]

The problems that a certain type of reader has with the more discursive passages of *Jerusalem* are in fact those which he has with the long poem in general. As C. S. Lewis, writing of the misapprehension of Milton, remarks:

The unfortunate reader has set out expecting 'good lines'—little ebullient patches of delight—such as he is accustomed to find in lyrics, and has thought he was finding them in things that took his fancy for accidental reasons during the first five minutes; after that, finding that the poem cannot really be read in this way, he has given it up. Of the continuity of a long narrative poem, the subordination of the line to the paragraph and the paragraph to the Book and even of the Book to the whole, of the grand sweeping effects that take a quarter of an hour to develop themselves, he has had no conception.[2]

Blake's verse techniques, as we have seen, are not precisely Milton's; nor is the Prophetic structure of *Jerusalem* equatable with the narrative structure of *Paradise Lost*, a subject to be discussed in Chapter VI. Nevertheless, Lewis's statement holds true of Blake's mode of the long poem as well as of Milton's: the work is not a quarry to be worked by industrious editors, despite attempts to extract its riches in anthologies[3] or to

[1] *The Tempest*, II. i. 150–2.

[2] *A Preface to Paradise Lost* (London: Oxford University Press, 1959 [1942]), p. 1.

[3] W. B. Yeats, in his Muses' Library edition of *The Poems of William Blake* (London, 1893), set a doubtful precedent by printing passages from *Jerusalem* prefixed by Yeats's own titles.

present it in a 'simplified version'.[1] Such attempts may be helpful in that by giving the reader an idea of what *Jerusalem* is like they encourage him to read the whole. Too often, however, the implication of such selections is that *Jerusalem* can be read only for its 'terrific numbers' in contradiction to Blake's own view that all three modes of poetic discourse 'are necessary to each other'.

There is one further aspect of the poetry of *Jerusalem* which, though not one of Blake's three categories, needs to be discussed: the lyric, represented by rhymed passages from four to eighty-eight lines in length on plates *3, 26, 27, 37/41, 52,* and *77*. Of these the poems on *27, 77,* and *52* stand out in importance. The last, a poem of seven quatrains beginning 'I saw a Monk of Charlemaine', is closely related to the Pickering MS poem 'The Grey Monk': both derive from a *Notebook* poem probably written in 1803 or 1804.[2] As Erdman suggests, the original impetus for the poem was probably Blake's own suffering of mind as he was charged with sedition in a former Grey Friars church in Chichester.[3] 'The Grey Monk' is a ballad which presents a dramatic situation and then develops it in a brief narrative to an ironical conclusion. 'I saw a Monk' is not a version of this poem but derives independently from the *Notebook*, containing twelve lines of the *Notebook* draft that do not appear in the longer Pickering MS poem. 'I saw a Monk' is a visionary poem which serves as an introduction, linked by the favourable references in the prose of *52* to monks and Methodists, to the chapter addressed 'To the Deists'. The figures of Charlemaine, Gibbon, Voltaire, Rousseau, Titus, Constantine, and even Satan are appropriate here, in the context of Prophecy, as they would not be in 'The Grey Monk'. The scene is Goyaesque in its macabre, lurid

[1] *Jerusalem: A Simplified Version* (London: George Allen and Unwin), ed. William R. Hughes (London, 1964).

[2] See Erdman, *Notebook*, p. 13 and note to N 8 transcript. The Pickering MS has usually been dated *c.*1805, but Bentley (*Blake Books*, p. 342) dates it '? after 1807'. Nevertheless, as Bentley also assigns 'The Grey Monk' to 1803, the date of the holograph need not concern us here, especially as 'I saw a Monk of Charlemaine' is really another poem rather than a version of 'The Grey Monk'.

[3] See *Blake: Prophet*, pp. 414–15. As Erdman points out, in the original draft, the Monk, like Blake, was accused of being 'seditious' (*Notebook*, N 8 transcript). I cannot agree, however, that the wife and children in the poem are meant to be the Monk's.

quality. 'I talkd with the Grey Monk as we stood / In beams of infernal light' has the matter-of-factness of the *Caprichos* etchings as well as of the Memorable Fancies of *The Marriage of Heaven and Hell*. Gibbon and Voltaire are surreally depicted wielding medieval instruments of torture, in accord with Blake's conviction that 'Voltaire . . . was as intolerant as an Inquisitor'.[1] These personifications mingle with abstractions—'The Schools', 'clouds of learning', 'War'—to create a symbolic frame of reference in which there flows, nevertheless, real blood. Imagery of weapons links up with that of the torture chamber, though unfortunately the *Notebook*'s brilliant 'Glory & Victory a phallic Whip'[2] is not included. Satan's black bow, reminding us of the bent triple bow of the *35* design, is marvellously transformed along with the Roman sword at the end of the poem. Unlike 'The Grey Monk', which ends with a deliberately ironical ending appropriate to a manuscript that includes the cyclical 'Mental Traveller', 'I saw a Monk' concludes with a triumphant statement of non-violent victory:

For a Tear is an Intellectual thing;
And a Sigh is the Sword of an Angel King
And the bitter groan of a Martyrs woe
Is an Arrow from the Almighties Bow!

These lines concluded the poem in the *Notebook* too, thus dominating the stanza in which the successful tyrannicide becomes 'a Tyrant in his stead'.[3] That ending is appropriate to 'The Grey Monk', which remains close to being a ballad and needs a sense of narrative closure; the *Jerusalem* ending opens out immediately to the first line of the following plate —'But Los, who is the Vehicular Form of strong Urthona / Wept vehemently over Albion . . .' (*53*: 1–2).

Of the remaining rhymed poetry in *Jerusalem*, two examples are single quatrains which require little discussion. 'Each Man is in his Spectre's power', which appears in mirror writing in the *37* design, is a doctrinal statement which originally was written on the same *Notebook* page as 'I saw a Monk of

[1] *A Vision of the Last Judgment*, E. 553.
[2] *Notebook*, N 8; cf. the *21* design.
[3] *Notebook*, N 8, and 'The Grey Monk', E. 481.

Charlemaine', The famous 'I give you the end of a golden string' (*77*) introduces 'To the Christians' with fine epigrammatic thrust. Two passages of distichs, on *3* and *77*, are primarily expository rather than lyrical; the latter especially is closely related to the crabbed, gnomic style of *The Everlasting Gospel*. But Blake's lyric power at its highest intensity is seen in the long 'The fields from Islington to Marybone' (*27*) and its pendant 'England! awake! awake! awake!' (*77*). Here the central subject-matter of *Jerusalem* is expressed masterfully in lyric form.

'The fields from Islington to Marybone' is a lyrical epitome of the whole of *Jerusalem*. As Damon observes, this poem moves through three distinct phases from Innocence to Experience to Redemption.[1] It combines personal recollection with myth, juxtaposing places remembered from Blake's childhood with symbolic figures and topographical symbolism characteristic of Blake's late works. Employing iambic tetrameter quatrains rhyming abab, it generates through a strong accumulative sense of rhythm an excitement characteristic of some Methodist hymns,[2] which it also resembles in its sense of intense personal intimacy with the divine. There is at least one older model for 'The fields from Islington to Marybone': the 'Jerusalem' hymn dating back to the sixteenth century and known to us chiefly through the examples of 'Hierusalem my happy home'—itself existing in several forms[3]—and 'The Bellman's Song'.[4] The first of these was published in 1801-2 in versions by James

[1] *William Blake: His Philosophy and Symbols*, p. 447.

[2] On the Methodist hymn and the relation of Blake's poetry to Charles Wesley's, see Martha Winburn England, *Hymns Unbidden* (New York Public Library: New York, 1966), pp. 31-112.

[3] Three versions are distinguished by Stephen A. Hurlbut, *The Picture of the Heavenly Jerusalem* (Washington, DC, 1943), part II, as follows: 1. 'A Song mad[e] by F. B. P.: to the tune of Diana', printed in *The Song of Mary the Mother of Christ* (1601). 2. 'Hierusalem, thy joyes divine' (MS title 'A prisoner's songe'), likewise printed in *The Song of Mary*. 3. 'O Mother deare Hierusalem', printed in *The Glasse of vaineglorie* by W. Prid (1585). All three are included in BL Add. MS 15,225, a compilation of hymns made in the reign of James I. Their common source is the book known as *The Meditations of St. Augustine*, actually by the eleventh-century author Jean de Fécamp, first translated into English in 1558 (incompletely) and completely translated in 1581 by Thomas Rogers; see below, Chapter III, pp. 144-5.

[4] For this suggestion I am indebted to the late Ruthven Todd.

Montgomery,[1] the poet and journalist who was a friend of Fuseli's patron William Roscoe and who knew of Blake through the 1808 *Grave* if not earlier.[2] In this magnificent poem, the speaker apostrophizes Jerusalem from the perspective of a world in which

> Wee that are here in banishment
>   Continually doe mourne
> We sighe and sobbe, we weepe and weale
>   Perpetually we groane[3]

—very much the world of the middle section of Blake's lyric, with its weeping, groans, and woe, just as F. B. P.'s pastoral vision of Jerusalem is suggestive of Blake's:

> Thy gardens and thy gallant walks
>   Continually are greene
> There groes such sweet and pleasant flowers
>   As no where else are seene[4]

The less powerful 'Bellman's Song' is perhaps verbally closer to the short *77* lyric, calling 'Awake, awake, good people all; / Awake and you shall hear'[5] as Blake calls 'England! awake! awake! awake!' in *77* (cf. also 'Awake! Awake Jerusalem!' in *97*: 1). Blake's apparent debt to traditional lyrics in both instances casts a new light over the tradition itself, bringing vividly to us an expression of longing for Jerusalem that goes back through English hymnody to Psalm 137 and to Lamentations.

[1] Noted by John Julian, *A Dictionary of Hymnology* (London: John Murray, rev. edn., 1908), pp. 580–3, as follows: 1. Hymn no. 193, signed 'Eckington C.', in Edward Williams and James Boden's *Collection of Above 600 Hymns designed as a New Supplement to Dr. Watts's Psalms & Hymns* (Doncaster, 1801). 2. *Psalms for Public or Private Devotion* (Sheffield, printed by James Montgomery At *The Iris* Office, 1802). 3. James Montgomery's *Christian Psalmist*, No. 129. Julian points out that Montgomery printed a collection of hymns for the use of the Eckington Parish Church Choir (1796–1800) and that 'Hierusalem, My Happy Home' was included there.

[2] See Robert N. Essick and Morton D. Paley, *Robert Blair's* The Grave *Illustrated by William Blake*, pp. 11, 13, 21, 23–5, 28.

[3] *Hymns as Poetry*, ed. Tom Ingram and Douglas Newton (London: Constable, 1956), p. 43.

[4] Ibid., p. 44.

[5] *The Oxford Book of Carols*, ed. Dearmer, Williams, and Shaw (London, rev. edn., 1964), p. 89. Note, too, in stanza 4: 'The fields were green as green could be'; cf. 'In Englands green & pleasant bowers' in *J 77*.

The poem itself begins with an evocation of a time which is at once the archetypal *illud tempus* when (as in the *Milton* lyric) Jerusalem and Albion were one, and Blake's own childhood, when we imagine that he rambled through open fields north of the metropolis past places like the Jew's Harp House tea-garden and the Green Man Inn, between Islington and Marylebone. The dominant colours of the first twenty lines are green and gold, evocative here of a feeling of primal innocence,[1] a feeling reinforced by images of children, diminutives —even the meadows are 'little'—and syntactic inversions reminiscent of children's verse—'The Pond where Boys to bathe delight'. In the *now* of the poem, emphasized by the sudden shift to present tense in line 25, this Paradise is about to be regained. The 'golden builders' (cf. 'The singing masons building roofs of gold' in *Henry V*, I. ii. 198) bring us back to the 'pillars of gold' of line 3, perhaps in reference to the greening of London that seemed to be taking place in 1811 when Regent's Park was established, linking Marylebone to Primrose Hill to the north-east, and to St. John's Wood to the north-west. Thus the natural delights of the north of London are seen as restored, but with the difference of cultivation and architecture, for Blake's idea of the regenerate state is not a wilderness but (as Frye has emphasized) a city and a garden. The golden builders are probably constructing the Nash terraces[2] facing the Park to the south (and later to the east and west).[3] Seen from the vantage-point of Primrose Hill (where Blake once conversed with the Spiritual Sun),[4] their splendid, Bath-stone-coloured stucco façades with their pillars and pilasters would have appeared 'golden'.[5] Thus the lyric goes from the evocation of an Edenic past to regenerative activity in the present, but it then diverges to a fallen

[1] Cf. the similar thematic use of these colours in Dylan Thomas's 'Fern Hill'.

[2] As suggested by Stanley Gardner, *Blake* (London: Evans Bros., 1968), pp. 143–5.

[3] On the great architectural plans of which the terraces were part, see John Summerson, *Georgian London* (Harmondsworth, Middlesex: Penguin Books, rev. edn., 1962), pp. 177–90.

[4] As Blake told Crabb Robinson in 1825. *BR*, p. 313.

[5] The first of the Nash Crescents was Park Crescent, begun in 1812, opening off the New Road. The Jew's Harp House, the Green Man, and Willan's Farm were all on or just off the New Road.

past 'Where Satan the first victory won' (28). This fallen past, which continues until the present tense reappears in line 67, is of course not the archaic *illud tempus* but the interim of history in which take place the psychic division of Albion, the institution of retributive justice, and the outbreak of war.

The first section of the poem is comparatively regular (with the exception of the pentameter line 24) and is marked by a euphonious assonance of open vowels, as in 'Shine upon the starry sky' (12). These qualities, mimetic of primal innocence, are superseded in the second section by variation of stressed syllables in the form of spondees and trochees:

> Albions Spectre from his Loins
> Tore forth in all the pomp of War!
> Satan his name: in flames of fire
> He stretch'd his Druid Pillars far.

By artful variation the disjunctive nature of the Spectre is emphasized. With the word 'far', the imagery shifts from a world in which the largest distance—from St. Pancras to St. John's Wood—is less than three miles, to the map of the earth. Jerusalem begins her fall in Lambeth, where Blake conceived the mythology of his long poems, and continues eastward—the direction of the progress of England's armies. Her fall continues from Poplar, in the East End Docks, and Bow just north of it, north and east about fifty miles to Maldon and Colchester on the Essex coast. Maldon, perhaps significantly located on the river Blackwater (cf. *4*: 10 'A black water accumulates'), is of course the site of the Old English *Battle of Maldon* where the heroic Byrhtnoth was killed with a poisoned spear. Colchester was at various times a citadel of the ancient Britons, the Romans, the Saxons, and the Normans, associated with Boadicea, Constantine, and William I, all of whom are identified with war or tyranny in *Jerusalem*.[1] This terrible progress continues to the Continent, to the scenes of Napoleonic battles on the Rhine and the Danube;

[1] On Boadicea and Constantine, see *Blake Dictionary*, s.v. 'William' is one of a (deleted) list of rulers of England in *73*: 37. He built at Colchester the largest castle keep in Europe; the Royalist city held out for eleven weeks against Fairfax's army in the Civil War.

and at this point, as Erdman points out, the topographical allusions make contact with those in Chapter 1 of *The Rise and Fall of the Roman Empire.*[1] Modern warfare reiterates ancient warfare, and continues to do so as Satan stands on the Euphrates, dominating Asia and exercising his powers over Palestine (where British defenders were besieged at Acre by Napoleon in 1799). Thus present-tense limited motion in an insular space ('She walks upon our meadows green') is replaced by enormous motion eastward across the map of the world; and the place-names of remembered personal intimacy by those of ancient military tradition and of modern newspaper headlines.

The last part of this second section is bound together by the anaphora of 'He witherd up' in lines 49, 51, and 53. The images of withering and of the Worm that the Human Form becomes are then qualified by the word 'translucent' (56), a semi-technical Swedenborgian term which enters Blake's vocabulary only after 1800 along with a number of other Swedenborgian terms and conceptions.[2] The entry of light implied by 'translucence' then leads in the next two stanzas to the assumption of the human form by Jesus, and with this the third, redemptive portion of the poem begins. A sense of exalted momentum is then generated by a series of apostrophes, exclamations, questions, and commands. In the four quatrains from line 65 to line 80 there are three interrogatives and five imperatives, and in 75 the declarative statement framed by apostrophes has a triumphant assertiveness:

> Spectre of Albion! warlike Fiend!
> In clouds of blood & ruin roll'd:
> I here reclaim thee as my own
> My Selfhood! Satan! armd in gold.

At 67 the present tense enters the poem for the first time

[1] See *Blake: Prophet*, p. 468.

[2] In *Apocalypse Revealed* (Manchester: C. Wheeler, 1791), Swedenborg writes: 'By precious Stones, when speaking of the Word, is signified Divine Truth in the literal sense of the Word transparent or translucent in it's spiritual sense. . . . The reason why it is translucent, is because Divine Truth in the literal sense is in spiritual Light, wherefore when spiritual light flows into natural light with a Man, who is reading the Word, he is illuminated, and sees truths there, for the objects of spiritual Light are Truths.' (No. 911, vol. II, pp. 547–8.)

since line 25, bringing us back from the fallen past to the regenerative present. Finally, in the last stanza, two reiterated future tenses project the redemptive meaning into the millennial future of the continuing city:

In my Exchanges every Land
Shall walk, & mine in every Land,
Mutual shall build Jerusalem:
Both heart in heart & hand in hand.

'From Islington to Marybone' is Blake's longest poem in a verse form he particularly liked to employ, the iambic tetrameter quatrain rhyming abab. Because of its extraordinary beauty it is sometimes taken by critics hostile to Blake's long poems as evidence that at least he had not lost his lyric gift. Indeed he had not, but it should be emphasized that this poem does not stand apart from the rest of *Jerusalem*, depending as it does for its meaning upon symbols established elsewhere in the work. Lyric in form, it is nevertheless a Prophecy in miniature, an epitome of the whole. With the other, shorter lyrics in *J* it constitutes a fourth mode of poetic statement, and its success as a poem is an indication not that Blake mistook his calling but that he understood how the various parts of his great work demanded different types of poetry. Of the relations of those parts to one another, of the form of the whole, much needs to be said. If *J* is not to be considered a collection of fragments, then the subject of its coherence must be discussed. Yet this cannot be done with respect to the poetry alone, for *J* is also a work of art. Furthermore, such an overall view of the work will make more sense after a consideration of its thematic arguments and of its constituent myths.

Supplementary note

Some changes are primarily contextual; that is, the alterations are made primarily to adjust a *FZ* passage to new narrative circumstances in *J*. Such a revision occurs in the *FZ* text that became *J 43/29*: 33–82. The lines of *FZ* 39: 17–20, 40: 1–20, 41: 1–18, 42: 1–19—a continuous passage in the manuscript—were emended in numerous details, most of which can be described as follows:

1. Albion is named in *J* in place of *FZ*'s 'Eternal / Fallen / Darkning Man', 'Man', 'Eternal / Fallen One'. Having found a name for his central

figure, Blake evidently meant to use it. However, at four points in the MS passage Albion is named, although three times in a third revision and once in a second revision. Once *J* actually uses the earlier 'fallen Man' (*43*: 65) where the third *FZ* revision reads 'Albion'.

2. Pronominal reference is changed, since the *FZ* speech is made by Ahania to Urizen (first to second person), while the account in *J* is recounted by 'two Immortal forms', the Spectre and Emanation of Los. At various points in the speech, lines spoken in the first person by Ahania are either excised in *J* or changed to the second person (the latter following revision in the MS), three lines of this sort being deleted.

3. Five more lines (*FZ* 41: 5–9) were omitted in *J*. Considering how carefully Blake transcribed most of the rest, we can only conclude that these rather emptily rhetorical lines addressed by Ahania to Urizen could not be adapted for Blake's purpose in *J*, in which case they properly belong in category 2 above, or that he did not care for them enough to adapt them to the new context.

4. Two lines already deleted in *FZ* (39: 20–1) were not incorporated. Only one substantial change seems to have been made for other than contextual reasons. In *FZ* 42 Blake had added the lines 'Whether this is Jerusalem or Babylon we know not / All is confusion All is tumult & we lone escaped' (E. 751)—which, as the plural pronoun shows, was meant not for Ahania, the speaker in *FZ*, but for the two Immortal forms of *J*. In further revision for *J*, he changed the first of these lines to 'Whether of Jerusalems or Valas ruins congenerated, we know not' (81). 'Congenerated' is one of a number of words used in a semi-technical sense in *J*—Latinate words like 'conglomerating', 'conjoined/conjoining', and 'assimilate/assimilating' become more important in Blake's vocabulary from *The Four Zoas* on. It is interesting that 'congenerated' did not appear in the late *FZ* addition and that Blake took the opportunity to add it in *J*.

Other parallel passages may be described as follows:

1. Some of the Daughters of Albion are (differently) listed in *FZ* 25: 29–30 and in *J 5*: 43–4.

2. A line spoken by Enion to Tharmas in *FZ* 4: 18 (an added passage) is taken over with reference to Albion in *J 22*: 1, where Vala says 'Albion thy fear has made me tremble; thy terrors have surrounded me.' Eight new lines follow in *J*, and then three more lines are borrowed without substantial change from *FZ* 4: 19–21 (an added passage) for *J 22*: 10–12. After two more new *J* lines, the borrowing continues, this time from a passage written discernibly after lines *4*: 18–26 in the MS:

> I have lookd into the secret soul of him I lovd
> And in the Dark recesses found Sin & cannot return

J 22: 14–15 takes these lines over almost verbatim, only changing 'cannot' to the stronger 'can never'. After three new lines in *J*, the borrowing takes up once more with Tharmas's reply to Enion (30–4), written vertically in the right-hand margin of the MS, now transferred to Jerusalem addressing Albion (*22*: 20–4). Here again the changes are minor: 'number' for 'examine' and 'dark' for 'Death'. In all, ten *FZ* lines are adapted for *J 22*, from at least two 'layers' of additions to the original manuscript. Although it cannot be proved that the traffic goes from *FZ* to *J* here, it seems as if Blake were quarrying material from his nearly abandoned Zoas myth for the later myth of Jerusalem and Albion.

3. *FZ* 18: 18–13 (part of an added passage) was emended for greater rhythmical effect in *J 23*. The original reads:

> Now Man was come to the Palm tree & to the Oak of Weeping
> Which stand upon the edge of Beulah & he sunk down
> From the supporting arms of the Eternal Saviour . . .

In *J 23*: 24–7, Blake changes 'Man' to 'Albion' in the first line, and breaks the second line at 'sunk', enjambing to 'Down in sick pallid languour!' in the third.

4. A line about the Spectre appears with variations twice in *FZ* and once in *J*:

> They said The Spectre is in every man insane & most / Deformd
> (*FZ* 5: 38–9)

> Thou knowest that the Spectre is in Every Man insane brutish
> (*FZ* 84: 36)

> The Spectre is, in Giant Man; insane, and most deform'd. (*J 33*: 4)

Both *FZ* passages come from additions to their respective MS pages, the one on the much reworked page 5 being part of a second column of vertically written additions in the right margin.

5. An interesting reworking of lines occurs in *FZ* 59: 11–16 / *J 36*/*40*: 37–42. Lines relating to Urthona are reworked so as to refer to the fallen Albion. The *FZ* lines are, as is often the case in that poem, discrete enough to be used as units that can be rearranged:

> Torn by black storms & ceaseless torrents of consuming fire
> Within his breast his fiery sons chaind down & filld with cursings
>
> And breathing terrible blood & vengeance gnashing his teeth with pain
> Let loose the Enormous Spirit in the darkness of the deep
> And his dark wife that once fair crystal form divinely clear
> Within his ribs producing serpents whose souls are flames of fire

In *J*, Blake rewrote the first line of the passage ('And curses, with his mighty arms brandish'd against the heavens'). Line 3 became the second line, the initial 'and' only being omitted. Line 1 followed, with the addition of 'his own' to 'consuming fire'. In line 2, now the fourth line, 'fiery sons' was changed to 'mighty sons'. The last two lines are the same in both passages, with the exception of the technical term 'Eon' substituted for 'wife' in the first of them. (In Blake's works 'Eon', meaning 'Emanation', appears only in *Milton* and *Jerusalem*—see *Blake Dictionary*, p. 127.) The fourth line of the *FZ* passage, displaced by the new first line in *J*, was discarded. This revision is primarily interesting as an example of how whole lines of *FZ* could be moved and yet retained in a single passage.

6. Locational references vary from *FZ* 25: 39, where the dead wail 'In Ulro beneath Beulah', to *J 36/40*: 57, where it is 'In Bowlahoola & Allamanda'. In *FZ* 25: 39, the dead wail once again 'In Ulro beneath Beulah'; in *J 48*: 52 'In the ends of Beulah'. Both *FZ* lines are additions to page 25, the second being part of a passage written in a stanza break. The symbolic topography changes from vertical to horizontal in both instances.

7. Two lines in *J 44/30* are adapted from a powerful passage in *FZ* 80. The subject is the pauperization of the poor, advocated by Urizen in the MS and delivered in the imperative mood, described in the third person by the narrative voice in *J*. The *FZ* passage of seven lines was expanded to thirteen (80: 3–16) but is reduced to two lines (*44/30*: 30–1) in *J*:

> They compell the Poor to live upon a crust of bread by soft mild arts:
> They reduce the Man to want: then give with pomp & ceremony.

In *FZ* 80 (lines 3, 16) 'They' does not occur in the first line; the second reads 'Magnify small gifts reduce the man to want a gift & then give with pomp'. There is certainly less power in the *J* version.

8. Los sees the finger of God touch the seventh furnace in a section added to the end of Night IV—*FZ* 56: 24–5 and in *J 48*: 44–5. In *J 12* he beholds the finger of God in terrors, and in 10–11 'I saw the finger of God go forth / Upon my Furnaces . . .'.

9. 'Eternity groand & was troubled at the image of Eternal Death' (*FZ* 18: 9) is repeated verbatim, with the addition of punctuation, in *J 48*: 12. It is interesting to note that in this and a number of other instances, an unpunctuated *FZ* line which might be presumed to end with a full stop ends with an exclamation mark in *J*. The MS line is at the beginning of an added section on the page.

10. Also from the beginning of an added section is 'Lord. Saviour if thou hadst been here our brother had not died', *FZ* 56: 1; this is repeated without 'Lord. Saviour' in *J 50*: 11.

11. 'In eternal torment of love & jealousy' in *J 69*: 7 may or may not be regarded as parallel to 'The Torments of Love & Jealousy in' from a very late addition, written in pencil, on *FZ* 1: 4.

12. In *FZ* 115: 5–6 occurs a list of Churches which has four names in common with a list in *J 75*: 15–16. *J 75*: 2–3 has a reference to Rahab and her cup loosely similar to the reference to the Harlot and her Cup in *FZ* 111: 6–7.

13. On *FZ* 30: 48 occur the lines, referring to Urizen and Ahania, 'Two wills they had two intellects & not as in times of old'; this is repeated with punctuation in *J 86*: 61 but with reference to Enitharmon and Los.

14. 'I know I was Urthona keeper of the gates of heaven' (*FZ* 48: 19) is in *J 82*: 81 'I know I am Urthona keeper of the Gates of Heaven'.

Figures

1. *Jerusalem*, copy F, plate *33/37*

46

Leaning against the pillars, & his disease rose from his skirts
Upon the Precipice he stood: ready to fall into Non-Entity.
Los was all astonishment & terror: he trembled sitting on the Stone
Of London: but the interiors of Albions fibres & nerves were hidden
From Los; astonishd he beheld only the petrified surfaces:
And saw his Furnaces in ruins, for Los is the Demon of the Furnaces;
He saw also the Four Points of Albion reversd inwards
He seizd his Hammer & Tongs, his iron Poker & his Bellows,
Upon the valleys of Middlesex, Shouting loud for aid Divine.
In stern defiance came from Albions bosom Hand, Hyle, Koban,
Gwantok, Peachy, Brertun, Slaid, Huttn, Skofeld, Kock, Kotope
Bowen, Albions Sons: they bore him a golden couch into the porch
And on the Couch reposd his limbs, trembling from the bloody field.
Rearing their Druid Patriarchal rocky Temples around his limbs.
(All things begin & end, in Albions Ancient Druid Rocky Shore.)

2. *Jerusalem*, copy F, plate *46*/*32*

3. *Jerusalem*, copy F, plate *76*

4. J. Matham, engraving after Tintoretto. *The Miracle of the Slave* (detail)

5. *Jerusalem*, copy F, plate *31*/*35*

6. *Biblia Pauperum*. Detail of the creation of Eve

7. (*below*) Hartman Schedel, *Liber Chronicorum* (Nuremberg, 1493, folio 6). Creation of Eve

8. *Jerusalem*, plate *28*. First proof state

9. *Jerusalem*, plate *28*. Second (intermediate) proof state

10. *Jerusalem*, copy I (posthumous), plate *28*

11. *Jerusalem*, copy F, plate *51*

12. *Jerusalem*, plate *51*. Separate plate

13. Pencil drawing related to *Jerusalem*, plate *51*

14. *Jerusalem*, plate *1*. Proof state

15. Anonymous engraving, probably after Mantegna. *The Descent to Hell*

16. Marcantonio Raimondi, engraving after an unknown artist. *Vulcan, Venus, and Cup*

17. The [*First*] *Book of Urizen*, copy G, plate 21

18. *Jerusalem*, copy F, plate *100*

II. *Jerusalem*, copy E, plate *100*

Chapter II

Art

Thanks principally to the works of the art historians Anthony Blunt, Martin Butlin, and David Bindman,[1] we are now in a position to understand the development of Blake's art. We can see that just as Blake's thought evolved, sometimes gradually, sometimes in dramatic leaps, so did his theory and practice of art. What is especially clear now is that for about a decade beginning in the mid-1790s, Blake's art went through a period of transition during which Blake made several kinds of exploration from the neo-classical base that was almost always his point of departure. He experimented with colour-printing from copper, producing several copies of illuminated books and other graphic works,[2] and he developed a distinctive method of creating colour prints from millboards.[3] In painting he allowed himself to be tempted to emulate 'demons'—as he was later to call them[4]—like Titian and Rubens, experimenting with colour and chiaroscuro. Then, in the first few years of the new century, Blake consolidated what may be called the beginning of his mature style, one characterized by the predominance of line and form over colour and masses, by a high degree of linearity, and at first by a tendency to emphasize the intersection of strong verticals with an emphatically flat picture plane. (Butlin demonstrates

[1] Anthony Blunt, *The Art of William Blake* (New York: Columbia University Press, 1959); David Bindman, *Blake As an Artist* (Oxford: Phaidon Press, 1977); Martin Butlin, *William Blake* (London: The Tate Gallery, 1978).

[2] On Blake's colour-printing technique, see Ruthven Todd, *William Blake the Artist* (London: Studio Vista, 1971), p. 37, and Robert N. Essick, *William Blake, Printmaker* (Princeton: Princeton University Press, 1980), pp. 125–35.

[3] See Martin Butlin, 'The Evolution of Blake's Large Color Prints of 1795', *William Blake: Essays for S. Foster Damon*, pp. 109–16. More recently, Butlin has shown that at least one of these colour prints, the Tate Gallery's *Newton*, was produced in 1804–5. See 'A Newly Discovered Watermark', *Blake*, XV (1981), 101–3.

[4] In *A Descriptive Catalogue* (1809); see Edward J. Rose, ' "A Most Outrageous Demon": Blake's Case Against Rubens', *Bucknell Review*, XVII (1969), 35–54.

this development by contrasting *The Soldiers Casting Lots for Christ's Garment* (Fitzwilliam Museum, 1800) with water-colours such as *The Magdalene at the Sepulchre* (Yale Center for British Art, *c.* 1805).[1]) In the years following 1805, Blake's style relaxed somewhat, becoming less austere at times and more deliberately irregular, yet maintaining the 'primitive' quality that is characteristic of *Milton* and *Jerusalem*. The rich colouring of copy E of *Jerusalem* as well as of some other late coloured illuminated books[2] is a still later feature which also characterizes the more finished Dante water-colours and other drawings and paintings of Blake's last years.

The hinge on which these changes turned was, in Blake's mind, his visit to the Truchsessian Gallery in October 1804: 'Suddenly, on the day after entering the Truchsessian Gallery of Pictures, I was again enlightened with the light I enjoyed in my youth, and which has for exactly twenty years been closed from me as by a door and by window-shutters.'[3] As I have elsewhere attempted to reconstruct Blake's Truchsessian Gallery experience, the details need not be repeated here.[4] In the display of over nine hundred pictures Blake found a re-confirmation of his earlier ideas about art, and his recent intuitions crystallized into a coherent artistic programme. He would reject the eclecticism which, however interesting the results, had come to represent for him a deviation from his true vocation. He thought of this as a return to origins: in painting, to Raphael, Michelangelo, and Giulio Romano; in graphic art to Dürer, Marcantonio Raimondi, and other 'old' engravers. In doing this, Blake was emphasizing elements of his earlier work as well, work which clearly partakes of what Robert Rosenblum has called 'the International Style of 1800'.[5] The non-illusionistic nature of the *Jerusalem*

[1] *William Blake* (London: Tate Gallery, 1978), p. 92.

[2] One must of course beware of circular reasoning in calling the richly coloured copies of the illuminated books 'late'; but two good examples are copy D of *Milton* (Library of Congress) and copy O of *America*, the former having watermarks of 1815 and the latter of 1818.

[3] Letter to William Hayley, 23 October 1804, *Letters*, p. 107. Blake's previous letter to Hayley is dated 28 September 1804; presumably the visit to the Truchsessian Gallery occurred in the interim.

[4] 'The Truchsessian Gallery Revisited', *Studies in Romanticism*, XVI (1977), 165–77.

[5] 'The International Style of 1800: A Study in Linear Abstraction', New York

designs, their use of line rather than colour to define masses, and their conscious relationship to classical tradition (even when deliberately distorting classical forms and attitudes)—all these characteristics link the art of *Jerusalem* with similar aspects of the art of Fuseli, Flaxman, Romney, Carstens, Runge, and even Ingres.[1]

During the sixteen or more years that he was working on *Jerusalem*, Blake expressed his views about art in ways that may help us to understand his purposes but that too often have been interpreted as a programme which we are bound to accept or reject. For some there is a temptation to give Blake bad marks in art history for his dismissal of Rubens, Correggio, and Titian; or, conversely, to identify with Blake in his running quarrel with Reynolds's *Discourses.*[2] To embrace either alternative is, however, to misunderstand the necessity that drove Blake to his polemical positions. Blake and some of his contemporaries faced the dilemma of the artist in what Matthew Arnold called 'an epoch of concentration'. In such an age society does not provide the creative power with 'a current of ideas in the highest degree animating and nourishing to the creative power' characteristic of an 'epoch of expansion', but 'books and reading may enable a man to construct a kind of semblance of it in his own mind, a world of knowledge and intelligence in which he may live and work'.[3] Blake shows his intense awareness of this predicament. In order to accomplish his great task, Blake had to place himself within a tradition. He could have said, altering Los's

University, Ph.D. thesis, 1956; see also Rosenblum, *Transformations in Late Eighteenth Century Art* (Princeton: Princeton University Press, 2nd printing, 1969), pp. 154–8.

[1] On the general subject, see once more Rosenblum, 'International Style' and *Transformations*. Of particular importance from this perspective is the catalogue prepared by David Bindman for the Blake exhibition in the Hamburger Kunsthalle series 'Kunst um 1800': *William Blake* (Hamburg: Prestel, 1975). On Romney, see Jean H. Hagstrum, 'Romney and Blake: Gifts of Grace and Terror', *Blake in His Time*, ed. Robert N. Essick and Donald Pearce (Bloomington, Ind.: Indiana University Press, 1978), pp. 170–97.

[2] Blake's ideas about art are discussed in my *William Blake* (Oxford: Phaidon, 1978), pp. 49–54.

[3] 'The Function of Criticism At the Present Time', *Lectures and Essays in Criticism*, ed. R. H. Super (Ann Arbor: University of Michigan Press, 1973 [1962]), p. 262.

word but not its essential meaning: 'I must create a Tradition or be enslaved by another Mans.' He did this by assimilating elements of works of art which he often knew only through engraved or painted reproductions. Finding the institutional resources available to him insufficient for his purposes, Blake set about forming an art school of the mind. He frequented sales, studied the pictures that were exhibited, and formed his own print collection despite his poverty.[1] Most important of all, he continued to develop as a graphic artist. As Robert N. Essick has shown,[2] and as comparisons between Blake's early and late engravings dramatically testify, Blake developed from a competent print-maker to a great one—from an engraver whose best work was perhaps equal to the excellent William Sharp's to the master who created the *Illustrations of the Book of Job*.

Blake's search for authenticity was also a search for the archaic in a special sense of that word. He believed there had been a golden period in the state of the arts—the word 'ancient' recurs in connection with this idea—and that the great works of both classical and modern art were but copies of 'wonderful originals'[3] produced in an antediluvian age. To the extent that the qualities of those mythical originals were approximated in later art, the latter participated in the 'ancient' qualities of the former. Thus Raphael and Michelangelo could be seen as primitive. There is, in this Blakean view, no progress in art, only the periodic rediscovery of permanent truth. By this strategy of displacement Blake tried to cope with an age in which artistic activity—as measured by academies, sales, and exhibitions—had remarkably increased within recent memory, and yet in which his own talents were denigrated. 'In this Plate', declares Blake of his *Canterbury Pilgrims*, 'M^{r} B has resumed the style with which he set out in life of which Heath & Stothard were the awkward imitators at that time it is the style of Alb Durers Histries & the old Engravers which cannot be imitated by any one who does not

[1] On Blake's early print-collecting, see Benjamin Heath Malkin, *A Father's Memoir of His Child* (1806), *BR*, p. 422. Late in life, in 1821, Blake was forced by poverty to sell his print collection to Colnaghi; see *BR*, p. 276.

[2] *William Blake, Printmaker* (Princeton: Princeton University Press, 1980).

[3] *Descriptive Catalogue*, E. 422. See my essay '"Wonderful Originals"—Blake and Ancient Sculpture', in *Blake and His Time*, pp. 170–98.

understand drawing.'[1] Of course this does not mean that Blake set out to produce a print that could literally be mistaken for one by 'the old Engravers'. The distinction is well characterized by Bo Lindberg:

Blake's artistic revolution was a reaction, exactly as the revolution of the renaissance had been. But when a man moves back to the past, he enters that past time with a knowledge of all that had taken place in between. Thus Blake could interpret the times of a Dürer in a way that Dürer could not. He could also, by his profound knowledge of the past, interpret his own times in another way than his contemporaries. By melting past and present together, he could create something that was not present either in his own time or that of Dürer. He could create something that was new, and fit for time to come.[2]

The old engravers mentioned favourably in Blake's later writings are Marcantonio Raimondi, Dürer, Goltzius, Sadeler, Edelinck, Lucas van Leyden, Hisben [Hans Sebald Beham], and Aldegrever.[3] To this list we may almost certainly add other names, thanks to the collecting interests of Blake's friend George Cumberland. In *Some Anecdotes of the Life of Julio Bonasoni* (London, 1793) Cumberland laments the undervaluation of pure outline in engraving, criticizes those who fail to appreciate Marcantonio, and praises Bonasone as 'a great and original genius' whose manner is 'purely ideal, founded on the principles of nature and the antique'.[4] In a later work, Cumberland praises Mantegna, comparing the Roman Triumph at Hampton Court with Tassie's Greek gems.[5] Blake's friendship with Cumberland was a close one,[6]

[1] 'Public Address', E. 561.

[2] *William Blake's Illustrations to the Book of Job*, p. 176.

[3] As noted by Bindman, *Blake As an Artist*, p. 212.

[4] *Some Anecdotes of the Life of Julio Bonasoni . . . Accompanied by a Catalogue of the Engravings . . . To Which Is Prefixed, A Plan for the Improvement of the Arts in England* (London, 1793), pp. 26–7.

[5] *An Essay on the Utility of Collecting the Best Works of the Italian School; Accompanied by a Critical Catalogue* (London, 1826). Though published only the year before Blake's death, the introductory essay was written in 1816. Blake borrowed the manuscript in 1823 (see *BR*, p. 279), but it is likely that he had long been acquainted with Cumberland's ideas. Todd points out the influence of Bonasone on the second state of *Mirth and Her Companions* (notes to Gilchrist's *Life*, p. 368), but suggests that this influence occurred only towards the end of Blake's life.

[6] On the Blake–Cumberland relationship, see Geoffrey Keynes, 'George Cumberland and William Blake', *Blake Studies*, pp. 230–52.

and we may assume that Blake knew Cumberland's great collection of prints by Bonasone, Mantegna, and other Italian masters. Blake may also have been familiar with the researches of another scholar-collector, William Young Ottley, into the origins of engraving. Although it was only late in life that Blake met Ottley,[1] Blake could have read Ottley's richly illustrated book, *An Inquiry into the Origin and Early History of Engraving*, published in 1816. Here he would have found reproductions not only of early Italian engravings but also of pages from the *Biblia Pauperum* and other 'Gothic'[2] block-books.

The taste of Blake, Cumberland, and Ottley for prints with archaic qualities was part of the primitivist tendency which also found expression in the International Style of 1800. By the second decade of the nineteenth century this older art was exciting the imaginations of young men of a new age. In 1818, for example, John Keats discovered with excitement a book of engravings after Orcagna and Giotto:[3] 'it was finer to me than more accomplish'd works—as there was so much room for Imagination'.[4] Keats's 'more accomplish'd' may be regarded as a synonym for Blake's 'high finished', and one could not find a better description than this of the artistic intention of the designs for *Jerusalem*.

In addition to his knowledge of European art, classical and post-classical, Blake was also familiar with engraved reproductions of some of the art of ancient Egypt, Persia, China, and

[1] Ottley was one of the owners of the original *Jerusalem* (perhaps copy A; see *Blake Books*, p. 259). On 25 April 1827 Blake was looking forward to meeting Ottley; see *Letters*, p. 163. Ottley was also a talented artist, and Bindman suggests an affinity between some of his work and Blake's, especially Ottley's 'remarkable set of illustrations to Genesis in 1797 and . . . *Life of Christ* in 1796, which combine visionary fervour with a firm, unyielding outline'. See *Blake As an Artist*, p. 107.

[2] Ottley (p. 136) quotes this term from a description by Heineken of a block-book comprising thirty-two subjects from the Book of Canticles: *Historia seu Providentia Virginis Mariae, ex Cantico Canticorum.*

[3] Keats does not name either the book or the artists, but Ian Jack argues persuasively that the volume was Benjamin Robert Haydon's copy of *Pitture al Fresco del Campo Santo di Pisa intagliate da Carlo Lasinio* (1812), reproducing frescoes by Giotto and Orcagna among others. See *Keats and the Mirror of Art* (Oxford: The Clarendon Press, 1967), pp. 98–9.

[4] Letter to George and Georgiana Keats, section dated 31 December 1818, *The Letters of John Keats*, ed. Hyder Edward Rollins (Cambridge, Mass.: Harvard University Press, 1958), II. 19.

India. From his student days, as I have argued elsewhere,[1] he would have known such compilations as Bernard de Montfaucon's *Antiquity Explained, and represented in Sculptures*[2] and the Comte de Caylus's *Recueil d'antiquités Égyptiennes, Étrusques, Grecques, et Romaines.*[3] In carrying through his claim to 'copy Imagination',[4] Blake drew upon images such as these, images originally acquired through study and copying but transformed by his own imagination into new artistic conceptions. The bird-headed man of *Jerusalem 78* for example, may well derive from bird-headed human figures in both Montfaucon and Caylus, especially from a hawk-headed figure identified as Osiris in *Antiquity Explained.*[5] A rich variety of Indian imagery was reproduced in the 105 plates of Edward Moor's *The Hindu Pantheon,*[6] and one figure from this book appears in *Jerusalem 41/46* (see below). Blake's use of such imagery, as well as his adaptation of imagery from Michelangelo, Raphael, and the old engravers, is once more related to his archetypal theory of art itself. As Blake had an art school of the mind, so he had a mental picture gallery stocked with 'the bright Sculptures of / Los's Halls' (*16*: 61–2), certain images of which are re-created in *Jerusalem*.

Types and Symbols, or How to Read Blake's Pictures

'Never before surely was a man so literally the author of his own book',[7] wrote Gilchrist, and in the study of Blake today we tend to assume that Blake's illuminated works must be

[1] See 'Wonderful Originals'.

[2] Paris 1719; English translation by David Humphreys (London, 1721–5).

[3] Paris, 1752–67.

[4] 'Public Address', E. 563.

[5] Vol. II, pl. 39, nos. 10, 11. See also Caylus, vol. III, pl. VI, no. i (an ibis-headed man with a long decurved beak) and vol. IV, pl. V, nos. iii and iv (a man with the head of a sparrow-hawk).

[6] Published by Joseph Johnson in 1810; many of the plates, however, are dated 1st Jan. 1809. Blunt, p. 38, notes the resemblance of the *Jerusalem 53* design of a female figure seated in a sunflower to plate 50c of *The Hindu Pantheon.* For other suggestions about Blake's probable indebtedness to Moor's book, see Joseph Burke, 'The Eidetic and the Borrowed Image: an Interpretation of Blake's Theory and Practice of Art', in *The Visionary Hand*, ed. R. N. Essick (Los Angeles: Hennessey and Ingals, 1973), pp. 290, 295.

[7] *Life of William Blake*, ed. Todd, p. 61.

experienced as works of 'composite art'.[1] This assumption has been strengthened by the accomplishment of the William Blake Trust, which, by publishing its magnificent facsimile reproductions has made it all but impossible to ignore the visual aspect of Blake's works in general and of *Jerusalem* in particular. During the first half of the twentieth century such a view was by no means prevalent. In that period Blake's text was carefully established, but the designs for *Jerusalem* were largely ignored. Most literary critics preferred the typeset text, detached from Blake's designs, a preference still held by some today;[2] while art critics were slow to discover the beauty and interest of Blake's illuminated pages. Ironically, this situation was the inverse of the one Blake encountered. To the very limited extent that Blake found appreciative buyers for the longer illuminated books, these seem to have been interested in the works for their pictorial value. On 9 June 1818, Blake wrote to Dawson Turner:

> Those [works] I Printed for Mr Humphry are a selection from the different Books of such as could be Printed without the Writing, tho' to the Loss of some of the best things. For they when Printed perfect accompany Poetical Personifications & Acts, without which Poems they never could have been Executed.[3]

My own approach to *Jerusalem* is therefore to consider it as 'Printed perfect'—a work comprising both text and design engaged in fruitful interrelationship.

Before we consider ways of discussing the visual part of Blake's composite art, a few words should be said about two of its aspects: colour and calligraphy. In Blake's own words only one copy of *Jerusalem* was 'finished': copy E, which,

[1] The term was first used, as far as I know, by Jean H. Hagstrum (*William Blake: Poet and Painter*, Chicago: University of Chicago Press, 1964, pp. 10–20).

[2] Harold Bloom, for example, writes: 'I read one of the most eloquent descriptive passages in the language; I stare, disbelievingly, at an inadequate engraved illumination, and then I try, too strenuously, to isolate an image that Blake, as a poet, knew better than to isolate.' 'The Visionary Cinema of Romantic Poetry', in *William Blake: Essays for S. Foster Damon*, ed. Alvin Rosenfeld (Providence: Brown University Press, 1969), pp. 18–19.

[3] *Letters*, p. 139. As Keynes notes, the works without texts to which Blake refers are probably those now known as *A Large Book of Designs* and *A Small Book of Designs* in the British Museum Print Room. Blake's price list for Turner includes *Milton* but not *Jerusalem* (which evidently was not yet ready).

according to Allan Cunningham, 'he wrought incessantly upon . . . tinting and adorning it, with the hope that his favourite would find a purchaser'.[1] The others are either incomplete or uncoloured, but as these 5¼ copies have elsewhere been described in bibliographical detail,[2] we need not repeat those descriptions here. Our concern is the significance of the differences among the copies, and particularly of those between the complete coloured copy E and the monochrome copies, as this is what defines Blake's final artistic intention in *Jerusalem*. The monochrome copies do exhibit some differences of detail, but, as one would expect, these are not of the same order as the distinctions between copy E and the four uncoloured copies (and, for plates *1–25*, copy B).

In colouring copy E, Blake created, to put it simply, one of the masterpieces of Western art which is at the same time one of the great long poems of the nineteenth century. In addition to the extraordinary beauty of the colouring, however, copy E possesses a dimension of meaning which the other complete copies lack. This is due to Blake's significant use of colouring to establish symbolic and thematic meanings. Some of these are relatively simple, involving the use of a single colour to produce a significance that would otherwise not be possible. The colours green, blue (usually in conjunction with white), and russet brown are frequently used in this manner. Conjunctions of these three colours are often used to make more complex visual statements. This use of colour in *Jerusalem* is not based on any mysterious key, but rather evokes associational and contextual responses on the part of the reader/viewer.

One of the primary colour effects of copy E is the thematic use of green. The irregular black areas at the bottoms of plates *16* and *61* in copies A, C, D, and F become green and blue landscapes in E (olive green ones in B). Pastoral associations are evoked by more extensive green areas in the turf below Los in *44/30* and under the great trilithon of *70*. In

[1] *BR*, p. 501, from *Lives of the Most Eminent British Painters, Sculptors, and Architects* (1830).

[2] See p. 8 above and Bentley, *Blake Books*, pp. 224–60.

several of the last plates, the colouring emphasizes England's green and pleasant land: below and behind the mourning figure of *92*, likewise behind and beneath Brittania and Albion in the dawn of *94*, under the fallen three-headed giant at the top of *94*, and beneath the feet of the dancing Los in *97*. In the margin of *7* a naked man stands before a green flame (not in B) of vegetation, as does a naked woman in the margin of *43*; perhaps we ought to unite these two in our minds as an Adam and Eve separated by thirty-six plates. The colour may also be used contrastively. In *29/33* the contrast of green hills with brown ploughed earth is a simple visual effect, but in *31/35*, where Albion-Adam lies on the green earth amid flames, there is a vivid symbolic contrast between Wrath and Hope. The green earth at the bottom of *35/39* partially offsets the sinister triple archer at the top. In general, the use of green in copy E reinforces the optimism underlying *Jerusalem*.

Blue, often in conjunction with white, establishes the presence of water and sky when we otherwise would not be aware of it. This can have figurative meaning as well. In *14* a blue sea (darker blue in B)—the Sea of Time and Space—breaks in white foam against the couch of the recumbent Albion. *33/37* displays only a few waves in the monochrome copies, but in E blue water covers the entire foreground and right side, showing that the sleeping Albion is floating on his bier. The mass at the bottom of *22* is in E discerned to be water covering more than half of the great gear wheels, thus relating this design more closely to the water-mill described in *15*: 15-20. The colouring of parts of the right side of *38/43* (behind the praying or aspiring figure, for example) makes the text appear to be written in a cloud behind which patches of blue can be seen. With such clues from the colouring, the viewer/reader may learn to construe some of these details in the monochrome copies as well, but without reference to E his understanding of them would be imperfect at best. It is indeed hard to discriminate at times between details that have been added in E and those which have been clarified by colouration.

Russet, the colour of the etched text of E, has an especially important meaning, for it is used to represent the 'Fibres' out of which the bodies of all living things are made. This can be a matter of mere emphasis, as when Blake accentuates the 'fibrous' nature of vegetating forms in the margins of *34/38, 36/40,* and *49*. An equation is thus made between the constituent elements of vegetable matter and those of the human body. This equation is emphasized in *47* by the russet colouration of the exaggerated muscles and blood vessels of the three figures. Interestingly, the 'golden string', which Blake encourages the reader/viewer to wind into a ball on plate *77*, is visually depicted as russet brown, although Blake achieved striking effects in gold elsewhere in copy E. It seems clear that Blake wished to bring out the positive aspect of his fibre imagery here: the golden string with which we wind our way to Jerusalem's gate is after all the same substance that is woven into our own bodies—and that is also shaped into the text of *Jerusalem*.

More complex visual meanings may be established in *Jerusalem* by the interrelationships of colours—particularly of the colours green, blue (with white), and russet brown. One frequent combination is that of the 'green and pleasant land' motif with the 'fibres of life motif' in the conjunction of the colours appropriate to them. Such simple juxtapositions occur in *15*, where the russet thicket entangling the figure at the right is set off against the green land; in *52*, where the uniform black of the monochrome copies is startlingly transformed into a russet arterial tree spreading its roots and branches in a green valley; in *74* where the fibres imprisoning the recumbent figure grow into (or out of?) the green earth; and in *85*, where Los and Enitharmon rest on the green earth while she draws fibres bearing grapes from his body and fibres bearing flowers (lilies?) from her own. Another group of colour contrasts involves the green land with the blue sea breaking in white foam against it, making us aware that Blake's Giant Forms are carrying on their drama on an island which, in such plates, appears oddly small for them. In copy E we are aware of the sea breaking at the feet of the despairing Albion as he sits above his green land (*37*). The dramatic confrontation of Vala with Jerusalem and her daughters occurs on a green peninsula with the sea breaking in a thin lip of foam (*46/32*). The giant Hand sits not on a stark rock but on a green promontory, against which the sea breaks, in E (*50*).

The meaning of such colour combinations is not mechanical but it does tend to be forceful and relatively simple.

In some designs the colouring may make an especially intense statement, as in *14*, where what appears in monochrome to be an arch of solid matter is shown to be a rainbow, presumably 'Erins lovely Bow' (*50*: 22) with its message of redemptive hope. Thus we can see why Blake regarded only copy E as 'finished', even though all the copies he produced have independent authority, and despite the power of some of the designs as monochrome graphic works. Especially striking in the uncoloured copies are the remarkable effects of white-line engraving in some plates, effects which were to some extent retained in copy B but not in the more intensely coloured copy E. Nevertheless, *Jerusalem* was probably never conceived as a monochrome work and only became one by default. While giving due attention to the glories of the other copies, we should bear in mind that Blake regarded all but copy E as unfinished.

A further distinctive aspect of Blake's composite art is his calligraphy.[1] Like the text of most of the other illuminated books,[2] *Jerusalem*'s script is written out in a highly distinctive hand.

The *technique* by which Blake achieved his final result—whether by a transfer process or by writing in reverse with a brush[3]—is yet debated, but the *status* of his handwritten text may be described without reference to this. A comparison of any page of *Jerusalem*'s text with Blake's normal hand, as displayed in his letters, will show that his calligraphic hand does not correspond to his letter-writing hand, though there are of course numerous resemblances. That should not surprise

[1] Some varying opinions on the merits of the calligraphy are collected by Mona Wilson, *The Life of William Blake*, rev. edn., ed. Geoffrey Keynes (London, Oxford, New York: Oxford University Press, 1971), pp. 382–3.

[2] *All Religions are One* and *There is No Natural Religion* [a] and [b] are printed in an idiosyncratic roman style; *The Book of Los* and *The Book of Ahania* are written out in engraver's hand; *The Gates of Paradise* presents several styles of lettering; all the other books are written in Blake's calligraphic hand.

[3] The leading proponents of these two explanations are, respectively, Ruthven Todd and Robert N. Essick. See Todd, 'The Techniques of William Blake's Illuminated Printing', in *The Visionary Hand*, ed. Robert N. Essick (Los Angeles: Hennessey and Ingals, 1973), pp. 19–44; Essick, *William Blake, Printmaker*, pp. 89–92.

Luvah was cast into the Furnaces of affliction & sealed
And Vala fed in cruel delight, the furnaces with fire
Stern Urizen beheld urg'd by necessity to keep
The evil day afar, & if perchance with iron power
He might avert his own despair; in woe & fear he saw

Luvah was cast into the Furnaces of affliction and sealed.
And Vala fed in cruel delight, the Furnaces with fire:
Stern Urizen beheld; urgd by necessity to keep
The evil day afar, and if perchance with iron power
He might avert his own despair: in woe & fear he saw

Example I. Comparison of Copperplate Hand with calligraphic script.
(*FZ* 25: 25: 40–4 (reduced); *J* 7: 30–4)

us, but what is worth noting is that comparison of the calligraphic hand with what Bentley terms Blake's Copperplate Hand and his Modified Copperplate Hand in *The Four Zoas*[1] shows all to be significantly dissimilar. The Copperplate Hand, the elegant engraver's script which Blake employed in the *Four Zoas* manuscript, may be compared with the calligraphic hand in the parallel passages *FZ* 25: 40–4 and *J* 7: 30–7 (see Example I). The differences between the calligraphic hand and the Modified Copperplate Hand are readily apparent in a comparison of *FZ* 18: 11–12 with *J 23*: 24–6 (see Example II). With such examples before us, extensive verbal analysis is hardly necessary. The calligraphic hand is not a script at all but rather a substitute for a fount of type—one in which, however, the letters of each word can be fluently linked. MCH relaxes, as it were, towards Blake's normal hand but remains a cursive script essentially unlike the calligraphic printing. Paradoxically, CH, though a form of handwriting, is less distinctive than calligraphic printing: it would require an expert eye to identify Blake rather than some other late eighteenth-century engraver as the inditer, but the calligraphic printing looks like nothing else. It is of course radically different from an actual fount of type in being as individual as the painter's brush-stroking or the whorls of a fingerprint. It establishes a sensuous intimacy with the reader's eye as no printed type can. As Nelson Hilton has pointed out, it makes possible visual puns such as 'moon/moan' and 'worshipped/warshipped',[2] with consequent extensions of meaning that could not otherwise be achieved. Furthermore, while the purpose of set type is usually to make one forget that one is reading, to facilitate access to the referents behind the signs, Blake's calligraphy seems to float on the page as on a thin film. This appearance is intensified by the fact that the inked copperplates produce designs and text from the same coloured substance. We perceive a single field of action in reading the pages of *Jerusalem*, aware of both text and design as vehicles of symbolic statement.

[1] See G. E. Bentley, Jr., *Vala or The Four Zoas* (Oxford: The Clarendon Press, 1963), pp. 210–13.

[2] See *Literal Imagination: Blake's Vision of Words* (Berkeley, Los Angeles, London: University of California Press, 1983), pp. 14–15.

Now Man was come to the Palm tree & to the Oak of Weeping
Which stand upon the Edge of Beulah & he sunk down

He stood between the Palm tree & the Oak of weeping
Which stand upon the edge of Beulah; and there Albion sunk

Example II. Comparison of Modified Copperplate Hand with calligraphic script.
(*FZ* 18: 11–12 (reduced); *J* 23: 24–5)

One last general consideration before I turn to some of the individual designs: any discussion of them requires a statement about method. The variety of interpretations of certain plates and the number of disputed interpretations demand such a statement. How do we go about determining the meaning of the designs? Are they necessarily representations of events in the text? Do they have single meanings or are they susceptible of being understood in different senses, each of which is equally valid? How much do they depend upon meanings established visually elsewhere in *Jerusalem* or in other works by Blake? How much art-historical knowledge must we have to understand their iconography? How, in fact, to use a contemporary term which Blake would have understood, are we to read Blake's pictures?

In the ensuing discussion, I hope to answer these and other questions through a critical analysis of some especially interesting plates. My approach derives from a close examination of minute particulars as well as from my experiential responses to whole compositions. I do not believe there is an occult solution or diagrammatic key to Blake's meaning. Occasionally we may be helped by a (more or less) general rule, such as Wicksteed's discovery that in Blake's *Job* the right is the spiritual side and the left the material one.[1] Such insights derived from one work, however, may only with great caution be applied to another. More consistently useful is a knowledge of Blake's vocabulary of forms as established through the wide range of his work. Sometimes we can also benefit from recognizing Blake's allusive use of sources, but here I bear in mind what S. Foster Damon stressed to his students: the most important thing about Blake's sources is how he departed from them. Above all, we should trust our informed intuitions of how particular designs work in their particular contexts, remembering that these images are not hieroglyphs but educts of the imagination. Blake dismissed the figures in Thomas Taylor's edition of Plato because Taylor reduced myth to 'Mathematical Diagrams'.[2] In contrast, he praised the engravings in the 'Law edition' of Boehme, telling Henry Crabb Robinson that Michelangelo could not have done

[1] *Blake's Vision of the Book of Job, passim.*

[2] The *Laocoön*, E. 271.

better.[1] The full-bodied illustrations to Boehme are indeed symbolic, but they also possess an imaginative reality utterly lacking in Taylor's diagrams. We should remember this contrast in thinking about Blake's own pictorial works.

In choosing plates for discussion in this chapter, I have used two related criteria. First, it is recognized that certain designs in *Jerusalem* have a different status in the structure of the work than do the others. The book has a frontispiece, a pictorial title-page, and full-page designs at the end of each chapter. Chapters begin with headpieces and end with tailpieces. Thus there are fourteen designs the positions of which are predetermined. Second, there are a number of designs which were obviously planned as occupying the space they do. For example, in *31/35* (Fig. 5) a magnificent white-line engraving occupies about two-thirds of the pages above and below the text, so that we are made to imagine the text as floating in front of a relatively small design area behind it. The dramatic confrontation of Vala and Jerusalem in *46/32* (Fig. 2) virtually overwhelms the fifteen lines of text that occupy less than a quarter of the page. So by their place in the book, by their design areas, and by their placement on the page we may distinguish the major designs of *Jerusalem* from the frequently interesting but less important marginal and interlinear images. Some of these major designs, however, are, because of their subject-matter, best discussed in other chapters of this book. From among the rest I have selected five which exemplify various ways in which Blake establishes visual meanings in *Jerusalem* and which in some cases have led to instructively varying critical interpretations.

25

Jerusalem 25 is one of the pages in which the relationship of text and design is contrapuntal. In the former there is a lamentation from Beulah, calling upon the Lamb of God to 'Descend . . . & take away the imputation of Sin' (12); the latter shows a scene of horror: Albion being literally unwoven by three women. The central, Michelangelesque-captive figure had been used by Blake in his water-colour *The Blasphemer*

[1] *BR*, p. 313, from Robinson's diary entry of 10 December 1825.

(London, Tate Gallery), but in two drawings[1] Blake changed the patriarchal executioners to females, and in the *25* design he grouped the torturers in their present positions. These women are at the same time the three Fates and (from left to right) Blake's Rahab, Vala, and Tirzah.[2] Albion is tattooed with the sun, moon, and stars (including Orion's belt and the Pleiades), from which we can infer that his fall is just beginning, for after the fall 'The Starry Heavens all were fled from the mighty limbs of Albion' (*70*: 32). These heavenly bodies also associate Albion with the similarly depicted 'Ancient Britains' in John Speed's *Historie of Great Britain* (London, 1623).[3] The composition of this plate, the visual sources behind it, and its relationship to other parts of *Jerusalem* provide a striking example of Blake's symbolizing imagination at work.

In the Keynes and the Fogg drawings an altar at the right suggests that the victim is to be the subject of a ritual sacrifice as pictured in *Jerusalem 69* and described in *67*: 24–5:

> Tirzah sits weeping to hear the shrieks of the dying: her
> Knife
> Of flint is in her hand: she passes it over the howling
> Victim[.]

It seems likely that Blake first executed the pencil drawing for the *25* design,[4] introducing the victim from *The Blasphemer*

[1] One of these is a pencil drawing in the collection of Sir Geoffrey Keynes, repr. *Drawings of William Blake*, ed. Keynes (New York: Dover, 1970), no. 35; the other is a red chalk drawing in the Fogg Museum of Art, repr. Paley, *William Blake*, pl. 105.

[2] See Wicksteed, *Jerusalem*, p. 155; Erdman, *Illuminated Blake*, p. 304; Mitchell, *Blake's Composite Art*, p. 201. Damon, however, thinks they are 'Daughters of Albion'. Since the Daughters can combine into Tirzah, Rahab, and Vala (see *5*: 40–5 and *64*: 6), this is not an important difference; but I think the more specific identifications can be sustained.

[3] As pointed out by Deirdre Toomey, 'Two Pictorial Sources for *Jerusalem*', 25, *Blake* V (1971–2), p. 190; an engraving entitled 'The Portraitures and Paintings of the Ancient Britains' is reproduced from Speed, Book V, Chap. 6, p. 39. See also David Worrall, 'Blake's *Jerusalem* and the Visionary History of Britain', *Studies in Romanticism*, XVI (1977), 189–216.

[4] Both drawings are known as *The Death Chamber*, a title given to them by William Michael Rossetti. According to Martin Butlin's *catalogue raisonné*, which Mr Butlin has kindly allowed me to consult in proof, in style the pencil drawing is less similar to sketches for biblical water-colours datable *c.*1800 (such as *The Blasphemer*) than to those for *Jerusalem*. Butlin thinks the pencil drawing 'may well be an early project, subsequently altered save for the foreground figure, for plate 25' of *Jerusalem*. See Butlin, *Catalogue*, no. 564.

and making the executioners female in accord with the symbolism in *Jerusalem*. Then, in the red chalk drawing, he gave two of the females knives. At the same time he intensified the sexual content by substituting for the praying figure of the pencil drawing a female nude in a seductive posture similar to that of Vala in *47*.[1] In the etched version, however, there occurs a brilliant rearrangement of the female forms, deriving from an anonymous engraving known as *Le Tre Parche*, after Il Rosso Fiorentino.[2] As Deirdre Toomey observes, 'Blake's debt to the Rosso design . . . can be seen in his use of the unusual pyramidical composition of three female nudes; in the torso and outstretched arms of the central figure and the bundles of cord-like structure that she holds; in the relationship of her arms to the heads of the other two figures; and in the head, features, tear-stained face and hunched pose of the right-hand figure.'[3] In so recognizably connecting his female executioners with the three Fates, Blake widened the symbolic reference of the *25* design and connected it thematically with other parts of *Jerusalem*.

Weaving and spinning compose a central theme, which I have discussed elsewhere in detail,[4] of Blake's later works. Somewhere behind all Blake's weavers are the three Fates who spin, measure, and cut the threads of our lives. For Blake these beings symbolize the insensate forces that govern physical existence, but weaving itself may be positive or negative, depending on the context, in *Jerusalem*. The stripping-away of garments generally has a negative valence, as when the Daughters of Albion sacrifice their victim in *66*: 26–7: 'They take off his vesture whole with their Knives of flint: / But they cut asunder his inner garments . . .'. Envisaging the human body as a woven network of fibres, Blake can

[1] Butlin terms the red chalk drawing 'an elaboration' of the pencil drawing (*Catalogue*, no. 565), and he discerns a 'Rubensian' quality in the face of one of the standing women. The latter detail accords with Blake's idea of the seductive nature of Rubens's style.

[2] See Toomey, 'Two Pictorial Sources', p. 188. The engraving, reproduced on p. 189, has been attributed alternatively to the Fontainebleau engravers René Boyvin and Pierre Millan.

[3] Ibid., p. 188.

[4] 'The Figure of the Garment in *The Four Zoas, Milton*, and *Jerusalem*', in *Blake's Sublime Allegory*, ed. Stuart Curran and Joseph Anthony Wittreich, Jr. (Madison: University of Wisconsin Press, 1973), pp. 119–40.

imagine the stripping-away of these so as to leave nothing but a mass of insatiable need, a poor, ravening Spectre. In *25* Blake creates a horrifying variation of the weaving theme by making the subject the *un*weaving of Albion's body. This action has been variously interpreted as 'winding a clue of "vegetation" from his navel', 'drawing out the umbilical cord from his navel', and 'disembowelment'.[1] Actually, it is all three: bowels and umbilical cord are composed of fibres of vegetation. Lachesis/Tirzah winds these fibres out of Albion's body in *25*, while other fibres emanate from Clotho/Vala and stream down the back and sides of the picture. This identity of substance is most apparent in copy E, where the same russet colour is used for the fibres throughout. This winding of Albion's 'bowels of compassion' (*56*: 34) into a ball may be seen as a parody by anticipation of *77*, where in both text and design the reader is urged to wind Blake's golden string into a ball. In *25* one might expect to see a knife ready to cut the fibres of life, but here Blake has suppressed the literal detail of the red chalk drawing. Instead, Albion, head thrown back, is mesmerized by the sexual allure of Rahab. Here, as in the Petrarchan tradition, the lady's most powerful weapon is her eyes.

The symbolic meaning of the picture can thus be established in part by its affect, in part by references to the body of Blake's mythology, and in part by recognizing allusions to sources. There also exists a strong candidate for a pictorial source for the victim-figure in *The Martyrdom of St. Erasmus* by Nicolas Poussin (Pinacoteca del Vaticano). Poussin was a painter for whom Blake, in his annotations to Reynolds's *Discourses on Art,*[2] expresses admiration; he may have become interested in the *St. Erasmus* through a report by Henry Fuseli, who saw the painting in the Louvre (to which it had been moved from Rome by Napoleon) in 1802. Fuseli considered the picture too horrifying, according to the summary of his view by John Knowles: 'The actual martyrdom of St. Erasmus is one of those subjects which ought not to

[1] Damon, *William Blake*, p. 470; Wicksteed, *Blake's Jerusalem*, p. 155; Martin Butlin, *William Blake: a Complete Catalogue of the Works in the Tate Gallery* (London: The Tate Gallery, rev. edn., 1971), p. 45.

[2] See E. 644, 650.

be told to the eye—because it is equally loathsome and horrible; we can neither pity nor shudder; we are seized by qualms and detest.'[1] The very horridness of the subject—St. Erasmus was martyred by having his entrails drawn out and wound on a winch—would have made it an appropriate prototype for *Jerusalem 25*. An engraved reproduction by Joseph Marie Mitelli[2] was readily to hand, and Blake appears to have drawn upon it, shifting the supine suffering figure (which may also be the source of the design at the bottom of *91*) to a contorted posture.[3] At the same time he introduces his own thematic concerns, showing Albion's entrails as made up of the same fibres as those which constitute the natural world, drawn out and wound by Tirzah and at the same time cascading as the veil of Vala.

Is the identification of these sources necessary for an understanding of the picture? In a sense it is not, for the affect of the design is very strong, and we can place this picture in relation to the rest of Blake's myth. The conjunction of Fates and martyr does extend the thematic resonance of the scene, however, while simultaneously making us aware of how Blake has assimilated these traditional images to his own conception. As for Blake's myth, a knowledge of that is essential to an interpretation of the design. In these respects *25* is typical of the major illuminations in *Jerusalem*. Certain elements, such as expression and gesture, provide clues to the meaning without any reference to the mythical content, but the design cannot stand independently of that content, which is primarily established by the text throughout the work. A recognition of sources (to some of which Blake may deliberately allude) widens the signification established by the other two elements but cannot substitute for them; and the same may be said of comparisons with preparatory drawings. In *Jerusalem* most of the major designs are typological constructions which encourage us to wander back and forth

[1] *The Life and Writings of Henry Fuseli* (London, 1831), I. 270–1.

[2] This engraving is mentioned as one of Mitelli's 'principal works' by Michael Bryan in *A Biographical and Critical Dictionary of Painters and Engravers* (London, 1816), II. 76.

[3] C. H. Collins Baker hypothesizes an unspecified source in Flaxman; see 'The Sources of Blake's Pictorial Expression', *Huntington Library Quarterly*, IV (1940–1), 365.

through the work in order to construe the thematic relationships of one part with another. This can be seen more clearly in the course of considering some other plates.

31/35

Four points about this remarkable plate (Fig. 5) ought to be emphasized. These concern the arrangement of the design on the page, the nature of the upper figure, the nature of the lower figure(s), and the thematic connections of *31/35* with other parts of *Jerusalem*. The important status of this design is shown not only by its size, covering about three-quarters of the page, but also by its position. The plate had to be planned to accommodate this large visual conception, with the text appearing to intervene between the reader/viewer and the visual background, which can be imagined as continuing behind the text. Blake learned this technique from the necessities of his illustrations for Young's *Night Thoughts*, where the engravings are conceived as partially blocked by the inset letterpress. In *Jerusalem* Blake used this kind of arrangement by choice for some important subjects, as in *11, 33/37, 35/39, 93,* and *94*. The fact that *31/35* is also a dramatically placed interpolation deliberately interrupting the episode of Los and Reuben[1] demands further consideration.

The scene is the creation of Eve by Christ from the sleeping body of Adam, with the surrounding flames suggesting 'the burning fiery furnace' of Daniel, where 'the form of the fourth is like the son of God' (3: 21, 25). That the flying figure is Jesus we know by the stigmata on his hands and feet.[2] Closely related in conception is *The Creation of Eve*[3] in the *Paradise Lost* illustrations, where Jesus, standing, is depicted as a bearded young man. But in *31/35* the presence of the resurrected Jesus also implies his Incarnation and his Crucifixion, events which are subjects of the text in *27* and

[1] See Sloss and Wallis, I. 509; David V. Erdman, 'The Suppressed and Altered Passages in William Blake's *Jerusalem*', *Studies in Bibliography*, XVII (1964), 21.

[2] Stigmata on hands and feet are visible in all copies save E, where they are seen only on the feet.

[3] Versions in Huntington Art Gallery, Boston Museum of Fine Arts, and National Gallery of Art, Melbourne. See also the design in plate 5 of *All Religions are One*, where Jesus creates Adam.

in *61* and of the full-page design *76*. It could be said that in *31/35* Jesus initiates the process that will lead to his own birth, his suffering on the cross, and the redemption of humankind.

Behind the presence of Jesus here there is an iconographical tradition which Blake employs to establish a symbolic meaning. William Young Ottley, for example, observed of a Creation of Eve by Robetta:

> Eve appears coming out of his side; her hands are joined together, and she bends forwards towards the Creator, who is standing on a bank of earth, on the right. It is remarkable, that the Almighty is represented in this print as a very young man, and not, as usual, with a long beard.[1]

Blake almost certainly knew that there was an alternative tradition for representing the creation of Eve, since, in addition to the Robetta engraving, there are depictions of Eve created by the Son in the *Nuremberg Chronicle* and in the *Biblia Pauperum.*[2] In view of his frequently expressed interest in old prints and in the history of his craft, Blake can hardly have been ignorant of these representations. That the choice could be a conscious matter of considerable weight is evident in the remarks of Henry Fuseli on his own *Creation of Eve* (Kunsthalle, Hamburg). In a letter to his friend and patron Thomas Roscoe dated 14 August 1795, Fuseli wrote of the ambiguous creator in his painting: 'for believers, let it be the Son, the visible agent of the Father; for others it is merely a superior Being entrusted with her creation, and looking for approbation of this work to the inspiring power above'.[3] As this painting was exhibited in Fuseli's Milton Gallery in 1799, Blake could have seen his friend's picture before rendering his own, decidedly less equivocal, treatments of the subject.

In the lower part of *31/35* Blake represents male and female as a composite being budding into two separate sexual identities. In this way he links the creation of Eve to his myth, developed in *The Book of Urizen* and in *The Four*

[1] *History of Engraving* (London, 1816), I. 460–1. Ottley cites Bartsch's Catalogue of Robetta, no. 1.

[2] See Figs. 7 and 6. I owe the reference to the *Liber Chronicorum* (Nuremberg, 1493, folio 6) to Dr Ellen Kelley.

[3] Quoted by Gert Schiff, *Johann Heinrich Füssli, 1741–1825* (Zurich and Munich: Verlag Berichthaus and Prestel-Verlag, 1973), I, no. 897, p. 517.

Zoas, of sexual division. This myth, deriving from the fable narrated by Aristophanes in Plato's *Symposium*, is in the earlier works presented pessimistically, but here the division of androgynous humanity into two sexes is viewed as an act of Divine Mercy. It is described as such in *42*: 29–34:

> There is a limit of Opakeness, and a limit of Contraction;
> In every Individual Man, and the limit of Opakeness,
> Is named Satan: and the limit of Contraction is named
> Adam.
> But when Man sleeps in Beulah, the Saviour in mercy
> takes
> Contractions Limit, and of the Limit he forms Woman:
> That
> Himself may in process of time be born Man to redeem

This Blakean version of the paradox of the fortunate fall offers an alternative perspective to the grim myths of sexual division discussed in Chapter IV below. For this reason, Blake deliberately chooses to follow a tradition in which the Creator is the Son, not the Father, and in which Adam and Eve possess a composite body—the tradition of Robetta, of the *Biblia Pauperum*, and of the *Nuremberg Chronicle* rather than that of the Sistine ceiling, which Blake knew through engravings,[1] in which God can be seen to be the Father by his long beard and Eve's body is completely distinct from Adam's. In choosing his iconographical details Blake imbues them with his own symbolic significance, which is also expressed in the passage from *Jerusalem 42* quoted above.[2]

One further, and curious, pictorial source should be noted here. The flying figure of Jesus strikingly resembles that of St. Mark in Tintoretto's *Miracle of the Slave*[3] as engraved

[1] Among the engravings of the Sistine ceiling that Blake could have known are those of I. Bonato, Domenico Cunego, and Julio Bonasone, examples of which are in the British Museum Print Room. The Bonasone engraving was in the collection of George Cumberland (see Cumberland's *Catalogue*, p. 61, no. 75).

[2] Blake rewrote the Lord's Prayer to begin 'Jesus our Father' (Annotations to Thornton's *The Lord's Prayer*, E. 658), a view compatible with John 10: 30, where Jesus says 'I and my Father are one.'

[3] I owe this suggestion to Professor Hugh Richmond. This painting was seen in Paris during the Peace of Amiens by Henry Fuseli, who noted: 'The miracle of St. Marc derives all its merit from that whirlpool of execution, which sweeps undistinguished all individual merit into one mighty mass. As a whole, of equal compre-

by J. Matham (Fig. 4). Tintoretto was, of course, one of those Venetian painters whom Blake dismissed with the words 'They could not Draw.'[1] If his imitation is deliberate here, this aspect of *31/35* could be regarded as a challenge on Blake's part—as Blake's demonstration that he could achieve, in this beautifully articulated white-line engraving, greater effects than 'the Laboured fabrications of Journey-work'.[2]

41/46

Unlike the two plates discussed so far, both of which have immediately definable subjects whatever the difficulties of interpreting them may be, *41/46* is so obscure as to present almost a Rorschach test for Blake scholars. This design is notable both for its iconographical complexities and for its partial dependence upon the recognition of esoteric visual allusions. Though difficult, it is understandable: its components can be traced either to related examples of Blake's pictorial idiom or to traditional sources, from both of which (in this particular instance) we can construe the meaning of the pictorial statement. Some representative critical views should first be considered, as *41/46* presents a good example of both the pleasures and the perils of reading Blake's pictures.

For Damon the design portrays 'The Sage in his Inspiration as Elijah in the chariot of flame, whose structure is composed of the Serpent of Nature . . . drawn by the human-headed bulls of Luvah. . . .'[3] Thus its basic thrust would be prophetic vision using but transcending the natural world. For Wicksteed the chariot represents Time; the two riders in it are Albion and Jerusalem looking back into the past, while the three-headed serpent signifies past, present, and future.[4] The

hension, energy, and suavity, it astonishes the common man of organs, and the artist who enters into the process of this amalgama, equally; but when the first charm is over, and we begin to examine the parts, we shall not find they were drawn forward, distanced, or excluded by propriety and character.' (Knowles, *Life and Writings*, I. 276.)

[1] Annotations to Reynolds's *Discourses*, E. 635. [2] Ibid.

[3] *William Blake*, p. 471. The small winged riders are identified as 'possibly Gnomes'.

[4] *Jerusalem*, pp. 185–6. The function of the winged riders ('harpies') is seen as the inscribing of history.

meaning would then be ambiguous, presenting the illusion of Time along with the possibility of penetrating that illusion. John Beer sees the picture as an allegorical satire on the doctrine of atonement where 'two horned tyrants with animal bodies [are] harnessed to a chariot of snakes'; the creatures on the backs of these tyrants are 'recording angels' who 'enact a profitless moral judgment' of the sins of the riders in the chariot, identified as Jerusalem and Albion.[1] Erdman suggests that the animals drawing the vehicle are the 'unicorns' referred to in Job 39: 9, the vehicle itself an illustration of 'the Plow of Jehovah, and the Harrow of Shaddai' referred to in the text (line 14) of this plate. The passengers are or will become 'the woman England or Brittania, the man Albion as Jehovah' of plate *96*: and the whole is seen as Blake's 'yoking of the arts to produce *Jerusalem*'.[2] For Mitchell, the riders are Albion and Jerusalem or Vala; the small winged creatures 'prophetic eagle-men' of whom the nearer is Los or Blake himself; and the whole 'a self-parody, a satiric vision of Blake's own epic machinery, the elements of his craft'.[3] Such a welter of critical opinions is at first disheartening, particularly in view of the widely differing interpretations of detail. Since the *41* design is more complicated than most of the other *Jerusalem* pictures, I propose to discuss its constituent elements, remembering that what is taken apart must be put together in the end. I distinguish the components as the chariot, the passengers in the chariot, the drawers of the chariot, and the small winged riders.

The chariot. It clearly *is* a chariot and not a plough or a harrow. Damon's suggestion of a resemblance between this chariot and that of Blake's 1795 colour-printed drawing is well taken. However, although chariots may be vehicles of vision, they are not necessarily so. In *Jerusalem 65*, for example, 'They forg'd . . . the chariot of war', and the horses of Urizen are harnessed 'to the chariot of love' ironically 'to trample the corn fields in boastful neighings' (47, 49). Now that it is known that Blake's title for the 1795 colour print was 'God Judging Adam', the flame-surrounded chariot there

[1] *Blake's Visionary Universe*, p. 187.
[2] *Ill. Bl.*, p. 320. [3] *Blake's Composite Art*, p. 216.

takes on a sinister meaning—as here. There is, in addition, a striking pictorial source for the unusual conception of a serpent-wheeled chariot. Among the engravings in Montfaucon's *Antiquity Explained, and Represented in Sculptures* is one of a serpent-wheeled chariot in which Ceres rides in search of her abducted daughter Proserpine.[1] Blake, of course, assimilates the serpents to his own characteristic meaning, which suggests the energies of nature (as does the similarly coiled but not so elongated Orc serpent of the *Europe* title-page) and cyclical recurrence.

The passengers. The most likely candidate for the veiled female form is obviously Vala, clothed as she is in the designs on plates *4* and *46*. The male figure takes the patriarchal form of Urizen but could well be Albion in his Urizenic state of self-accusation. The Montfaucon design is followed by another showing the abduction of Persephone by Pluto in a conventional, horse-drawn, chariot; what Blake has in effect done is to put his Pluto and Persephone into the serpent-wheeled chariot suggested by the preceding engraving.

The drawers. It was long ago noticed that the man-headed bulls were similar to sculptures at Nineveh and Persepolis,[2] and possible engraved sources have been discussed by Keynes and by Blunt, among them plates in Jacob Bryant's *New System, or An Analysis, of Ancient Mythology* (London, 1774–6), for which Blake did apprenticeship work under Basire.[3] Once again, Blake assimilates the source of his system: these are Luvah's Bulls (cf. Night VIIa of *The Four Zoas*, where in the caves of Orc 'The bulls of Luvah breathing fire bellow on burning pastures' (77: 16)). The human-headed bull is an apt embodiment of the dual nature of the *Zoa* of passion. They are crowned with laurel in parody of Petrarchan poet laureates; one reaches for a quill pen, perhaps to indite a love poem, with the hand at the end of his flexible horn.

[1] I, pl. 20, upper design; text on p. 49. Reproduced in *Blake in His Time*, Fig. 103.

[2] See Gilchrist, *Life of William Blake*, ed. Todd, p. 211.

[3] See Geoffrey Keynes, *Blake Studies* (Oxford: The Clarendon Press, 2nd edn., 1971), p. 26 and pl. 11; Anthony Blunt, *The Art of William Blake*, pp. 86–7 and plates 50, 54a, and 54b. On other possible examples of ancient Eastern influences on Blake, see Mary Jackson, 'Blake and Zoroastrianism', *Blake*, XI (1977), 72–85.

The riders. There is an extraordinary visual source for these in Edward Moor's *Hindu Pantheon*, where the eagle-headed god Garuda is depicted riding on a multi-headed serpent. Moor describes Garuda in terms reminiscent of the Covering Cherub of Blake's mythology, a symbol which Blake derives from Ezekiel 28: 13, taking it to represent the Law which blocks humanity's way back to Paradise. 'He [Garuda]', Moor writes, 'is sometimes described in the manner that our poets and painters describe a griffin, or a cherub, and he is placed at the entrance of the passes leading to the *Hindu* garden of Eden, and he appears in the character of a destroying angel, in as far as he resists the approach of serpents, which in most systems of poetic mythology, appear to have been the beautiful, deceiving form that sin originally assumed.'[1] The riders, then, are neither gnomes nor harpies but cherubs directing a course away from Paradise. The fact that one of them holds the pen for which the horn-hand reaches may be an ironical indication that Petrarchan love poetry, with its idealization of woman and its attendant suffering, is a result of the Fall.

The *41/46* design is unusually dependent upon the recognition of allusions to esoteric sources. Trying to interpret it is something like trying to interpret *The Waste Land* without T. S. Eliot's notes. To that extent—and to that extent only—it might be regarded as a self-parody. Yet the picture also produces an overall effect which is greater than the sum of its parts—a dark, even a demonic feeling. This atmosphere is generated in the uncoloured copies by the way in which the white-line engraving highlights the chariot, its occupants, and the surrounding flames against a background of deep darkness. In copy E a corresponding effect comes from the intense colouration of the flames. This is truly a Chariot of Wrath, drawn by the passions and cyclical natural energies, directed by Covering Cherubs. In it the drooping couple Vala and Albion[2] make their way as Pluto and Persephone into the lower world.

[1] p. 340. The engraving is reproduced in *Blake in His Time*, Fig. 104. Garuda is also portrayed in Moor's plate 10.

[2] Vala is referred to as Albion's 'wife' four times in *Jerusalem*.

46/32

Here is an example in which the protagonists are clearly identifiable and in which the reader/viewer is given clear indications of meaning despite the absence of the precise situation from the text. *46/32* (Fig. 2) does not illustrate any passage of *Jerusalem* but rather complements several. Vala thrusts her body-length veil at Jerusalem, who stands transfixed while three of her daughters implore her to fly upward. The situation is a significant variation of that pictured in *3*, where Jerusalem leads the same three daughters through the sky towards the inscription meaning 'Jesus alone', leaving the earth-bound Vala trying to control the two male figures below. Here Jerusalem, again displaying naked beauty, meets Vala on Albion's shore. In the text of the preceding plate (in either order) Jerusalem calls upon Vala to awake and exclaims that she feels Vala's 'iron threads of love & jealousy & despair' (*45/31*: 49) around her limbs; and the design at the bottom of that plate shows Vala passing the threads from a spindle in her right hand, between her legs via her left hand, to enmesh Jerusalem in a net. Vala's purpose in both designs is to restore their loosely assimilated combination as it was before Albion's act of phallic aggression. But the separation of Jerusalem and Vala is irrevocable, and Vala's desire to bring about a false unity through entrapping Jerusalem in the veil cannot succeed, although Jerusalem does remain sadly vulnerable to Vala's imputations of sin and guilt.

Jerusalem is presented here, as also in *3*, as a Caritas figure. Blake was of course cognizant of the depiction of Charity as a mother surrounded by children, as found, for example, in Cesare Ripa's *Iconologia.*[1] His own rendering of such a group may be found in an untitled print, executed *c.*1789, in the British Museum.[2] Jerusalem is, in the words of *The Four Zoas*, 'Mother of myriads redeemd & born in her spiritual palaces'.[3] Here in *46/32* Jerusalem supports two of her daughters while a third leaps skyward. Jerusalem looks at the

[1] See *Iconologie, ou Explication Nouvelle de Plusieurs Images, Emblèmes, et autres figures* (Paris: Mathieu Gillemot, 1644), pt. II, p. 112. Three children are depicted here.

[2] Repr. Essick, *Printmaker*, pl. 122.

[3] Night IX, 122: 19, E. 376.

threatening Vala with dismay but stands her ground[1]—yet the implication may be that she ought to fly upward as urged by the daughter on her left.

In the background at either side are buildings which are thematically associated with, respectively, the Jerusalem-principle and the Vala-principle. To our right is a Gothic cathedral, suggestive of Westminster Abbey, which in *Jerusalem* and other later works Blake consistently associates with true, spiritual religion and the artistic imagination. To our left is the dome of St. Paul's surmounted by a cross, Blake's icon of state religion and the letter that killeth. Similar architectural juxtapositions occur in *57*, where St. Paul's and a Gothic cathedral labelled 'Jerusalem' are at the antipodes of a central disc; and in *84*, in which the two structures are next to each other.[2] The use of these buildings in *46/32* came as a late thought to Blake. In his preliminary drawing, Jerusalem and her three daughters appear, but there is only a heap of stones to their left.[3] Furthermore, he somewhat changed the effect of the design when he coloured copy E. In the monochrome copies only the dome of St. Paul's is cast in shadow, but in E part of the Gothic church is shadowed too, and clouds obscure a section of the nave. (Clouds are present in the uncoloured copies also, but they are rendered transparent so that the whole nave can be seen.) In contrast, the coloured proof of *46/32* has no shadow on either church and shows the Gothic nave visibly through the cloud. Thus we can see Blake developing his conception through several phases. The implication in copy E is that even the purer manifestations of Christianity are threatened by corrupting forces.

The *46/32* design employs, as we have seen, two simple juxtapositions. The symbolic meanings of Jerusalem and Vala are thematically reinforced by the two structures associated

[1] Her expression varies slightly from copy to copy, being most definite in the posthumous ones. Erdman sees her as 'almost mesmerized' by Vala (*Ill. Bl.*, p. 325).

[2] A similar juxtaposition occurs in *The Chaining of Orc*, an etching dated 1812 (National Gallery of Art, Rosenwald Coll.; repr. Essick, *Printmaker*, pl. 168).

[3] Erdman suggests that these stones are 'the ruins of the Temple' referred to in *45/31*: 41. See *The Notebook of William Blake*, ed. David V. Erdman with the assistance of Donald K. Moore (Oxford: The Clarendon Press, 1973), p. N 80. The drawing is reproduced.

with them in this picture. A context for these meanings is provided by other parts of *Jerusalem* and by other works by Blake. The interpretation so established is reinforced and enriched by reference to a traditional emblematic figure. Certain shades of meaning are also suggested by the variations in detail among the different copies, particularly by differences between the monochrome copies and copy E. The challenges which this design poses are relatively simple: anyone with a knowledge of Blake's visual vocabulary will have little difficulty here, although there are bound to be some disagreements in reading the expression on Jerusalem's face from one copy to another. Although no one would wish to argue that Blake's iconography is immediately self-revealing, the mode of statement of *46/32* is more characteristic of *Jerusalem* than is that of the exceptionally difficult *41/46*.

76

One would think that such a statement should also apply to the deeply moving full-page Crucifixion of *76* (Fig. 3). Indeed, this picture posed no problem for Blake's earlier commentators. Damon places it 'among the greatest Crucifixions ever painted' and interprets it as showing the Dark Night of the Soul in which Albion, adoring Jesus, beholds 'the torture and death of his highest faculties'.[1] Wicksteed, too, takes the design at face value;[2] and the notion that plate *76* is a positive representation of man's imitation of Christ is probably still the prevalent one.[3] One recent critic goes so far as to say: 'Only once in *Jerusalem* does Blake epitomize his meaning simply and totally upon a single plate. On the full-page illumination of Plate 76, Albion, stretching his arms wide in unconscious sympathy, contemplates the crucified Christ.'[4] Yet there is also an alternative reading of *76*, according to which the crucified Jesus is to be viewed ironically as the 'vegetated Christ, the hermaphroditic blasphemy, the

[1] *William Blake*, p. 473.

[2] *Blake's Jerusalem*, p. 220.

[3] See Anne K. Mellor, *Blake's Human Form Divine*, pp. 321–3; David Bindman, *Blake As an Artist*, p. 179.

[4] Stuart Curran, 'The Structures of Jerusalem', *Blake's Sublime Allegory*, p. 346.

Evil-One'.[1] The Albion figure has been seen as positive in contrast to a negative Jesus, 'For the dancelike movement of Albion in both *Albion rose* and *Jerusalem* 76 is the subtle but central quality which distinguishes Albion, the living human, from the passive, crucified Jesus.'[2] The design has also been interpreted from *both* perspectives: 'Albion is at the acme of Satanic worship of a vegetated Christ; but he has now made the crucial identification, and the clues in this rehearsal of the true awakening instruct him that the natural sun could be setting, the sun of imagination bursting forth in noonday glory.'[3] There are, then, two quite different views of the figure of Jesus, positive and negative views corresponding to 'naïve' and 'sophisticated' readings of the picture. How are we to decide between them?

Those who believe plate *76* depicts a 'vegetated Christ' cite as support the passage in *90*: 34–8, where Los cries:

> A Vegetated Christ & a Virgin Eve, are the Hermaphroditic
> Blasphemy, by his Maternal Birth he is that Evil-One
> And his Maternal Humanity must be put off Eternally
> Lest the Sexual Generation swallow up Regeneration
> Come Lord Jesus take on thee the Satanic Body of Holiness

What is meant by this passage, and can it be applied to *J 76*? By 'Vegetated Christ' and 'Virgin Eve' Blake refers to the literal conceptions of historical Christianity according to which Jesus was conceived by an act of magic, performed other acts of magic called miracles, and then paid for our sins by allowing himself to be murdered to appease the wrath of a vengeful father god. The idea that Jesus must 'put off' (= take off, as a garment) his Maternal Humanity is one that would have been familiar to Blake through the writings of Emanuel Swedenborg. Swedenborg, for example, asserts 'that the Lord successively put off the humanity which was taken

[1] Henry Lesnick, 'The Antithetical Vision of *Jerusalem*', *Blake's Visionary Forms Dramatic*, ed. D. V. Erdman and J. E. Grant (Princeton: Princeton University Press, 1970), p. 399.

[2] Janet A. Warner, 'Blake's Use of Gesture', *Blake's Visionary Forms Dramatic*, p. 179.

[3] Erdman, *Ill. Bl.*, p. 355.

from the Mother, and put on the humanity from the Divinity in Himself, which is the Divine Humanity and the Son of God'.[1] The false body of literal doctrine worshipped by the Churches is actually Satan, while the true Jesus is the brother and friend who sacrifices himself for Albion:

Jesus said. Wouldest thou love one who never died
For thee or ever die for one who had not died for thee
And if God dieth not for Man & giveth not himself
Eternally for Man Man could not exist! for Man is Love:
As God is Love: every kindness to another is a little
 Death
In the Divine Image nor can Man exist but by Brother-
 hood[2]

The question is, then: which of these two Christs is worshipped by Albion in *76*? In Jean H. Hagstrum's comprehensive and enlightening essay 'Christ's Body', the only pictorial example of the 'darker side' in Blake's works is the tempera *Virgin and Child* (1825, Yale Center for British Art).[3] This picture is indeed dark, both physically and emotionally, but there is no similar portrayal of the adult Jesus. Perhaps a clue as to how Blake would have drawn the vegetated Christ may be found in the *Notebook* poem 'To English Connoisseurs':

I understood Christ was a Carpenter
And not a Brewers Servant my good Sir (E. 505)

The second line refers to Rubens, and presumably a fleshy Rubenesque Christ could have been seen by Blake as representing Christ's Maternal Humanity. But the Jesus of *76* is a spiritual being, a man of sorrows acquainted with grief. The starkness of depiction recalls early Italian Renaissance painting, particularly Mantegna, and the execution of the plate,

[1] *The Doctrine of the New Jerusalem Concerning the Lord* (London: R. Hindmarsh, 3rd edn., 1791), no. 35. On the relation of Blake's thought to Swedenborg's, see my article, ' "A New Heaven Is Begun": William Blake and Swedenborgianism', *Blake*, XIII (1979), 64–90.

[2] *96*: 23–8. Mitchell (*Blake's Composite Art*, p. 210) also refers to this passage in refuting the 'vegetated Christ' interpretation.

[3] *William Blake: Essays in Honour of Sir Geoffrey Keynes*, ed. M. D. Paley and M. Phillips (Oxford: The Clarendon Press, 1973), p. 137.

with its white-line technique expressing spiritual light gleaming in spiritual darkness is especially reminiscent of Bonasone. For example, Bonasone's mixed method print *The Resurrection*[1] displays white lines of radiance emerging from Christ's body and condensing into intense areas of white light composing his halo and the aura of the lower part of his body. Blake does not include the latter, but does introduce a rising sun[2] which echoes the radiance emanating from Christ's body. This sun cannot be responsible for the gleams of light on Albion's body; if it were natural light, his back and right side ought to be in shadow. Here Blake is perhaps challenging comparison with Rembrandt's chiaroscuro just as his rendering of Christ's idealized, muscular form may challenge comparison to the emaciated Christs of Rembrandt's etchings. For the figure of Albion himself, Blake went back to a conception associated with one of his most famous compositions. There is in the Victoria and Albert Museum a pencil drawing executed on both recto and verso, each showing the corresponding sides of a nude male. The front view provided the basis for the great print *Albion rose.*[3] For *Jerusalem 76* Blake elaborated the back view, presenting an Albion whose imitation of Christ consists in 'Giving himself for the Nations' just as Jesus gives himself for Albion in *96*: 17–22:

> So Jesus spoke: the Covering Cherub coming on in darkness
> Overshadowd them & Jesus said Thus do Men in Eternity
> One for another to put off by forgiveness, every sin

[1] See Adam Bartsch, *Le Peintre Graveur* (Vienna: J. V. Deagn, vol. XV, 1813), p. 121, no. 45. This print, dated 1561, was owned by George Cumberland. See *Catalogue*, p. 50, no. 30.

[2] Critics differ as to whether the sun is rising or setting, and their views do not necessarily agree with their positions on whether the Christ is 'vegetated' or not. Damon, for example, thinks the sun is setting (*William Blake*, p. 473). Wicksteed (*Blake's Jerusalem*, p. 220) sees it as rising, as do Lesnick (op. cit., pp. 399–400) and Bindman (*Blake As an Artist*, p. 179). Erdman thinks there are two suns, a natural one setting and a sun of imagination which is behind Jesus's head (*Ill. Bl.*, p. 355).

[3] The colour print (British Museum, Huntington Library), executed *c.* 1795–6, is often referred to by the Gilchrist title *Glad Day*, but the only title Blake himself gave this design appears as the caption of the final state of 1804: 'Albion rose from where he laboured at the Mill with Slaves / Giving himself for the Nations he danc'd the dance of Eternal Death.' For the dating of the states, see Essick, *Printmaker*, pp. 70–1, 182–3.

Albion replyd. Cannot Man exist without Mysterious
Offering of Self for Another, is this Friendship & Brotherhood
I see thee in the likeness & similitude of Los my Friend

There is, of course, no way in which this or any other interpretation can be established so as to persuade those who wish to believe that the design is a parody of its ostensible subject. All one can say is that the 'naïve' view of this picture, deriving from its immediate affect, fully accords with the central doctrine of *Jerusalem* as stated in the passage above, a doctrine which we find almost everywhere in Blake's works. 'Therefore God becomes as we are, that we may be as he is',[1] and Albion could not become as God is by imitating a vegetated Christ. This reading is also reinforced by Blake's iconography elsewhere. In the *Paradise Lost* illustration *The Archangel Michael Foretelling the Crucifixion,*[2] the figure of Christ on the Cross is almost exactly as in *Jerusalem 76,*[3] while Adam is to Christ's left, adoring him with hands placed together in an attitude of prayer. For *Jerusalem*, Blake changed the posture of Albion/Adam to indicate imitation rather than mere worship. In the third and last version of the *Paradise Lost* design,[4] he introduced a dazzling nimbus around the figure of Christ, making it even more like the *Jerusalem* depiction.

There *is* a vegetated Christ in *Jerusalem*. Hand in *26* stands cruciform, hands pierced by nails,[5] enveloped in a Satanic

[1] *There is No Natural Religion* [b], E. 2.

[2] I refer here to all three versions: Huntington Library, Boston Museum of Fine Arts, and Fitzwilliam Museum, produced in 1807, 1808, and 1822 respectively.

[3] The head of Jesus inclines to his left and Adam is to the left of him in the *Paradise Lost* illustrations, while in *Jerusalem 76* his head inclines to his right and Albion is below on his right. Of course in the copperplate for *76*, the directions would have been the same as in the Milton designs; they would have been reversed in printing.

[4] See Butlin, *William Blake*, pp. 116 and 117 for reproductions of the Boston Museum and the Fitzwilliam Museum versions.

[5] The monochrome copies show nails in both his feet and in one ankle. The latter detail is not visible in copy E, and in that copy what have been interpreted as stigmata (see *Ill. Bl.*, p. 305) may actually be attempts to cover the nails with flame colour. In the pencil drawing (British Museum) for this plate there are neither nails nor stigmata, and Hand's face has a more obviously anguished expression.

nimbus of flame that swathes his head with a false halo. As Christ's receptive audience is Albion, so Hand's is Jerusalem —but her reaction is not imitation but repulsion; she extends her forearms, palms outward in a pathos-formula of horror. The resonance of *76* extends back over the fifty plates to contrapose sacrifice of Self with Satanic Selfhood. The two designs invite the reader/viewer to identify with the observer in each picture and to respond accordingly; both designs, while not illustrating texts, are related to various passages in the poem. *26* would have little meaning if it were not defined by the myth of Albion's giant Sons, to be discussed in Chapter IV. *76*, although not similarly dependent on the text for its significance, connects passages in which Jesus appears as saviour, brother, and friend.

The foregoing discussion of five major designs leads us to some more general reflections on how to read Blake's pictures in *Jerusalem*. As I have said, there is no occult key to Blake's 'system', which is rendered meaningful only contextually, by the words and images of the work itself. There are, however, principles of interpretation which emerge as a result of having had one's faculties roused to act by Blake's admitted obscurity.[1] I see these principles not as substituting for an empathic experience of the designs as works of art, but as informing and deepening such an experience.

1. The designs are seldom without a pronounced immediate effect. Although Blake is capable of undermining the apparent surface meaning, we ought to credit our emotional responses to the designs unless the argument for an ironical reading is a compelling one.

2. Interpretations according to which mutually exclusive meanings are seen as equally valid are not likely to be helpful. We should remember Blake's love of the definite.

3. The traditions of art mattered to Blake, and they must matter to his critics as well. The identification of sources alone should not be the main object of enquiry here, but a recognition of what Blake does with his sources will often help us understand his iconography.

[1] See Blake's letter to the Revd John Trusler, 23 August 1799, *Letters*, p. 29.

4. Variants among the 5¼ original copies may be significant, but their significance is one of emphasis. Only occasionally does a variant change the meaning of a design. In a sense, the rule-proving exception could be *28*, in which the two figures were originally in a copulating position (see discussion in Chapter IV below); but this is a change from a proof state to the final state in all copies.

5. Although many of the designs are in no sense illustrations to the text but are, rather, related thematic statements, the reference of the designs exists in a frame of meaning defined by the text.

Chapter III

Millennium

The millenarian theme of *Jerusalem* was recognized as early as Gilchrist's *Life*, where we read: ' "Jerusalem" is once spoken of as Liberty; she is also apostrophized as "mild shade of man", and must, upon the whole, be taken to symbolize a millennial state.'[1] It need hardly be said that the association of Jerusalem with a regenerate human community comes to Blake from the Bible—from the Prophets of the Old Testament and from John of Patmos in the New. From the Prophets, Blake derives the idea of a Jerusalem tested by suffering, emerging as part of a new order of being after cataclysmic events:

For, behold, I create new heavens and a new earth: and the former shall not be remembered, nor come into mind.
But be ye glad and rejoice forever in that which I create: for, behold, I create Jerusalem a rejoicing, and her people a joy. (Isaiah 65: 17–18).

Revelation 21 presents the descent of the New Jerusalem as an eschatological event involving all humanity:

And I saw a new heaven and a new earth: for the first heaven and the first earth were passed away; and there was no more sea.
And I John saw the holy city, new Jerusalem, coming down from God out of heaven, prepared as a bride adorned for her husband. (1–2)

In *Jerusalem*, Blake transmutes this Prophetic-Apocalyptic situation into one applicable to his own immediate time and place, and in so doing he becomes part of a millenarian tradition that extends from biblical times to the early nineteenth century and beyond. A proper history of that tradition would require volumes,[2] but here it must at least be sketched

[1] Ed. Todd, p. 203.

[2] An excellent general study is *Millennium and Utopia* by Ernest Lee Tuveson (Berkeley and Los Angeles: University of California Press, 1949). *The Pursuit of the Millennium* by Norman Cohn (New York: Oxford University Press, 3rd edn., 1974) is a rich study of revolutionary millenarianism in the Middle Ages. Its conclusions, however, need not apply to later millenarianism and do not apply to

and Blake's relation to it indicated so that its importance for *Jerusalem* may be fully understood.

History

In the early Christian church it was generally believed that history would culminate, after six millennia, with a great Sabbath, the seventh day of a world-week. The early Church Fathers, including Lactantius, Irenaeus, and Tertullian, agreed that before the end of the world the saints would live in Jerusalem under the rule of Christ. Justin Martyr declared: 'I and whosoever are, *in all things*, of sound Christian doctrine, know that there shall be both a resurrection of the flesh, and 1000 years in Jerusalem, built, and adorned, and enlarged, as the prophet Ezekiel and the rest confess.'[1] Tertullian spoke of 'that middle space of time, which lieth open between'[2] as a period in which the whole human race would be resurrected to await the Last Judgement in Jerusalem. Lactantius regarded each day of Genesis as equivalent to one thousand years, with the seventh day being a thousand-year reign of peace and justice.[3] St. Augustine, who was later to repudiate the idea of the millennium, at first assigned the resurrection of the flesh to the world's Sabbath, reserving the spiritual millennium for the mysterious eighth day of the world-week. 'That eighth day', he wrote, citing John 20: 26, 'signifies the new life at the end of the world; the seventh the rest of the saints, which shall be on the earth.'[4] However, in *The City of God*, Augustine,

Blake's, in any event. Particularly valuable for its discussion of the world-week and other conceptions of time is *Cosmos and History* by Mircea Eliade (trans. Willard R. Trask, New York and Evanston: Harper and Row, 1959 [1949]). A useful collection of essays by various hands is *Millennial Dreams in Action*, ed. Sylvia L. Thrupp (The Hague: Mouton, 1962). *Primitive Rebels* by E. J. Hobsbawm (Manchester: Manchester University Press, 1959) is devoted to several later nineteenth-century and twentieth-century millenarian movements.

[1] Quoted by C. Dodgson, *Tertullian* (Oxford: Parker, 1842), I. 123.

[2] 'The Book of Apology Against the Heathen', *Tertullian*, I. 101.

[3] 'Necesse est, ut in fine sexti millesmi anni malitia omnis aboleatur e terra, et regnet per annos mille iustitia; sitque tranquillitas, et requies a laboribus, quos mundus iamdiu perfert.' Quoted from *Divina Institutionum Liber Septimus* by Marjorie Reeves, *The Influence of Prophecy in the Later Middle Ages* (Oxford: The Clarendon Press, 1969), pp. 296–7.

[4] Quoted by Dodgson, *Tertullian*, I. 128.

while holding to the conception of a world-week in which the Sabbath is followed by an eighth day, rejects the notion that there would be a physical millennium.

> Now this opinion would be tolerable up to a certain point, if it were believed that in the sabbath some few spiritual delights were to fall to the lot of the saints through the presence of the Lord; I, too, was once of this opinion. But since they say that those who are to rise again will enjoy a holiday of most immoderate carnal feasts, in which food and drink will be so plentiful that not only will they observe no limits of moderation but will also exceed all bounds even of incredulity, all this can be believed only by the carnally minded. Those who are spiritually minded call those who believe these things, in Greek, chiliasts, and we may in Latin translate the term literally as 'millenarians.'[1]

The very elements which made the idea of the millennium unacceptable to Augustine would have made it attractive to Blake. In Blake's most extensive treatment of the millennial theme, Night IX of *The Four Zoas*, Day of Wrath is followed by Resurrection, and in the ensuing 'bright feast' Luvah rises 'drunk with the wine of ages', and Tharmas and Urthona are 'satiated / With Mirth & Joy'.[2] The conclusion of *Jerusalem*, while shorter and less detailed, is no less concerned with the renovation of the body. In terms of the world-week, plates *95–100* involve a transition from the Sabbath of Blake's Seventh Eye of God, Jesus, to the 'regenerations terrific' of the nameless Eighth Eye. In imagining the conclusion of history as a vast celebration of risen bodies, Blake is consistent with the millenarian tradition of early Christianity, as he may well have known through an account such as that of J. L. Mosheim in *An Ecclesiastical History, Ancient and Modern*, published in English in 1765.[3]

After its displacement as a central tenet of Christian faith, millenarianism persisted in forms such as the Sybilline Prophecies and popular folk beliefs. Norman Cohn has shown what extraordinary power the latter could assume, impelling

[1] *The City of God Against the Pagans* (Cambridge, Mass.: Harvard University Press, 1960), trans. William Chase Greene, p. 285. Needless to say, the statement does not represent the views of Lactantius and Tertullian fairly. For discussion, see Reeves, op. cit., pp. 297–8.

[2] 126: 8, E. 380; 135: 22, E. 388; 137: 7–8, E. 390.

[3] London, trans. Archibald Maclaine. See vol. I, pp. 145–6, where controversies concerning the millennium are discussed.

masses of men to acts of astonishing collective violence.[1] With the medieval dream of the military capture of Jerusalem, Blake could have had little sympathy, nor with the sentimentalization of that dream in the Renaissance. Blake's Jerusalem Liberated is of a different order from Tasso's; it is a free human community conceived in terms of biblical prophecy and apocalyptic. There did, nevertheless, exist in the Middle Ages a view of history similar in many respects to Blake's—that of Joachim of Fiore, whom Dante places in Paradise as 'the Calabrian abbot Joachim, endowed with prophetic spirit'.[2] For Joachim there are three ages of world history, corresponding to the Father, the Son, and the Holy Spirit. Temporally, these correspond to the period of the Old Testament, the period of the New Testament, and that of a new age about to begin. In this new Age of the Spirit both the secular law and the sacraments of the Church will be unnecessary; humanity will live in a state of perfect freedom, conceived as a Sabbath within history, the seventh day of the world-week.[3] The similarities between these ideas and Blake's could have been reinforced by indirect influence, for Joachim of Fiore was a powerful force in the intellectual history of Europe. He was taken up by the Spiritual Franciscans; he deeply affected Dante;[4] and his *Figurae*—the allegorical illustrations accompanying his texts—are thought to have found their way into the imagery of *Piers Plowman*.[5] The similarity of his thought to that of the English Ranters in the seventeenth century is considerable,[6] and it has also been argued that Blake's writings exhibit striking verbal parallels with certain Ranter texts.[7] The affinities between Blake's form of millenarianism and Joachim of Fiore's are, in any event, remarkable.

[1] See Cohn, *The Pursuit of the Millennium.*

[2] *The Paradiso of Dante Alighieri*, trans. P. H. Wicksteed (London: J. M. Dent, 1958), p. 151.

[3] See Reeves, *The Influence of Prophecy*, pp. 295–305.

[4] See Marjorie Reeves and Beatrice Hirsch-Reich, *The Figurae of Joachim of Fiore* (Oxford: The Clarendon Press, 1972), pp. 317–29.

[5] See Reeves and Hirsch-Reich, pp. 312–14. For some further comparisons and suggestions as to the possible transmission of Joachite ideas to Blake, see Désirée Hirst, *Hidden Riches: Traditional Symbolism from the Renaissance to Blake* (London: Eyre and Spottiswoode, 1964), pp. 8, 101–2.

[6] On the Ranters, see Cohn, *The Pursuit of the Millennium*, pp. 287–330.

[7] See A. L. Morton, *The Everlasting Gospel* (London: Laurence and Wishart, 1958).

Millenarianism became once again a subject of public debate in seventeenth-century England, as vigorously argued among dissenters and divines as it had once been among Church Fathers and heresiarchs. The political and social consequences of millenarian views were at least as important as their theological implications. 'Milton', suggests Christopher Hill, 'shared this widespread millenarianism, as was appropriate for a man educated at Joseph Mede's college.'[1] Mede, whose literary effect on Milton has been discussed by Joseph A. Wittreich, Jr.,[2] presented a formidable millenarian argument based on the Bible and early Church history. Like his predecessors of the third century, Mede interpreted the 'new heaven, and a new earth' of Revelation 21: 1 as looking back to the promises of Isaiah 65: 17 and 66: 22. 'Surely', writes Mede, 'whosoever shall read, I should marvel, if he should conceive that it shall be fulfilled anywhere but on earth.'[3] The seventh trumpet of Revelation announces '*the glorious . . . appearing of our Lord in flaming fire*', to be followed by the 'reigne of the thousand years granted to new Jerusalem, his most holy Spouse, upon the earth'.[4] Mede supplements his view with an annotated translation of Justin Martyr's dialogue with Typho the Jew, affirming the millennium, and with seven pages of quotations from rabbinical commentaries. The latter support the idea of a Day of Judgement constituting a seventh millenary after the six thousand years of world history. 'Even as every seventh year of seven years, is a year of release: so of the seven thousand years of the world, the seventh thousand year shall be the year of release.'[5] Although we cannot tell whether Blake read Mede's famous book,[6] it is clear that the tradition of the world-week upon which he draws is extra-

[1] *Milton and the English Revolution* (Harmondsworth, Middlesex: Penguin Books, 1979 [1977]), p. 281.

[2] *Visionary Poetics: Milton's Tradition and His Legacy* (San Marino, California: Huntington Library, 1979), pp. 16, 20, 22, 36, 37–8, 40, 43, 47, 63, 75.

[3] *The Key of the Revelation* (London: 2nd edn. in English, 1643), p. 123.

[4] Ibid., p. 122.

[5] Ibid., p. 131, quoting '*Gemara Sanhedrin, Perek Chelek*'.

[6] Mede's millenarian arguments are referred to by, among others, Joseph Priestley and Thomas Hartley. Priestley mentions them to disagree with their literalness; see *The Institutes of Natural and Revealed Religion* (1772–4), *Theological and Miscellaneous Works* (London, 1817), pp. 366–7. Hartley summarizes them with sympathy in *Paradise Restored: or a Testimony to the Doctrine of the Blessed Millennium* (London, 1764); see discussion below.

biblical and that Mede was one of its most important exponents. Blake's version of the world-week in *Jerusalem* is of course the Seven Eyes of God, elected by the Eternals in *55*: 1-2, with the Eighth Eye not yet ready to appear ('he hid in Albions Forests').

What of a possible connection between Blake's millenarian theme and the ideas of what Hill terms the 'third culture' of the sixteenth century, with its radicalism, its printing activity, and its interpretations of prophecy and apocalypse?[1] Some affinities are indeed striking, and it is intriguing to imagine how Blake might have responded to the revolutionary social writings of Gerrard Winstanley and the messianic doctrine of James Nayler. Blake's notion of the indwelling human imagination as Christ also has much in common with the beliefs of the Familists, his view of the fundamental innocence of the body with those of the Ranters, his political ideas with those of the Fifth Monarchy Men, his apocalyptic visions with those of the Muggletonians. It is difficult to believe that Blake was entirely ignorant of the visionary politics of the Commonwealth era;[2] at the very least we can assume that he knew that the building of Jerusalem in England's green and pleasant land had previously been envisaged.

During the Restoration, millenarian thought became both politically dangerous and remote from the intellectual concerns of the age; though tolerated after 1688, it never regained a place in the main stream of political discourse. Nevertheless, speculation about the millennium persisted. Thomas Beverley announced the imminent arrival of the Kingdom of Christ, basing his argument both upon scriptural exegesis and on 'the Assistance of the *Spirit of Prophecy*'.[3] Both Jakob Boehme and Emanuel Swedenborg, though neither was in the strict sense a millenarian, promoted doctrines which were susceptible of a millenarian interpretation by their followers. Boehme

[1] See *Milton and the English Revolution*, pp. 93–116.

[2] See A. L. Morton, *The Everlasting Gospel*. E. P. Thompson informs me that his forthcoming book on Blake will explore parallels with the Muggletonians, among other groups. For comparisons between Blake and the Puritan divines of what Hill calls the second culture, see Harold Fisch, *Jerusalem and Albion* (New York: Schocken, 1964), pp. 11–15, 274–80.

[3] *An Apology for the Hope of the Kingdom of Christ, Appearing within This Approaching Year, 1697* (London, 1697), p. 3.

postulated an 'Enochian period' in which the human race would attain a happier state, an aspect of his thought adopted by Jane Leade and her Behmenist circle, which became the Philadelphian Society.[1]

Mrs Leade's successor as leader of the Society, Richard Roach, became influenced by the millennial notions of the French Prophets or Camisards, and published in 1725 *The Great Crisis: or, the Mystery of the Times and Seasons Unfolded.* This book includes an account of 'the several *Ages* or *Periods* of the Christian Church, as Represented by the *Seven Churches* of *Asia*, from the Time of Christ's Coming in the Flesh to his Second Appearance in his Millennial Kingdom; and from thence to the end of this World, and the Consummation of all Things: Together with a *Scheme* or *Figure* representing their Process, and the Manner of their Succession; with Proper *Emblems* representing the most Material Characters, or Events therein'.[2] 'The Scheme or Figure' is a fold-out engraving that was re-published in 1727 with Roach's *The Imperial Standard of the Messiah Triumphant.* In it Christian history is represented by a series of seven overlapping circles, each representing a Period, with each successive circle beginning in the centre of its predecessor. In each period there exists a redemptive possibility, just as in *Jerusalem 75* Los walks continually up and down the twenty-seven Heavens and their Churches. Writes Roach: 'the little Circles, or *Centers* . . . passing thro' the whole Church Series, become the *Central Power* of the Ages of it; Proceding and Returning in Circulation, thro' all the Times and Variations of the Church States, as the Victorious and Overcoming Part, or the *Spirit of Christ*, which Constitutes and Conducts the Course and Periods of it from the Beginning to the End'.[3] The sixth period, the Philadelphian, concludes with the Millennial Kingdom in which Christ reigns among the saints in their resurrected bodies. After one thousand years, Christ re-ascends to heaven in the Laodicean Period, 'but the *New Jerusalem* still continues to Overshadow and rest upon the *Jerusalem City*

[1] See Nils Thune, *The Behmenists and the Philadelphians: a Contribution to the Study of English Mysticism in the Seventeenth and Eighteenth Centuries* (Uppsala: Almqvist and Wiksell, 1948). Thune points out that Thomas Beverley was connected with the Philadelphian Society, though not a member (p. 110).

[2] p. 209.

[3] p. 239.

and *Church* remaining on earth'.[1] Just so, after the abolition of Time in *Jerusalem*, the great City of Golgonooza still exists in the Shadowy Generation, and exulting voices come from it.

In the period before the organization of the (Swedenborgian) Theosophical Society in the 1770s, an important disseminator of millenarian doctrine was the Revd. Thomas Hartley, Rector of Winwick in Northamptonshire. Hartley was both a Behmenist and a Swedenborgian; he had known Swedenborg personally; and he was co-translator of the edition of *Heaven and Hell* owned by Blake. Hartley's *Paradise Restored*, published in 1764, contains numerous ideas that would have struck a responsive chord in Blake. Unfallen Adam, argues Hartley, 'had a body of unspeakable beauty' and 'had doubtless an intuitive knowledge of all things within the sphere of his kingdom, and was not left to painful researches, and slow procedure of the human understanding in its present state'.[2] Like some other early Swedenborgians, Hartley condemns the slave-trade, and like a number of them he is a millenarian. Hartley adduces detailed arguments from the Bible, from the Church Fathers, and from Joseph Mede to demonstrate that there will be a resurrection of the flesh lasting one thousand years in a rebuilt and enlarged Jerusalem. 'In this new heaven and new earth, after the first heaven and first earth are passed away, will gloriously appear the new Jerusalem come down out of heaven, prepared as a bride adorned for her husband, wherein God will tabernacle with men, and drink the new wine of the kingdom with his disciples.'[3] Like Blake, Hartley views regeneration as accessible for the individual before and apart from the advent of a millennial society, and he defends William Law and Methodists against their attackers. Hartley shows a support very similar to Blake's for all forms of spiritual Christianity, but perhaps the most notable aspect of his book is its recension of millenarian doctrine.

The early Swedenborgian movement in England served as a virtual clearing-house for seekers after the millennium. It may be that Swedenborg's declaration that the Last Judgement had occurred in 1757 meant that in that year the

[1] p. 237.
[2] pp. 10, 15.
[3] p. 179. Hartley discusses the millenarian views of Justin Martyr, Irenaeus, Tertullian, and Lactantius, among others.

millennium had begun, but nevertheless the atmosphere of the early New Jerusalem Church was decidedly millenarian. The Revd. Jacob Duché, at whose church in Lambeth numerous Swedenborgians worshipped from 1785 until 1789, wrote to his mother-in-law in America: 'The New Church from above, the Jerusalem of the Revelation, is come down upon earth. Look henceforward for an Internal Millennium.'[1] Two of the Swedish delegates to the General Conference of 1789, Augustus Nordensköld and Carl Bernhard Wadström, planned to found the New Jerusalem in Africa, motivated both by abolitionist conviction and by Swedenborg's belief that the Africans of the interior maintained a direct intuitive communication with God.[2] Robert Hindmarsh was moved, in the heady atmosphere of the General Conference of 1789 to write: 'The tree of life, whose roots are planted in the gardens and streets of the New Jerusalem, as well as on either bank of its river, spontaneously sprang up before our eyes, luxuriant in foliage, and laden with the sweetest fruits of paradise in endless variety and abundance.'[3] This text could well accompany one of Blake's drawings such as the design for Revelation 22: 1-2 called *The River of Life* (Tate Gallery), and the fervour of statements like Hindmarsh's shows what drew William and Catherine Blake to attend the General Conference.

Among the pursuers of the millennium who passed through Swedenborgian circles in the 1780s was 'Count' Thaddeus Grabianka,[4] emissary of the group known variously as the *illuminés* of Avignon, the Prophets of Avignon, or the Avignon Society.[5] Count Grabianka attended meetings of the Theo-

[1] Letter, 5 May 1785, quoted by Clarke Garrett, 'The Spiritual Odyssey of Jacob Duché', *Proceedings of the American Philosophical Society*, CXIX (1975), 143-55.

[2] See ' "A New Heaven Is Begun" ', pp. 83-5.

[3] Robert Hindmarsh, *Rise and Progress of the New Jerusalem Church*, ed. the Revd Edward Madeley (London: Hodson and Son, 1861), p. 107.

[4] On Count Grabianka, see M. L. Danilewicz, ' "The King of the New Israel": Thaddeus Grabianka (1740-1807)', *Oxford Slavonic Papers*, NS, I (1968), 49-73. Although his title was fictitious, Grabianka was, Danilewicz points out, the enormously wealthy owner of three castles and fourteen large estates in Poland.

[5] On the Prophets of Avignon, see Joanny Bricaud, *Les Illuminés d'Avignon: Étude sur Dom Pernety et son groupe* (Paris, Librarie Critique Émile Nourry, 1927); and Clarke Garrett, *Respectable Folly: Millenarianism and the French Revolution in France and England* (Baltimore: Johns Hopkins University, 1975), pp. 97-120.

sophical Society in London in 1786, both in the Middle Temple and at the Duché house in Lambeth. Robert Hindmarsh reports:

All were delighted with his company: all were anxious to shew him tokens of their affection and esteem. He was particularly desirous of *eating bread*, and *drinking wine* (as if in commemoration of the Lord's Supper), at each of our houses, or at least of the houses of those whom he esteemed the leading members of the Society. . . . He distinguished *twelve* from the rest, and marked them, in his own mind, as resembling in character, person, or manner, the twelve apostles of the Lord. One he called *Peter*; another, *James*; a third, *John*; and so on with the rest. . . . It is remarkable, that in almost all the meetings, which Count Grabianka attended, he gave us to understand, that he and his Society were in possession of some *grand secret*, which he was not then at liberty to divulge, because the time proper for its disclosure *was not yet arrived*.[1]

Although he did not succeed in persuading most of the London Swedenborgians of the affinity of their beliefs with those held at Avignon, Count Grabianka addressed a letter to the Theosophical Society in 1787, announcing the imminence of the Second Coming: '*For, very dear brethren, the angel that stands before the face of the Lamb, is already sent to sound his trumpet on the mountains of Babylon, and give notice to the nations that the God of heaven will soon come to the gates of the earth, to change the face of the world, and to manifest his power and glory.*'[2] 'There was still something about the whole of their communication, which was not entirely satisfactory', writes Hindmarsh;[3] and indeed the group at Avignon was a Masonic lodge whose members were engaged in deep alchemical researches and who believed that the Virgin Mary was the fourth person of the Trinity. Such convictions were hardly compatible with Swedenborgianism as it was understood in England, and in 1795 Benedict Chastanier, one of the early translators and editors of Swedenborg's works, attacked the Avignon group as being the 'synagogue of Satan'.[4] There was nevertheless traffic between London and

[1] *Rise and Progress*, pp. 42–3.

[2] Dated 12 February 1787 and signed by Grabianka with five others, this letter was printed by Hindmarsh as a leaflet in 1787 and reprinted by him in *Rise and Progress*, pp. 46–7.

[3] *Rise and Progress*, p. 45.

[4] *A Word of Advice to a Benighted World*. Blake also uses this term in his late works, including *Jerusalem* (*52*), meaning the corrupt and worldly church (see

Avignon as a result of Grabianka's visit, and at least one of the seekers was a member of the Duché circle—Thomas Spence Duché, artist and son of the clergyman.[1]

The fact that Count Grabianka's mission was for a time entertained seriously by the London Swedenborgians indicates something of their sense of millenarian expectation. The story of John Wright and William Bryan is also illustrative of millenarian currents then moving. Wright was a carpenter in Leeds when he heard the Swedenborgian preachers Joseph Salmon and Ralph Maher, and was subsequently called by the Spirit to go to London.[2] There he was disappointed to find that the new church adhered to the old forms of worship, 'although called by the blessed name of *New Jerusalem*, in which these old forms have neither part nor lot'.[3] Then Wright met William Bryan, a copperplate printer who had been set up in business by William Sharp.[4] Bryan was a fervent opponent of war and slavery who believed 'that in the restoration of the house of Israel they [Jesus and the twelve apostles] will have a manifestation in this world, together with all the old prophets and holy men spoken of in the scriptures, it being the time of the first resurrection, and the commencement of the period mentioned by St. John, in his Revelation, in which the Lord shall reign with his saints upon the earth, when Paradise shall be again revealed unto man, and evil shall disappear'.[5] Bryan was in contact with the Avignon Society, and in January 1789 he and Wright set out

Damon, *Blake Dictionary*, p. 394). In appropriating this typological symbol from Rev. 2: 9 and 3: 9, both Chastanier and Blake (and Chastanier's sources, identified as H. Jones and Sarah Flaxmer) exhibit the millenarian tendency to interpret contemporary history in apocalyptic terms.

[1] See Albert Frank Gegenheimer, 'Artist in Exile: the Story of Thomas Spence Duché', *Pennsylvania Magazine of History and Biography*, LXXIX (1955), 3–26.

[2] See John Wright, *A Revealed Knowledge of Some Things that Will Speedily be Fulfilled in the World* (London, 1794), pp. 1–3.

[3] Ibid., p. 4.

[4] According to Clarke Garrett, *Respectable Folly: Millenarianism and the French Revolution in France and England* (Baltimore and London: Johns Hopkins University Press, 1975), p. 176.

[5] William Bryan, *A Testimony of the Spirit of Truth, concerning Richard Brothers* (London, 1795), p. 6. Bryan says the Lord communicated this to him 'ten years ago'. It is interesting that Bryan's booklet, like Blake's *Jerusalem*, consists of parts addressed to different audiences: 'To the Reader', 'To the Children of Israel', and 'To the Gentiles called Christians'.

for Avignon, where they stayed with the illuminés for seven months. On returning to England, they published their spiritual testimonies, including (in Wright's) a transcript of some exchanges they had had with the Holy Word at Avignon. Bryan, furthermore, gave Robert Southey information about the Prophets of Avignon for use in *Letters From England by Don Manuel Alvarez Espriella.*[1] Wright was converted to the cause of Richard Brothers, self-styled 'Prince of the Hebrews' and 'Nephew of the Almighty'; and Bryan, after having a dream of Brothers in the New Jerusalem, followed suit but later moved on (with William Sharp) to become a follower of Joanna Southcott.

The quests of Wright and Bryan, and to some extent Sharp's as well, were motivated by a sense of millenarian expectation that was shared by William Blake. All four had sought satisfaction in the teachings of Swedenborg and had been disappointed.[2] Blake, however, associated with no movement after that. What sets him off from contemporaries like Wright, Sharp, and Bryan is that for him the millennial state became a theme to be advanced in art and poetry.

Of the various millenarian figures of the time, perhaps the most interesting to compare with Blake is Richard Brothers.[3] In 1794, the year in which Blake published two works which he himself entitled prophecies, *America* and *Europe*, Brothers brought out in two instalments *A Revealed Knowledge of the Prophecies and Times*. Like Blake, Brothers predicts the defeat of monarchy, the ruin of empire, and the frustration of Britain's attack on the French Revolution. Like Blake,

[1] Southey, *Letters from Spain* (London, 1807), vol. III, pp. 227–53. Southey's copy of *A Testimony of the Spirit of Truth*, bound with *A Revealed Knowledge*, is in the Bodleian Library. On the flyleaf facing the title-page is a manuscript note below Southey's signature: 'These are two of the most curious pamphlets in my possession. There is an account of them in Espriella's Letters, where what is said of Bryan is from my personal knowledge of him, when he lived in Bristol in the winter of 1794–5. R.S.'

[2] Sharp had been a member of the Theosophical Society and then of the New Jerusalem Church. Blake attended the General Conference of 1789. Wright was drawn to London by the New Jerusalem Church. Bryan, according to Clarke Garrett, asserted that Swedenborg had been divinely taught at first but had introduced many of his own fantasies into his writings. (See *Respectable Folly*, p. 110.)

[3] Brothers is discussed in detail in my article 'William Blake, the Prince of the Hebrews, and the Woman Clothed with the Sun', *William Blake: Essays in Honour of Sir Geoffrey Keynes*, pp. 260–93.

too, Brothers anticipates the imminent appearance of the prophet Elijah, a role that in *Jerusalem* is accorded Los.[1] Blake can hardly have been indifferent to the fate of Brothers, who was arrested on 4 March 1795 on the charge of 'unlawfully, maliciously, and wickedly writing, publishing, and printing various fantastical prophecies, with intent to cause dissension and other disturbances within the realm, contrary to the Statute'.[2] Blake must have realized that he himself could easily have been so charged, and it seems more than coincidence that after publishing eleven illuminated books from 1789 to 1795 Blake produced no new works in this mode for more than a decade. It nevertheless remains true that Blake was never a prophet in the literal sense claimed by Brothers. The Prince of the Hebrews attracted great attention by predicting events like the assassination of Gustav III of Sweden, and his intention was to establish a kingdom with its seat in Jerusalem. Blake, in contrast, wrote: 'Every honest man is a Prophet he utters his opinion both of private & public matters Thus If you go on So the result is So He never says such a thing Shall happen let you do what you will.'[3] Blake's Jerusalem is to be built in England's green and pleasant land, and his manner of building it is in the practice of art and poetry.

In the aftermath of the French Revolution, prophecies of the millennium flourished. Joseph Priestley saw in the post-Revolutionary state of Europe a prelude to the fulfilment of biblical prophecy, and he preached the imminent advent of the millennium.[4] In a series of discourses entitled *The Signs of the Times*, Joseph Bicheno, M.A., of Newbury opposed the war against France, protested against the curtailment of liberty, and predicted the literal accomplishment of 'a new heaven and a new earth' to be preceded by the restoration of

[1] See *39/44*: 30–1, where the Friends of Albion 'gave their power to Los / Naming him the Spirit of Prophecy, calling him Elijah'.

[2] The text of this law, which goes back to Elizabeth I, is printed in 'The Prince of the Hebrews', p. 362.

[3] Annotations to *An Apology for the Bible*, by R. Watson, Bishop of Llandaff (London, 1797), E. 606–7.

[4] *The Present State of Europe* (London, 1794). Garrett discusses the influence upon Priestley of the American millenarian evangelist Elhanan Winchester (*Respectable Folly*, p. 137).

the Jews to Jerusalem.[1] Nathaniel Brassey Halhed, M.P., followed Richard Brothers in calculating the date of the millennium as 19 November 1795.[2] Francis Dobbs, member of the Irish Parliament for Charlemont, declared in 1800 that the Second Coming would take place in time to forestall the Act of Union; this would fulfil the belief of the first teachers of Christianity 'that they should live again on this earth, and enjoy one thousand years of happiness, under that Messiah, who died upon the cross'; the Jews would be restored to Jerusalem, 'and then, as is foretold, nation shall rise up against nation no more'.[3] Writers such as these shared with Blake the conviction that the conditions of life were about to be transformed, that Scriptural prophecy would be fulfilled, and that a new era of peace and justice would shortly begin.

The era of political millenarianism faded as the Napoleonic wars continued into the nineteenth century and the publication of prophecies continued to be dangerous. Prolonged war, political repression, dearth, and rising prices produced an atmosphere conducive to what E. P. Thompson aptly calls 'the chiliasm of despair'.[4] The great exemplar of this type of millenarianism was Joanna Southcott, daughter of a Devonshire farmer, who began to publish prophecies in 1801.[5] Thirteen years later, having attracted thousands of followers and published an enormous amount of doggerel verse dictated by the Spirit, she announced that she was with child by the Holy Ghost. She was to give birth to a saviour called Shiloh, but after a highly publicized lying-in, she died and was found not to be pregnant.[6] As I have elsewhere compared Southcott's ideas with Blake's, some main points only need be repeated.[7]

[1] The textual history of this series of pamphlets is complicated, as Bicheno kept adding to and revising former editions. The most extensive I have consulted is dated (London) 1799. See also Bicheno's *The Restoration of the Jews, the Crisis of All Nations* (London, 1800).

[2] *A Calculation of the Millennium* (London, 1795).

[3] *A Concise View from History and Prophecy of the Great Predictions in the Sacred Writings, That Have Been Fulfilled; Also of Those That Are Now Fulfilling, and That Remain to be Accomplished* (London, 1800), pp. 61–2, 147, 168.

[4] *The Making of the English Working Class*, pp. 411–40.

[5] Her first book was *The Strange Effects of Faith* (Exeter, 1801).

[6] See Richard Reece, M.D., *A Correct Statement of the Circumstances That Attended the Last Illness and Death of Mrs. Southcott* (London, 1815).

[7] See 'William Blake, the Prince of the Hebrews, and the Woman Clothed with the Sun'.

Joanna Southcott's message, in contrast to Brothers's, scarcely urges social justice. It is possible to stress Southcott's humble agricultural origins, the importance of Woman in her doctrine, and the predominance of artisans, labourers, and women in her movement;[1] yet the content of her teaching is quietistic. Brothers, for example, tells how he was physically thrown out of Parliament, where he had gone to denounce the war then impending, and his incarceration as a madman was obviously politically motivated.[2] Southcott's only 'trials' were the ones she herself promoted, trials at which no adversary appeared. Southcottonian preachers went to great lengths to stress their loyalty to the existing order, and if they did otherwise, they were quickly checked by their prophetess.[3]

Blake's view of Joanna Southcott's pretensions to bear the Son of God is clear; he recorded it in his *Notebook*:

On the Virginity of the Virgin
Mary & Johanna Southcott

Whateer is done to her she cannot know
And if youll ask her she will swear it so
Whether tis good or evil none's to blame
No one can take the pride no one the shame[4]

Blake's antagonism derives from his lifelong hostility to the doctrine of the Virgin Birth, with its concomitant exaltation of celibacy and its condemnation of sensual enjoyment. For Blake true virginity resides in the innocent love of characters like Oothoon and Jerusalem herself, while merely external virginity is the province of 'Babylon the City of Vala, the Goddess Virgin-Mother' (*18*: 29). Blake's reaction to Joanna Southcott may also have been expressed in *Jerusalem*, in the

[1] As pointed out by J. C. F. Harrison, *The Second Coming* (New Brunswick, NJ: Rutgers University Press, 1979), pp. 86–134.

[2] This is not, of course, to question that Brothers was technically insane.

[3] Harrison notes that Peter Morrison of Liverpool was rebuked by Joanna for saying that 'all the property of the rich would be taken away and given to the sealed people' (*The Second Coming*, p. 127).

[4] E. 492. This poem was written long before Joanna Southcott announced her pregnancy, but her earlier writings are full of veiled predictions that her followers were not slow to apply. William Sharp, for example, told Dr Reece that he had bought flannel for her accouchement fifteen years before the event (*A Correct Statement*, pp. 83–4). Blake's epigram may have been written as a reaction to Sharp's effort to convert him, reported by Henry Crabb Robinson on information from John Flaxman (*BR*, p. 435).

episode of Gwendolen and Hyle. Gwendolen, the would-be virgin mother, claims in *82* to have produced a man-child unaided.

> Look I have wrought without delusion: Look! I have wept!
> And given soft milk mingled together with the spirits of flocks
> Of lambs and doves, mingled together in cups and dishes
> Of painted clay; the mighty Hyle is become a weeping infant;
> Soon shall the Spectres of the Dead follow my weaving threads. (5–9)

Triumphantly, 'she drew aside her Veil from Mam-Tor to Dovedale' (45)—rock formations suggestive of breasts and vagina[1]—but all she produces is the monstrous worm of mortality that winds its way up the right-hand margin of the *82* design. In contrast, the episode of Joseph and Mary, where Mary does not deny the charge that she is 'a Harlot & an Adultress' (*61*: 6), emphasizes the purity of love and culminates in the birth of a human infant who is received by Jerusalem 'in the Visions of Jehovah' (48).[2]

The idea of the millennium finds its most memorable expression in the renovated Jerusalem of the Prophets and of Revelation. It is to this idea of Jerusalem, sometimes conceived as a city, sometimes as a woman, that post-biblical millenarianism keeps returning. Blake's millenarian theme in *Jerusalem* is deeply imbued with this tradition. 'The Nations wait for Jerusalem. they look up for the Bride' (*72*: 37).

[1] See Damon, *Blake Dictionary*, p. 107.

[2] It is interesting that *61* is clearly an insertion, the speech at the end of *60* being continued on *62*, with the script of *61* being considerably larger and more flowery than that of the two others; while the existence of two deleted half-lines in *82* leads Erdman to say that this plate 'was prepared in a condition of unusual haste, or inattention, or illness' ('The Suppressed and Altered Passages in Blake's *Jerusalem*', *Studies in Bibliography*, XVII (1964), 31). Haste would seem more likely in the case of one of the last plates to be etched than in an early one, and the later the date of etching the more likely that *82* was completed after the death of Joanna Southcott. *61* may then have been inserted, perhaps having been originally conceived for another purpose, as a thematic counterpoise.

Throughout *Jerusalem*, Los labours to build Golgonooza, which is Blake's version of the ultimate city and which may be seen as a revision of the one alluded to by Paul: 'For here we have no continuing city, but we seek one to come.' (Heb. 13: 14.) Blake's continuing city is both here 'the great City of Golgonooza in the Shadowy Generation' (*98*: 55) *and* to come, for it exists after the abolition of Time.[1] That city and its associated symbols are the central embodiment of Blake's millenarian theme.

City and Temple

The mind delights in cities. In constructing mental models of cities, writers long before and long after Blake have devised frames of reference for the meanings of their works. Sometimes the city is a microcosm of the universe, as the Dublin of Joyce's *Ulysses*; sometimes it is the encapsulation of an imagined ideal, as Yeats's Byzantium. Both heaven and hell are frequently pictured as cities. Rome, Paris, London, Jerusalem—all have provided enabling myths by which both human history and individual experience may be given meaning. For Blake, the ultimate city is Golgonooza, a name combining the place of Christ's sacrifice of self with the primeval ooze of existence. It combines the quotidian reality of Blake's London, its streets, buildings, and public places, with the visionary New Jerusalem. Or, rather, Los works continually to build the second from the mundane materials of the first, and by this process creates Golgonooza. Blake's continuing city, unlike Paul's, *is* 'here'—but it is also 'there', continually in the act of being formed. It takes its bricks and mortar from London ('Oxford Street is in Jerusalem'), but as a city of the imagination it is a transformation of the idea of Jerusalem deeply embedded in our cultural history and developed by writers from the time of the Old Testament to Blake's own day. This tradition centres on the structure of Solomon's Temple or of the rebuilt Temple of Zerubabel,[2] which thus

[1] See Chapter V, p. 267 below.

[2] In the subsequent discussion I do not distinguish between the two Temples (or between these and the Temple as modified by Herod) unless it is necessary for historical reasons.

becomes an analogy of an analogy, the microcosm of the world city, with its gates, walls, courtyards, and towers. An understanding of this tradition sheds light, as one would expect, on Blake's use of it, but the converse is also true: Blake's re-creation of City and Temple shows us this traditional representation of Jerusalem as the representation of total human fulfilment.

Blake's mental model of the continuing city is presented in the extensive passage beginning at *12*: 45 and ending after fifty-one lines at *13*: 33. It is possible to make a diagram of this model, and, if we remember that such a diagram is only ancillary, it may be helpful to consult the one in *A Blake Dictionary*.[1] But we should remember that Blake, who was capable of diagramming for the reader's benefit (see *Milton* 33), did not do so here. Perhaps two-dimensional representation would be inadequate for what is four-dimensional. Golgonooza is neither a square nor a cube, but a tesseract, and Los moves through time as well as space as he 'views the City of Golgonooza, & its smaller Cities . . . all that has existed in the space of six thousand years' (*13*: 56, 59). Blake refers to this passage throughout *Jerusalem* and it is worth quoting in its entirety, so that we may afterwards do the same in this study.

> Fourfold the Sons of Los in their divisions: and fourfold, *12*
> The great City of Golgonooza: fourfold toward the north
> And toward the south fourfold, & fourfold toward the east & west
> Each within other toward the four points: that toward
> Eden, and that toward the World of Generation,
> And that toward Beulah, and that toward Ulro:
> Ulro is the space of the terrible starry wheels of Albions sons:
> But that toward Eden is walled up, till time of renovation:
> Yet it is perfect in its building, ornaments & perfection.

[1] p. 163.

And the Four Points are thus beheld in Great Eternity
West, the Circumference: South, the Zenith: North,
The Nadir: East, the Center, unapproachable for ever.
These are the four Faces towards the Four Worlds of Humanity
In every Man. Ezekiel saw them by Chebars flood.
And the Eyes are the South, and the Nostrils are the East.
And the Tongue is the West, and the Ear is the North.
And the North Gate of Golgonooza toward Generation;
Has four sculpturd Bulls terrible before the Gate of iron.
And iron, the Bulls: and that which looks toward Ulro,
Clay bak'd & enamel'd, eternal glowing as four furnaces:
Turning upon the Wheels of Albions sons with enormous power.
And that toward Beulah four, gold, silver, brass, & iron:

13

And that toward Eden, four, form'd of gold, silver, brass, & iron.

The South, a golden Gate, has four Lions terrible, living!
That toward Generation, four, of iron carv'd wondrous:
That toward Ulro, four, clay bak'd, laborious workmanship
That toward Eden, four; immortal gold, silver, brass & iron.

The Western Gate fourfold, is closd: having four Cherubim
Its guards, living, the work of elemental hands, laborious task!
Like Men, hermaphroditic, each winged with eight wings

That towards Generation, iron; that toward Beulah, stone;
That toward Ulro, clay: that toward Eden, metals.
But all clos'd up till the last day, when the graves shall yield their dead

The Eastern Gate, fourfold: terrible & deadly its ornaments:
Taking their forms from the Wheels of Albions sons; as cogs
Are formd in a wheel, to fit the cogs of the adverse wheel.

That toward Eden, eternal ice, frozen in seven folds
Of forms of death: and that toward Beulah, stone:
The seven diseases of the earth are carved terrible.
And that toward Ulro, forms of war: seven enormities:
And that toward Generation, seven generative forms.

And every part of the City is fourfold; & every inhabitant, fourfold.
And every pot & vessel & garment & utensil of the houses,
And every house, fourfold; but the third Gate in every one
Is closd as with a threefold curtain of ivory & fine linen & ermine.
And Luban stands in middle of the City. a moat of fire,
Surrounds Luban, Los's Palace & the golden Looms of Cathedron.

And sixty-four thousand Genii, guard the Eastern Gate;
And sixty-four thousand Gnomes, guard the Northern Gate:
And sixty-four thousand Nymphs, guard the Western Gate:
And sixty-four thousand Fairies, guard the Southern Gate:

Around Golgonooza lies the land of death eternal; a Land

Of pain and misery and despair and ever brooding
melancholy:
In all the Twenty-seven Heavens, numberd from Adam
to Luther;
From the blue Mundane Shell, reaching to the Vegetative Earth.

The continuing city that is laid out verbally here has its chief Old Testament model in the plans for the new temple and city presented in Ezekiel 40–7.[1] Elsewhere Blake shows a sense of identity with Ezekiel as prophetic visionary. In *Night Thoughts* water-colour 474 (British Museum), he depicts the wheels full of eyes of Ezekiel 1: 18 from the perspective of Ezekiel himself. *Ezekiel's Wheels* (water-colour, Boston Museum of Fine Arts)[2] again shows the eyed wheels, this time surrounding one of the cherubim (who is, however, shown with three visible human faces rather than the man, lion, ox, and eagle faces of Ezekiel 1: 10). The description of Golgonooza obviously departs from Ezekiel's detailed architectural schema, but one is aware throughout of Ezekiel's prototype for Blake's city of four gates, one of which is closed. Of course Blake freely alters or invents details. He substitutes Wheels for Eagles, closes the Western rather than the Eastern gate, gives his Cherubim eight wings rather than four. Some of these changes indicate that, in Damon's words, 'Golgonooza, however, is not perfect as yet'.[3] In Ezekiel the eastern gate is closed because the glory of God went in by that route; in *Jerusalem* it is the western gate because in Blake's psychic cartography the West leads to Eden, which cannot (yet) be re-entered. The Wheels at the Eastern gate are not the wheels within wheels shown in the two water-colours, but are seen 'Taking their forms from the Wheels of Albions sons; as cogs / Are formd in a wheel, to fit the cogs of the adverse wheel.' Golgonooza partakes of the nature of Generation in all its

[1] See Damon, *William Blake*, p. 440; Harold Bloom, *Blake's Apocalypse* (Garden City, NY, 1963), pp. 378–80; Stevenson, *Poems of William Blake*, notes to pp. 648–9.

[2] Reproduced Butlin, *William Blake* (1978), no. 170, p. 90. This picture is sometimes referred to under other titles, but only the title *Ezekiel's Wheels* has Blake's authority; see *BR*, p. 572.

[3] *William Blake*, p. 441.

ambiguity. At its centre is not the sanctuary and altar of the Temple, but Luban—the place of sexual fertilization. Yet there can be no doubt that in Golgonooza generation achieves an ultimately positive valorization, as the contiguity of the Looms of Cathedron, where human bodies are woven, to Los's Palace inside the moat of fire at the centre of Golgonooza suggests. Cathedron, taking its name from the common first name of Blake's mother, sister, and wife, is where Los and Enitharmon harmoniously co-operate in the long addition to Night VIIa of *The Four Zoas*, providing garments for the otherwise naked Spectres and also creating works of art. It is fitting that, by implication, such activities go on in the centre of Golgonooza: this is not the Platonic idea of a city but a city in process, taking its form from biblical descriptions of the Temple of Solomon in Chronicles and in Kings, from Ezekiel's vision, from the New Jerusalem of Revelation, and possibly from other, later sources—all as re-shaped by Blake's imagination.

In the New Testament it is of course Revelation 21 that provides a prototype for Golgonooza. 'I see the New Jerusalem descending out of Heaven', exclaims Los in *86*: 19, thus establishing his affinity with John of Patmos in Revelation 21: 2: 'And I, John, saw the holy city, new Jerusalem, coming down from God out of heaven, prepared as a bride adorned for her husband.' As with Ezekiel, so Blake also identifies in his visual art with John. In his water-colour *The Angel of the Revelation* (Metropolitan Museum of Art)[1] Blake creates a pendant to *Ezekiel's Wheels*. Once again the visionary is depicted as a relatively tiny figure and the object of his vision is a gigantic form in *contraposto* position in the centre of the design. In both instances, the small figure is a surrogate for Blake as artist and for us as viewers. In *Jerusalem* it is Los who is the viewer, singing:

> O lovely mild Jerusalem! O Shiloh of Mount Ephraim!
> I see thy Gates of precious stones: thy Walls of gold &
> silver (*85*: 22–3)

John's description of the New Jerusalem is behind this passage

[1] Reproduced Butlin, *William Blake* (1978), no. 185, p. 95. Like *Ezekiel's Wheels, The Angel of the Revelation* was painted for Thomas Butts *c.* 1805.

as it is in part behind the cityscape of Golgonooza in *12–13*. John's city is a 'rebirth', to use Austin Farrer's term,[1] of the imagery of Ezekiel 40–7, which is itself a transformation of the accounts of Solomon's Temple earlier in the Old Testament. These progressive re-envisagings give Blake an ample basis for his own version of the continuing city. He uses some of the materials of his predecessors and adheres to a basic plan which they established, but he also freely invents new features and adapts old ones.

One other ancient description of city and temple deserves mention here, both because of its importance in its own right and because Blake was probably familiar with it: *The Wars of the Jews* by Flavius Josephus. The works of Josephus went through numerous editions in the eighteenth century, and those of Dr George Henry Maynard (first published *c.*1786, with four subsequent editions in the 1790s to *c.*1800) include at least three plates engraved by Blake.[2] Although these were probably originally executed for the Revd Edward Kimpton's *A New and Complete Universal History of the Holy Bible* (?1781),[3] Blake is likely to have known an easily available work of such great interest. Maynard's edition is a great aid to the visualizing and locating of the locales of the Bible. It includes 'Various Copious INDEXES, particularly of the Countries, Cities, Towns, Villages, Seas, Rivers, Mountains, Lakes, &c.' of the Holy Land. There are 'An accurate map of the Holy Land with the adjacent countries' and 'An exact representation of Solomon's Temple.' The latter represents the Temple as a magnificent, three-storeyed Renaissance palace surmounted by four oriental-looking attics and a pagoda-like central tower, fronting an enormous piazza. A large, anonymously engraved fold-out map of Jerusalem shows the location of the twelve gates, the Fuller's Field, the Lower and Higher Fountains of Gihon, the King's Wine-Press, Golgotha ('Region of Death'), Solomon's Temple, and other details.

[1] *A Rebirth of Images* (Gloucester, Mass.: Peter Smith, 1970 [1949]).

[2] For bibliographic details, see Bentley, *Blake Books*, pp. 585–9. In addition, one more Blake engraving (after Stothard) was probably made either for Maynard's Josephus or for Kimpton's Bible. (Reproduced by G. E. Bentley, Jr. in 'A Handlist of Works by William Blake in the Department of Prints & Drawings of the British Museum', *Blake*, V (1972), 242.)

[3] See *Blake Books*, pp. 589–91.

Josephus' text also emphasizes the magnificence of the Temple to the eye:

The curiosity and beauty of the outside of the temple was charming to a degree, being faced every where with substantial golden plates, that sparkled like the beams of the sun, and dazzled the eye of the beholder. Where there was no gilding, the parts were so delicately white, that it appeared at a distance to travellers like a marble mountain, or pillar of snow.[1]

Josephus also appreciates the symbolic meaning of the Temple, both as conveyed by its parts and by the structure as a whole. Before the golden doors of the temple hung 'a piece of Babylonian tapestry . . . interwoven with blue, purple and scarlet, in a most curious manner'. Josephus continues:

Nor was this mixture of colours without a mystical interpretation, as it alluded to the four elements, either by the colours themselves, or the matter of which they were composed; the scarlet representing the fire, the silk the earth that produced it, the azure the air, and the purple the sea, from whence it comes. So that this veil or hanging was in miniature an emblem of the universe.[2]

Here is a basis for Blake's symbolic use of the Temple veil as representing materiality, a subject to be discussed in Chapter IV. Blake could also have found in Josephus' idea of the Temple's structure another emblem of the universe, where, as Eliade puts it, 'the three parts of the sanctuary correspond to the three cosmic regions (the court representing the sea—that is, the lower regions—the Holy Place the earth, and the Holy of Holies heaven)'.[3] Eliade remarks, 'The builders of the Temple not only constructed the world; they also constructed cosmic time'; and in like manner, Los constructs Golgonooza in both space and time.

After the destruction of the Temple and the expulsion of the Jews from the Holy Land, the Jerusalem of Ezekiel and the New Jerusalem of John become subjects of a long tradition of biblical exegesis from the period of the Church Fathers to Blake's own time. Here we can only sketch the history of

[1] *The Wars of the Jews with the Romans, Works*, n.d., p. 431.

[2] Ibid., p. 431.

[3] *The Myth of the Eternal Return*, p. 77, citing *Antiquities of the Jews*, III. 7. 7.

the idea of Jerusalem in so far as that idea can fruitfully be related to Blake's. Briefly, two types of view are distinguished by the great historian of medieval exegesis, Henri de Lubac.[1] One view, represented by Richard of St. Victor, takes Ezekiel as an inspired architect and the material of Ezekiel 40–7 as a realizable architectural plan. This literalist view, later revived by the Jesuits Pradus and Villalpandus (see below), may at first seem to have little in common with Blake's, but a mental reconstruction of the Temple in detail could well have stimulated his own imagination, labouring well the minute particulars. More obviously in line with the way in which Blake uses Ezekiel is the exegetical tradition, going back at least to Origen, represented by Saint Jerome and by St. Gregory (Gregory I). According to Jerome, the temple of Ezekiel is a mystical temple and its description is to be understood in a spiritual sense.[2] St. Gregory, writes de Lubac, regards Ezekiel's temple as not having substance outside the prophet's imagination but as 'le symbole d'une réalité d'un autre ordre, réalité qui est, pour le chrétien, "sanctae Ecclesiae aedificium, caelestis civitatis aedificium" '.[3] Such an approach to the interpretation of vision is also shared with respect to John's New Jerusalem by Richard of St. Victor: 'Tantae civitatis mirabilis structuram secundum spiritualem intelligentiam elucidandam ingressuri . . .'.[4] Blake carries the process of interpretation into a different realm. Like Dante in *Purgatorio* xxix–xxxiii, Blake incorporates elements of biblical vision with his own vision, integrating both.

The New Jerusalem was also a great theme of medieval and Renaissance literature, art, and architecture. Its walls and towers rose in manuscript illuminations (to which, however, Blake would not have had easy access) and in woodcut illustrations to the Bible, such as Nicolai de Lyra's *Biblia Latina* (Venice 1489), which shows the city's four walls, twelve gates, and central Temple. A literary source may have been known to Blake, even if indirectly: as mentioned in Chapter I, behind at least one of the 'Jerusalem' lyrics printed in the

[1] *Exégèse médiévale: les quatre sens de l'écriture* (Paris: Aubier), vol. I (parts i and ii), 1959; vol. II (parts i and ii), 1964.

[2] *Exégèse médiévale*, II. i. 399.

[3] Ibid., II. i. 396 (quoting Gregory *In Ez.*).

[4] Ibid., II. i. 400 (quoting Richard *In Ap.* 1. 7, prol. [CXCVI, 859A]).

sixteenth century is the *Liber Meditationum* once ascribed to St. Augustine but actually written by Jean de Fécamp (995?–1078) and later augmented. The first complete English translation, by Thomas Rogers in 1581, includes a poignant evocation of the city imagined by John:

Oh, happie that my soule be, yea happie and alwaies happie shal I be, could I once get to behold thy glorie, thine happines, thy beautie, thy gates, and thy walles, and thy streetes, and thy manifold mansions, thy noble citizens, and thy mightie king in his maiestie.

For thy walles are of pretious stones; thy gates of the richest pearles; and thy streetes of the purest golde, wherein is soong the ioieful Halleluiah without intermission; thy manifolde buildings are founded upon squared stones, builded upon Saphires, inclosed with golden walles, whereinto none shal enter but the cleane, and it no uncleane person shal inhabit.[1]

The work, re-translated under various titles, could have been known to Blake—an edition entitled *Pious Breathings*, translated by George Stanhope, Dean of Canterbury, was published in 1701.

In architecture the heavenly Jerusalem was recapitulated in the iconology of Romanesque churches, churches which were, moreover, thought of as prefigured by the Tabernacle and Temple.[2] As the builder of Golgonooza, Los may be thought of as analogous to the medieval builder whose church represented in spatially symbolic form the *Jerusalem Celestis* of the Apocalypse. Renaissance architects and theorists like Francesco Georgi[3] also adhered to the notion that the Temple was the symbolic prototype of Christian churches, and some carried this idea further to mean that the temple was in a more literal sense the divinely inspired historical basis of later buildings. Philibert de l'Orme, in *Le premier tôme de l'architecture* (Paris, 1567), advanced a theory of Divine Proportion which Blunt summarizes as follows:

The basic principle . . . was to deduce the true laws of proportion from the account given in the Old Testament of the various buildings the

[1] Reprinted in Stephen A. Hurlbut, *The Picture of the Heavenly Jerusalem*. Printed by the author at the St. Albans Press, Washington DC, 1943. VII. 27–9.

[2] See Frans Carlsson, *The Iconology of Tectonics in Romanesque Art* (Lund, 1976), pp. 15–20.

[3] See Rudolf Wittkower, *Architectural Principles in the Age of Humanism* (London: Alec Tiranti, 1952), pp. 90–4.

design of which was dictated by God to the Jews, that is to say the Ark of Noah, the Ark of the Covenant, the Temple and the House of Solomon, and the Temple as revealed to Ezekiel in his vision. These proportions were divinely dictated but they were also in accordance with those of the human body, which is itself the Temple of God.[1]

Such ideas form a bridge from the architectural theories of Renaissance humanism to the architectonics of Blake's *Jerusalem*. Blake is of course unlikely to have read the works of Philibert, but Blunt suggests that he may have known the commentary on Ezekiel by Pradus and Villalpandus, published with enormous engraved illustrations in 1596–1605.[2] These Jesuits also argued that the Temple described by Ezekiel was the architectural model for later buildings, a view which accords well with Blake's ideas about painting and sculpture.

The idea of the New Jerusalem appears, as we would expect, with great force in the writings of the visionaries of the seventeenth century. Its importance to the Familists can be seen even in the title of Hendrik Niclas's *A true Testification of the Spiritual Lande of Peace; which is the spirituall Lande of Promise, and the holy Citee of Peace or the heavenly Jerusalem; and of the Holy and spirituall People that dwell therein: as also of the Walking in the Spirit, which leadeth thereunto.*[3] The book itself has many resemblances to Bunyan: a traveller journeys from the Lande of Ignorance through a wilderness and then to 'the pleasant Waye of the knowledge of Good and Evell'; but this leads only to the country of Babylon, which the traveller must leave 'and not have regarde anymore to the knowledge-of-good-and-evil'.[4] (Cf. Los's 'I care not whether a Man is Good or Evil'—*91*: 54.) At the end of his quest, the traveller, like Blake's reader following

[1] *Philibert de l'Orme* (London: A. Zwemmer, 1958), p. 124.

[2] *The Art of William Blake*, p. 18. As Blunt observes, this work was much studied throughout the seventeenth and eighteenth centuries, partly because of the plates showing the authors' reconstruction of the Temple; the commentary, however, is in Latin, a language which Blake could not read proficiently. He could have known the substance of Villalpandus's ideas on this subject from English sources (see below).

[3] 'Translated out of Base-almayne'; no date, translator's name, or place of publication on title-page, but according to a pencil note in the Cambridge University Library copy, the book was published in Amsterdam. The British Library dates its copy 1575 [?].

[4] p. 40.

the golden string to a gate built in Jerusalem's wall, receives a key:

This key is named, *Equitee*: and with the same, the Travailer goeth thorow the Gate named *The-nature-of-god*: and so cometh into the holy Citee of Peace, named *Gods-understanding*, for to possesse in heir-like-maner, the everlasting Good 'the heavenly Jerusalem' wheare there is nothing but everlasting Lyfe and Joye: and wheare all Sorrow and Teares are don-away.[1]

Some Behmenists, following Jacob Boehme's distinction between a true and a false Jerusalem, discussed the imminent fall of Sardian Jerusalem and the rebuilding of Philadelphian Jerusalem.[2] During the English Revolution some millenarians saw Jerusalem as about to be built in England's green and pleasant land while others envisaged this rebuilding as taking place in the Holy Land. The Ranter Mary Cary, for example, wrote *A New and more Exact Mappe or Description of New Jerusalems Glory* in 1651 to show that in 1645 Christ began to establish his kingdom in England;[3] while Thomas Tany, also a Ranter, declaimed, 'Jerusalem shall be built in Glory, in her own land, even on her own Foundation, as the Lord hath shown mee, though it seeme never so impossible in the Judgement of Men.'[4] The Seeker William Erbery, as A. L. Morton notes, linked the new Jerusalem with a third age in the history of the spirit:

For the Nations of them that are saved, shall walk in the light of the New Jerusalem, and men shall dwell in it, and there shall be no more destruction, but Jerusalem shall be safely inhabited . . . this new Jerusalem being the third dispensation differing from the Law and Gospel-Churches, yet comprehending both, as the glory of the Gospel was above that of the Law, and darkened the light thereof, even as the rising Sun doth the Moon when it shines at the full.[5]

Such varying views of the *locus* of the New Jerusalem, whether limited to a small group or extended to the nation at large, do not obscure the fact that the figure was commonly used

[1] p. 42. [2] See Thune, *Behmenists and Philadelphians*, p. 110.
[3] Quoted by Christopher Hill in *The World Turned Upside Down* (Harmondsworth, Middlesex, 1975 [1972]), p. 322.
[4] *I Proclaim the Return of Jesus* (broadsheet, London, 1650).
[5] *The Everlasting Gospel*, p. 56, from Erbery's *A Call to the Churches* (1653), pp. 35–7.

in the 'third culture' as representing the ultimate realization of human community—not only used, but lovingly elaborated.

In the 'second culture', there was during this period of the English Revolution considerable discussion of the idea of the New Jerusalem. This interest was not limited to millenarians: it is found, for example, in David Pareus (whose writings on Revelation antedate the period but were translated from Latin in 1644). In discussing Revelation Chapter 21, Pareus says:

> Here is exhibited unto John the renovation of the world that shall bee, as also the Heavenly glory of the godly, under a *two-fold Type*, viz. of a *Bride* gloriously attired, and of a most magnificent *City*: The illustration of which Type, this whole Chapter so sets forth, as that the wit, art, hand or tongue of man is able to expresse nothing more beautifull, more magnificent, more glorious, and sumptuous than this structure. For whatsoever may seem to conduce to the glory and comlinesse of an Earthly City in respect of wals, gates, foundation, figure, streets, Temples, Air, and lastly wealth of all the Citizens, ornament and pleasantness of life, all this *John* here sees to be most eminent and glorious in this *Heavenly Jerusalem.*[1]

David Pareus was a resolute anti-millenarian, but here it is not his view of the millennium that concerns us but his interest in the New Jerusalem as a structure and his praise of it as such, something which he shares with the millenarian Joseph Mede —and with William Blake.

> And in the North Gate, in the West of the North. toward Beulah
> Cathedrons Looms are builded. and Los's Furnaces in the South[.]
> A wondrous golden Building immense with ornaments sublime
> Is bright Cathedrons golden Hall, its Courts Towers & Pinnacles (*59*: 22–5)

Joseph Mede, for his part, comments on 'the Analogy of new Jerusalem' in its use of the number twelve, deriving from the twelve Apostles, 'in the frame whereof, and the dimensions of the Gates, Foundations, Court, compass of the walls,

[1] *A Commentary Upon the Divine Revelation of the Apostle and Evangelist John* (Trans. Elias Arnold, Amsterdam, 1644), pp. 546–7.

longitude, latitude, altitude, the same number of twelve, or multiplication of twelve, is used'.[1] Mede also publishes a plan of the Temple's two courts: a large outer one which all the people could enter, and an inner court which included the Tabernacle and the altar, and which only the high priests and the Levites could enter. Blake, in *Milton*, conceives 'Jerusalems Inner Court' to be Lambeth, no doubt because it was the residence of the Bishop of London;[2] in *Jerusalem* when Jesus rends the Veil of the Temple, he 'the whole Druid Law removes away / From the Inner Sanctuary: a False Holiness hid within the Center' (*69*: 39–40). Such imagined structures have a mental fascination which has been well characterized by Gaston Bachelard, who in *The Poetics of Space* speaks of 'literary prints'—poems which, in creating houses, produce the effect of engravings.[3] Bachelard's 'oneiric house' is a personal dwelling, while the structures of the imagined Jerusalem are grand and public, but all share the characteristic of inviting the reader to invest their spatial forms with his own imaginative power.

It may seem at first incongruous to associate Blake's use of architectural conceptions in *Jerusalem* with those of David Pareus, Joseph Mede, and others whose mode of discourse is not primarily poetic, but behind these verbal (and pictorial) creations of Jerusalem, New and old, there is one similar motive. In describing the structure of the Temple, all these writers relate themselves—and us—to a model of reality, and this is of course also true of the accounts in Ezekiel and Revelation. The Old Testament and Jewish Apocrypha are themselves involved in creating a tradition in which such a model is re-created, in their describing the Tabernacle, the Camp, and the two Temples as recapitulations of a preceding

[1] *The Key of the Revelation*, p. 74.

[2] It was of course Blake's too, for almost the entire decade of the 1790s, and as such is mentioned with special importance in *Jerusalem*. Lambeth is, then, at the same time associated with the State Religion that Blake sees as dead and with his own poetic inspiration. Erdman has discussed the *M* passage in detail in *Blake: Prophet*, pointing out that the reason 'Jerusalems Inner Court, Lambeth' is seen as 'ruin'd and given / To the detestable Gods of Priam, to Apollo . . .' lies in the existence of the Apollo Gardens and two other pleasure gardens, a 'mouldering paradise', in Lambeth (pp. 288–9).

[3] Translated from the French by Marie Jolas (New York, 1964 [Paris, 1968]), p. 50.

structure. The original structure precedes its embodiments. 'Not only does a model precede terrestrial architecture', writes Eliade, but the model is also situated in an ideal (celestial) region of eternity. 'This is what Solomon announces: "Thou gavest command to build a sanctuary in thy holy mountain, And an altar in the city of thy habitation, A copy of the holy tabernacle which thou preparest aforehand from the beginning." '[1] The writer who describes City and Temple as Blake does in the long quoted passage on *12–13* in effect builds both again, newly elaborating the original model.

In the seventeenth century the most ambitious of such constructions was John Lightfoot's extraordinary book *The Temple: Especially As it stood in the dayes of our Saviour.*[2] Recommended by Mede to his readers, Lightfoot's work is a scholarly study, largely relying on Jewish sources, in which the Temple is literally described room by room. It devotes considerable attention to certain details which are also of special interest to Blake, notably the Veil, the Temple Ornaments, and especially 'these living *Creatures* or *Cherubims* [that] are never mentioned but in vision or Hieroglyphick'.[3] And while Lightfoot's elaborate descriptions are founded on documentary sources, he recognizes the divine analogy of the whole, characterizing the Temple as 'of a heavenly resemblance, use and concernment, as figuring Christ's body'.[4] Lightfoot leaves it to the reader to imagine 'What Streets, Houses, Turrets, Gardens and beauteous buildings were to be seen in *Jerusalem* as it lay before you' and proceeds to sketch the environs of the Temple as traced by the brook Siloam in its progress eastwards from the Fuller's Field to Solomon's Pool and westward 'along the broad wall, the Tower of the Furnaces, the valley gate, and dung gate, and . . . into the *Poole of Siloam*'.[5] Thus the entire setting is conceptualized. Blake similarly wants to place the Temple in relation to its surroundings. 'The Temple', he writes in *A Vision of the Last Judgment*, 'stands on the Mount of God from it flows on each side the River of Life on whose banks Grows the tree of

[1] *The Myth of the Eternal Return*, p. 8; quoting Wisdom of Solomon 9: 8, from R. H. Charles, *The Apocrypha and Pseudepigrapha of the Old Testament in English* (Oxford, 1913), I. 459.

[2] London, 1650. [3] p. 253. [4] p. 169. [5] pp. 14–15.

Life among whose branches temples & Pinnacles tents & pavilions Gardens & Groves display Paradise with its Inhabitants walking up & down in Conversations concerning Mental Delights' (E. 552).

Something of Lightfoot's empirical brilliance can be seen in the way he relates Jerusalem's architecture to London's, as in his explanation of the waters described as issuing eastwards from the threshold of the building in Ezekiel 47: 1–8: 'The waters then from that fountaine *Etam* being gathered into this well or great cisterne, were from hence dispersed into the severall offices and places where the water was necessary (as the new river from the water house into *London*) a wheele being used to raise it and force it up into the pipes or conveyances that were to carry it into the several receptacles and uses.'[1] In characterizing the architectural style of the First Temple, Lightfoot once more relates the biblical to his own England, saying that '*Solomon's* Temple did very truely resemble one of our Churches, but onely that it differed in this, that the Steeple of it (which was the porch) stood at the East end.'[2] It seems, moreover, from Lightfoot's account, that the Temple as restored by Herod resembled a church of a particular style of architecture—the Perpendicular Gothic.

> The roof was not a perfect flat, as was the roof of other houses, but rising in the middle . . . *till the very crest of the middle came up as high as the height of the battlement*; as *Kings Colledge Chappell* may herein be a parallel also; And the like battlements and pinnacles are likewise to be allotted to the lower leads.[3]

Blake too thought of the Temple in Christ's time as a building very like King's College Chapel, as we can see in the background of the tempera *The Body of Christ Borne to the Tomb* (Tate Gallery)[4] with its high steeples, as well as in the *Paradise Regained* water-colour *Christ Placed on the Pinnacle of the Temple* (Fitzwilliam Museum).[5] These are visual equivalents

[1] p. 142. [2] p. 39.

[3] p. 51. The ellipsis in the quoted sentence is in Lightfoot's text a Hebrew quotation from his Midrashic source.

[4] Reproduced in Butlin, *William Blake: a Complete Catalogue of the Works in the Tate Gallery*, p. 44, no. 28. (As Butlin notes, the title is Rossetti's; the painting is often referred to as *The Procession from Calvary*.)

[5] Reproduced in Bindman, *An Illustrated Catalogue of the Works in the Fitzwilliam Museum*, pl. 32; Cat. 34 J.

of the golden halls of bright Cathedron, surmounted by 'Towers & Pinnacles' (*59*: 25). Imagining the Temple as Gothic would for Blake have been an extension of his conception of painting and sculpture as Hebraic in origin. The idea of the Temple as a prototype of later architecture, advanced by Villalpandus, disseminated by Fischer von Erlach, and argued in detail by John Wood of Bath (as will shortly be discussed) was evidently shared by, among others, Lightfoot and Blake.

Blake writes that the western gate of Golgonooza 'is perfect in its building, ornaments & perfection' (*12*: 53), evidently thinking of the Temple ornaments devised by Hiram in I Kings 7; Cathedron is 'A wondrous golden Building immense with ornaments sublime' (*59*: 24). Lightfoot also attaches great importance to the Temple's ornaments and ceremonial objects. The seven-branched candlestick, glowingly depicted by Blake in the tempera *Zacharias and the Angel* (New York, Metropolitan Museum of Art),[1] is characterized as 'These seven lamps (which denoted *the seven Spirits of God*, Rev. 4.5 & 5.6 which the *Jewes* call the *Seven Spirits of Messias*, from *Esay* 11. 1,2,3).'[2] 'God', writes Lightfoot, 'by these candles did as it were enlighten the people to teach them spirituall things by these corporall.'[3] He vividly describes the imagery decorating the pillars and walls of Solomon's Temple, emphasizing that the decorations were engraved. Following his source in Kings, Lightfoot characterizes the engravings on the pillars Jachin and Boaz as being 'As vines or thickets . . . that are caught and infolded one within another', 'like the branches of Palme trees', and 'With thickets of branch-work and wreaths of chaine-work'; below the capital was 'a large border or circle of lilly-work'.[4] Over the doors of Herod's Temple was 'a great golden vine' with 'bunches of grapes as big as the proportion of a man'. The veils were 'Babylonian tapestry work, of blue purple scarlet and fine twined linnen'.[5] The Laver, which Lightfoot suggests was the source of Ezekiel's visionary wheels, had a square base with a wheel on every side and was decorated with engraved 'Cherubins, Oxen,

[1] Reproduced in Bindman, *Blake As an Artist*, pl. II.
[2] p. 83. [3] p. 84. [4] pp. 62, 69.
[5] pp. 73, 78. Lightfoot gives Josephus as his source for the Veil.

and Palme trees'.[1] The Molten Sea, hemispherical in shape and resting on twelve brazen oxen, was bordered with the engraved heads of oxen in ovals. Most of these motifs are employed by Blake both in his pictorial and his written works. The *42* border design culminates in a giant bunch of grapes slightly larger than the topmost human figure climbing up to it; a chain descends the right border of *65*. Palm trees abound in Blake's designs—see the top design (left) in *33*—but perhaps the most notable use of the palm as a motif occurs in *Job* 19, where vertical and horizontal palm leaves dominate all four margins of the engravings.[2] In the *Paradise Lost* water-colour, *The Archangel Raphael with Adam and Eve* (Boston Museum of Fine Arts),[3] a tracery of lilies follows the lines of a Gothic arch formed by two palms, while the chairs on which Adam and the archangel sit are formed of intertwined stems and leaves of various kinds. An ox's head in an oval is one of the four representations of Evangelist-Zoas in the illustration to Dante entitled *Beatrice Addressing Dante from the Car* (Tate Gallery). As for the Veil, it is one of the major symbolic images in *Jerusalem* and must be discussed in connection with the myth of Albion and Vala in Chapter IV. In *59*: 55, Blake refers to the common source of Lightfoot and Josephus, Exodus 35: 25–6, when he describes the daughters of Los 'weaving in bitter tears / The Veil of Goats-hair & Purple & Scarlet & fine twined Linen'. In both poetry and art Blake tries to go back to authentic Hebrew images as he imagined them to be, just as Lightfoot tried to re-create them from the historical and interpretive texts at his disposal.

Perhaps the most striking parallelism between *The Temple* and *Jerusalem* concerns the description and positioning of the Cherubim. As we can see from the description of Golgonooza on *12–13*, among many such examples in Blake's works, the Cherubim of Ezekiel's vision, usually fused with the Living Creatures of John's, are of the most compelling importance to Blake. The tradition of representing Ezekiel's Cherubim in a manner felt to be historically correct goes

[1] Reproduced in Lindberg, *William Blake's Illustrations to the Book of Job*, pls. 64 and 65.

[2] Reproduced in Butlin, *William Blake* (1978), pl. 221.

[3] Reproduced in Paley, *William Blake*, pl. 112.

back at least to the engraved illustrations for the commentary of Villalpandus, where the Cherubim are shown as gentle-looking furred creatures with wings. Blake's contemporary Philip Jacques de Loutherbourg, in a painting for the Macklin Bible Gallery,[1] showed Ezekiel's vision of a six-winged cherub with a human torso and three faces—eagle, human, and lion—the fourth (ox) face presumably looking away from the viewer. Blake in his *Descriptive Catalogue* speaks of his visions of 'those wonderful originals called in the Sacred Scriptures the Cherubim',[2] and as we have seen, Blake rendered his own version of one of the 'living creatures' in *Ezekiel's Wheels*. It is interesting that almost all Blake's written references to the Cherubim can be dated 1800 or later,[3] one of the numerous indications of Blake's intense interest in Hebrew art after that date. Lightfoot devotes an extensive chapter, entitled 'The Emblem of the Divine Glory at the Temple', to the subject of the Cherubim and their wheels, saying of them: 'They therefore being thus constantly held out in a doctrinall and significative tenour, as visions and *Hieroglyphicks* are, they are to be expounded to such a doctrinall and figurative sense, and so is the whole body of glory, as I may so call it, the whole visionary theatre or spectacle that is before us to be taken.'[4] The memorable phrase 'visionary theatre or spectacle' could well be applied to *Jerusalem*, and we shall consider this further, along with Mede's idea of an 'Apocalyptick Theater'[5] in Chapter VI. The details of Lightfoot's exposition also present some highly interesting parallels to Blake's rendering of the Cherubim and of the imagery associated with them.

According to Mede, the four faces of the Cherubim correspond to the four standards at the cardinal points of the Tabernacle: lion, bullock, man, and eagle. These 'were engraven upon the walls of the temple', with 'two of their faces being drunk up (as it needs must be in such engraving) on the plain of the wall',[6] leaving the human and lion faces represented. Blake displays a similar assumption in delineating his

[1] Engraved by J. Fitler for the Macklin Bible in 1796. [2] E. 522.

[3] The word in all numbers and cases occurs 49 times in the *Concordance*, of which all save three are datable 1800 or after. *Milton* and *Jerusalem* account for 34 of the occurrences.

[4] *The Temple*, p. 253.

[5] *The Key of the Revelation*, p. 30. [6] Ibid., p. 32.

continuing city according to the cardinal points, and in so creating a grid on which to place his imagined gates and living creatures. For the details of the interior of the Temple, however, Mede refers his reader to Lightfoot, his own concern here being a brilliant argument to the effect that the imagery of Revelation consists of a visionary transformation of the real temple objects which Mede presumes John to have seen. Lightfoot represents the Cherubim as having human bodies with four heads, each with a human, an eagle, a lion, and a bullock face. They had six wings, the uppermost for flying, the middle ones for covering their faces, the lowest ones for covering their secret parts. 'These living Creatures are called Cherubins by the Prophet very often', says Lightfoot, '. . . as the *Cherubins* upon the Mercy seat and the *Cherubins* wrought in the Tabernacle Curtaines, and carved upon the Temple wals, &c. namely, of this four-fold feature or having so many faces; saving that in the imbroidery of the Curtaines and sculpture upon the wals, only two of the four faces could be made to appear.'[1] Blake too imagines the Cherubim as variously 'sculptured and painted on walls',[2] woven into 'a Veil of Cherubim' (*64*: 3), and 'bowd over the Ark'.[3]

Perhaps most striking of all is the attention given by both Blake and Lightfoot to what Keats would have called the 'stationing' of the figures. As we see in the description of Golgonooza on *12–13*, Blake presents the Living Creatures of Ezekiel's vision in a complex arrangement in relation to the cardinal points. Lightfoot relates the Cherubim of Exodus, Ezekiel, and Revelation as follows:

There is intimation enough in *Ezekiel*, that the four living Creatures stood square, with a fire in the middest of them, and the wheeles in

[1] *The Temple*, p. 244.

[2] *Descriptive Catalogue*, E. 522.

[3] *A Vision of the Last Judgment*, E. 552; cf. 'The Cherubim bowing over it' [the Tabernacle] in Blake's letter to Ozias Humphrey describing his Last Judgment water-colour (*Letters*, first draft dated 18 January 1808, p. 130; second draft dated February 1808, p. 132). The water-colour (National Trust, Petworth House; rep. Paley, *William Blake*, pl. 50) depicts two angels with their wings forming an ogee arch very like that of *The Angels hovering over the Body of Jesus in the Sepulchre* (Victoria and Albert Museum; rep. Paley, *William Blake*, pl. 84) and very unlike the cherub of *Ezekiel's Vision*. We do not, of course, know what the bowed Cherubim of the lost *Last Judgment* looked like, but in the design on *22* the Cherubim (cf. 'Wings of Cherubim' in the text, *22*: 35) are depicted much as in the Petworth drawing. Evidently Blake had two conceptions of Cherubim, one associated with the visionary Living Creatures of Ezekiel, the other not.

a square on the outside of the square of the living Creatures: but in the *Revelation* it is yet more plain, for there it is said the foure living Creatures stood round about the Throne, which could not be but in a quadrature, one before, another behinde, and one of either side; for how else could four stand round about it? The Throne then meaning the Temple as was shewed before, this double quadrature about it, doth call us to remember the double camp that pitched about the Tabernacle upon the four sides of it, East, West, North, and South: when the Lord did first platforme and order the incamping of *Israel* in the Wildernesse.[1]

Blake too conceives of the Camp of the Israelites in relation to visionary art:

> For the Sanctuary of Eden. is in the Camp: in the Outline,
> In the Circumference: & every Minute Particular is Holy:
> (*69*: 41–2)

The two typical shapes governing these conceptions are the square—the Camp, the fourfold City with its gates—and the circle—the visionary wheels. In *12–13*, as already discussed in connection with Ezekiel, Blake combines both. Lightfoot imagines a composite view of four-faced cherubim with their wheels in a quadrilateral space. 'Their quadrangular standing was . . . lozenge-wise, or after the Diamond square; one looking toward the South with his humane face, and another with his humane face towards the North, a third with the same face toward the East, and the fourth with the same towards the West.'[2] As for the wheels they stood 'on the four sides or faces of the square body as it stood; namely, a wheele before every one of the living creatures on the out-side of the square . . . and so you have the four severall faces on the outside of the square, and the four severall faces on the inside of it, and the four wheeles standing before on the outside staves'.[3] Blake's view over Golgonooza posits a quadrilateral grid, with the Wheels stationed at the Eastern gate in place of Ezekiel's eagles. The 'wheel in the middle of a wheel' of Ezek. 1: 16 is described by Lightfoot as 'one wheele put crosse within another, so that they [the Cherubim] could runne upon either of these crossing rings as there was occasion: were they to go Eastward, they ran upon the one ring, but were they

[1] *The Temple*, p. 254. [2] Ibid., pp. 247–8. [3] Ibid., p. 248.

suddainly to turn South, then they ran upon the crosse ring.'[1] The wheels of the Eastern gate of Golgonooza are a representation of the mechanical gear-wheels of Albion—'as cogs / Are formd in a wheel, to fit the cogs of the adverse wheel' (*13*: 13–14), while in contrast the wheels of Eden 'Wheel within Wheel in freedom revolve in harmony & peace' (*15*: 20).

Perhaps no other scholarly reconstruction of the Temple combined particular detail with intense imagining as did Lightfoot's. There were, nevertheless, other literary restorations of the Temple which could have been of considerable interest to Blake. One of these comprises the fifth chapter of Isaac Newton's *The Chronology of Ancient Kingdoms Amended,*[2] a copy of which was owned by William Hayley.[3] Unlike Lightfoot, Newton confines himself to Old Testament sources. By ingeniously conflating these, he is able to present a detailed description of the Temple supplemented by three floor plans showing its walls, gates, courts, and other architectural features. Like Lightfoot, Newton emphasizes the Temple's quadrilateral structure. In Plate I, *A Description of the Temple of Solomon*, a square altar is shown at the centre of a square court which in turn is surrounded by a square pavement. Outside the pavement is the Court of the People, also square, surrounded by another square pavement. A square wall encloses the whole. Before we dismiss the possible relevance of these plans to Blake's conceptions on the ground of Blake's well-known dislike of geometry and of Newton, we should recall *72*: 5–8:

> For Albion in Eternity has Sixteen Gates among his Pillars
> But the Four towards the West were Walled up & the
> Twelve

[1] *The Temple*, p. 248.

[2] London, 1728. A new edition was included in the set of Newton's works (*Opera Quae Exstant Omnia*) edited by Samuel Horsley (London, vol. V, 1785). Part 2 of this volume contains Newton's *Observations upon the Apocalypse of St. John*, in which Newton quotes Justin Martyr to the effect that 'there shall be a resurrection of the flesh, and a thousand years life at Jerusalem built, adorned, and enlarged'. Newton adds: 'Which is as much as to say that all true Christians in that early age received this prophecy: for in all ages, as many as believed the thousand years, received the Apocalypse as the foundation of their opinion: and I do not know one instance to the contrary' (p. 446).

[3] See *Sale Catalogues of the Libraries of Eminent Persons*, ed. A. N. L. Munby (London: Mansell, 1971), vol. II, p. 156, no. 2184.

That front the Four other Points were turned Four
Square
By Los for Jerusalems sake & called the Gates of Jerusalem

The enormous positive importance of the quaternary in *Jerusalem* has rightly been stressed by George Mills Harper;[1] in the ground-plans[2] published with Newton's *Chronology* Blake could have found visual corroboration of the fourfold nature of the Great City of Golgonooza.

The ideas of Villalpandus reappeared in the eighteenth century in published works by two great architects: Johann Bernhard Fischer von Erlach and John Wood of Bath. Fischer von Erlach designed the Karlskirche, Vienna, according to the then prevailing image of the Temple of Solomon, which, Hans Aurenhammer points out,[3] was represented in Mannerist prints as a building with a massive dome and a porch flanked by two great columns.[4] Fischer von Erlach's *Entwurff einer Historischen Architecture*, a book from which Blake seems to have borrowed at least two visual conceptions,[5] begins with a description of the Temple of Solomon based on Pradus and Villalpandus as well as on other authorities, including Lightfoot. Plate I is 'A Ground-Plan of the Temple of Solomon, With all it's Courts, according to Villalpandi, who has given the best *Designs* of this *Building* out of the *Holy Scripture*'. Plate II is 'A View of the Temple, As it appears from the Side of Mount Morea, taken out of the Prophet *Ezekiel*, and after him from Villalpandi'. This book was published in an English

[1] 'The Divine Tetrad in Blake's *Jerusalem*', *William Blake: Essays for S. Foster Damon*, pp. 235–55.

[2] The unsigned plates of 1728 were re-engraved in James Basire's studio for the edition of 1785.

[3] *J. B. Fischer von Erlach* (London: Allen Lane, 1973), p. 135.

[4] Aurenhammer reproduces (fig. 86) an engraving by Philipp Galle after Martin van Heemskerck showing the Temple as such a building (p. 134, no date or title given).

[5] There is a striking resemblance between the Colossus of Rhodes as pictured in Fischer von Erlach's Book I, plate VIII and the central figure of *The Angel of the Revelation* (Metropolitan Museum of Art, New York: repr. Butlin, *William Blake*, 1978, fig. 185). Blake's water-colour *The Sunshine Holiday*, illustrating lines from Milton's *L'Allegro* (Pierpont Morgan Library, New York; repr. *Blake*, IV (1971), 124), appears to derive from Book I, plate XVIII, showing Mount Athos cut into a gigantic statue of a man, with a town in his lap.

translation by Thomas Lediard in 1730,[1] and so its text as well as its designs was easily available to Blake. The author argues: 'It would be a Subject of a vast Extent, but might be prov'd, that the *Roman Architecture*, and the *Corinthian Order* owe their Perfection to the excellent *Structure* of this *Temple*. The *Phoenicians* having first discover'd the Beauty of it to the *Greeks*, & these to the *Romans*.'[2] This theory of the originality of Hebrew architecture and the derivative nature of classical and later architecture found its fullest exposition in a book by one of the foremost architects of the eighteenth century, John Wood of Bath: *The Origin of Building: or, the Plagiarism of the Heathens Detected.*[3]

Wood's view, substantiated by references to the Bible and to Josephus, was that the Tabernacle was the first of four sacred structures in which the same relationships of dimensions were observed, the others being the three successive temples. The Tabernacle's floor plan is the subject of plates 2 and 3; plates 12 and 13 show the disposition of the tribes of Israel around the tabernacle in the camp; and the following plates show the dispositions of individual tribes. Three pages of text are devoted to a list and enumeration of the twelve tribes, making Blake's long enumeration of the tribes in *16* and *32* appear in perspective less singular. (Of course Wood places the tribes entirely according to Numbers 12: 3, in four camps consisting of three tribes each, one for each direction; while in Blake's analogical transformation the equivalent is England, Scotland, Wales, and Ireland, with 'Gates looking every way / To the Four Points' [*16*: 32–3] from Wales.) The Temple, Wood argues, was an architectural elaboration of the Tabernacle. Plates 24 and 25 show the Temple plan as rectangular—a double square rather than a single square as in Newton's *Chronology*. The city of Jerusalem is represented in plates 29–30 with its wall, twelve gates, and streets dividing the city into twelve great squares with a grand Piazza at the centre.

[1] First published in English in 1730; the edition consulted in the British Library is dated (London) 1737 and entitled *A Plan of Civil and Historical Architecture*. On the continuity of ideas from Pradus and Villalpandus to Fischer von Erlach to John Wood of Bath, see R. Wittkower, 'Federico Zuccari and John Wood of Bath', *Journal of the Warburg and Courtauld Institutes*, VI (1943), 221.

[2] *A Plan of Civil and Historical Architecture*, p. 1.

[3] Bath, 1741.

The Temple interior, as Wood describes it, is in some respects like Los's halls, with their 'bright Sculptures' representing 'every pathetic story possible to happen from Hate or / Wayward Love & every sorrow & distress' (*16*: 63–4). According to Wood, the structure of the Tabernacle was 'intended as an Hieroglyphical Representation of the past *History of the World*',[1] and this representation was carried further in the Temple with consummate art:

In this *Temple*, GOD Himself was the Historiographer of the most beautiful and explicit Kind of History the World ever produced; all the Ornaments of the *Tabernacle* were there collected together and improved to the utmost Degree, beyond Imagination itself. . . . The Cherubims above [the inside entablature], and the Pillars below, represented the Inhabitants of Heaven, and those of the Earth; the first in their real Shapes, and the last Hieroglyphically.[2]

Thus both Los's Halls in Golgonooza and Solomon's Temple in Jerusalem as described in Wood are palaces of art in which universal history is represented. 'In this Temple', writes Wood, 'a Man might have seen all that Art was capable of producing, adorned with the choicest and richest Productions of Nature', and by it, '*Architecture* was brought to the greatest perfection it ever arriv'd to'.[3]

According to Wood, the plan of the Tabernacle was copied by the pagans and also by the Druids, 'And if we were to scrutinize all the Works of the Druids, we shou'd find them to have been copied from the work of the *Jews*.'[4] Stonehenge is specifically mentioned. Like Blake, Wood thinks the original meaning of the symbolism of the Jews to have been lost by the pagans: 'Those People, by neglecting the *Real Part of the Law* . . . also forgot the *Symbolical*, nor could they tell us to what divine Matters the various Parts of their Sacred Edifices referr'd!'[5] This idea of an ancient vocabulary of representation is very similar to Blake's. In *The Laocoön*

[1] *The Origin of Building*, p. 90.

[2] Ibid., pp. 123–4. It is not clear to me why the inhabitants of *earth* are not represented in their real shapes and those of heaven hieroglyphically.

[3] Ibid., pp. 134, 136.

[4] pp. 220–1. Wood mentions Toland's history of the Druids as a source of information.

[5] *The Origin of Building*, p. 235.

Blake presents the statue as 'copied from the Cherubim of Solomons Temple by three Rhodians & applied to Natural Fact or. History of Ilium'. The Druids likewise did not comprehend the symbolic truths of which they were possessed: 'the Druidical age . . . began to turn allegoric and mental signification into corporeal command, whereby human sacrifice would have depopulated the earth.'[1] The 'wonderful originals' of Hebrew art—and, by extension, architecture—are seen by Blake as expressive of a lost language, the meaning of which can be recovered by returning (in vision) to the original sources. Similarly, for Wood, 'From the *Tabernacle* and *Temple* . . . the *Dorick, Ionick* and *Corinthian Orders* of Columns were taken'; while in British buildings, the proportions and figures of the sacred buildings of the Jews could be found 'disguised under *Gothick Dress*'.[2] In the oldest church in Britain, according to Wood the Cathedral of Llandaff, these Hebrew origins could be seen most distinctly in the east part, which 'was built to imitate *Solomon's Temple*'.[3] Thus both Blake and Wood believe that the lost language of the arts of the ancient Jews can be recovered and employed in England.

In Blake's lifetime, the interest in re-creating Jerusalem continued to stimulate the imagination of prophets, visionaries, and artists. In the writings of Emanuel Swedenborg, the meaning of the New Jerusalem was largely confined to the idea of a new Church; though elaborated in great detail in *The Heavenly Doctrine of the New Jerusalem, The Apocalypse Revealed*, and other books by Swedenborg, the New Jerusalem remains an allegorical concept rather than a city imagined to be real. As frequently in Swedenborg's works, in the Memorable Relations of the *Apocalypse Revealed* a more concrete and poetic element can be found. In no. 926 Swedenborg has a vision of a woman in a scarlet robe which turns out to be an effect of phantasy caused by infernal spirits; angels then give him a vision of the tabernacle 'as a Temple like that at Jerusalem'. Swedenborg's vision then begins to sound much like a passage from *Blake's Descriptive Catalogue*, as he writes: 'I saw the foundation stone, under which the

[1] *The Laocoön*, E. 270; *A Descriptive Catalogue*, E. 533.
[2] *The Origin of Building*, p. 222. [3] Ibid., p. 221.

word had been deposited, set with precious stones, from which something like Lightning shone upon the Walls, upon which there were forms of Cherubims, and variegated with beautiful Colours.'[1] Blake, who almost certainly had read at least parts of *The Apocalypse Revealed,*[2] is more likely to have been impressed by a vision such as this than by Swedenborg's rather mechanical expositions of the doctrinal meaning of the new Jerusalem as a city. '*Ezekiel* and St. *John* in the Revelations', writes Hartley, 'are particular in the description of the new *Jerusalem* . . . and the latter specifies the glories of the place, its foundations, walls, and gates, as made of the richest materials in nature, as precious stones and transparent gold.' To the view that these are figures, Hartley replies, 'Be it answered, that figures imply realities, otherwise they would be but figures of figures.'[3] So Hartley can assert 'There shall be a resurrection of the flesh to a life of a thousand years in *Jerusalem*, which shall be new built, richly adorned, and enlarged, as the prophets *Ezekiel, Isaiah*, and others have foretold.'[4]

The idea of the New Jerusalem was also powerful among Masons. The Masonic temple of the Prophets of Avignon was reportedly built in the proportions of the Temple of Solomon, and Count Grabianka expected the fulfilment of a prophecy according to which he would become king of Poland and then transfer his capital to Jerusalem.[5] When Cagliostro returned to London in 1786, he advertised for 'All true Masons in the name of Jehovah to form a plan for the reconstruction of the New Temple of Jerusalem.'[6] With such literal ideas Blake can have had little sympathy, but their currency reveals to what extent his work was created amid a contemporary ferment of ideas about what Jerusalem was or ought to be. Also of interest in this respect are the views of Francis Dobbs, whose prophecy of the millennium has already been mentioned. Dobbs had frequented the Duché circle, where he

[1] *The Apocalypse Revealed* (Manchester: C. Wheeler, 1791), vol. II, p. 568.

[2] The fact that in *The Marriage of Heaven and Hell* Blake parodied the technique of the Memorable Relations suggests familiarity with at least some of these.

[3] *Paradise Restored*, p. 103.

[4] Ibid., p. 169.

[5] See Danilewicz, 'The King of the New Israel', pp. 50, 65.

[6] Quoted by Garrett in *Respectable Folly*, p. 155.

met Count Grabianka in 1786.[1] In *A Concise View from History and Prophecy*, published some fourteen years later, Dobbs declares: 'The city of Jerusalem, which will be built after the House of Israel are gathered together, will surpass all that has ever appeared in the world.'[2] Perhaps following the doctrine of Swedenborg's *Conjugial Love*, Dobbs also asserts that the inhabitants of the New Jerusalem are to have 'their female partners of eternity', because 'male and female constitutes man'.[3] In his rather pedestrian 'poem on the Millennium' Dobbs envisages the New Jerusalem as a masterpiece of urban architecture.

> And lo! her palaces and temples rise,
> In true magnificence. In polish'd marble,
> Exquisitely wrought, the diff'rent orders
> Are with the justest taste dispos'd—Her lofty spires
> The Streets adorn—and strictest symmetry
> In all her buildings is display'd. What'er
> Babylon, of old renown'd, or later Rome—
> Or Paris, or London, now can boast—is here
> So far excell'd, as not to be compar'd.[4]

Like Blake, Dobbs takes the architecture of the existing city in order to imagine a model for the continuing city, though Dobbs's poetic style is hardly adequate for his subject.

Richard Brothers's millenarian prophecies also emphasized the urban character of Jerusalem. From his confinement in Dr Simmons's madhouse, Brothers published in 1802 *A Description of Jerusalem* and in 1805 *A Letter to the Subscribers for Engraving the Plans of Jerusalem, the King's Palace, the Private Palaces, College-Halls, Cathedrals, and Parliament-Houses*. The first of these is illustrated with engraved plans of the projected New Jerusalem, at least one of

[1] See *A Concise View from History and Prophecy*, pp. 247–51.

[2] Ibid., p. 272.

[3] *Conjugial Love* was first published in English in its entirety in 1794. Of course, as we have seen, such ideas about the New Jerusalem were held in the early Christian church. Brothers's disciple, Nathaniel Brassey Halhed, commenting on Romans 20: 1–6, writes: 'This passage all the ancient Millenarians took in a sense grossly literal, and taught, that during the Millennium, the saints on earth were to enjoy every bodily delight' (*A Calculation on the Commencement of the Millennium*, p. 8).

[4] From an extract published with Dobbs's *Memoirs* (Dublin, 1800).

them by Wilson Lowry,[1] whose portrait Blake was later to engrave with John Linnell.[2] Brothers's idea of the city is a beatific transformation of contemporary town planning.

Look at London or Paris [he complains], those two great and wealthy cities, there are no such regular streets in either, or healthy accommodations as in ours. Their streets in general are narrow, and very crooked, their houses in many parts are confusedly crowded together, some high, some low, and very few with gardens except those of the most wealthy men. But with us every house throughout the city has its regular portion of ground for a garden, where the poorest families may walk and enjoy themselves—where their children may play in safety, to acquire daily fresh health and strength.[3]

Brothers's idea of a perfect city is to some extent indebted to such plans as those of Mecklenburgh Square and Brunswick Square (proposed by Samuel Pepys Cockerell in 1790[4]) and the New Town of Edinburgh.[5]

His [the king's] residence will be a noble palace, on the north side of the square that incloses the park, or Garden of Eden, for the public to walk in. The square is formed by a range of twelve private palaces on each side, including the king's, which makes forty-eight in all. Each palace is 444 feet long, with a space of 144 feet between each; to every one is a lawn in front, and behind is a spacious garden. What a noble square to excite admiration! Each side of it is near a mile and a half in length! Such is to be the centre of the future Jerusalem, and round it the city is to be built. . . . I have delineated the whole under God's direction, as he ordered to be laid down about 2,360 years ago, in the last nine chapters of Ezekiel.[6]

A comparison of such passages with the description of Golgonooza in *12–13* shows how Blake, drawing upon the same biblical source as Brothers, constructed a mental city which has much in common with the New Jerusalem as Brothers envisaged it.

[1] 'Plan of the Holy City the New Jerusalem', rep. in 'The Prince of the Hebrews and the Woman Clothed with the Sun', p. 274. The plate is signed 'Lowry'; no other Lowry is recorded as a working engraver in London at that time, and Wilson Lowry specialized in architectural and mechnical subjects.

[2] Rep. Geoffrey Keynes, *Engravings of William Blake* (Dublin: Emery Walker, 1956, pl. 44).

[3] *A Description*, p. 34.

[4] See Summerson, *Georgian London*, pp. 167–8.

[5] See A. J. Youngson, *The Making of Classical Edinburgh, 1750–1840* (Edinburgh: Edinburgh University Press, 1966).

[6] *A Letter*, pp. 18–19.

Not all imaginative reconstructions of Jerusalem were millenarian in motive. In 1804 was published an enormous engraving entitled *A Scenographic View of Jerusalem*, by John Daniel Hertz, 'Senr. Topographer and Engraver to His Imperial Majesty'. Relying on the Bible, Josephus, 'and the Observations of the Moderns', Hertz created an impressive panoramic view showing in painstaking detail the city with its walls, gates, and buildings ('Every House minutely described'), with the Temple dominating the upper central portion of the design. The streets are not shown empty, as in an architectural plan, but thronged with people; and in various parts of the engraving scenes from the life of Jesus can be seen taking place. An accompanying printed key identifies 159 details in the engraving! Bearing the same date as Blake's *Jerusalem* title-page, Hertz's scenographic view attests to the powerful attraction of the Holy City for the imagination. It is literal in its mode of presentation, while Blake's work is figurative, but Hertz's engraving nevertheless appeals to our desire to invest city and temple with our own sensibilities, an invitation made even more appealing by the synchronic presentation of episodes in the story of Christ in Jerusalem. Hertz's *Scenographic View* anticipates on a relatively small scale the appeal, later in the century, of Burford's Panorama—one of the subjects of which was, inevitably, Jerusalem.[1]

'I observe', wrote David Hume, 'that many of our complex ideas never had impressions, that corresponded to them, and that many of our complex impressions never are exactly copied in ideas. I can imagine to myself such a city as the *New Jerusalem*, whose pavement is gold and rubies, tho' I never saw any such.'[2] Blake's continuing city takes its origin from a synthesis of literary antecedents with Blake's experience of real cities. The antecedents have been discussed at length; the real cities should at least be mentioned. Most important is, of course, London, 'a Human awful wonder of God!' who declares 'My Streets are my, Ideas of Imagination. . . . My Houses are Thoughts' (*34/38*: 29, 31, 33). London

[1] See Richard D. Altick, *The Shows of London* (Cambridge, Mass.: Harvard University Press, 1978), p. 138.

[2] *A Treatise of Human Nature*, ed. L. A. Selby-Brigge, rev. P. H. Nidditch (Oxford: The Clarendon Press, 2nd edn., 1978), p. 3.

aspires to become Golgonooza, 'the Spiritual Fourfold London' (*53*: 18–19) as Golgonooza aspires to become the Jerusalem of *illud tempus*. Second only to London is, as Thomas Wright was the first to suggest,[1] Chichester—'a very handsome City, Seven miles from us' Blake called it shortly after moving to Felpham.[2] The importance of Chichester in this regard is conveyed by a passage from William Camden's *Britannia*:

> The city is of a circular form within the walls, and washed on all sides by the little river *Levant*. It has four gates pointing to the four quarters of the world, from which the streets run in a strait line, and intersect each other in the centre, where stands the market-place, and where Bishop Robert Read built a beautiful piazza of hewn stone.[3]

Here we can see how Chichester, a circle transected by roads laid out according to the cardinal points and intersecting at the centre, could also be a prototype of Golgonooza. Golgonooza is the realization of the city envisaged by Milton in *Areopagitica*: 'Behold now this vast City, a city of Refuge, the mansion house of liberty.'[4] Such cities take their place in a tradition of urban models of reality, a tradition going back to Ezekiel and forward to Joyce's *Ulysses* and to Doris Lessing's *The Four-Gated City*. In such cities extrapolation from buildings, streets, and town plan creates an analogical grid on which take place the events of myth.

[1] *The Life of William Blake* (New York: Burt Franklin, 1969 [Olney, 1929]), vol. I, pp. 107, 152–5.

[2] Letter to Thomas Butts, 2 October 1800, *Letters*, p. 48.

[3] Enlarged by Richard Gough (London, 1789), vol. I, p. 186. The frontispiece was engraved by Basire.

[4] *Complete Prose Works of John Milton*, ed. Don M. Wolfe (New Haven: Yale University Press), vol. II, 1969, pp. 553–4.

Chapter IV

The Myth of Humanity

The Sexual Myth

The death of Albion and the ensuing fragmentation of humanity in *Jerusalem* is presented as the disastrous result of a primordial sexual encounter. This sexual myth is recounted in the text of plates *19* and *20*, and it is also the subject of the design on plate *28*, but its ramifications extend throughout the first ninety-five plates of the work. From this episode arises the sadistic dominance of Albion's affections as Sons and Daughters, the casting-out of Jerusalem, the triumph of Vala, and the death of Albion himself. Understanding this sexual myth is therefore prerequisite to a comprehensive understanding of the work, especially as the myth epitomizes the ambiguous attitude towards sexuality that pervades *Jerusalem*. One critic goes so far as to speak of 'the radical dubiety in this myth that makes it difficult to arrive at any unified interpretation'.[1] Yet if we can reconcile ourselves to seeing in the later Blake a much more complex attitude towards sexuality than is manifest in *The Marriage of Heaven and Hell*, then we can find in that dubiety itself a profound, albeit disturbing, meaning.

When Albion, turning from the divine vision, flees from Eden to Beulah, he encounters what at first appears to be a sexual paradise.

> He found Jerusalem upon the River of his City soft repos'd
> In the arms of Vala, assimilating in one with Vala
> The Lilly of Havilah: and they sang soft thro' Lambeths
> vales,
> In a sweet moony night & silence that they had created
> With a blue sky spread over with wings and a mild moon
> (*19*: 40–4)

[1] John E. Grant, 'Two Flowers in the Garden of Experience', *William Blake: Essays for S. Foster Damon*, p. 355.

Havilah is in Genesis a land watered by one of the rivers of Paradise:

And a river went out of Eden to water the garden; and from thence it was parted, and became into four heads. The name of the first is Pison: that is it which compasseth the whole land of Havilah, where there is gold . . .[1] (2: 10–11).

So Albion at first seems to be in the position of Adam in *The Marriage*, about to re-enter Paradise. But the next lines add a disquieting note:

> Dividing & uniting into many female forms: Jerusalem
> Trembling! then in one comingling in eternal tears,
> Sighing to melt his Giant beauty, on the moony river.
> (45–7)

Their union is unstable; it is pre-sexual, and their emerging sexuality manifests itself in their tempting Albion. They become Sirens or Loreleis, and in this way they resemble the Sons and Daughters of Rahab who try to lure Milton across the river Arnon in *Milton* 17. Unlike Blake's Milton, however, Albion is willing to be tempted. Telling Vala the rest of the episode retrospectively, Jerusalem says:

> When Albion rent thy beautiful net of gold and silver twine;
> Thou hadst woven it with art, thou hadst caught me in the bands
> Of love; thou refusedst to let me go: Albion beheld thy beauty
> Beautiful thro' our Love's comeliness, beautiful thro' pity. (*20*: 30–3)

At this point Albion seized the initiative:

> Albion lov'd thee! he rent thy Veil! he embrac'd thee! he lov'd thee!
> Astonish'd at his beauty and perfection, thou forgavest his furious love (36–7)

Consequently, Jerusalem redounded from Albion's bosom to become the Bride and Wife of the Lamb of God, who gave

[1] See Damon, *Blake Dictionary*, p. 176.

Vala to Albion. This occurred *in illo tempore*—'Then was a time of love: O why is it passed away!' (41.)

Several aspects of this sexual myth are worthy of remark. Jerusalem is the Bride not of Albion—though she is his Emanation—but of Jesus. Vala is the wife of Albion, and at first a willing one who admires her husband's beauty and perfection and who forgives the 'furious' quality of his love. The initial sexual act, then, results in a temporary harmony. From Yeats[1] on, commentators have rightly emphasized that the subsequent disharmony results not from the sexual act but from Albion's feeling of guilt about it. Had Albion continued his furious love towards Vala, the 'time of love', as Jerusalem calls it, would have continued. Instead, Albion sees Vala as a powerful mother-figure—the Goddess Nature—and is consumed with Oedipal guilt at his act of phallic aggression. 'The disease of Shame covers me from head to feet', he says, become a self-afflicted Job; '. . . Every boil upon my body is a separate & deadly Sin' (*21*: 3–4). Thus sexuality is seen as powerfully enticing but destructive in its results.

The ambiguity of the sexual myth is epitomized in the transformations of the much-discussed design on plate *28* (Fig. 10). There are almost as many interpretations of this beautiful picture (especially glorious in the coloured copy E, reproduced in Plate I) as there are major interpreters. Damon, comparing the full-page design on plate 5 of *The Song of Los*, identifies the figures as the King and Queen of the Fairies, representing 'natural joys' embracing in the Lilly of Havilah.[2] Wicksteed too sees the characters as male and female, but implies that in copy E alone they are not sexually differentiated.[3] Erdman sees them as male and female in their original proof state—which we will shortly discuss—but as both female in all final states.[4] John E. Grant sees them as intended to be Albion and Vala, but suggests that in the revised state

[1] As mentioned in the Introduction, according to Yeats, Albion repeats Adam's sin, which was 'not the nakedness of which he was ashamed, but the following of beauty's act with misguided opinion,—the belief that the state of innocence—an eternal state—was no more'. (Ellis and Yeats, *Works*, II. 191.)

[2] *William Blake*, p. 470.

[3] *Blake's Jerusalem*, p. 160.

[4] *Illuminated Blake*, p. 307.

there may be 'some unintended ambiguity'.[1] To Mitchell this headpiece 'illustrates the ambiguous lesbian union of Jerusalem and Vala'.[2] Thus critics disagree not only about the identities of the figures but also about the sex of each; and even those who view them as male and female may disagree as to which figure is male and which female. The difficulty lies in Blake's own ambiguity, whether intended or not—in the ambiguity of Blake's sexual myth itself.

The existence of the Morgan Library proof and the discovery of another proof state[3] (also in the Morgan Library; see Fig. 9), reworked in pen and ink, help us to understand the meaning of this design, though the reason for its revision must remain a matter for speculation. 'The primary change', as Erdman puts it, '. . . involved turning the legs of the two nude figures from a position in which they can be assumed to be copulating to one in which they cannot.'[4] To do this, Blake refashioned a new right leg for the right-handed figure, placing the buttock so that the left leg could be imagined parallel to the right, though unseen by the viewer; and he made what had been the left leg of the right-hand figure become the left leg of the left-hand figure, thus disengaging the lower parts of the bodies of the two figures. The general effect of the couple in the first state is suggestive of the spherical androgynous creature of Aristophanes' myth in *The Symposium*. In reworking the plate, Blake reduced this 'spherical' impression. He also excised the caterpillar on the petal, though it still haunts the uncoloured copies as a ghost. The total effect of these changes is to make the design less explicitly sexual and, possibly, to change its symbolic reference.

Blake's original motive was almost certainly to depict two

[1] 'Two Flowers in the Garden of Experience', in *William Blake: Essays for S. Foster Damon*, p. 358.

[2] *Blake's Composite Art*, p. 206.

[3] The figures have been redrawn and the caterpillar clumsily erased, evidently in preparation for reworking the copperplate to the final state; but this proof displays the rounded petal ending (lowermost right) of the final state and not the pointed petal ending of the first state. Some reworking of the plate had, then, evidently been done, and more was to follow. (Both proofs are watermarked 'Edmead & Pine 1802'.)

[3] 'The Suppressed and Altered Passages in William Blake's *Jerusalem*', *Studies in Bibliography*, XVII (1964), 18.

fairies miming the love-making of Albion and Vala, as recounted by Jerusalem in the lines already cited, *20*: 30–41. Blake pictures this according to the Song of Solomon 2: 6: 'His left hand is under my head, and his right hand doth embrace me.'[1] (This is to assume, as not all viewers have, that the figure on the *left* is Albion.)[2] The point of departure is no doubt the mythopoetic version of plant sexuality in Erasmus Darwin's *Loves of the Plants*; Blake magnifies the sexual loves of the vegetable world to the ecstatic encounter of the Giant Forms Albion and Vala. There are, however, some disquieting details. Blake has made his Lilly of Havilah a water-lily, and has extended the imagined area of water by decorating marginal and interlinear spaces with images of fish, seaweed, and crustaceans. In Blake's symbolic imagery such marine life generally suggests 'fallen', materialized existence—as the human-legged hermit crab on the right reminds us. A related symbol, the phallic caterpillar on the petal, is associated with the cycle of birth, copulation, and death, as in plate 1 of *The Gates of Paradise* and the related verses

The Caterpiller on the Leaf
Reminds thee of thy Mothers Grief[3]

When Blake changed the position of the embracing figures in the flower, he also burnished out the caterpillar, reducing still further the sexual connotations of the picture. Now the design could be taken to refer to *19*: 40–7:

He found Jerusalem upon the River of his City soft
   repos'd
In the arms of Vala, assimilating in one with Vala
The Lilly of Havilah: and they sang soft thro' Lambeths
   vales,
In a sweet moony night & silence that they had created
With a blue sky spread over with wings and a mild moon,

[1] As noted by Stevenson, p. 681.

[2] What is sometimes interpreted as musculature appears to me to be a network of blood vessels. Cf. the design on plate 17 of *The Book of Urizen*, especially copy G.

[3] The plate was first issued in *For Children* in 1793 and reissued in a second state in *For the Sexes* in 1818. The verses belong to the later work; they are revised from 'Auguries of Innocence' in the Pickering Manuscript (?1807).

Dividing & uniting into many female forms: Jerusalem
Trembling! then in one comingling in eternal tears,
Sighing to melt his Giant beauty, on the moony river.

The beauty of the final, water-coloured illumination is once more misleading, but in a different way from that of the original proof state. In the latter, heterosexual love is attractively presented only to be undermined by visual–symbolic clues; in the former, what ought to be differentiated is instead presented as 'assimilating', a word which tends to have a negative valence in Blake, suggesting the incorporation of disparate values into a speciously unified whole.

In the *19* text, Jerusalem and Vala are siren figures who want to tempt Albion to lose his sublime identity (= 'melt') in the deceptive pathos of sexual adoration. In the final *28* design, Albion is absent, but the viewer is now placed in the position of Albion, watching the 'comingling' of Jerusalem and Vala much as Artegall in *The Faerie Queene* is tempted by nymphs wrestling in the waters of the Bower of Bliss. Albion, no Artegall, is excited by the spectacle of the endearments of the two females, 'Beautiful thro' our Love's comliness', as Jerusalem says. This aspect of the myth is strangely premonitory of the situation in Mallarmé's 'L'Après-Midi d'un Faune'. Mallarmé's Faun too encounters two embracing female beings and is moved to commit an aggressive sexual act in a flowery landscape. The Faun, too, feels guilt, referring to his act as 'mon crime' and imagining 'sûr châtiment', but his actual punishment seems to be a typically modern one: 'Couple, adieu; je vais voir l'ombre que tu devins.'[1] He first relegates the erotic experience to memory and then contemplates it, unsure of its reality. Albion's recourse is more traditionally puritanical: he finds sin in himself, in Vala, in Jerusalem, and in his daughters.

The Anterior Myth

In the disaster which overtakes Albion, the terrible results of the rending of the veil are not seen as arbitrary; they are determined by an anterior myth which is recounted at several

[1] *Mallarmé*, ed. Anthony Hartley (Baltimore: Penguin, 1965), p. 56.

points in *Jerusalem*. It is the myth of Albion, Luvah, and Vala. The anterior myth is first recounted in part by the Spectre of Los in plate *6*: 'Luvah was cast into the Furnaces of affliction and sealed, / And Vala fed in cruel delight, the Furnaces with fire' (30–1). The result of Luvah's torture, according to the Spectre, is 'To prepare the Spectre of Albion to reign over thee O Los' (40); but the role of Albion is not supplied here. That dimension is first provided by Albion himself: 'For I see Luvah whom I slew. I behold him in my Spectre' (*22*: 31). Further details are given in the long speech of the Spectre and Emanation of Los in *43/29*, telling how 'Luvah strove to gain dominion over Albion' (62), and smote him with boils, leaving him 'prostrate upon the crystal pavement' (63). In revenge, Albion forced Luvah to materialize and exiled Luvah and Vala to the Human Heart. As a result, the vast form of nature was generated in the shape of a serpent, and the Heart 'where Paradise & its joys abounded' was invaded by 'jealous fears & fury & rage'. An alternative version, supplied by Vala in *80*: 16–29, makes Vala herself the murderer of Albion. She says that her father Luvah fought in wars against Albion; Luvah was slain, but, revived by Vala, he commanded her to murder Albion. Lest Albion rise again to kill Luvah, Vala says: 'I . . . keep his body embalmed in moral laws / With spices of sweet odours of lovely jealous stupefaction' (27–8). Like the Marys who embalmed Christ, Vala preserves the dead body instead of the living spirit.

These accounts may at first seem at variance, but if we remember that we are considering a myth rather than a sustained allegory, we can see that the core of the myth is consistent in the several accounts. Albion, instead of being the passive victim of the war between Urizen and Luvah as in *The Four Zoas*, is himself the antagonist of Luvah. In other words, the anterior myth is a *psychomachia* describing man's repression of his sexual passion and its destructive consequences: thereafter, consummation can only be followed by guilt. The result of this in the external political world is war.

> Luvah tore forth from Albions Loins, in fibrous veins, in rivers
> Of blood over Europe: a Vegetating Root in grinding pain.

Animating the Dragon Temples, soon to become that Holy Fiend
The Wicker Man of Scandinavia in which cruelly consumed
The Captives reard to heaven howl in flames among the stars
Loud the cries of War on the Rhine & Danube, with Albions Sons,
Away from Beulahs hills & vales break forth the Souls of the Dead,
With cymbal, trumpet, clarion; & the scythed chariots of Britain.

And the Veil of Vala, is composed of the Spectres of the Dead (*47*: 4–12)

On this level of the symbolism Luvah as France is both aggressor and victim. 'Luvah slew Tharmas the Angel of the Tongue & Albion brought him / To Justice in his own City of Paris, denying the Resurrection'[1] (*63*: 5–6). Internally, Luvah moves from his original place (the East) to Urizen's (the South),[2] usurping the role of reason in the little world of man. This act of hubris precipitates, as inexorably as in a Greek tragedy, *sparagmos.*[3] In a shocking display of the Romantic Agony's latent content become manifest, the Sons and Daughters of Albion torture and sacrifice Luvah:

Go Noah [says Tirzah] fetch the girdle of strong brass, heat it red-hot:
Press it around the loins of this ever expanding cruelty
Shriek not so my only love! I refuse thy joys: I drink
Thy shrieks because Hand & Hyle are cruel & obdurate to me (*67*: 59–62)

Thus in both macrocosm and microcosm the principle of desire overreaches itself, is cruelly repressed, and consequently manifests itself in perverted forms. In the grand

[1] For the reference to 'the two occupations and the two Treaties of Paris in 1814 and 1815', see Erdman, *Blake: Prophet*, p. 466.

[2] See Damon's useful table of fourfold correspondences in *Jerusalem* (*William Blake*, p. 433).

[3] Frye is especially enlightening on this theme. See *Fearful Symmetry*, pp. 387, 397, 403.

design of the work, Luvah must be regenerated and 'identified' along with all other human forms, but this cannot occur until the consequences of Albion's fall have been fully worked out.

One concomitant of Albion's repression of Luvah is alienation—not in the almost meaningless journalistic sense in which the term is often used, but in the precise meaning later employed by Feuerbach, Nietzsche, and Marx. In *43/29* the Spectre and Emanation of Los tell how Albion created the Old Testament God as an object of worship:

> Above him rose a Shadow from his wearied intellect:
> Of living gold, pure, perfect, holy: in white linen pure he hovered
> A sweet entrancing self-delusion a watry vision of Albion
> Soft exulting in existence; all the Man absorbing!
>
> Albion fell upon his face prostrate before the watry Shadow
> Saying O Lord whence is this change! thou knowest I am nothing!
> And Vala trembled & coverd her face! & her locks were spread on the pavement (37–43)

Albion hypostatizes a God and then addresses him in a psalmodic utterance, expressing his own helplessness in contrast to the omnipotence of the reified image he has created. This is the view of Nietzsche in *The Genealogy of Morals*, a view which Blake anticipated as early as 1790–3, with his own genealogy of the gods in *The Marriage of Heaven and Hell*. 'Choosing forms of worship from poetic tales', men confused the creations of the imagination with externally existent 'Gods', and 'Thus men forgot that All deities reside in the human breast' (E. 37). The deity that Albion worships is his own Spectre, the Urizen in him, and until he can annihilate this self-created persecutor—which is to say until *Jerusalem* is ready to conclude—Albion suffers from feelings of sexual guilt, frustrated rage, and powerlessness. This is nowhere more evident than in his helplessness before the sexual power of Vala and his condemnation of Jerusalem as a harlot.

Thus Albion, rending the veil and embracing Vala, makes a gesture toward sexual unity which his own psyche cannot accommodate. He has in effect programmed himself for guilt. This inner division also predetermines the nature of Albion's love: 'He felt that Love and Pity are the same; a soft repose! / Inward complacency of Soul: a Self-annihilation!' (*23*: 14–15.) Blake may be taking himself as a source here, and Albion's problems may be more Blake's own than has been realized. According to Frederick Tatham, Blake at the age of twenty-four fell in love with a young woman named Polly Wood, who, 'as obstinate as she was unkind', rejected him.

> He became ill & went to Kew near Richmond for a change of air & renovation of health & spirits & as far as is possible to know lodged at the House of a market Gardener whose name was Boutcher. . . . He was relating to the daughter, a Girl named Catherine, the lamentable story of Polly Wood, his implacable Lass, upon which Catherine expressed her deep sympathy, it is supposed in such a tender & affectionate manner, that it quite won him, he immediately said with the suddenness peculiar to him 'Do you pity me?' 'Yes indeed I do' answered she. 'Then I love you' said he again. Such was their courtship.[1]

The literary prototype of this—and Blake must have been aware of living at times according to such prototypes—is in *Othello*. Othello told Desdemona the story of his life,

> And often did beguile her of her tears,
> When I did speak of some distressful stroke
> That my youth suffer'd. My story being done,
> She gave me for my pains a world of sighs:
> . . . .
> Upon this hint I spake:
> She loved me for the dangers I had pass'd,
> And I loved her that she did pity them.[2]

Blake loved Catherine Boutcher because she pitied him; Albion 'felt that Love and Pity are the same'; Othello loved Desdemona because she found his story 'pitiful . . . wondrous pitiful' (161). In all three instances the result was, to use Blake's subtitle for *The Four Zoas*, 'The torments of Love & Jealousy'.

The dichotomous perception of female by male described in *Jerusalem* is of course deeply embedded in our culture; it is, for example, described by Leslie Fiedler in *Love and Death*

[1] *Life of Blake, BR.*, pp. 517–18.

[2] I. iii. 156–9, 166–7.

in the American Novel.[1] The tendency is to bifurcate women into two aspects: the sexually alluring figure who represents the threat of castration precisely because she is desired, and the passively sympathetic woman whose *métier* is to be possessed by the male. Some Victorian and early modern critics could at the same time admire William Blake as a hero of sexual liberation and Catherine Blake as her husband's *alter ego.*[2] Largely through the careful study of Blake's manuscript poems we now realize that the torments of love and jealousy were very much part of the Blakes' domestic life. The type of dual perception of woman that characterizes Albion is also the problem of the eponymous hero of 'William Bond' (E. 487–80), who of course stands for Blake himself. William Bond, like Blake after his rejection by Polly Wood and like Albion stricken by guilt after rending the veil, is 'very ill'. His illness is precipitated by repressed desire for a woman who 'is ruddy & bright as day', while he is engaged to the 'Melancholy Pale' Mary Green. The choice is something like that of Lawrence's Paul Morel between Miriam Leivers and Clara Dawes. Mary Green precipitates a solution of sorts by becoming ill herself; this enables her to share William's bed, causing him to reject Eros for Agape.

> Seek Love in the Pity of others Woe
> In the gentle relief of anothers care
> In the darkness of night & the winters snow
> In the naked & outcast Seek Love there
>
> (E. 489)

This Dostoevskeian solution may work for the poem, but it did not work for the Blakes, at least not at the time that 'William Bond' was written, *c.*1804,[3] as is shown by the struggles between Los and Enitharmon and by the torments of Albion.

[1] New York: Criterion Books, 1960.

[2] For discussion of Blake's ideas about the sexes, see Irene Tayler, 'The Woman Scaly', *Bulletin of the Midwest Modern Language Association*, VI (1973), 74–87; and two articles forthcoming in *Blake*: 'Blake's Sexism', by Anne K. Mellor and 'Desire Gratified and Ungratified: William Blake and Sexuality', by Alicia Ostriker.

[3] I agree with Erdman's view (E. 777) that the poems of the Pickering Manuscript 'appear to belong to the late Felpham period', although of course the fair copy may have been made considerably later—'probably between 1807 and 1824' according to G. E. Bentley, Jr. ('The Date of Blake's Pickering Manuscript *or* The Way of a Poet with Paper', *Studies in Bibliography*, XIX (1966), 232–43).

It is difficult to disengage various portions of the myth, although this must be done for the purposes of discussion. Jerusalem, Vala, and Albion can hardly be said to exist except in relation to one another, and yet we will be in a better position to understand their interrelationships if we first consider them as separate figures, each having traditional antecedents which were synthesized and transformed by Blake.

Jerusalem

It is fitting to begin with the title figure of the work. *In illo tempore* Jerusalem and Vala are virtually a composite being. Their synthesis is Brittania. In *32/36* we are told that in the wars of the zoas—that is, in what I have called the anterior myth—'England who is Brittannia divided into Jerusalem & Vala' (28). Presumably this synthesis is, with much else, restored near the end of the work when 'England, who is Brittannia entered Albions bosom rejoicing' (*96*: 2), which is also the subject of the design on *96*. But the body of the work, with the exception of the flashback to the sexual myth in which they assimilated in one, Jerusalem and Vala are presented as discrete beings. The basis of their differentiation is Paul's interpretation in Galatians 4: 22–6 of the story of Abraham, Sarah, Hagar, and their children:

> For it is written, that Abraham had two sons, the one by a bondmaid, the other by a freewoman.
> But he who was of the bondwoman was born after the flesh, but he of the freewoman was by promise.
> Which things are an allegory: for these are the two covenants; the one from the mount Sinai, which gendereth to bondage, which is Agar.
> For this Agar is mount Sinai in Arabia, and answereth to Jerusalem which now is, and is in bondage with her children.
> But Jerusalem which is above is free, which is the mother of us all.[1]

Paul wants to 'Cast out the bondwoman and her son' (30), while Blake characteristically wants to redeem the bondwoman through the freewoman and reunite them. Neverthe-

[1] As pointed out by Albert S. Roe, *Blake's Illustrations to the Divine Comedy* (Princeton: Princeton University Press, 1953), p. 12, Paul's statement in turn refers back to Isaiah 54: 1.

less, Jerusalem and Vala maintain their separate roles through most of *Jerusalem*.

Jerusalem as a figure first appears in *The Four Zoas*, in much the same sense as in *Milton* and in *Jerusalem* itself,[1]

> . . . the Lamb of God Creates himself a bride & wife
> That we his Children evermore may live in Jerusalem
> Which now descendeth out of heaven a City yet a Woman
> Mother of myriads redeemd & born in her spiritual palaces
> By a New Spiritual birth Regenerated from Death
> (122: 16–20, E. 376)

Jerusalem as a city was discussed in Chapter III; here we are concerned with Jerusalem as a woman. The female personification of Jerusalem derives, of course, from the Old Testament Prophets, whom Blake follows in presenting her both as the chosen bride of God and as the transgressor. In Isaiah 52, for example, the prophet calls:

> . . . Put on thy beautiful garments, O Jerusalem, the holy city: for henceforth there shall no more come into thee the uncircumcised and the unclean.
> Shake thyself from the dust; arise, and sit down, O Jerusalem: loose thyself from the bands of thy neck, O captive daughter of Zion. (1–2)

Passages such as these are the prototypes of Blake's presentations of the redeemed Jerusalem, the greatest of which occurs in Los's Watch Song in *86*: 1–32, beginning 'I see thy Form O lovely mild Jerusalem'. Jerusalem as harlot has its paradigmatic expression in Ezekiel 16, where the word of the Lord says:

> . . . Thou wast cast out in the open field, to the lothing of thy person, in the day that thou wast born.
> And when I passed by thee, and saw thee polluted in thine own blood, I said unto thee when thou wast in thy blood, Live . . .
> I have caused thee to multiply as the bud of the field, and thou hast increased and waxen great, and thou art come to excellent ornaments: thy breasts are fashioned, and thine hair is grown, whereas thou was naked and bare. (5–7)

[1] This is not in any way to suggest that all references to Jerusalem in *The Four Zoas* are earlier than those in *Milton* and *Jerusalem*. Indeed, Blake may for a time have had all three works in process concurrently. What is important is that of the four pages devoted to 'Jerusalem' and 'Jerusalem's' in the *Concordance*, only three entries occur before *The Four Zoas*, and in all three Jerusalem is merely a place-name.

The Lord goes on to denounce Jerusalem for her subsequent harlotry and to prophesy her humiliation. Perhaps Blake's most eloquent evocation of the fallen Jerusalem is in the magnificent passage beginning 'Naked Jerusalem lay before the Gates upon Mount Zion' on *78*: 21 and continuing through the next plate to *80*: 5 with her deeply moving lamentation. Of course in Blake's conception Jerusalem's harlotry is in the eyes of the beholders—of the guilt-obsessed Albion and his terrible sons; the actual whoredoms are Vala's.

One could fill a volume with comparisons between the biblical personification of Jerusalem and Blake's adaptation of it. What is important here, however, is not so much the sources of individual passages as the centrality of the tradition of Blake's Jerusalem. The common elements are a woman (yet a city) who exists *in illo tempore* in a state of primal innocence, who is then rejected as a sexual transgressor, and who is elevated in her regenerate form as the mother of us all. These same elements are seen, though not in sequential order, in the designs in which Jerusalem is represented.[1]

In illo tempore Jerusalem and Vala are pictured united in their love play in the second state of *28*, as discussed early in this chapter. Divided from each other, they yet collaborate productively on *18* in a design related to line 7: '(For Vala produc'd the Bodies. Jerusalem gave the Souls).' Vala is probably the figure at the right, wearing a chaplet of lilies, for she is called 'Vala / The Lilly of Havilah'[2] in *19*: 41–2 and is twice connected with lilies in *The Four Zoas*.[3] Jerusalem is then the androgynous-looking winged figure at the right, crowned with roses.[4] The successful union of feminine body

[1] David Wyatt goes so far as to argue that the illustrations in which Jerusalem appears stand in relation to the text as a 'counterplot' (see 'The Woman Jerusalem: *Pictura* Versus *Poesis*', *Blake Studies*, VII, 105–24). Whether or not such a consistent pattern exists, Wyatt is certainly correct in his view that Jerusalem is frequently seen from different perspectives in text and in design.

[2] *Pace* Erdman, who finds no reference to either flower in *Jerusalem* (*Ill. Bl.*, p. 297). Erdman identifies the figure on the *left* as Jerusalem, as do Damon (*William Blake*, p. 469) and Wicksteed (p. 297). Grant considers the left-hand figure 'probably male' and the right-hand one as female ('Two Flowers', p. 312), and this is also the view of Stevenson (p. 661).

[3] *64*: 30, E. 337; *83*: 8, E. 351. The association of the Virgin Mary worshipped in churches (as opposed to the Mary of Blake's Maternal Line, discussed below) with lilies would reinforce this.

[4] The late Ruthven Todd suggested to me in correspondence that these roses

and masculine soul—the latter possibly 'Shiloh the Masculine Emanation' (*49*: 47)—is signified by two redemptive moon-arks;[1] but the parenthetical status of line 7 indicates the anteriority of this episode. In *4* the two go completely asunder. Naked Jerusalem leads three of her daughters up towards the crescent moon, in which is inscribed Μονος ὁ Ἰεσους—'Jesus alone', referring to the Transfiguration, where Peter, James, and John see 'Jesus only'.[2] In contrast, the cowled, sybilline Vala (cf. *America* 14 and emblem 16 of *The Gates of Paradise*) remains below, trying to hold down two male figures. A confrontation between the two (which does not occur in the text) is the subject of *46/32*, where Jerusalem defies Vala[3] who, dressed like the Beatrice of Blake's great Dante illustration,[4] threatens to cover Jerusalem with her veil. Each is flanked by an appropriate icon[5] —Vala by the dome of St. Paul's, Jerusalem by Westminster Abbey. (These structures, suggesting, respectively, State Religion and spiritual Christianity, do not appear in the preparatory sketch on page 80 of Blake's *Notebook*.)[6] The three daughters of Jerusalem reappear, this time in differentiated attitudes. One leans on Jerusalem for support; one indicates that the way to go is upward; and one has already begun to

could be the English dog rose, which has a single rather than a double flower; Blake could have seen it in hedgerows around Felpham.

[1] On this general subject, see Nicholas O. Warner, 'Blake's Moon-Ark Symbolism', *Blake*, XIV (1980), 44–59.

[2] The Greek words are ὁ Ἰησοῦς μόνος; see Wicksteed, p. 117; Luke 9: 36, Matt. 17: 8, Mark 9: 8.

[3] Erdman (*Ill. Bl.*, p. 325), on the contrary, sees Jerusalem as 'almost mesmerized by Vala'. Wicksteed (pp. 204–5) thinks Jerusalem's expression is changed from 'hatred, even horror' in the monochrome copies to 'yielding to the dark way' in copy E.

[4] *Beatrice Addressing Dante from the Car* (Tate Gallery).

[5] On this general subject, see my essay 'The Fourth Face of Man—Blake and Architecture', in *Examining the Sister Arts*, ed. R. Wendorf *et al.*, the University of Minnesota Press (forthcoming).

[6] This indicates that the association of each figure with an architectural icon was deliberately made after the original conception had been formed. There are some significant changes with respect to the Gothic cathedral from the monochrome copies to copy E. In A, C, D, and F, and also in the unique coloured proof (National Gallery of Art, Canberra, Australia) only the dome of St. Paul's is in shadow; but in E Westminster Abbey is also partly in shadow and its nave is obscured. This may indicate increased pessimism on Blake's part about the prospects for spiritual Christianity in England.

soar in a cursive line.[1] Jerusalem is here a *caritas*-figure,[2] 'Mother of myriads'; Vala, significantly, is pictured without children.

The conflict between Jerusalem and Vala brings us from *illud tempus* to historical time and space, as indicated by the wave-lashed shore on which both stand in *46/32*. In that conflict, Jerusalem must necessarily be the loser, as she embodies the values of primordial innocence which must be eclipsed in historical time and are only to be regained by a process of regeneration. So in *47* Jerusalem, arms outstretched in a gesture of vain entreaty to Albion, is trodden down by Vala; Albion holds his hands to his head in despair[3] as Vala lures him with her 'beauty contest' attitude (cf. her similar pose in the margin of *24*). In *45* Vala weaves a net around the apparently sleeping Jerusalem, passing a thread from a spindle in her right hand so that it goes between her legs, is guided by the fingers of her left hand, and then weaves around Jerusalem's body. Thus is re-established 'thy beautiful net of gold and silver twine' in which Vala caught Jerusalem 'in the bands / Of love' in *20*; but here there is no commingling but mere entrapment. Related imagery occurs in *57*, where the network in which Jerusalem, at the bottom, is entrapped, is formed of fibres which appear to grow out of her. (Yet there may also be a positive implication here, for the fibres also suggest the vines of Rosamond's Bower, referred to in line 7 of the text on this plate.)

As Jerusalem's being enwoven by fibres is one image of her temporal helplessness, so is her sleep, pictured in *2, 23,* and *33/37*. A fairy figure on the title-page mimes the sleep of Jerusalem in Beulah, lying in a posture that Erdman rightly calls a parody of Henry Fuseli's *The Nightmare.*[4] Her recumbent, winged figure lies recumbent on *23*, on the Peak in

[1] In the *Notebook* drawing, this girl is the smallest of the three and is leaning against Jerusalem. The drawing can be dated as before 1810 because the writing around the drawing belongs to that year. See Erdman, *Notebook*, p. N 80.

[2] Compare the untitled etching of a similar subject included in copies B, C, and D of *Songs of Innocence and of Experience*. (Bentley, who designates this plate a, sees a male figure (*Blake Books*, p. 404), but it appears clearly female to me.)

[3] On this general subject, see Janet A. Warner, 'Blake's Figures of Despair: Man in His Spectre's Power', in *William Blake: Essays in Honour of Sir Geoffrey Keynes*, pp. 208–24.

[4] *Ill. Bl.*, p. 283.

Derbyshire.[1] Intestines wind out from behind her head almost to both margins, suggesting that she has descended to the level of merely visceral life known as Bowlahoola, which Blake elsewhere defines as 'the Stomach in every individual man'.[2] This in turn links the image to the text of *89*: 43–4:[3] 'But in the midst of a devouring Stomach, Jerusalem / Hidden within the Covering Cherub as in a Tabernacle'. Nevertheless there is redemptive hope in the *23* design, figured in the flowers on either side of Jerusalem—the Lily of Calvary and the Star of Bethlehem.[4] Most sinister is Jerusalem's sleep under the enormous outspread wings of the vampire-bat Spectre (*33/37*). Nevertheless, the sleeper is borne safely on a floating bier which, like the ark of *39*, preserves the divine vision on the Sea of Time and Space.[5]

Jerusalem in the designs is never wholly lost, but her role is largely passive: except in the two plates in which she opposes Vala, her attitude is one of helplessness. Plate *26*, in which she shrinks in horror before the ghastly spectacle of Hand, is not an exception. But her mourning posture in *92* is different; here the theme of redemption is not rendered by an accessory object (flower or bier) but by Jerusalem herself. In contrast to the palms-forward attitude of repulsion in *26*, her hands are palms up in *92*, embodying Blake's pathos-formula of self-surrender.[6] This *mater dolorosa* mourns the four fallen Zoas around her as a prelude to the regenerative action of the last few plates.[7] Her own role in that action is

[1] The caverned mountain of *23* is suggestive of the Peak district, with its mines and caves, which figures in the text of *57*: 5 and *64*: 35. See Damon, *Blake Dictionary*, p. 102; and David Worrall, 'Blake's Derbyshire: A Visionary Locale in *Jerusalem*', *Blake*, XI (1977), 34–5.

[2] *Milton* 24: 67, E. 120.

[3] As suggested by Wicksteed, p. 154.

[4] See Piloo Nannavutty, 'A Title-Page in Blake's Illustrated Genesis Manuscript', *Journal of the Warburg and Courtauld Institutes*, X (1947), 117–18.

[5] See Wicksteed, p. 25; Erdman, *Ill. Bl.*, p. 312, and Stevenson, p. 601. Damon (*William Blake*, p. 470) appears to be alone in regarding the sleeper as male.

[6] If the Jerusalem of *26* were to straighten out her arms, she would approximate the impotent, fearful gesture of the old man in *Europe* 8 (11 in the *Blake Books* numeration). If the Jerusalem of *92* extended her arms upwards, her gesture would become that of her joyful embrace in *99*. On this general subject, see Janet A. Warner, 'Blake's Use of Gesture', *Blake's Visionary Forms Dramatic*, pp. 174–5.

[7] As Erdman (*Ill. Bl.*) notes, this image is related to Isaiah 3: 26: 'And her [Jerusalem's] gates shall lament and mourn; and she being desolate shall sit upon the ground.' Blunt suggests a source for the design in *The Prodigal Son* engraved by Martin de Vos (see *The Art of William Blake*, p. 81 and pl. 49*b*).

seen in *99*, where, with arms held obliquely and palms up, she enters the embrace, at once both physical and spiritual, of Jehovah.[1]

Jerusalem Surrogates

A number of other female figures are so closely linked with Jerusalem as to be in effect her surrogates. Jerusalem's Daughters are obviously among these. In two designs that have been discussed, *4* and *46/32*, they are three in number, making for an interesting comparison with C. Nesbit's wood engraving after John Thurston, *The Daughters of Jerusalem*. This was one of the illustrations to *Religious Emblems,*[2] a book published by Rudolph Ackermann in 1809, with an interpretive text by Blake's patron the Revd. Joseph Thomas[3] (one of the subscribers was 'William Blake, Esq.'). The Thurston–Nesbit picture shows the three daughters as clothed, but, like Blake's Daughters of Jerusalem, they are associated with love. The accompanying text in *Religious Emblems* is from the Song of Solomon 5: 8: 'I charge you, O daughters of Jerusalem, if you find my beloved, that you tell him, that I am sick of love.' Thomas's commentary gives the traditional Christian interpretation of this passage as expressing the longing of the soul for her redeemer. In *Jerusalem*, of course, the Daughters are aspects of Jerusalem herself—'my infant loves & graces' (*20*: 28), as she puts it. Sometimes distinguished from Jerusalem's Sons, sometimes included with them as her Children, they share Jerusalem's tribulations: are scattered abroad, condemned by Albion, woven false bodies by Vala, and protected by Los.

In addition to the Daughters of Jerusalem, there are five other important Jerusalem surrogates: Erin, Dinah, Rosa-

[1] Note the similar embrace of the couple at the lower left in the illustration of the Last Judgement in Blair's *Grave*; see Essick and Paley, *Robert Blair's* The Grave *Illustrated by William Blake*, p. 52.

[2] *Religious Emblems, Being a Series of Engravings on Wood, Executed by the first Artists in that Line, from Designs . . . by J. Thurston, Esq. The Descriptions written by the Rev. J. Thomas, A. M., Chaplain to the Earl of Corke and Orrery*. For details about this book and other information about Joseph Thomas, see Leslie Parris, 'William Blake's Mr. Thomas', *TLS*, LXVII (5 Dec. 1968), 1390.

[3] He was the original owner of the sets of illustrations to *Paradise Lost* and *Comus* now in the Huntington Library.

mund, Oothoon, and Mary. Each represents an aspect of redemption through female love. The largest role is given to Erin, who reflects Blake's sympathy for Irish freedom in the aftermath of the Act of Union of 1800.[1] So Erin is given a tremendous speech (*48–50*) in which spatial conceptions are used to convey the possibility of liberty. She commands the Amorite kings Sihon and Og, defeated by Joshua, to 'Remove Eastward from Bashan and Gilead'; in other words, to go across the Jordan from the Holy Land in order 'to give a Place for Redemption' (*48*: 63–4). Jerusalem, she says, must be drawn away from Albion's mountains and hidden away; and she calls upon the daughters of Beulah to lament for Albion all over Ireland. She is conceived as a preserving and protective maternal figure. She is the 'Maternal Love [who] awoke Jerusalem' in *48*: 18; she is the watcher at Albion's tomb in *48*, and in *94*: 13 we find Erin still faithfully 'sitting in the Tomb', protecting Albion's body from his terrible sons. 'Erins lovely Bow' (*50*: 22) is an image of the Covenant, associated with the hope that Albion shall rise again. In *48*: 48 she assumes the role that was given to the earth-mother Eno[2] in *The Four Zoas*, taking a Moment of Time and bending it 'Into a Rainbow of jewels and gold' (35).[3] In her association with Albion's arched tomb, with the curved rainbow, and with 'the Spaces of Erin, / In the Ends of Beulah' (51–2), Erin is the custodian of womb-like containers which protect vision until the world is ready to receive it.

Erin too has surrogate figures, or rather a surrogate and a demonic parody. The latter is

> . . . a Sexual Machine: an aged Virgin Form.
> In Erins Land toward the north, joint after joint & burning
> In love & jealousy immingled & calling it Religion
>
> (*39/44*: 25–7)

[1] On this, see Erdman, *Blake: Prophet*, pp. 481–4.

[2] As the 'aged Mother, / Who the chariot of Leutha guides' (E. 89)—i.e. as the maternal principle which impels female sexuality—Eno recites the proem to *The Song of Los*, and at one point she had a similar function in *The Four Zoas* (see E. 739).

[3] This line, being specifically associated with Erin, does not appear in the *FZ* version. For details of the revision, see Chapter I above.

This is the personification of xenophobic nationalism and religious orthodoxy which James Joyce represents as Old Gummy Granny in *Ulysses*. As Stephen Dedalus refuses the knife she proffers, so Blake rejects violence as a solution to the sufferings of Ireland. Instead, he presents a positive alternative in *74*: 52–4:

> I see a Feminine Form arise from the Four terrible Zoas
> Beautiful but terrible struggling to take a form of beauty
> Rooted in Shechem: this is Dinah, the youthful form of
> Erin

Like Jerusalem and Erin, Dinah is an emanation who becomes a victim. In Genesis 34 she is ravished by the Hivite prince Shechem, who, however, marries her and undergoes circumcision in order to be allowed to do so, only to be murdered by Dinah's treacherous brothers Simeon and Levi. Her combination of beauty and terror is derived from Eve in *Paradise Lost*[1] and will be passed on to the Irish heroes of Yeats's 'Easter 1916'. As the youthful form of Erin, Dinah embodies the possibility of saving the oppressor through love, an idea similar to William Faulkner's conviction that the descendants of black slaves would save the descendants of slave-holders in the American South. 'Pacifism' may be too weak a word to convey such a message; perhaps more adequate is the word that Gandhi coined for non-violence: *satyagraha*, or 'truth-force'.[2]

Dinah's status as the violated woman links her to Oothoon, who is mentioned only twice in *Jerusalem*, though she is the central figure of *Visions of the Daughters of Albion*, where like Jerusalem herself she combines the attributes of love and freedom. Her palace, which is the joy of sexual love, holds both Jerusalem and Vala 'in soft slumberous repose' (*37/41*: 21), accommodating both the spiritual and the physical, albeit in suspended animation. The fulfilment of both together is too dangerous to be practised openly. 'Oothoon?', asks Los. 'Where hides my child? in Oxford hidest thou with Antamon?'

[1] Satan refers to Eve as 'fair, divinely fair, fit Love for Gods, / Not terrible, though terror be in Love / And beauty . . .' (IX. 489–91, *Complete Poems and Major Prose*, pp. 389–90).

[2] See M. K. Gandhi, *The Story of My Experiments with Truth* (Ahmedabad, India: Navajivan Press, 1929), II. 153–4.

(*83*: 27–8). 'Prince of the pearly dew' in *Europe* 14: 15, Antamon is the semen; his union with Oothoon in *Jerusalem* must be concealed 'In graceful hidings of error: in merciful deceit / Lest Hand the terrible destroy his Affection' (*83*: 29–30). They hide in Oxford because that is the locale of Rosamond's Bower, mentioned in *57*: 6. Rosamond (de Clifford), another Jerusalem surrogate, was the mistress of Henry II, who supposedly hid her in a labyrinth at Woodstock; but she was nevertheless discovered and murdered by Queen Eleanor. Blake did an engraving in 1783 (after Stothard), *The Fall of Rosamond*, on this subject, and he seems to have intended to illustrate it himself later: a pencil drawing depicting one woman giving another a presumably poisoned cup probably represents Eleanor and the unfortunate Rosamund.[1] Here they stand in the relation of Vala and Jerusalem in *88*: 57: 'Jerusalem took the Cup which foamd in Vala's hand', and somewhere behind both pairs of figures are the Whore of Babylon with her cup of abominations and the woman clothed with the sun (Rev. 17: 4 and 12: 1).

Mary is a Jerusalem surrogate by virtue of her motherhood and her love. She is not the Virgin worshipped in the churches, for, Los says:

> A Vegetated Christ & a Virgin Eve, are the Hermaphroditic
> Blasphemy, by his Maternal Birth he is that Evil-One
> And his Maternal Humanity must be put off Eternally
> (*90*: 34–6)

Blake may have derived the idea of putting off the Maternal Humanity from Emanuel Swedenborg,[2] who declared that 'the Lord Successively put off the humanity which was taken from the Mother, and put on the Divinity in Himself, which is the Divine Humanity and the Son of God'.[3] For Blake, however, this dismissal of the Maternal Humanity involves only the theological tenet that Jesus was conceived by an act

[1] The subject was correctly identified by George Goyder and the drawing reproduced under the title of *The Fall of Fair Rosamund* and dated *c.* 1815 by Martin Butlin in *William Blake* (1978), p. 125, no. 256.

[2] Damon, *Blake Dictionary*, p. 264.

[3] *The Doctrine of the New Jerusalem Concerning the Lord* (London: R. Hindmarsh, 3rd edn., 1791), no. 3.

of magic without sexual intercourse. 'If he intended to take on Sin', says *The Everlasting Gospel*, 'The Mother should an Harlot been' (E. 794). The human aspect of Mary is treated with deep sympathy in *61*, a plate which may have been inserted[1] to counterpoise the false virgin birth announced by Gwendolen in *82*. Like Oothoon, Dinah (and therefore Erin), Rosamond, and Jerusalem herself, Blake's Mary engages in sexual experience outside the Law. In this she also resembles her namesake Mary Wollstonecraft, who may have been a model for Oothoon[2] and who seems again to have been in Blake's thoughts at about the time that he was beginning *Jerusalem*. The Pickering Manuscript poem 'Mary' (E. 478–9) is a village tragedy in which the heroine, at first described as 'An Angel . . . from the heavenly Climes', is rejected and humiliated because of her lack of conventional modesty. Consequently 'her lillies & roses are blighted & shed', and she laments in words that Blake elsewhere applies to himself 'O why was I born with a different Face'.[3] Blake may have been thinking about Mary Wollstonecraft at this time because of the abusive reviews that appeared for years following William Godwin's publication of *Memoirs of the author of a Vindication of the Rights of Woman* in 1798.[4] If so, the Mary of *Jerusalem* may be in part a tribute to the woman Blake had known a decade or more before.

The episode in *61* derives from the account in Matthew 1, where Joseph, upon discovering Mary's pregnancy, 'was minded to put her away privily' (19) but is prevented by an angel. Blake may also have had in mind some version of the traditional 'Cherry Tree Ballad', in which Joseph angrily

[1] *61*, which interrupts the dialogue of the Divine Voice and Jerusalem that goes from *60* to *63*, is one of three plates written in a larger, more flowery script than any others in *Jerusalem*. (The others are *30/34* and *56*.) If, as Bentley maintains, 'absence of decoration and lateness are associated with each other' in the plates of *Jerusalem* (*Writings*, I. 728), then *61* is among the later plates. Of course this does not tell us when the poetry was originally written.

[2] See Henry H. Wasser, 'Notes on *The Visions of the Daughters of Albion* by William Blake', *Modern Language Quarterly*, IX (1948), 292–7.

[3] This is also the first line of a poem Blake wrote about himself, included in a letter to Thomas Butts, 16 August 1803, *Letters*, p. 74. For Mary Wollstonecraft as a prototype for 'Mary', see Schorer, *William Blake*, pp. 208–9.

[4] Some of these, as well as equally abusive poems and novels, are discussed by Ralph M. Wardle in *Mary Wollstonecraft: A Critical Biography* (Lincoln, Neb.: University of Nebraska Press, 1972), pp. 316–22, 357.

accuses Mary only to be confronted with a miracle—in this case the bowing of the cherry tree. In Blake's account, however, Mary does not deny her adultery. Instead she regards it as a *felix culpa*:

> . . . if I were pure, never could I taste the sweets
> Of the Forgive[ne]ss of Sins! (11–12)

Persuaded by a voice in his sleep, Joseph voices Blake's conviction that God does not demand Atonement as a debt to be paid, and concludes with an adaptation of Matthew 1: 20: 'Fear not to take / To thee Mary thy Wife, for she is with Child by the Holy Ghost' (26–7). The link between Mary and Jerusalem is made explicit when, after the memorable passage in which Mary flows like a river through Paradise, Blake speaks in his own person:

> And I heard the voice among
> The Reapers Saying, Am I Jerusalem the lost Adultress? or am I
> Babylon come up to Jerusalem? (33–5)

The 'voice' incorporates both Jerusalem and Vala, perceived in their potential unity—the answer to the question is 'Either, or both'. This interpolated plate concludes with Jerusalem receiving the divine child from Mary and then assuming Mary's role at the Crucifixion, hearing the divine voice proclaim the doctrine of Individuals and States: 'Every Harlot was once a Virgin: every Criminal an Infant Love!'

Vala

Jerusalem and her surrogates are not the opposite of Vala, but are located at one end of a spectrum along which Vala is free to move. As we have seen, Jerusalem and Vala were united *in illo tempore*; Brittannia, who comprised that union, will revive in the last pages of the poem; but in the interim the two are divided, and Vala asserts her dominance. Her prototypes are many: the goddess Vala in the Elder Edda,[1] the combined Fates and Norns, Milton's Dalila, and all personifications of Nature as a goddess are among them. Her two

[1] See Frye, *Fearful Symmetry*, p. 270.

surrogates, Tirzah and Rahab, represent respectively the Virgin and the Whore in her nature.[1] Blake would have been reminded of her in reading Swedenborg's account of a visit from a Satan and his Harlot. 'She was', Swedenborg writes, 'of the Tribe of Sirens, who have the Art to assume all Habits and Figures of Beauty and Ornament; at one Time they put on the Beauty of a Venus, at another they adorn themselves with Crowns and Robes like unto those Queens, walking in great State, with Wands of Silver in their Hands.'[2] That Blake was thinking of this figure in *Jerusalem* is suggested by Vala's derisive address to the Spectre Arthur in *64*: 16–17: 'O Woman-born / And Woman-nourishd & Woman-educated & Woman-scorn'd!' Swedenborg's Satan asks, having displayed his harlot: 'Is not the Universe therefore a God, and Nature a Goddess, who like the Wise of the Universe conceiveth, bringeth forth, educateth, and nourisheth her young offspring?'[3] But Swedenborg and Blake believe that mere nature is an unnourishing mother; Vala devotes both her consort and her offspring to torture, destruction, and death.

In addition to being portrayed with Jerusalem, as discussed above, Vala is depicted in the designs on *51* and *53*. In the full-page design *51*[4] she wears the spiked crown of dominion, an emblem which Blake associated with her as early as the *Night Thoughts* illustrations,[5] and she holds a fleur-de-lis sceptre as do the angels in *Europe* 11. Despite these signs of material power—or because of them—she is in an attitude of despair, one huge hand drooping listlessly, the other supporting her down-bent head. A superficially more attractive aspect of Vala is presented by a fairy miming her in *53*. Seated in a sunflower and winged with butterfly wings displaying the earth, moon, and stars, this goddess is so delusively beautiful

[1] Tirzah is the name both of Zelophehad's fifth daughter (on which, see Frye, p. 127) and of the capital of the southern kingdom of Israel, opposed to the northern capital, Jerusalem. Rahab, the harlot of Jericho in Josh. 2, is identified by Blake with the Whore of Babylon.

[2] *True Christian Religion*, pp. 114–15 (no. 80). [3] Ibid.

[4] In the coloured proof copy in the collection of Sir Geoffrey Keynes, this figure is labelled 'Vala'.

[5] Blake seems to have developed the conception of Vala in the course of illustrating *Night Thoughts*: see my 'Blake's *Night Thoughts*: An Exploration of the Fallen World', in *William Blake: Essays for S. Foster Damon*, ed. Alvin Rosenfeld (Providence: Brown University Press, 1969), pp. 142–5.

as once to mislead even Damon, who identified her as 'Beulah, mercifully veiling the Sun of Eternity from our eyes'.[1] But this brooding, despondent figure, wearing a triple crown suggestive of the papal tiara,[2] is surely Vala or a Vala surrogate, as John Beer and others have maintained.[3] Her butterfly-winged throne *blocks* the light of Eternity behind it. Later, Blake combines aspects of both these plates in Dante illustration 99 (National Gallery of Art, Melbourne) showing Mary enthroned in a sunflower and holding a mirror and a fleur-de-lis sceptre. This is of course not Mary as we encountered her in *61*, but the idealized Virgin who, like her companion Beatrice in this design, is a manifestation of Vala.

In the text Vala is given a certain plausibility which makes her more interesting than a personified abstraction could be. She is in many ways a believable character—a beautiful and charming woman, power-driven and deceptive, at times self-deceptive. She has as much affinity with Becky Sharp as with Duessa. Particularly in the earlier parts of the poem, she is allowed to impose on the reader's sympathy. Her first speech strikes a note of pathos that is often characteristic of her, and that marks her first words in the poem:

When winter rends the hungry family and the snow falls:
Upon the ways of men hiding the paths of man and beast,
Then mourns the wanderer: then he repents his wanderings & eyes
The distant forest; then the slave groans in the dungeons of stone. (*20*: 12–15)

The elegiac note, however, is subtly turned to an accusation of Jerusalem as a sinner:

Thou art my sister and my daughter! thy shame is mine also!
Ask me not of my griefs! thou knowest all my griefs. (19–20)

[1] *William Blake*, p. 472. Damon corrects this in *A Blake Dictionary*, p. 300, identifying the figure as Vala.

[2] Blunt suggests a source in Edward Moor's *Hindu Pantheon*; see *The Art of William Blake*, p. 38 and pls. 50 c and 50 d.

[3] See Beer, *Blake's Visionary Universe*, p. 213; also Wicksteed, *Blake's Jerusalem*, p. 207; and Grant, 'Two Flowers', p. 357. Grant identifies her as 'a pernicious threefold Rahab'.

Here we have Vala as an all-too-credibly guilt-inducing mother. Jerusalem, for her part, is only too willing to accept Vala at her own valuation. In reality, Vala is but the Shadow of Jerusalem—'A shadow animated by thy tears O mournful Jerusalem!'[1]—but Jerusalem mistakenly regards her as a sister, addressing her as 'beloved Virgin daughter of Babylon . . . beautiful daughter of Moab' (27–8), and begging her for the mercy and love of which these ironical references to the enemies of Jerusalem show Vala to be incapable.

In Vala's false-elegiac speeches there are two suspect elements. One is her nostalgia: her reference to 'Stringing them [moments] on their remembrance as on a thread of sorrow' (*20*: 18) has at least as much reference to herself as to the imagined captives. The other is analysis. For Vala's second speech (*22*: 1–15) Blake borrowed part of Enion's speech to Tharmas in *The Four Zoas* (1: 17–27), including:

I have looked into the secret Soul of him I loved
And in the dark recesses found Sin & can never return.
(*22*: 14–15)

Thus Vala recapitulates Albion's obsession with finding the sources of sexuality and declaring them sinful. Imagining herself as once the generous creator of a love of which the sinful Albion and Jerusalem were unworthy, she makes her third speech (*29*: 36–*30*/*34*: 1) in the pride of self-idealization. She arrogates to herself the attributes of Jerusalem—'I was a City & a Temple built by Albions Children. / I was a Garden planted with beauty . . .'. She believes that she offered her 'Sacrifice of fanatic love' in vain, and therefore denies all possibility of the realization of love. 'Wherefore did I loving create love, which never yet / Immingled God & Man . . .'. But the answer to her question 'why loved I Jerusalem!' is given by Los in *17*: 24–5: Vala's 'love' masks destructive envy:

Vala would never have sought & loved Albion
If she had not sought to destroy Jerusalem; such is that
false
And Generating Love: a pretence of love to destroy love

The specious self-justification of Vala's early statements, though undermined by interpretive comments by Los and his

[1] So say the children of Los in *11*: 25.

children, is bound to enlist the reader's sympathy to some degree. Like the Satan of the early parts of *Paradise Lost*, Vala is made all the more dangerous by her ability to elicit such a response.

Later in the poem, Vala's true nature is directly stated in her own words. Or it might be truer to say that she resolves her own ambivalence and straightforwardly expresses her domineering possessiveness and her destructive intentions towards Jerusalem. 'Albion is mine!' she cries; Jerusalem is the 'harlot daughter! daughter of despair' who must be cast out for her sins (*45/31*: 50, 58). Now her true intentions toward Jerusalem become apparent, as 'she triumphs in pride of holiness / To see Jerusalem deface her lineaments with bitter blows / Of despair' (*60*: 45–7). As a war goddess, she is invoked by the Spectre Sons of Albion in *65*:

> Lift up thy blue eyes Vala and put on thy sapphire shoes:
> O melancholy Magdalen behold the morning over Malden break;
> Gird on thy flaming zone, descend into the sepulcher of Canterbury.
> Scatter the blood from thy golden brow, the tears from thy silver locks. . . . (37–40)

The true Magdalen is Jerusalem herself (see *62*: 14); Vala is a ghastly parody—a blonde, blue-eyed Snow Queen or Valkyrie. Paul Miner has called attention to the indebtedness of passages such as these to Thomas Gray's *The Fatal Sisters*, one of the poems by Gray illustrated by Blake in 1798, and the notes accompanying it.[1] As her destructiveness becomes more explicit, she is increasingly described in parodic terms:

> Her Hand is a Court of Justice, her Feet: two Armies in Battle
> Storms & Pestilence: in her Locks: & in her Loins Earthquake. (*64*: 9–10)

In the Song of Solomon the beloved is described hyperbolically as 'beautiful . . . as Tirzah, comely as Jerusalem, terrible as an army with banners' (6: 4), but Blake's unvisualizable

[1] See 'William Blake: Two Notes on Sources', *Bulletin of the New York Public Library*, LXII (1958), 203–7.

passage goes beyond hyperbole into travesty. It is an appropriate mode for Vala, who in her most extreme manifestation is Rahab, presented, as we have seen in Chapter I, as a parody of Burkeian Beauty in *70*: 17–31.

The power of Blake's satire in such passages has not been sufficiently appreciated, perhaps because it is connected with a characteristic which critics have been reluctant to accept: Blake's ambivalence about women. Both are correctly yoked by Sloss and Wallis:

> 'The Monstrous Regiment of Women' takes on a new and more devastating meaning as the most perilous antagonism to visionary aspiration. Its symbols betray Blake's dread of the power of sex in life: woman and its embodiment, a spiritually malign influence, perverse and subversive, fascinating but deadly, terrible but lovely. Such criticism shows how inadequately the phrase 'gentle visionary Blake' describes him and how the dubious gain of a mystical gospeller is paid for with the loss of a notable ironist.[1]

Putting aside the sneer at Blake's visionary tendencies, we can see that at times Blake's ranging of female figures along the lines of the Jerusalem-principle and the Vala-principle threatens to become congruent with the old cultural bifurcation mentioned early in this chapter. There is no simple solution to this problem, for Blake is inconsistent about it. Sometimes his motive seems almost like Trollope's in *The Way We Live Now*, where the highly sexualized Mrs Hurtle becomes too interesting and must somehow be alienated from the reader's sympathy so the hero can marry the virtuous, dull heroine. But at its most resolved Blake's vision holds Jerusalem as a positive image of naked beauty and courageous love while Vala is merely negative, spurious good, as in the *46* design.

One further aspect of Vala should be discussed: the Veil, which in *Jerusalem* takes on a life of its own, becoming as it were a figural character. Only an animated cartoon could do full justice to the fluidity it displays. As the Veil which Albion rent in making love to Vala in *20*, it is both the hymeneal membrane and, by analogy, the veil of the Temple as described by Josephus and by interpreters such as Lightfoot:

> It was woven of four colours, blew, purple, scarlet, and fine white linnen yearn, every one of these threads twisted six double and woven

[1] *Prophetic Writings*, I. 441.

upon hair for the warp, of 72 haires twisted into every thred. These two vails rent at our Saviours death from the top to the bottome, (*Matt.* 27.5) and gave demonstration of those Ceremonious things which had hitherto been reserved in such reclusiveness and singularity.[1]

The rending of the veil is, then, an archetypal act of knowing. Like some mesozoic organism, however, the Veil has the power to regenerate itself, and in *21*: 50 we find Vala 'spreading her scarlet Veil over Albion'. This is the blood-red life of the mortal body in which Albion exists imprisoned: 'My soul is melted away, inwoven within the Veil' (*23*: 4). It then becomes a kind of fish-net in which Albion entraps humankind in his system of Law:

> He drew the Veil of Moral Virtue, woven for Cruel Laws,
> And cast it into the Atlantic Deep, to catch the Souls of
> the Dead. (*23*: 22–3)

Here Albion is a parody of Peter, whom Christ made a fisher of men in order to save them, not entrap them. Albion presents the Veil to Jerusalem 'for a Law, a Terror & a Curse!' (32), and then he takes it as his own cerement: 'while in the Veil I fold / My dying limbs' (35–6). Then, at the end of Albion's dying speech in *24*, it becomes a hawser that he cannot control. 'Thundring the Veil rushes from his hand Vegetating Knot by / Knot' (61–2).

It is with such unpromising material as the Veil that Los must work to create a structure for reality, making possible regeneration and redemption. So in *42*: 81 he builds the Mundane Shell, which 'is the Net & Veil of Vala, among the Souls of the Dead'. This may appear at first to be a negative act, but all such acts in *Jerusalem* have a contextual definition. If the Veil is (at least in one of its aspects), as Damon defines it, 'the film of matter which covers all reality',[2] then it is this that Los, that labourer in the rough basement of English, must use as building material. So in *59* the negative Veil imagery of *22–4* is picked up and inverted in value:

> For the Veil of Vala which Albion cast into the Atlantic
> Deep
> To catch the Souls of the Dead: began to Vegetate &
> Petrify

[1] *The Temple*, p. 88. [2] *Blake Dictionary*, p. 432.

Around the Earth of Albion. among the Roots of his Tree
This Los formed into the Gates & mighty Wall, between the Oak
Of Weeping & the Palm of Suffering beneath Albions Tomb.
Thus in process of time it became the beautiful Mundane Shell,
The Habitation of the Spectres of the Dead & the Place
Of Redemption & awaking again into Eternity (2–9)

This transformation of the Veil is another instance of Blake's use of multiple perspectives in *Jerusalem*. Furthermore, by a kind of metonymy the metamorphosis of the Veil suggests the redemption of that part of Vala that can be redeemed: the natural world as re-ordered in our perceptions by the imagination.

Albion

Albion, the Father of us all, is depicted as female in the frontispiece to Michael Drayton's *Poly-Olbion*;[1] she/he later undergoes a sex change and becomes suitor to the river Poole, begetting three children (islands) by her. This is of course only one precedent for Blake's Albion[2]—Milton's *History of Britain* is another, cited by Blake himself[3]—but it is as far as I know the only other explicitly androgynous one; and Blake's Albion, like Drayton's, is a frequenter of rivers.[4] His phallic aggression and its guilt-induced traumatic result have been discussed earlier: through most of *Jerusalem* he is portrayed and described as either falling or fallen, and it is only in the final plates of the work that his regeneration occurs. Like other elements of *Jerusalem*, the myth of Albion has a tripartite structure, but most of it is middle. It 'begins', as we have seen, with a retrospective account *in illo tempore*, 'before' which occurred the anterior myth in which Albion slew Luvah.

[1] London, 1622. With engraved maps and notes by George Selden.

[2] For others, see Frye, *Fearful Symmetry*, pp. 125–7; and Damon, *Blake Dictionary*, p. 9.

[3] In *A Descriptive Catalogue*, E. 534.

[4] *Poly-Olbion*, p. 26.

Self-maimed, he must fall, and it is in his fallen state that we encounter him on the first page of verse, *4*. The nature of his fallen existence is the explicit subject of much of the text from *4* to *57* and of designs interspersed through the first ninety-four plates. A major concern of more than half the work as a whole is, then, Blake's diagnosis of the disease that afflicts Albion. Before being cured the patient indeed grows worse, lapsing into almost total quiescence from plate *58* until his fallen condition is once more described in *94* as a prelude to his rising in *95*. These States, as Blake says, we now explore.

In *The Four Zoas*, the subject of which is announced as Albion's torments, his division is represented by his analysis into his constituent Zoas, each in turn separated from his respective Emanation. There are Zoas in *Jerusalem*, but their effective role is much reduced. The myth of division is transferred to paternity and to geography, Albion's sons and daughters and his regions. When Albion asserts 'My mountains are my own, and I will keep them to myself', he is drawing upon the traditional idea of mountains arising from the imperfections of the world.[1] He is also selective in his claims, for thematic reasons. Of the five mountains or ranges he names, three are associated with borders:[2] the Malvern Hills separate Herefordshire and Worcestershire; the Cheviot is the highest peak in a range between England and Scotland; Plinlimmon is on the border between Cardiganshire and Montgomeryshire in Wales. These, then, are appropriate topographical accomplishments to a myth of division. Snowdon is the highest mountain in either Wales or England as well as being the site of the suicide of the last bard, depicted and described by Blake,[3] and so for two reasons can be associated with a fallen world.[4] The Wolds are no doubt included for their undulating shape, which can be associated with the serpentine temples that Albion participates in building elsewhere.

[1] *4*: 29. See Marjorie Hope Nicholson, *Mountain Gloom and Mountain Glory* (Ithaca, NY: Cornell University Press, 1959).

[2] See Damon, *Blake Dictionary*, pp. 81, 260, 329.

[3] See *Descriptive Catalogue*, E. 532. The tempera is in the Tate Gallery. Blake also executed water-colours for this poem as part of his series of illustrations to the poems of Gray (in the collection of Mr and Mrs Paul Mellon).

[4] Or, conversely, Albion may be trying to possess the home of Blake's last Ancient Britons, who dwell there in 'naked simplicity' (*Descriptive Catalogue*, E. 534).

The two rivers of this discourse, too, are symbolically appropriate. In book IV, canto ix, of *The Faerie Queene*, Spenser celebrates the marriage of the Thames and the Medway; by *hiding* his Emanation upon these 'rivers of Beulah', Albion represses the joyful love that Spenser extols.

Albion's topographic references are apposite. Battersea and Chelsea mourn because they are separated by London's river. The Peak is the highest mountain in England and is also associated with other geological formations in Derbyshire which carry for Blake sinister sexual connotations.[1] There are ancient fortifications on top of the mountains Dhinas-Bran and Pemaenmawr.[2] Maldon is the site of the battle in which Beorhtnoth was killed by Vikings who went on to sack London; Colchester was a fortified town in Celtic, Roman, and Norman times (its river, the Blackwater, may have suggested 'a black water accumulates' in *4*: 10). Manchester and Liverpool are fittingly 'in tortures of Doubt & Despair'— the former because of its new urban squalor and human dislocation, the latter because of its role as the principal port for the slave-trade. Lincoln, Norwich, Edinburgh, and Monmouth are cathedral cities which as such will be among the Friends of Albion who, later in the text, try to save him but fail because of the spiritual weakness of institutional Christianity in Britain. Thus what may at first appear a farrago of place-names is actually carefully chosen to bring out a rich texture of meaning.

In his divided condition, Albion takes on many of the characteristics assigned to Urizen-figures in Blake's earlier works. In the *41/46* designs, as we have seen in Chapter II, he is a white-bearded patriarch seated in his chariot much like the God of the colour-printed drawing *God Judging Adam*. At the beginning of Chapter 2 we find him setting up as 'punisher and judge'. From his seat 'by Tyburns brook', scene of the triple gallows that Blake regards as London's Golgotha, Albion condemns the sinful sources 'Of loves: of unnatural consanguinities and friendships / Horrid to think of when

[1] See Worrall, 'Blake's Derbyshire: a Visionary Locale in *Jerusalem*'.

[2] Damon, *Blake Dictionary*, p. 103. Nelson Hilton suggests that 'Dhinas-bran' may actually refer to Dîn Brëon, which is named in Edward Davies's *Myths and Rites of the British Druids* (London, 1809, p. 6) as 'the Hill of Legislature . . . the sacred mount, where the ancient judges of the land, assembled to decide causes'. Hilton, 'Blake and the Mountains of the Mind', *Blake*, XIV (1981), 199.

enquired deeply into' (*28*: 7–8). He has, as it were, learned the right method from Freud but drawn the wrong conclusions: the roots of 'consanguinities' and friendship are indeed libidinal, but the Sin of which the hills and valleys are 'accursed witnesses' is Albion's own conviction of guilt, derived, as we have seen, from the maiming of self described in the anterior myth. He therefore wills 'That Man be separate from Man' in a state that represents, to use Norman O. Brown's term, 'Universal Otherhood'. There then follows in lines 13–19 of *28* a description of the growth of the Tree of Mystery, recapitulating similar passages in *The Book of Ahania* 3: 61–73 and in *The Four Zoas* (VIIa) 78: 4–12, but with Albion now taking the place of Urizen.

As Urizenic Lawgiver and priest, Albion is in the power of his Spectre. Unlike Los, who resists his own Spectre and finally integrates him with his whole psychic identity, Albion submits to the Spectre's reasoning. At first it may seem inappropriate that Albion, the practitioner of an irrational religion of human sacrifice, should be dominated by a Spectre who calls himself 'your Rational Power'; what interests Blake, however, is not the content of belief but its form, uniting what he sees as authoritarian religion with an equally authoritarian rationalism. 'Many are Deists', he writes in *A Vision of the Last Judgment*, 'who would in certain Circumstances have been Christians in outward appearance Voltaire was one of this number he was as intolerant as an Inquisitor.' (E. 553.)

Albion's is a learned Spectre, combining philosophical jargon with biblical references. Man is a 'Worm' as in Job 17: 14. He lives 'In fortuitous concourses of memorys accumulated & lost'—a view which the Cambridge Platonists accused the empiricists of holding.[1] The human worm is stopped by 'A stone of the brook' as David killed Goliath;[2] it 'creeps forth in a night & is dried in the morning sun' like Jonah's gourd.[3] All that is left in the end is 'my deluge of forgotten remembrances over the tablet'—Locke's *tabula rasa*. Armed with this parody of a rationalist world-view, Albion's Spectre challenges Christ in *54*, demanding in the tone of a bar-room bully: 'Where is that Friend of Sinners! that Rebel against my

[1] See *Energy and the Imagination*, p. 254.
[2] 1 Sam. 17: 40. [3] See Stevenson, p. 683.

Laws! / . . . Come hither into the Desart & turn these stones to bread' (19, 21). He is now the tempter who speaks in Matthew 4: 3 and who is pictured as a Urizenic old man in Blake's *Paradise Regained* illustration 'The First Temptation' (Fitzwilliam Museum). Christ's reply in Matthew 4: 4—'It is written, Man shall not live by bread alone, but by every word that proceedeth out of the mouth of God'—would have no meaning for the Spectre, who can conceive of such belief in the Word only as belief 'in a World of Phantasy upon my Great Abyss!' Like some extremely literal-minded Freudians, he conceives the constructions of the Imagination to be merely wish-fulfilment fantasy: 'A World of Shapes in craving lust & devouring appetite'. On the political level, this view is encapsulated in the literalization of the Arthurian mythos into a nationalistic legend, and therefore 'the hard constrictive Spectre . . . is namd Arthur'. In this Spectre's power, Albion falls further down, 'Into his own Chaos which is the Memory between Man & Man' (*54*: 8) and which is therefore a parody of true community, 'The Mystic Union of the Emanation in the Lord' (*53*: 24).

Albion's fall, precipitated by his sexual guilt, also has further sexual consequences. Ignoring Jerusalem's pleas in *19*, *22*, and *23*, Albion rejects her love and turns instead to Vala. The *47* design is a sort of caricature of the Choice of Hercules *topos*, in which Albion-Hercules chooses the easier, sinister way. Guilt-stricken by his murder of Luvah, he sees his own repressed sexuality return in constricted form—'I behold him in my Spectre' (*22*: 31)—and he calls upon Vala to come 'with knife & cup: drain my blood / To the last drop!' (29–30.) Thus his maimed sexuality makes Albion a willing candidate for the Romantic Agony, graphically depicted in the human sacrifices of *25* and *69* (where two Daughters, holding knives and a cup, dance round Albion/Luvah). As in the earlier sexual myth, there seems to be a strong personal element for Blake here as well. When Albion looks up from his 'furrowd field' in *29/33*, like Blake looking up from his contoured and inscribed copperplate, he beholds 'darkness immingled with light'. In other words, he sees chiaroscuro, which Blake condemned but was at times attracted by. And like Blake tempted by the spirit of Titian, Albion is seduced by the 'colours of autumn ripeness' of his emanation—now, in the fallen world, Vala instead of Jerusalem, whom Vala parodies by saying 'I was a City & a Temple built by Albions Children' (*29/33*: 36). Taken in by Vala's spurious claim to be 'Love / Elevate[d] into the Region of Brotherhood with my red fires' (*29/33*: 52–*30/34*: 1), Albion has a wet dream in which 'my members pour down milky fear!' As his sexuality becomes localized in a 'dewy garment', he becomes further removed from libidinal freedom. Blake's ambivalence about genital sexuality, sometimes manifest in his earlier works, is most deeply expressed in this aspect of the myth of Albion.

The structure that Los calls 'Sexual Organization' (*30/34*: 58) comprises the division of androgynous humankind into two sexes, the limitation of direct sensuous experience to one of the fallen Zoas (Tharmas), and the concentration of sexual pleasure in the genital organs. It is the third of these limitations that afflicts Albion in relation to Vala, 'a political arrangement', as Norman O. Brown calls it, 'arrived at after stormy upheavals in the house of Oedipus'.[1] Albion himself is dimly aware of this tyranny of delegation, exclaiming 'O Vala / In Eternity they neither marry nor are given in marriage' (*30*: 14–15).[2] Elsewhere in *Jerusalem* a doctrine of polymorphous perversity is stated further. 'Man in the Resurrection changes his Sexual Garments at will' (*61*: 51); 'Embraces are Cominglings: from the Head even to the Feet; / And not a pompous High Priest entering by a Secret Place' (*69*: 43–4). Just as the delegated religious representative enters the Holy of Holies in the Temple, so the phallus makes its way,[3] but at the cost of the full participation of the body. Even orgasm, which Blake had once viewed as a passage to Eternity,[4] is now seen as a fallen form:

> In Beulah the Female lets down her beautiful Tabernacle;
> Which the Male enters magnificent between her Cherubim:

[1] *Love's Body*, p. 127.

[2] The reference is of course to Matt. 22: 30.

[3] On this powerful analogy in Blake's works, see Paul Miner, 'William Blake's Divine Analogy', *Criticism*, III (1961), 46–61.

[4] In *Europe* iii: 5[3: 5 in Bentley's pagination], the Fairy says that through one of his five windows (= senses) man can 'himself pass out what time he please' (E. 59).

And becomes One with her mingling condensing in Self-love
The Rocky Law of Condemnation & double Generation, & Death. (*44/30*: 34–7)

'The Law' is the object of the participle 'condensing': like 'the young / In one another's arms', of Yeats's 'Sailing to Byzantium', the Male and Female loves here produce only dying generations. As lover, Albion is enslaved by his sexuality; as father, he contributes to the cycle in which his own sons and daughters must seek to destroy him. Thus 'Albion hath enterd the Loins the place of the Last Judgment' (*44/30*: 38).

Albion's fallen state is described and pictured at various points in the work. In *19* it is the subject of both text and design, the former being largely a beautiful passage reworked from Night IX of *The Four Zoas*.[1] The passage is marked by a rhetoric of inversion, in which all things either do the opposite of what they should do and/or are contrasted with their contrary aspect in an earlier, better state. Children are exiled, birds silent, flocks die, tents are fall'n, trumpets and harp silent. Crops are gathered in heat and rain, turning to thistles and poison. He once sat; he now walks. Songbirds become crows. Children's voices are now 'the cries of helpless infants'. 'Self-exiled' and separated from his Eon or Emanation, he wanders up and down in a world which has become 'a narrow house'—England, the narrow land. The design at the bottom of the page shows his fallen form, mourned by four of his Lilliputian children, three others of whom have been crushed by his falling body. This scene of deep pathos may be contrasted in some ways with the design in *9*, which has more sinister overtones concerning both Albion and his children. Here Albion lies on his back, head foremost, in what is at the same time an imitation and a parody of certain Renaissance perspectival effects, as that in Uccello's *Rout of San Romano* (National Gallery, London). It is a parody because Blake gives the foreshortening without perspective; there is no vanishing point. Albion's head is significantly below his loins, indicating the kind of subservience of Imagination and Reason to sexual passion which characterizes fallen man. The

[1] See Chapter I.

huge stars at his feet are emblems of fallen reason.[1] He is surrounded by five females, weeping, mourning worshippers, who may be identified with Zelophehad's daughters. These five women, by petitioning to receive an inheritance without having a male head of household, revealed their unconscious murder of their fathers.[2] (Blake sees a similarly sinister message in the 'Three Women around / The Cross' of *56*: 42–3.) Thus Albion's daughters are here seen as his murderers. (His open eyes don't *necessarily* signify that he is alive,[3] but his status is indeed dubious, as he remains in a state of Life-in-Death until plate *95*.)[4]

The horizontal Albion—and it is worth remarking that Los, no matter how severe his trials, remains vertical—is afflicted by disease, a thematic image which Blake had used as such as early as *An Island in the Moon*,[5] and one which appears with prophetic force in *America* and in the *Job* designs. He is a Job who needs no external Satan to smite him with sore boils, for he says 'The disease of Shame covers me from head to feet: I have no hope / Every boil upon my body is a separate & deadly Sin' (*21*: 3–4). He is also an Everyman who asks with genuine pathos: 'Will none accompany me in my death? or be a Ransom for me / In that dark Valley?' In the lines following this question, Albion alludes to the way in which the Jews were instructed to flee from Egypt after God's smiting of the firstborn. According to Exodus 12: 11, 'And thus ye shall eat it; *with* your loins girded, your shoes on your feet, and your staff in your hand . . .'. But Blake revises the biblical passage to bring out intimations of mortality: 'I have girded round my cloke, and on my feet / Bound these black shoes of death, & on my hands, deaths

[1] See Damon, *William Blake*, p. 469.

[2] On this Old Testament episode, see Frye, *Fearful Symmetry*, p. 127.

[3] See Erdman, *Ill. Bl.*, p. 288.

[4] The interlinear designs are not irrelevant to Albion's condition in the larger, lower design. As Damon points out, the progression goes from Innocence (the Shepherd piping to his flock) to the Fall (Eve taking the apple from the serpent's mouth while Adam-Albion sleeps) to Experience at the bottom. The middle design has caused some difficulty because the object in Eve's right hand is more egg-shaped than round and is also too large to be 'Eve's sweet pippin' (as Keats calls it). However, there is nothing to indicate that Blake took the modern apple to be the fruit of the Tree, and in his tempera of Milton (Manchester, City Art Gallery) in the *Heads of the Poets* series the fruit is in colour and shape like a lime.

[5] See E. 445–6, 453.

iron gloves.' Albion is also a parody of St. Paul's Christian warrior, wearing not 'the whole armour of God'[1] but 'petrified surfaces' (*46/32*: 5), life-denying armouring that stifles his own spontaneity and Joy:

> revengeful covering
> His face and bosom with petrific hardness, and his hands
> And feet, lest any should enter his bosom & embrace
> His hidden heart . . . (*33/37*: 12–*34/38*: 3)

The 'blue death' that Los sees in Albion's feet[2] identifies him as both practitioner and victim of Druidic human sacrifice, alluding to the woad, the 'poisonous blue'[3] with which the sacrificed Luvah is stained in *65*: 9. These diverse images of death combine to form a composite reminiscent of London in Defoe's *A Journal of the Plague Year*, a book which Blake seems to have had in mind in some of his earlier renditions of such subjects.[4] But Albion's disease, which 'Arose upon him pale and ghastly' (*36/40*: 2) is self-inflicted and is correctly diagnosed by Los as 'the infection of Sin & stern Repentance' (*38/43*: 75).

In Albion's extremity, his Friends try to save him. Their attempt occupies a group of seven plates in Chapter 2 from *36/40* to *42*. The Friends are the twenty-eight cathedral cities of England, sometimes represented by four of their number: Verulam, Canterbury, York, and Edinburgh. Edinburgh was not a cathedral city in fact, but, as Stevenson observes, Blake needed a full complement of twenty-eight for symbolic purposes.[5] The particular choice of Edinburgh, however, no doubt lies in Blake's sympathy for the Scottish radicals convicted during the years that *Jerusalem* was being written;[6] thus

> Edinburgh, cloth'd
> With fortitude as with a garment of immortal texture

[1] Eph. 6: 11.

[2] In copy A, the reading was emended to 'pale death', which is also the original reading in the unique Keynes proof. See Erdman, 'Suppressed and Altered Passages', pp. 23–4.

[3] See Damon, *William Blake*, p. 459.

[4] In addition to the full-page 'Plague' design for *Europe*, Blake executed five pictures on the subject of the Plague of London; see Butlin (*William Blake*, 1978), pp. 37–8.

[5] Stevenson, p. 696.

[6] See Erdman, *Blake: Prophet*, p. 476.

Woven in looms of Eden, in spiritual deaths of mighty
men
Who give themselves, in Golgotha, Victims to Justice . . .
(*34/38*: 51–4)

Others of the twenty-eight have particular associations for Blake. Chichester is the cathedral Blake would have seen frequently during his three years' slumber on the banks of Ocean in Sussex; his tribute to it encompasses the symbolism of the former see's, Selsey, being under water in Blake's time[1]—a fact taken by Blake as an image of self-sacrifice:

Selsey, true friend! who afterwards submitted to be
devourd
By the waves of Despair, whose Emanation rose above
The flood, and was nam'd Chichester, lovely mild &
gentle! Lo!
Her lambs bleat to the sea-fowls cry, lamenting still for
Albion. (*36/40*: 48–51)

Bath in its positive aspect is probably associated with the Revd. Richard Warner of Bath, author of anti-war sermons and tracts such as *War Inconsistent with Christianity* (1804) and *A Letter to the People of England on Petitioning the Throne for Peace* (1808).[2] Oxford, represented by its Bard, is associated with Edward Garrard Marsh, whom Blake met through William Hayley and about whom he wrote to Hayley on 27 January 1804, referring to him as 'Edward the Bard of Oxford'.[3] Another contemporary is associated with *41/46*: 3–4:

Hereford, ancient Guardian of Wales, whose hands
Builded the mountain palaces of Eden, stupendous works!

This is undoubtedly a tribute to Thomas Johnes of Hafod,[4] who grew up in Hereford, and later moved to his father's

[1] See Damon, *William Blake*, p. 48.

[2] As suggested by Martin K. Nurmi; see Erdman, *Blake: Prophet*, p. 476.

[3] *Letters*, p. 87. On Marsh, see Gilchrist, *Life*, p. 177; and Bishop, *Blake's Hayley*, pp. 290–1.

[4] On whom see my article, based on a suggestion from Ruthven Todd, 'Thomas Johnes, "Ancient Guardian of Wales" ', *Blake*, II (1968), 65–7; and Ruthven Todd, 'The Identity of "Hereford" in *Jerusalem*', *Blake Studies*, VI (1975), 139–52.

region of origin—Cardiganshire, Wales, where he built a famous 'Elysium' at Hafod.[1] According to his obituary in the *Gentleman's Magazine*, 'he employed the population in planting millions of forest trees upon the barrenness of the waste and mountains . . . and instituted schools, which he and Mrs. Johnes personally attended';[2] he also introduced a new, improved plough; and in his library was a copy of *Songs of Innocence* given him by Henry Fuseli. Men like Warner and Johnes must have seemed to Blake true friends of Albion who deserved to be immortalized for keeping the Divine Vision.

The attempt of the Friends to save Albion is carried on chiefly through Bath and Oxford. Bath, whose presentation would have originally been highly positive, becomes an ambivalent figure with the introduction of plates *37/41, 38/43*, and *39/44*.[3] Plate *36/40* ended 'benevolent Bath', but the interpolated *37/41* begins:

> Bath who is Legions: he is the Seventh, the physician and
> The poisoner: the best and worst in Heaven and Hell

Legions is of course the name of a demon cast out by Christ; it is also the name of the Roman military camp at Caerlon[4] and is evidently referred to as such in *Milton* 39: 35, where Legions is one of the four pillars of Albion's throne (E. 139). So the connotations of the first words of *40/45*, 'Bath, healing City!' which was inserted before *37/41*, are deliberately qualified. Bath's new ambivalence no doubt derives from his expanded role as a symbol. Now we are to think not only of Bath's healing waters but also of its status as a spa, a place of social ostentation and fortune-hunting as pictured in

[1] The term is applied by Blake and Johnes's mutual friend, George Cumberland, who also described Hafod by quoting from Milton's description of Eden (*An Attempt to Describe Hafod*, London, 1796). Benjamin Heath Malkin's introductory letter to *A Father's Memoirs of His Child* (London, 1806), with its now famous section on Blake, is addressed to Johnes.

[2] Vol. LXXVI, pt. 1 (1816), 563–4.

[3] Textual evidence suggests that the original sequence was *36–41*, with *40* inserted next, then *37, 38,* and *39*. See Erdman, 'The Suppressed and Altered Passages', pp. 24–5.

[4] See Damon, *Blake Dictionary*, p. 237. According to Ostriker, p. 1009, in Geoffrey of Monmouth's *History*, Merlin prophesies that Bath's healing waters will 'bring forth death'.

eighteenth- and nineteenth-century novels. (And for a comic aspect of Bath as poisoner, we may think of Smollett's Matt Bramble fainting from the Pump Room's fetid air in *Humphry Clinker.*) The amplification is evidently one of Experience supplanting Innocence, of the originally benevolent qualities of Bath being negated but not destroyed by its role in English society. So qualified, no wonder Bath's voice is 'faint as the voice of the Dead in the House of Death' (*39/44*: 44), and that his plea to Albion in *40/45* goes unheeded. For a moment, Bath takes comfort in the unchaining of Africa[1]—the slave-trade was abolished, at least in British ships, in 1807—but then he realizes that 'Albions sleep is not / Like Africa's: and his machines are woven with his life.' These 'mind-forgd manacles' grow too deep for external solutions to remove them.

Bath's attempt to get Albion to listen to Oxford's reading of 'leaves from the Tree of Life' is no more successful. According to Revelation 22: 2, these leaves, which are from the Tree in the midst of the streets of the New Jerusalem, are 'for the healing of nations'; their delivery by Oxford may refer to some now unknown verse setting by Edward Garrard Marsh of sentiments in writings by Richard Warner.[2] Oxford's weak speech has no effect except to cause him to faint, and the Friends' effort is foredoomed by the fact that they have 'caught the infection of Sin & stern Repentance' (*38/43*: 75). Although England can afford examples of heroic men and true altruism, its Christian institutions are, by and large, infected with the same sexual guilt that caused Albion's fall. And so the Friends not only fall—they are subverted. 'Strucken with Albions disease they become what they

[1] The fact that it was Africa himself who attached the chains has caused unnecessary puzzlement. Blake must have known that both slavery and the slave-trade existed in Africa before the coming of Europeans and continued to involve African slave-traders afterward. The anti-slavery writings of Charles Bernhard Wadström, whom Blake would have met at the Swedenborgian General Conference of 1789, give a detailed account of this (' "A New Heaven is Begun" ', pp. 84–5).

[2] According to Stevenson (p. 707), no poetry by Marsh is known. Marsh did edit a collection of hymns in 1837, but none of these express sentiments equatable with Bath's, nor do they seem otherwise capable of saving Albion. Yet Blake refers to 'Edward the Bard of Oxford whose verses still sound upon my Ear like the distant approach of things mighty & magnificent' (*Letters*, p. 87).

behold' (*39/44*: 32). They are like Coleridge snapping his squeaking baby-trumpet of sedition in 1798—a year in which Blake knew that a true defence of the Bible would cost a man his life.[1] As 'rebellious ingratitudes' they are seized by Albion's terrible sons Hand and Hyle (*42*: 48). They are divided so that as Spectres 'they curse their human kindness & affection . . . they repent of their human kindness' (*42*: 60, 62). Yet they retain 'human majestic forms' and so are capable of knowing how bad things are. They are Blake's portrait of men of good will who, deeply compromised in their own societal relations, are unable to act.

> They enquire after Jerusalem in the regions of the dead,
> With the voices of dead men, low, scarcely articulate,
> And with tears cold on their cheeks they weary repose.
> (*42*: 68–70)

They presumably remain in this state until after Albion awakens, when 'he Clothed himself in Bow & Arrows in awful state Fourfold / In the midst of his Twenty-eight Cities . . .' (*97*: 16–17).

Albion's 'death' and immolation is the subject of *47–50*, which occupy the same place in both sequences of plates in Chapter 2. He previously spoke his last words, 'relapsing' in the most literal sense, in *23*: 29–40, a speech which has aptly been compared to Satan's on Mount Niphrates.[2] Now his 'last words' are distilled into a short sentence which recalls both the last words of Christ and the inscription over the gate in the *Inferno*: 'Hope is banish'd from me' (*47*: 18[3]). After this terrible expression of despair, Albion collapses into the arms of the Saviour in the text of *48* as he does in the top design of *33/37*, where he falls backwards into the arms of the kneeling Christ, whose radiance is wonderfully conveyed in white-line engraving. Albion's right foot touches a winged disc, a symbol of eternity going back to ancient Sumerian cylinder seals. Between the palm and the oak, his situation is that described still earlier in the text:

[1] See Annotations to Bishop R. Watson's *Apology for the Bible*, E. 601.

[2] *Paradise Lost*, IV, 32–113; see Ostriker, *Complete Poems*, p. 1005.

[3] Blake originally etched this as line 1 but deleted the line. Damon (*William Blake*, p. 454) makes the comparison with Dante.

He stood between the Palm tree & the Oak of weeping
Which stand upon the edge of Beulah; and there Albion sunk
Down in sick pallid languour! (*23*: 24–6)

Thus by a series of recessions as it were, we are led back from *47–8* to *33/37* to *23*. *24*: 59–60 directs us forward to *47* again,

Look not so merciful upon me O thou Slain Lamb of God
I die! I die in thy arms tho Hope is banishd from me.

The first of these lines is an adaptation from the last speech of Dr Faustus: 'My God, my God look not so fierce on me.'[1] That Albion should dread God's mercy rather than his wrath is of course a characteristic Blakean irony. The utterance of Albion's last words and their repetition in *47* give something of the effect of the operatic hero who takes a very long time to die, but it also emphasizes the Life-in-Death state that is Albion's. At the same time, the reiterated presence of Christ delimits Albion's fall. This limitation eventually takes the form of the Tomb which the Divine Lord builds for Albion in *48*.

The building of Albion's tomb is of the greatest importance for the rest of the work.

In silence the Divine Lord builded with immortal labour,
Of gold & jewels a sublime Ornament, a Couch of repose,
With Sixteen pillars: canopied with emblems & written verse.
Spiritual Verse, order'd & measur'd, from whence, time shall reveal.
The Five books of the Decalogue, the books of Joshua & Judges,
Samuel, a double book & Kings, a double book, the Psalms & Prophets
The Four-fold Gospel, and the Revelations everlasting
(*48*: 5–11)

These sixteen 'books'—actually the list comprises twenty-seven books of the Old Testament and five of the New

[1] *The Works of Christopher Marlowe*, ed. C. F. Tucker Brooke (Oxford: The Clarendon Press, 1910), p. 194.

Testament—are precisely those which Emanuel Swedenborg says in *Arcana Coelestia* X. 325 have the internal sense of the Word.[1] Blake's construction of Albion's tomb with these sixteen pillars is one of several indications of Blake's reawakened interest in Swedenborg during the period in which *Jerusalem* was being written. This tomb composed of the true, symbolic meaning of the Bible will protect Albion's body of error until the time comes for him to arise. He is therefore appropriately a Lazarus figure. 'O Lord!', says Erin, 'If thou hadst been here, our brother Albion had not died' (*50*: 10–11), echoing the words of Martha to Jesus (John 11: 21).

Albion is pictured in his tomb in *14*, where he appears as a Flaxmanesque tomb effigy, or the caricature of one, with equally Flaxmanesque angels at his head and feet, reminding us of 'William Bond'. Sullen in expression, he peers in some copies (A, C, and D) through his own shut eyelids at the potentially redemptive figure of Erin, hovering above him on moth wings. That this is Erin is confirmed by the arched rainbow above her, for 'Erins lovely Bow' (*50*: 22) is a symbol of the Covenant of Hope, and Erin is closely associated with Albion's tomb in *48–50*. Described as 'Perusing Albions Tomb' (*48*: 41), she is in effect reading its canopy of 'emblems & written verse' in its internal sense. In *49*: 54–5, she defines its meaning, saying that Jehovah 'has builded the arches of Albions Tomb binding the Stars / In merciful Order, bending the Laws of Cruelty to Peace'. In other words, God has made it possible for the Law to be read as what Blake would call Allegory addressed to the Intellectual Powers. Such a reading would unravel the 'Druid' literalism by which, for example, the sacrifice of Self was misapplied to the blood sacrifice of victims; it would restore the original intellectual pleasures of War and Hunting. When Albion awakens, the true text will be there for him to read, for, like Ololon's Garment at the end of *Milton*, 'the Writing / Is the Divine Revelation in the Litteral expression' (*Milton*, 42: 13–14).

In *57*: 12–16, after succumbing to his Spectre in *54*, Albion

[1] As pointed out by Damon, *William Blake*, p. 454. G. E. Bentley, Jr. notes that the first General Conference reaffirmed belief in this among other Swedenborgian doctrines. ('Blake and Swedenborg', *Notes and Queries*, NS I (1954), 264–5.)

falls into the Furrow and is ploughed in among the dead by the Plow of Nations drawn by his own maddened Zoas. Thus he becomes raw material for resurrection, though this process will not begin until *95*. From *58* until *94*, a sequence comprising more than a third of *Jerusalem*, Albion is quiescent. He says and does nothing in these thirty-five plates, though we are reminded from time to time of his passive existence. His Tree, which grew about him like a labyrinth in *29*, is in *66*: 49–55 identified with the Polypus, that symbol of cancerously proliferating Selfhood. Jerusalem speaks of him in *79*: 17, punning once more on the etymology of England: 'And Albion is himself shrunk to a narrow rock in the midst of the sea!' He is pictured at the bottom of *67* as a human link in a great chain.

In *91*[1] we see him still supine but feet first as in *14*. From him fibres emanate to form two globes, one containing a Star of David (Jehovah) and the other an ear of wheat. These are the twin dispensations of Jehovah and Jesus, still seen as separate dispensations by fallen man, but perceived as united, as 'the Mutual Covenant Divine' (*98*: 41) in the Resurrection. Such occasional verbal and visual references as these only serve to reinforce our sense of Albion's palpable absence. This sense of voidness creates, as it were, a negative momentum, making us all the more expectant of Albion's revival in the last few plates of the work.

Sons and Daughters

The 'death' of Albion is abetted by the activities of his Spectre Sons and terrible Daughters, who visit upon him a literal return of the repressed, emerging from him in order to attack and destroy him. Along with their more general meanings as accusers, judges, and executioners, the Sons reflect Blake's none-too-tranquil recollection of his emotion upon being indicted and tried for sedition in 1803–4.[2] There is thus a personal edge to Blake's portrayal of the Sons, whose hostility

[1] Stevenson (p. 829) seems alone in interpreting this figure as female.

[2] On their specific identities, see Erdman, *Blake: Prophet*, pp. 458–9; Keynes, 'Blake's Trial At Chichester', *Blake Studies*, pp. 113–14; Damon, *Blake Dictionary*, pp. 15–16.

he counters with the aggressive activity of Los, his own Prophetic wrath. At the same time the Sons are an analysis of Albion himself, as was recognized as early as the Ellis–Yeats commentary, where the Sons are called 'his various misguided reasonings and moralities'.[1] They are of course much more than this, but this insight leaves room for their other meanings as projections of Albion's repressed feelings, perhaps most notably of his sadism masquerading as a zeal for Justice. Along with their personal, social, and psychological meanings, the Sons are part of a structure of myth which is best described in terms of Freud's Primal Father and Band of Brothers, a myth which governs the relations of Albion and his sons in various parts of *Jerusalem*.

> All his Affections now appear withoutside: all his Sons,
> Hand, Hyle & Coban, Guantok, Peachey, Brereton, Slayd & Hutton,
> Scofeld, Kox, Kotope & Bowen; his Twelve Sons: Satanic Mill! (*19*: 17–19)

Thus hypostatized, the Sons assume a life of their own and war against their progenitor. In *28* the guilt-obsessed Albion turns his hatred outwards to his own children, thereby initiating a cycle of victim and executioner in which he will soon move from the latter role to the former.

> From willing sacrifice of Self, to sacrifice of (miscall'd) Enemies
> For Atonement: Albion began to erect twelve Altars,
> Of rough unhewn rocks, before the Potters Furnace
> He nam'd them Justice, and Truth. And Albions Sons
> Must have become the first Victims, being the first transgressors
> But they fled to the mountains to seek ransom: building A Strong
> Fortification against the Divine Humanity and Mercy,
> In Shame & Jealousy to annihilate Jerusalem! (20–7)

Here Albion combines attributes of the patriarch Jacob and of Joshua, who 'built . . . an altar of whole stones. . . . And . . . wrote upon the stones a copy of the law of Moses . . . in

[1] *Works*, III. 182.

the presence of the children of Israel.'[1] This part of *Jerusalem* is in effect Blake's version of the story of Jacob and his twelve sons in the light of his reading of Hesiod and (probably) Sophocles. Blake was probably familiar with Hesiod's *Theogony* long before he began to engrave illustrations after Flaxman for it in 1814;[2] there he would have found the myth of how Zeus and his siblings escaped the murderous intentions of their father and then castrated him. Blake was interested in the conflict of father and sons from his early works on, as evidenced by the curse of the aged tyrant upon his sons in *Tiriel* and by the emblem entitled 'My Son! my Son!' in *The Gates of Paradise*, showing a youth with a spear attacking an old man. *The Book of Ahania* (1794) is a syncretic myth of father-son conflict.[3] In *Jerusalem*, 'The silent broodings of deadly revenge' that Albion bears toward his children spring from 'all powerful parental affection'—the Greek *storge*, to which Blake refers in describing the Oedipal situation of Los and Orc in *The Four Zoas*: 'Concenterd into Love of Parent Storgous Appetite Craving' (61: 10, E. 334).

In the war between patriarchy and fraternity, the band of brothers typically wins: republic succeeds monarchy, bureaucrat displaces robber baron. So in *46/32* Albion falls before his terrible Sons:

> In stern defiance came from Albions bosom Hand, Hyle, Koban,
> Gwantok, Peachy, Brertun, Slaid, Huttn, Skofeld, Kock, Kotope
> Bowen: Albions Sons: they bore him a golden couch into the porch
> And on the Couch reposd his limbs, trembling from the bloody field.
> Rearing their Druid Patriarchal rocky Temples around his limbs. (10–15)

[1] Joshua 8: 30–2, as noted by Stevenson, p. 681.

[2] A connection between Hesiod and the Tharmas-Enion myth of *The Four Zoas* is suggested by Frye, *Fearful Symmetry*, p. 284. On Blake's engravings for Flaxman's *Compositions from the Works and Days and the Theogony of Hesiod* (1817), see G. E. Bentley, Jr., *The Early Engravings of Flaxman's Classical Designs* (New York: New York Public Library, 1964), pp. 43–56; and *Blake Books*, 556–60.

[3] See *Energy and the Imagination*, pp. 81–6.

This is progress only in a negative or ironical sense. As Norman O. Brown remarks, in a passage that could serve as a gloss on the one above:

> It is the erotic sense of reality that discovers the inadequacy of fraternity, or brotherhood. It is not adequate as a form for the reunification of the human race: we must be either far more deeply unified, or not at all. The true form of unification—which can be found either in psychoanalysis or in Christianity, in Freud or Pope John or Karl Marx—is: we are all members of one body.[1]

That is of course the form of unification in *Jerusalem* as well, but first Albion must sleep, threatened by the power of the Giant Sons.

Two symbols are closely associated with Albion's Sons in their collective activity: the Polypus and the Wheel. The polypus is appropriate for obvious reasons, combining the images of a sea-creature, a network of associated beings, and a cancerous growth. In the first of these, referring to the freshwater hydra discovered by Linnaeus and described by Erasmus Darwin, we have what Karl Kroeber aptly calls 'Blake's understanding of the fallen natural world, a condition of endless multiplication through division'.[2]

> And Hand & Hyle rooted into Jerusalem by a fibre
> Of strong revenge & Skofeld Vegetated by Reubens Gate
> In every Nation of the Earth till the Twelve Sons of
>   Albion
> Enrooted into every Nation: a mighty Polypus growing
> From Albion over the whole Earth: such is my awful
>   Vision. (*15*: 1–5)

Like those science-fiction films which enlarge a lizard to a dinosaur, Blake makes this creature a monster with its head in Verulam (because of its association with Francis Bacon), its body in five Cathedral Cities, and its Fibres extending over the whole earth to Japan (*67*: 35–40). As a colonial organism, it parodies the brotherhood in which 'Man is adjoind to

[1] *Love's Body* (New York: Random House, 1966), p. 82.

[2] 'Delivering Jerusalem', in *Blake's Sublime Allegory*, ed. Curran and Wittreich, p. 360. Kroeber cites Darwin's *The Botanic Garden*, Part II ('The Loves of the Plants'), 4th edn. (London, 1799), II. 37. See also Damon, *Blake Dictionary*, pp. 332–3.

Man by his Emanative portion' (*39/44*: 38), for 'By Invisible Hatreds adjoind, they seem remote and separate / From each other; and yet are a Mighty Polypus in the Deep!' (*66*: 53–4.) It is also a 'ravening eating Cancer' into which all the males combine in *69*: 1–3, 'A Polypus of Roots of Reasoning Doubt Despair & Death'. As is frequently the case with Blake's multiple images, it is hard to keep these three aspects separate in our minds; what is important is their contiguity as representations of an antagonistic world formed by a pseudo-community of Selfhoods.

The Wheels of Albion's Sons are monstrous gear wheels which parody the visionary wheels of Ezekiel. Going in their same dull round, these wheels attempt to reduce everything to the Sons' will. They attack the primal father, separating him from his masculinity: 'Hoarse turn'd the Starry Wheels, rending a way in Albions Loins' (*18*: 44). Hyle attempts 'to draw Jerusalems Sons / Into the Vortex of his Wheels' (*74*: 29–30), and Jerusalem, at the Mills in the Dungeons of Babylon, succumbs for a time: 'Her reason grows like / The Wheel of Hand. incessant turning day & night without rest' (*60*: 42–3). These same wheels drive the Spectre of Los to separate from him (*6*: 1–2). The space of these Wheels is Ulro (*12*: 51), the hell formed by the illusion that the generated world alone is real. Although the Sons would extend their power, they are prevented from doing so by the redemptive activity of Erin:

> . . . all the Sons of Albion appeard distant stars,
> Ascending and descending into Albions sea of death.
> And Erins lovely Bow enclos'd the Wheels of Albions
> Sons. (*50*: 20–2)

As a kind of homeopathic magic, the ornaments of the Eastern Gate of Golgonooza are described as

> Taking their forms from the Wheels of Albions sons; as
> cogs
> Are formd in a wheel, to fit the cogs of the adverse wheel.
> (*13*: 13–14)

Thus Golgonooza is able to withstand the attack of Albion's Sons 'before the eastern gate bending their fury' (*5*: 28), and in general the Starry Wheels are contained until the end of Time, when

> The Breath Divine Breathed over Albion
> Beneath the Furnaces & starry Wheels and in the Immortal Tomb (*94*: 18–19)

The Wheels are one aspect of the furious activity of the Sons, who in general are the most active negative elements in *Jerusalem* as Los is the most active positive element. Affirming the doctrine of Atonement as a blood payment for Sin, they proclaim:

> That the Perfect,
> May live in glory, redeem'd by Sacrifice of the Lamb
> And of his children, before sinful Jerusalem.
> (*18*: 26–8)

They themselves are of course the Calvinist Perfect, the Elect of *Milton*, and for them to enjoy their perfection Jerusalem must be cast into the Potter's field, her children sacrificed, and her parents enslaved. Thus the captivity and dispersion of the Hebrews becomes another metaphor of repression for Blake. Unable to destroy either Jerusalem or their father, the Sons participate in the sacrifice of Albion's tormented sexuality, Luvah (*65–6*), and for this religious purpose they build 'a stupendous Building on the Plain of Salisbury' (*66*: 2)—Stonehenge.[1] As soldiers of all wars from the Old Testament to the crusade against Napoleon, they address a chorale to Vala in *68*: 29–55. Blake understands the source of their destructiveness to be 'unsatiated love': 'I must rush again to War', says a Warrior, 'for the Virgin has frownd & refusd' (*68*: 62–3). In a manner reminiscent of the armies of Tasso's *Jerusalem Delivered*,

> Albions Twelve Sons surround the Forty-two Gates of Erin,
> In terrible armour, raging against the Lamb & against Jerusalem,
> Surrounding them with armies to destroy the Lamb of God. (*78*: 12–14)

[1] On Blake's use of 'Druid' architecture, see 'The Fourth Face of Man'.

Their terrible armour is characterological, an expression of their self-deformation, but despite their armouring the Spectre Sons are to be transformed in Los's Furnaces (*78*: 7–9) and redeemed in the end.

The three Sons who play the largest roles in *Jerusalem* are Skofeld, Hand, and Hyle—all based on individuals about whom Blake had particularly bitter feelings. Schofield, man of war and false accuser, 'is Adam who was New- / Created in Edom' (7: 25–6) because he is the natural man, a wolf to man. As the natural man, he is associated with Reuben (see pp. 270–1), and 'like a mandrake in the earth before Reubens gate: / He shoots beneath Jerusalems walls to undermine her foundations!' (*11*: 22–3.) He himself incarnates Reuben's Oedipal wish, expressed in the foetus-shaped plant Reuben gave to his mother, and in his blind, visionless development he threatens Jerusalem. When the Daughters combined in Tirzah propose to combine Joseph and Skofield, 'to make / You One: to weave you both in the same mantle of skin' (*68*: 1–2), they wish to abolish the distinction between potential redeemer and irredeemable accuser. Joseph, the victim who forgave and saved his brothers, can never be made one with the man who caused Blake to be tried for a capital offence. There is an appropriate personal vehemence in Blake's depiction of Schofield, the only man we know Blake to have fought with physically and who, in Blake's words 'threaten'd to knock out my Eyes'.[1] In the *51* design, Skofield[2] is shown not 'bound in iron armour' (*11*: 21) but naked. Head shaven, manacled and chained hand and foot, Skofield is represented as either a madman (cf. Hogarth's dying Rake) or a convict, which is what he had wanted to make Blake. Blake had already used this figure once, for Despair in the colour-printed monotype *The House of Death* (1795). Now he reversed its direction and indulged himself by supplying thick flames so that Skofield could be seen, in the words of Gilchrist's *Life*, 'retiring fettered into his native element'.[3]

[1] Letter to Thomas Butts, 16 August 1803, *Letters*, p. 72.

[2] So spelt in the Keynes proof. Blake's deliberate misspelling of names is part of a strategy to render the Sons as grotesques. The substitution of *k* for *c* is a standard comic-book style today, as is the substitution of *x* for *ck*. So Schofield's friend and fellow false witness Private Cock becomes Kox, the tenth Son of Albion.

[3] *Life*, ed. Todd, p. 202.

Hand has long been recognized as deriving from the three brothers Hunt, whose *Examiner* attacked both Blake's *Grave* illustrations and his private exhibition.[1] In one sense he is a demonic parody of Los: Hand too has his Furnace—'on Highgates heights' (*90*: 23), perhaps owing to the indisposition Blake experienced in the northern parts of London.[2] In *70* Blake takes the opportunity to present Hand as a three-headed monster—Robert, John, and Leigh Hunt as Dante's Satan:

> His bosom wide & shoulders huge overspreading wondrous
> Bear Three strong sinewy Necks & Three awful & terrible
> Heads
> Three Brains in contradictory council brooding incessantly.
> Neither daring to put in act its councils, fearing each-other,
> Therefore rejecting Ideas as nothing & holding all Wisdom
> To consist. in the agreements & disagree[me]nts of Ideas.
> Plotting to devour Albions Body of Humanity & Love.
> (3–9)

This 'mightly threatning Form' is pictured in the last design of Chapter 2, plate *50*. As in the verbal description of *70*, he is 'sitting on Albions Cliffs' and the design further resembles the text in showing figures emanating from Hand's chest:

> . . . the key-bones & the chest dividing in pain
> Disclose a hideous orifice; thence issuing the Giant-brood
> Arise as the smoke of the furnace, shaking the rocks from sea to sea.
> And there they combine into Three Forms, named Bacon & Newton & Locke . . . (*70*: 12–15)

That the identities of the 'Three Forms' are the same in the design is shown by the one just budding out: it has two faces

[1] See Gilchrist, *Life*, p. 203; David V. Erdman, 'Blake's "Nest of Villains" ', *Keats–Shelley Journal*, II (1953), 61–71; Paley and Essick, *The Grave*, pp. 25–7, 31.

[2] 'When I was young, Hampstead, Highgate, Hornsea, Muswell Hill, & even Islington & all places North of London, always laid me up the day after, & sometimes two or three days, with precisely the same Complaint & the same torment of the Stomach', Letter to John Linnell, 1 February 1826, *Letters*, p. 153.

looking in opposite directions, as does the Roman god Janus, which Francis Bacon took for his own emblem.

Blake's major figures often have more than one form of visual representation, and this is true of Hand, who appears in at least three other guises. In *26* he walks through flames as a parody of Christ, arms cruciform with a serpent of flame twisted about them. In the monochrome copies there are nails through his hands and his left foot, but this perhaps melodramatic detail was not part of Blake's original conception, as its absence from the pencil drawing indicates; and in copy E he painted the nails over, tinting them red to blend in with the flames. Chunkier and more muscular in *21*, 'in stern accusation with cruel stripes / He drives them [three Daughters of Albion] thro' the streets of Babylon' (29–30); in keeping with his character, the whips in his hands are tripartite. As the triple accuser Anytus-Melitus-Lycon of Socrates in *93*, he points with three right hands, once more reminding us of the Hunts' editorial siglum; down he falls at the top of *93* as a prelude to Albion's regeneration. A fourth representation of Hand may occur in the pencil drawing for *51* (Hamburger Kunsthalle), which includes a fourth, baboon-like creature with preternaturally large hands (Fig. 13). Hand would have been an appropriate choice for a figure to place with Vala, Hyle, and Skofield; but Blake eliminated him for compositional reasons here.[1]

Hyle is in Blake's personal experience associated with his corporeal friend William Hayley and in a more universal sense with matter, the Greek word for which is transliterated *hyle* and used with this meaning in the Neoplatonist and Gnostic traditions. Although it has been argued that Blake's primary meaning was limited to one or the other of these two,[2] it is entirely consistent with Blake's syncretic habit of mind that Hyle refers to both or, in different contexts, either. When,

[1] The etched design of three figures has a much more concentrated emphasis; the four-figure design would also have been of the wrong proportions for Blake's page in *Jerusalem*.

[2] The generally accepted view is expressed by Damon, *Blake Dictionary*, p. 193. For the argument that Hyle is not Hayley but *hyle*, see Stuart Curran, 'Blake and the Gnostic Hyle: a Double Negative', *Blake Studies*, IV (1972), 117–33.

for example, Los is temporarily subdued by Hyle, the emphasis appears to be autobiographical:

> . . . Hyle roofd Los in Albions Cliffs by the Affections rent
> Asunder & opposed to Thought, to draw Jerusalems Sons
> Into the Vortex of his Wheels. therefore Hyle is called Gog
> Age after age drawing them away towards Babylon
> Babylon, the Rational Morality deluding to death the little ones
> In strong temptations of stolen beauty . . . (*74*: 28–33)

Here Blake is surely thinking of how his creative activity was diverted at Felpham to trivial channels, while Hayley usurped Blake's proper role of poet, even getting Blake to illustrate Hayley's own poems.[1] In contrast, the episode in which Hyle is born as a Worm in *80–3* refers to the life of merely vegetative man. When Gwendolen (see below, pp. 272–3) works on Hyle's organs, hiding them in his body, she parodies Los's action in bending the senses of Reuben. For example, 'Los folded his Tongue / Between Lips of mire & clay, then sent him forth over Jordan' (*32/36*: 5–6); 'she hid his tongue with teeth / . . . raving he ran among the rocks' (*80*: 69, 76). Where Los's motive is sternly compassionate, his actions directed towards giving the amorphous Reuben a way out of his self-enclosure, Gwendolen wants to imprison Hyle—'to keep / These awful forms in our soft bands' (*80*: 84–5). The 'two vessels of seed, beautiful as Skiddaws snow' she gives Hyle present a marvellously ambiguous image: cold, white sterility is not what we usually associate with the semen, 'the pearly dew' of *Europe* 14: 15. And while Gwendolen triumphantly presents him as the Christ Child—'the mighty Hyle is become a weeping infant' (*82*: 8), he is revealed in reality to be 'a winding Worm' (*82*: 47).

The worm of mortality, rich in biblical associations,[2] is at

[1] Of course Blake was at the time genuinely grateful for the opportunity; what we have here is a retrospective and mythologized account.

[2] Perhaps the most pertinent of these are Job 17: 14: 'I have said . . . to the worm, Thou art my mother, and my sister' (employed by Blake in *Gates of Paradise* 16) and Bildad's words in Job to the effect that since the stars are not pure in God's sight, 'How much less man, that is a worm? and the son of man, which is

this point in *Jerusalem* a symbol of life unredeemed by the imagination. As such, it reaches all the way to 'the Desarts of Great Tartary' (*86*: 46). Since, according to Swedenborg, 'that ancient Word, which was in Asia before the Israelitish Word . . . is still preserved amongst the People who live in Great Tartary',[1] the extension of the worm Hyle to this region threatens the extinction of the most ancient human knowledge of God. In his Winding Worm form, Hyle is moulded by Gwendolen in the upper half of the right-hand margin of *80*,[2] and he undulates up the entire right of *82*. In his human form, Hyle is presented in *51*, hunched over in abysmal despair. Whether man or worm, whether bad poet or principle of materiality, Hyle must in both his forms be re-cast in Los's furnaces in order to be redeemed.

If the Sons of Albion are the objects of his aggression disguised as Justice, the Daughters are the objects of his lust disguised as moral revulsion. In *21* he deplores the promiscuity he has discovered or fantasied in them. For him, the vaginal orifice is 'the deep wound of Sin', which he wishes could be sealed to produce the illusion of a seamless garment:

> . . . clos'd up with the Needle,
> And with the Loom: to cover Gwendolen & Ragan with costly Robes
> Of Natural Virtue . . . (*21*: 13–15)

Here Albion adapts Lear's words to Regan:

> Allow not nature more than nature needs,
> Man's life is cheap as beast's: thou art a lady;
> If only to go warm were gorgeous,

a worm?' (25: 6). Stevenson calls the winding worm 'a ballad expression' (p. 806), but gives no example. The *laily* (= loathly) worm is encountered in a number of ballads. In the best-known of these, 'The Laily Worm and the Machrel of the Sea', a young man is changed into the laily worm by his wicked stepmother. See Francis James Child, *The English and Scottish Popular Ballads* (New York: The Folklore Press, 1956), I. 316.

[1] *True Christian Religion*, trans. John Clowes (London, 1781), nos. 265, 278.

[2] The lower figure has been taken to be Cambel holding Hand; see Damon, *William Blake*, p. 473, and Erdman, *Illuminated Blake*, p. 359. But the figure that the lower figure is holding has the evident beginnings of a worm, and as it is only Hyle who becomes a worm, the two parts of the design may refer to different phases of the same process.

Why, nature needs not what thou gorgeous wear'st,
Which scarcely keeps thee warm.[1]

In contrast to Lear, for whom the fashionable garment represents the *difference* between humanity and nature, Albion takes it as an emblem of nature itself, hiding the humanity of the daughters—'for their Spiritual forms without a Veil / Wither in Luvahs Sepulchre' (15–16). Albion sees the naked passion of the Daughters as terrifying, and so extends his curse even to the two daughters who are usually taken as positive. Cordelia, who redeems nature from the general curse in *Lear*, and whom Blake depicts with great sympathy in his early water-colour *Lear and Cordelia in Prison* (Tate Gallery), is seen as a violated temple:

Thee whom I thought pure as the heavens in innocence & fear:
Thy Tabernacle taken down, thy secret Cherubim disclosed
Art thou broken? (*21*: 20–2)

And similarly treated is Sabrina, whom Blake pictured in his seventh *Comus* design (Huntington Library) as a liberating figure. According to the Spirit in Milton's poem, 'maid'nhood she loves, and will be swift / To aid a Virgin, such as was herself . . .';[2] but Albion exclaims: 'Ah me Sabrina, running by my side: / In childhood what wert thou? unutterable anguish!' (22–3.) In contrast to the 'lustful' infancy that delighted Oothoon in *Visions of the Daughters of Albion*, the origins of sexuality are seen by Albion as horrifying, and there is no innocence.

Recoiling from his harlot daughters, Albion has a nightmarish vision of them as dying and resurrected goddesses. This may, as Wicksteed ingeniously suggests, have its origin in the British defeat at Corunna in January 1809, when 'Sir John Moore's retreat and death . . . necessitated the abandonment of camp followers including the soldiers' wives and children'.[3] Albion sees his children 'Carried in Arks of Oak' —an allusion to the British navy and its song 'Hearts of Oak'

[1] *King Lear*, II. iv. 269–73. [2] Lines 855–6.
[3] *Blake's Jerusalem*, p. 153, n. 2.

—and 'worshipped'—which Nelson Hilton sees as a calligraphic pun on 'warshipped'.[1] These arks, demonic parodies of the redemptive arks pictured in *24* and *39/44*, become in turn the Old Testament Ark carried before the armies: Albion's children, like a collective representation of David, 'play before / The Armies'. So the wars of ancient Israel and of modern Britain, made parallel, are internalized by Albion as part of a psychodrama in which his daughters are sexually violated, murdered, and ironically resurrected.

The Daughters, rejected by their father and whipped through the streets of Babylon by their male counterparts, have reason for both lamentation and vengeance. At various points, they engage in either, and at some times in both together. This dichotomy is illustrated in *19*, where two pairs of daughters mourn at the head and feet of Albion, who has crushed some of his children in his fall, other sons and daughters ascend the right margin, and at the top three daughters and a son engage in a dance of death, staggering across the page with bloody knives. In the text, these two attitudes tend to be presented separately, though at times one may be imbued with a sense of the other. Los, addressing them as 'daughters of despair' in *56*, is not deceived by their claims to weakness. 'I mind not your laugh: and your frown I not fear!' he exclaims. Their reply is an unconvincing apology for mystifying the divine vision: 'We Women tremble at the light therefore: hiding fearful / The Divine Vision with Curtain & Veil & fleshly Tabernacle' (*56*: 39–40). The extent of their disingenuousness is evident in the lamentation which begins at *83*: 85 and continues throughout *84*. They start with a lyrical evocation of *illud tempus*:

> Our Father Albions land: O it was a lovely land! & the Daughters of Beulah
> Walked up and down in its green mountains . . .

But they go on to claim falsely that they were the builders of Jerusalem, and for their present activities, now that 'Jerusalem lies in ruins', they invoke necessity, the tyrant's plea:

> But here we build Babylon on Euphrates, compelld to build

[1] *Literal Imagination*, pp. 17–18.

And to inhabit, our Little-ones to clothe in armour of the gold
Of Jerusalems Cherubims & to forge them swords of her Altars (*84*: 8–10)

Their appeal to Los to 'come forth' may reflect a real ambivalence, but their dominant impulse is revealed in 29–30:

Thus sang the Daughters in lamentation, uniting into One
With Rahab as she turnd the iron Spindle of destruction.

The power of the Daughters to 'divide & unite at will' (*58*: 1), becoming Tirzah and Rahab (*5*: 40–5; *67*: 2–3) or Vala (*64*: 6), is associated with the manifest display of their 'jealousy and cruelty' (*58*: 5). This is sometimes given expression in their weaving, as in *64*: 2, where 'the Daughters of Albion Weave the Web / Of Ages & Generations, folding & unfolding it, like a Veil of Cherubim' (*64*: 2–3). This is the Veil of Vala in its crude material sense, not yet reconstructed into 'the Gates & mighty Wall' (*59*: 5) by Los. This destructive weaving is to be contrasted with the compassionate weaving of the Daughters of Los, pictured at their wheel in *59* as they create a garment of flesh for the disembodied Spectres. Theirs is the labour of self-sacrifice:

And one Daughter of Los sat at the fiery Reel & another
Sat at the shining Loom with her Sisters attending round
Terrible their distress & their sorrow cannot be utterd
And another Daughter of Los sat at the Spinning Wheel
Endless their labour, with bitter food. void of sleep,
Tho hungry they labour: they rouze themselves anxious
Hour after hour labouring at the whirling Wheel
Many Wheels & as many lovely Daughters sit weeping
(26–33)

In this passage, with its reiterated 'labour' and 'labouring', the Daughters of Los are at the same time the women weavers of England, 'weaving, late into the evening by candle or oil light'[1] and the forces that shape and give birth to the human

[1] E. P. Thompson, *The Making of the English Working Class* (Harmondsworth, Middlesex: Penguin Books, 1968), p. 318 (speaking of both male and female workers). Thompson's entire chapter 9, 'The Weavers', pp. 297–346, is pertinent to the background of weaving in *Jerusalem.*

body. As in Velázquez's great *Hilanderas* (Prado),[1] we glimpse behind the real women cloth workers the movement of mythological beings. In contrast to the beneficent garment-making of Los's Daughters, the Daughters of Albion, like Gray's Fatal Sisters,[2] weave the body of death.

In describing the weaving activity of the Daughters, Blake combines imagery associated with both the Valkyries and the Norns:

> Derby Peak yawnd a horrid Chasm at the Cries of
>   Gwendolen, & at
> The stamping feet of Ragan upon the flaming Treddles
>   of her Loom
> That drop with crimson gore with the Loves of Albion &
>   Canaan (*64*: 35-7)

Blake's sixth design to Gray's translation from Old Norse could virtually illustrate these lines, save that there are three sisters pictured; Gray's lines 9-14 are especially pertinent to Blake's:

> See the griesly texture grow,
> ('Tis of human entrails made)
> And the weights, that play below
> Each a gasping Warriour's head.
> Shafts for shuttles, dipt in gore,
> Shoot the trembling cords along.[3]

The imagery of this bloody weaving in *Jerusalem* is closely associated with the imagery of human sacrifice, the daughters' other enactment of the Romantic Agony. Pictured with their agonized victims in *66* and *69*, the Daughters are the tormentors of male sexuality as embodied in Luvah. This is represented as an undoing of the protective body-garment created by Los's Daughters: 'They take off his vesture whole with

[1] See José Lopez-Rey, *Velásquez: a Catalogue Raisonné of his Oeuvre* (London: Faber and Faber, 1963), pp. 89-92, 139-41. According to Lopez-Rey, this painting should correctly be entitled *The Fable of Arachne*.

[2] As pointed out by Paul Miner: 'William Blake: Two Notes on Sources', *Bulletin of the New York Public Library*, LXII (1958), 203-7.

[3] *The Complete Poems of Thomas Gray*, ed. H. W. Starr and J. R. Hendrickson (Oxford: The Clarendon Press, 1966), p. 29. For a discussion of the designs to this poem, see Irene Tayler, *Blake's Illustrations to the Poems of Gray* (Princeton: Princeton University Press, 1971), pp. 110-16.

their Knives of Flint: / But they cut asunder his inner garments . . .' (*66*: 26–7). In the manner of Aztecs performing human sacrifice,[1] they search 'with / Their cruel fingers for his heart' (27–8). Perhaps the most striking aspect of Blake's presentation of this scene of torture is his recognition that it is an act of perverted love. Combined into Tirzah, the Daughters cry:

> My soul is seven furnaces, incessant roars the bellows
> Upon my terribly flaming heart, the molten metal runs
> In channels thro my fiery limbs: O love! O pity! O fear!
> O pain! O the pangs, the bitter pangs of love forsaken
> (*67*: 52–5)

In this remarkable passage, the imagery of metal-working usually associated with Los's imaginative activity is demonically transferred to the Daughters, combining with the baroque image of the flaming heart as employed by Richard Crashaw:

> O HEART! the aequall poise of lou'es both parts
> Bigge alike with wounds & darts.
> Liue in these conquering leaues; liue all the same;
> And walk through all tongues one triumphant FLAME
> Liue here, great HEART; & loue and dy & kill;
> And bleed & wound; and yeild & conquer still.[2]

Although Blake probably never read his contemporary De Sade's works, he too perceived an erotic interchange in the scene of torture, and it is this that links the Daughters' spurious pathos with their furious passion: 'Shriek not so my only love! I refuse thy joys: I drink / Thy shrieks because Hand & Hyle are cruel & obdurate to me' (*67*: 61–2).

In the last appearance of the Daughters, it is Gwendolen who is most prominent, pointing a false moral in mirror writing to the others, who listen attentively in the *81* design. 'In Heaven the only Art of Living / Is Forgetting & Forgiving' is a good beginning, but it degenerates into special-interest

[1] It has been suggested that Blake knew of details through Clavigevo's *History of Mexico*, translated into English in 1787; see Stevenson, p. 768n.

[2] 'The Flaming Heart', *The Poems English Latin and Greek of Richard Crashaw*, ed. L. C. Martin (Oxford: The Clarendon Press, 1957), p. 326.

pleading—'Especially to the Female'—and then to the Satanic conclusion 'But if you on Earth Forgive / You shall not find where to Live.' Gwendolen was no doubt chosen for this role because of her vengefulness in pursuing Sabrina, the daughter of Gwendolen's husband Locrine by his mistress Estrild, to her death. The emotional coloration of the story may have been provided by a play, *The Lamentable Tragedy of Locrine. Locrine*, anonymously published in 1595 and later included in the third Shakespeare folio, emphasizes the cruelty of Gwendolen:

> *Guendoline* taking her by the chin shall say thus.
> *Guen.* Yes damsell, yes, *Sabren* shall surely die,
> Though all the world should seeke to save her life,
> And not a common death shall *Sabren* die,
> But after strange and greevous punishments
> Shortly inflicted upon thy bastards head,
> Thou shalt be cast into the cursed streames,
> And feede the fishes with thy tender flesh.[1]

Although Blake does not use the story itself, whether from Geoffrey of Monmouth, *Locrine*, or both, he does emphasize Gwendolen's wilful cruelty. 'I have mockd those who refused cruelty & I have admired / The cruel Warrior' (*81*: 1–2). Her cruelty is derived from her fear of sexuality, an attitude reinforced by the body language of her crossed legs in the *81* design and unforgettably expressed in her conviction 'That Love may only be obtaind in the passages of Death'. It is therefore fitting that she lay claim to producing a virgin birth.

I have already suggested that Gwendolen's aspiration may have been modelled on Joanna Southcott's. For this to be true in part need not necessarily date the text of *82* as late as 1814, when Joanna Southcott announced in her *Third Book of Wonders* that she was the virgin who would give birth to the new Messiah, Shiloh. As we have seen, Blake appears to have guessed the direction that Southcott's prophecies were taking earlier, in his epigram 'On the Virginity of the Virgin Mary & Joanna Southcott'. If, however, this episode were written after Southcott's death on 27 December 1814, then

[1] *The Lamentable Tragedie of Locrine*, ed. Ronald B. McKerrow (Oxford: The Malone Society, 1908), lines 2230–7, n.p.

the dramatic presentation of Hyle and its grotesque culmination would be appropriate to her dismal story. Gwendolen announces with pride:

> Look I have wrought without delusion: Look! I have wept!
> And given soft milk mingled together with the spirits of flocks
> Of lambs and doves, mingled together in cups and dishes
> Of painted clay; the mighty Hyle is become a weeping infant (*82*: 5–8)

When the time comes for the epiphany of this prodigy, Gwendolen draws aside her veil 'from Mam-Tor to Dovedale'—rock formations suggestive of the female breasts and vagina[1]—but she is no more able to produce an Infant Love alone than was Joanna Southcott. Hyle is discovered to be 'a winding Worm . . . & not a weeping Infant' (47–8). Conversely, Blake thinks of the conception of Jesus, as we have seen in *61*, not as immaculate but as the result of a sexual act outside the Law. It is interesting that plates *61* and *85*, so strongly contrastive in theme, both display peculiarities that suggest afterthought on Blake's part,[2] and it may well be that these pages are meant to counterpoise each other.

In the redemptive scheme of *Jerusalem*, the Sons and Daughters are not to be destroyed. What Jesus says of Luvah and Vala: 'I cannot leave them in the gnawing Grave' (*62*: 21) is also true of them. *In illo tempore*, as described in *71*, the Sons are united with Jerusalem's Sons above ('As the Soul is to the Body, so Jerusalems Sons, / Are to the Sons of Albion'); and Albion's Sons with their Emanations are assigned their proper places among the counties of England. In this golden age, even the terrible Hand and Gwendolen can be happy: 'All were his Friends & their Sons & Daughters intermarry in Beulah' (14), and likewise Hyle and Cambel can be part of a true human community. Hand is assigned Selsey, topographical symbol of self-sacrifice; and Hyle dwells in

[1] See Damon, *Blake Dictionary*, pp. 371–2.

[2] As previously mentioned, the script of *61* is larger and more flowery than that of the plates before and after it, which form a sequence into which *61* was clearly interpolated. Deletions and mistakes in *82* cause Erdman to conclude it was 'prepared in a condition of unusual haste, or inattention, or illness' ('Suppressed and Altered Passages', p. 31).

the cathedral city of Winchester, home of William of Wykeham's great school.[1]

> . . . and between Hand & Hyle arose
> Gwendolen & Cambel who is Boadicea:[2] they go abroad & return
> Like lovely beams of light from the mingled affections of the Brothers
> The Inhabitants of the whole Earth rejoice in their beautiful light. (22–5)

This unfallen state was lost in the catastrophe that is the subject of most of *Jerusalem*; it is, however, to be regained through self-sacrifice. Cambel begins this process in *82*. She seems an unlikely candidate for this task, for in *81* she stands in the attitude of the Medici Venus,[3] hands over breasts and pudenda. Despite her false modesty and the 'envious blight' (*82*: 56) produced by her jealousy of Gwendolen, Los draws her into his transforming furnace. Consequently she labours to humanize Hand, whom she had tormented in *80*, 'Soft: invisible: drinking his sighs in sweet intoxication' (60). Now, however, she offers Hand redemptive love: 'She minded not / The raging flames . . . she gave her beauty to another' (67, 69). Gwendolen, for her part, 'Began her dolorous task of love in the Wine-press of Luvah / To form the Worm into a form of love by tears & pain' (75–6). So both sisters 'Began to give their souls away in the Furna[c]es of affliction', an act parallel to Albion's imitation of Christ in the *76* design, as well as to Los's selfless activity throughout the poem. In the general awakening, therefore, the children of Albion too have a place in the story: 'And all the Cities of Albion rose from their Slumbers, and All / The Sons & Daughters of Albion on soft clouds Waking from Sleep' (*96*: 38–9).

[1] That the primary association of Winchester in this context is educational is shown by *71*: 53, where the four ungenerated sons of Jerusalem dwell in heavenly light over 'The Four Universities of Scotland, & in Oxford & Cambridge & Winchester'. This is an unfallen view of education, one which Blake seldom gives us.

[2] Two associations for Boadicea are provided by her role as a warrior queen (negative) who led British resistance to the Romans (positive).

[3] This is also the pose of Venus in Blake's *Judgment of Paris* (British Museum), as Erdman (*Ill. Bl.*, p. 360) observes.

Albion rose

Plates *95–9* form a group markedly different from any other in *Jerusalem*, for this segment is manifestly an *end*. It is both the apocalyptic termination of Blake's paradigm and the fictive conclusion of the work itself (as announced after the last line of verse in *99*), to apply the two terms which Frank Kermode so usefully employs in *The Sense of an Ending.*[1] As Kermode remarks, 'Men in the middest make considerable imaginative investments in coherent patterns which, by the provision of an end, make possible a satisfying consonance with the origins and with the middle.'[2] All through the enormous middest of *Jerusalem*, we await the apocalyptic regeneration of Albion to connect with the myths of the Fall. When this begins to happen, it is in a single line—*94*: 18. Plate *94* up to that point consists of a passage, closely related to the full-page design *Milton* 38, descriptive of the fallen Albion. The design, too, has its being in the fallen world: a woman lying prone over the supine figure of a man is for Blake virtually an icon of the disasters of war, and so it appears on the title-page of *America*. Here, however, the glow of dawn illuminates the Druid trilithons in the upper part of the design, thus adumbrating the declaration of line 18, 'Time was Finished!'[3] With the abolition of Time towards which the entire work has been tending, we anticipate Albion's awakening, which is the first of a sequence of events that commence on plate *95*.

Plate *95* was etched over a previous version of *94*,[4] giving Blake an opportunity to turn accident into substance. In the monochrome copies, traces of the aged Albion's body, particularly his protruding legs, can be seen in the lower part of the design. Blake worked up this part further in the unique coloured example so as to bring out the contrast between the Old and the New Man: a youthful, Los-like Albion rises in flames from the corpses of his former, fallen self. Blake had at first conceived of Albion as kneeling with his bow,[5] but

[1] New York: Oxford University Press, 1967. [2] p. 17.

[3] Alluding to Rev. 10: 6.

[4] See Erdman, 'Suppressed and Altered Passages', pp. 33–5.

[5] This drawing, now in the Yale University Art Gallery, was formerly known as 'Los kneeling', but is almost certainly a depiction of Albion, as the bow and

evidently changed his mind in order to concentrate on the theme of renewal. In copy E he also emphasized the garment-like covering of Albion, making what may once have been intended as flames become what Erdman describes as 'a sort of triple tail or threefold fleshy garment extending downward as part of the young man's back'.[1] This reminds us that, in the words from 1 Corinthians 15: 44 that Blake etched in 'To Tirzah', 'It is raised a spiritual *body*' [emphasis mine].

After the sleeper awakes, 'Albion rose / In anger: the wrath of God breaking bright flaming on all sides around / His awful limbs' (*95*: 5–7). This seems a deliberate reference to the inscription on the engraving *Albion rose*:

> Albion rose from where he labourd at the Mill with Slaves
> Giving himself for the Nations he danc'd the dance of Eternal Death[2]

The Albion of the engraving (which in this last state is contemporary with parts of *Jerusalem*) embodies the divine attribute of self-sacrificing love characteristic of Jesus in the Gospels. In *95*, however, Albion manifests the wrath of the Christ of the Parousia. In a trope in which tenor and vehicle merge, Albion becomes the Sun rising through heavy clouds. Recovering the unfallen forms of the Bow and Arrows (which had been given to Satan in the verse of *52*: 18–19 and to a demonic horseman in the *35/39* design), Albion compels three of his Zoas to their tasks. He also recovers the unfallen form of language, 'speaking the Words of Eternity in Human Forms' (8).[3] These events, unique and irrevocable, as are those that follow, are to be distinguished from the events of

arrow indicate. For discussion, see Frederick Cummings, 'Blake at Detroit and Philadelphia', *Blake*, II (1968–9), 46–8. See also Butlin, *Catalogue Raisonné*, no. 571.

[1] 'Suppressed and Altered Passages', p. 35. On this general subject, see my essay 'The Figure of the Garment in *The Four Zoas, Milton,* and *Jerusalem*'.

[2] The print has sometimes been called *Glad Day* and sometimes *The Dance of Albion*, but the only title Blake provided is the inscription (E. 660). For dating, see Robert N. Essick, *William Blake, Printmaker*, pp. 70–5.

[3] Sloss and Wallis (I. 631n) compare Swedenborg on the converse of spirits: 'For their speech is the universal of all languages, by means of ideas, the primitives of words' (*Arcana Coelestia*, no. 1641).

the postlapsarian world, the world of cyclical recurrence which occupies most of *Jerusalem* up to this point.

Even in these final plates, Albion retains the alternative form of an old man. In the *96* design, the horizontal couple of *94* suddenly becomes vertical and ascends in a cloud of glory. Perhaps this design is also meant to recall *41/46*, where Albion as a bearded old man sits stiffly beside the habited Vala. In contrast, *96* shows him as a benign patriarch embracing the naked Brittania: in the text, 'England who is Brittannia entered Albions bosom rejoicing' (2). Albion can now see Los in Jesus as 'Los my Friend' in contrast to 'the abhorred friend' he condemned in *42*: 47. He can understand Jesus's act of self-sacrifice and indeed replicates it by throwing himself into the Furnaces of Affliction. This too is an inversion of former action, for the death Albion suffered previously, the pale or blue death that Los saw in him, was the Life-in-Death of imprisonment in Selfhood. Now 'Self was lost in the contemplation of faith' (31). This single act, like the renunciation of the curse in *Prometheus Unbound*, makes possible the immediate transformation of the universe.

The first four lines of *97* consist of an aubade by Albion, indebted both to the Jerusalem carols[1] and to the Song of Solomon,[2] beginning 'Awake Awake! Jerusalem!' Albion is at this point identified with the benign aspect of God's fatherhood—'So spake the Vision of Albion & in him so spake in my hearing / The Universal Father' (5-6). At least one aspect of Los, too, is subsumed by Albion, whose Bow is described as 'laying / Open the hidden Heart' (13-14)—cf. Los's 'spiritual sword. / That lays open the hidden heart' in *9*: 18. Albion's being regains its prelapsarian inclusiveness to the point of his becoming once again androgynous: he grasps his Bow 'firm between the Male & Female Loves' (15). Thomas Frosch has rightly emphasized the dynamism of Albion in these last pages of the work:

> The imagery of Albion's new body is dynamic to the extent that it is more accurate to describe it as a risen activity than as a risen body. Its fourfoldness is difficult, deliberately, to imagine in static, naturalistic

[1] On Jerusalem lyrics, see above, pp. 73–4.

[2] 2: 10–11: 'Rise up, my love, my fair one, and come away. For lo, the rain is over and gone.' (As noted by Ostriker, *Complete Poems*, p. 1034.)

terms; but it appears instead in the constant activity of the bow and arrow, the expansion and contraction of the faculties, and the chariots always 'going Forward Forward irresistible from Eternity to Eternity' (*98*: 27).[1]

This sense of never-ending activity, as well as of the restored comprehensiveness of Albion, is mirrored in the verse of *98*, the characteristics of which I discussed in Chapter I. The lines are extraordinarily long, even for *Jerusalem*. They are heavily enjambed—from line 6 to line 42 there is no punctuation of any kind at the end of a line, which is unusual even for *Jerusalem*. It is as if the passage were one enormous run-on sentence, and the effect of hurtling through apocalypse is intensified by present participles—there are seven in the first six lines of *98* alone. All this contributes to what I have called a sublimity striving to burst through the very boundaries of expression. With one backward glance at Albion's former state as 'Albions Spectre the Patriarch Druid' (48), the text flows on to the harmony of *99*, with 'All Human forms identified'. Thus from the middest we pass with amazing rapidity to 'The End of The Song / of Jerusalem'.

[1] *The Awakening of Albion* (Ithaca, NY: Cornell University Press, 1974), p. 143.

Chapter V

The Prophetic Myth

Los

One of the two central myths of *Jerusalem* is the myth of Los, the archetypal prophet-poet who labours to save Albion and who at the same time struggles to reunify his own divided identity as manifest in his Spectre and Emanation. Into this myth Blake put great personal feeling: on one level Los is Blake's creative identity in conflict with his barely repressed fears and hatred—his poor Jackself, as Hopkins would say. On this level Enitharmon is Catherine Blake, and her division from Los represents the marital discord that is also a theme in *The Four Zoas* and in some of the *Notebook* poems. The universal meaning of the myth concerns the endeavour of the prophetic imagination to raise humanity to a true perception of itself. In creating this myth, Blake builds the figure of Los—as he does all his major figures—on a variety of recognizable elements. Los is at the same time Old Testament Prophet, New Testament Evangelist, Miltonic Seraph, ancient British Bard, the classical Hephaistos/Vulcan, alchemist, blacksmith, and watchman; and in all these roles he is the Imagination of Humanity, shaping our perception of Time, perceiving history as a coherent shape, building the great city of Golgonooza. In analysing these aspects of Los, we must remember that Blake's method is syncretic. At different points in *Jerusalem*, one or other aspect of a figure may dominate, but all are combined in an identity that we perceive as an integral whole. In analysing the figure of Los we seek to understand better the synthesis that Blake has made.

In the Lambeth books Los was presented as spirit of Time, Eternal Prophet, husband of Enitharmon, and father of the revolutionary Orc.[1] His function is potentially redemptive, but he is subject to error, and at times is as vicious as Urizen

[1] See *Energy and the Imagination*, pp. 57–8.

(as when he calls his sons to the strife of blood in *Europe* or jealously binds Orc in *The Book of Urizen*). When Blake reorganized and augmented the mythology of the Lambeth books in *The Four Zoas*, he made Los the Zoa of Imagination and identified him as the generated form of an Eternal, Urthona. In the earlier written parts of *The Four Zoas* Los is merely first among his equals Tharmas, Urizen, and Luvah. But in the later written parts, such as the new ending of Night VIIa and the very late Night VIII, Los is distinctively different from the other Zoas.[1] He becomes the sole active agent in the regeneration of Albion; at the same time he is more closely associated with Blake as both poet and man. This prophetic aspect of Los is further magnified in *Milton*, where he can declare:

> I am that Shadowy Prophet who Six Thousand Years ago
> Fell from my station in the Eternal bosom. Six Thousand
>   Years
> Are finishd. I return! both Time & Space obey my will.[2]

In *Milton*, however, the most dramatic activity of the poet-prophet is necessarily assumed by Milton himself, whereas in *Jerusalem* it is Los alone who gives himself in love for fallen humanity. The Zoas have become residual; when the fallen Zoa of Imagination is referred to as such, it is as Urthona, lying in ruins to the north.[3] The *psychomachia* formerly dramatized through the zoas is now projected through the two major groups of figures in *Jerusalem*: the Albion (with Sons and Daughters)–Vala–Jerusalem constellation and the triad Los–Spectre–Enitharmon. Jerusalem, the one other positive figure among these, is mostly acted upon; so the burden of redemptive activity falls upon Los.

Of the various prototypes of Los, the Old Testament Prophet is perhaps the most immediately apparent. In part this aspect of Los's identity derives from the traditional identification of Poet and Prophet that I have discussed in

[1] *Energy and the Imagination*, pp. 156–61.

[2] *Milton* 22: 15–17, E. 116. The first line and a half also appear in Night VIII of *The Four Zoas* (113: 48–9, E. 365). Since Night VIII is so late, it may have been written after the completion of the text of *Milton, a Poem*, in which event the borrowing would go from *M* to *FZ*.

[3] See *59*: 11.

Energy and the Imagination.[1] The personal example of the Prophet is important here too: the Prophets were frequently rejected and even imprisoned by those whom they sought to aid, just as Los is rejected as 'the abhorred friend' by Albion.[2] Los frequently appropriates the language of Old Testament Prophetic discourse, but these borrowings are less important than the spirit of Los's great speeches to Albion, speeches in which the mode of the Writing Prophets has in effect been re-invented.

> What shall I do! what could I do, if I could find these
> Criminals
> I could not dare to take vengeance; for all things are so
> constructed
> And builded by the Divine hand, that the sinner shall
> always escape,
> And he who takes vengeance alone is the criminal of
> Providence;
> If I should dare to lay my finger on a grain of sand
> In way of vengeance; I punish the already punishd: O
> whom
> Should I pity if I pity not the sinner who is gone astray!
> O Albion, if thou takest vengeance; if thou revengest thy
> wrongs
> Thou art for ever lost! What can I do to hinder the Sons
> Of Albion from taking vengeance? or how shall I them
> perswade. (*45/31*: 29–38)

There is no biblical source for these lines, but their effect combines Prophecy and Gospel. Los speaks with authority and not as the scribes. In so doing he brings together the two Testaments and he incorporates one further element that runs from one to the other—apocalyptic. As Prophet, Evangelist, and apocalyptic visionary, Los delivers his message of Wrath and Love throughout *Jerusalem*.

At first Los's role as blacksmith may seem at a pole opposite

[1] pp. 19–21, 41–2, 161–4, 231–6.

[2] *42*: 47. Erdman (*E.* 188) emends to 'fiend', and Bentley (*Writings*, I. 506) notes that '"friend" may be a mistake for "fiend"'. But Albion's statement works well without emendation, and I prefer to follow Keynes in retaining it. (See *The Complete Writings of William Blake*, London: Oxford University Press, 1966, p. 670.)

to his prophetic identity. But some of the metalworking imagery associated with Los comes directly from the Prophets,[1] while elsewhere his activity is clearly Prophetic in spirit, though not directly derived from biblical imagery:

> . . . I took the sighs & tears, & bitter groans:
> I lifted them into my Furnaces; to form the spiritual
> sword.
> That lays open the hidden heart: I drew forth the pang
> Of sorrow red hot: I workd it on my resolute anvil
> (*9*: 17–20)

This mighty artisan also has ancestors in classical mythology. Behind him is the classical Hephaistos/Vulcan, especially as transmitted through Renaissance art. In Marcantonio Raimondi's engraving (after an unknown artist) of Venus, Cupid, and Vulcan, the Vulcan figure is a powerfully muscled artisan who prepares to strike the metal on his anvil (Fig. 16). To this we may compare plate 21 of *The Book of Urizen* (Fig. 17), as well as Los at work in the designs on *32* and *73*, and Los leaning on his hammer in *6*. Blake could also have known through an engraved source Vasari's *Vulcan's Forge,*[2] where naked blacksmiths labour with hammers against a background of flames. Blake would, moreover, have understood such imagery according to an alchemical tradition in which the true alchemist was 'the Spiritual Vulcan', working to refine leaden humanity into gold.[3]

Of course the tenor must not obscure the importance of the vehicle. Los *is* a worker. Of all the major figures of the long poems of the Romantic period, Los is the only one who can call himself a 'labourer'.[4] His incessant work is directed towards saving Albion, and in that sense it is symbolic, but it is also real metalworking, meticulously described. In envisaging this mighty smith, Blake may have been affected by Joseph Wright of Derby's depictions of workers at the forge, particularly in *A Blacksmith's Shop* (1771) and *The Iron*

[1] See, for example, Ezekiel 22: 17–22, Isaiah 48: 10. The basis for the visions *in* furnaces in *Jerusalem* is of course Daniel.

[2] The original in the Uffizi Gallery was reproduced by an anonymous engraver; a photograph of the engraving is in the British Museum Print Room.

[3] See *Energy and the Imagination*, pp. 58–9.

[4] 'The labourer of ages in the Valleys of Despair!' *83*: 53.

Forge (1772). In the first of these, the smiths beat a piece of white-hot metal with their hammers; in the second, one man holds the glowing iron in a pair of tongs while the other stands in a rapt state.[1] Ronald Paulson has suggested that these pictures, with their intense light sources and barnlike settings involve 'the secularization of a miracle'—the Nativity.[2] In *Jerusalem* we are closer to an acknowledgement of myth than in Wright of Derby, but we are nevertheless conscious of Los as a real worker with real tools as the starting-point of the symbolism. His equipment—all depicted in the *J 6* design[3]—is hammer, anvil, tongs, chain, bellows, and furnace. Hammer and tongs are inescapably phallic, and much of the cumulative force of Los's role in *Jerusalem* has to do with his gradual actualization of potency—when he fights, his weapon is, if not his hammer, then an axe or a mace. Bellows and chain (for the damper of the furnace) are the means of creating 'the eddying wind' (*82*: 74) which suggests the Hebrew *ruah*, the Greek *nous*, and other conceptions of the wind as a creative power of the spirit. The anvil defines Los's position in the imagined spatial world of *Jerusalem*; it is in effect an altar transformed, at which Los stands intensely active rather than passively worshipping. The furnace is the energy source for the psychic transformation upon which Los's whole enterprise depends. Both the worker and his tools have multiple symbolic associations, but their existence is concretely imagined in both text and design.

Another role in which Los is cast is that of watchman. Here too there is a link between the ancient and the modern. In plate *1* of the uncoloured copies, Los is shown in the costume of a night-watchman of Blake's own time. One need only compare Hogarth's watchman in plates 3 and 6 of *A Rake's Progress* to see how accurately Blake has portrayed this familiar contemporary figure with his broad-brimmed hat, his dark coat, and his lantern. In the coloured copies,

[1] *A Blacksmith's Shop* (Mountbatten Coll.) was engraved by Richard Earlom for Alderman Boydell in 1771, *An Iron Forge* (Mellon Coll.) by Earlom for Boydell in 1773. See Benedict Nicolson, *Joseph Wright of Derby* (London: Paul Mellon Foundation for British Art, 1968), I. 237.

[2] *Emblem and Expression* (Cambridge, Mass.: Harvard University Press, 1955), pp. 190–1.

[3] In Copy B the tongs have been painted out.

however, Blake rings a change: Los here wears sandals which, along with his globe of radiant light, remind us of 'our friend Diogenes the Grecian', as Isaiah calls him in *The Marriage of Heaven and Hell* (E. 38). He also has biblical prototypes. 'Son of man, I have made thee a watchman to the house of Israel: therefore hear the word at my mouth, and give them warning from me' (Ezek. 3: 17). 'He calleth to me out of Seir, Watchman, what of the night? Watchman, what of the night?' (Isa. 21: 11.) In *83*: 75–6, 'Los arose upon his Watch, and down from Golgonooza / Putting on his golden sandals to walk from mountain to mountain', also reflects the angel's words to Peter in Acts 12: 8—'Gird thyself, and bind on thy sandals.' *85* and *86* are largely devoted to Los's great Watch Song. The link between the two identities of Watcher and Prophet is made explicit in *39/44*: 28–31, where the Family Divine

> with one accord delegated Los
> Conjuring him by the Highest that he should Watch over them
> Till Jesus shall appear: & they gave their power to Los
> Naming him the Spirit of Prophecy, calling him Elijah

Extending the divine analogy even further, Blake says in *96*: 'And the Divine Appearance was the likeness & similitude of Los' (*96*: 7); and another analogue of Los in *1* is the figure of Christ in the sixteenth-century Italian engravings, probably after Mantegna, *The Descent to Hell* (Fig. 15).[1]

As one who fearlessly speaks the truth regardless of the ingratitude and hostility of his listeners, Los also reminds us of the Seraph Abdiel in *Paradise Lost*. Abdiel, 'The flaming Seraph fearless, though alone / Encompass'd round with foes',[2] dares to denounce Satan in the midst of the host of revolted angels. Los's courage and determination are similar when he addresses the fallen Albion, the Spectre Sons, and

[1] According to Arthur M. Hind, the design probably belongs to the period of the Eremitani frescoes (1448–55), while the engraving was executed by a hand other than Mantegna's 'at a considerably later date than the period of the design'. (*Early Italian Engraving*, London: Bernard Quaritch for the National Gallery of Art, Washington, DC, I. 1948, p. 17.)

[2] V. 875–6.

the terrible daughters. The isolation of each, giving a further dimension to their heroism, is emphasized.

> Among the faithless, faithful only hee;
> Among the innumerable false, unmov'd,
> Unshak'n, unseduc'd, unterrifi'd
> His Loyalty he kept, his Love, his Zeal;
> Nor number, nor example with him wrought
> To swerve from truth, or change his constant mind
> Though single.[1]

So Los addresses Albion:

> Los answerd. Righteousness & justice I give thee in return
> For thy righteousness! but I add mercy also, and bind
> Thee from destroying these little ones: am I to be only
> Merciful to thee and cruel to all that thou hatest[?]
> Thou wast the Image of God surrounded by the Four Zoa's
> Three thou has slain! I am the Fourth: thou canst not destroy me.
> Thou art in Error; trouble me not with thy righteousness.
> (*42*: 19–25)

Abdiel fails to sway Satan and his minions, and through most of *Jerusalem* Los's exhortations are likewise unavailing; but each receives due recognition for witnessing to the truth in the most adverse of circumstances. Abdiel is praised by a mild voice from a Golden Cloud:

> Servant of God, well done, well has thou fought
> The better fight, who single hast maintain'd
> Against revolted multitudes the Cause
> Of Truth, in word mightier than they in Arms;
> And for the testimony of Truth hast borne
> Universal reproach, far worse to bear
> Than violence . . .[2]

Los is seen in *95* 'unwearied labouring and weeping', in his role as the Spectre of Urthona.[3]

[1] V. 897–903.

[2] VI. 29–35.

[3] Blake's terminology is not entirely consistent on this point, see below, p. 273.

Therefore the Sons of Eden praise Urthonas Spectre in songs
Because he kept the Divine Vision in time of trouble.
(19–20)

As a speaker of mighty verse, Los has a further identity as a poet closely identified with Blake himself. Here Blake's conception may again have been reinforced by the writings of William Owen Pugh, whose translations of the Welsh Triades and other antiquities were discussed in connection with the poetry of *Jerusalem* in Chapter I. Los is at times presented as a survivor of a primitive golden age, an ancient Britain conceived in terms very similar to Pugh's:

> In reviewing the various remains of the Ancient Britons . . . it is easily observed that poetry and music were among the necessary accomplishments of education, and formed a conspicuous trait in their civil institutions. . . . These rational amusements were cultivated, in a great measure, in consequence of the life of ease and of leisure, which the Britons led.[1]

> The Britons (say historians) were naked civilized men, learned, studious, abstruse in thought and contemplation; naked, simple, plain, in their acts and manners; wiser than after-ages.[2]

Such similarities make one suspect that 'The British Antiquities' which Blake says in his *Descriptive Catalogue* 'are now in the Artist's hands' are in part derived from Owen Pugh's writings.[3] This conclusion is reinforced by information that Robert Southey had from the Blakes themselves: 'Poor Owen found everything he wished to find in the Bardic system, and there he found Blake's notions, and thus Blake and his wife were persuaded that his dreams were old patriarchal truths, long forgotten and now re-revealed.'[4]

[1] Introduction to *A Dictionary of the Welsh Language, Explained in English* (London: E. Williams, 1803 [1793]), n.p.

[2] *A Descriptive Catalogue*, E. 533.

[3] A connection between Blake's writings and those of Owen Pugh is suggested by Ruthven Todd, *Tracks in the Snow*, pp. 50, 52, 54.

[4] *BR*, p. 399, from *The Correspondence of Robert Southey with Caroline Bowles*, ed. E. Dowden (London and Dublin, 1881), pp. 193–4. It is interesting to speculate whether there may have been a connection between Blake's association with Owen Pugh and his praise of Thomas Johnes of Hafod as 'Hereford, ancient Guardian of Wales'. In both *A Dictionary of the Welsh Language* (I, n.p.) and *The Myrvian Archailogy* (I. vii) Johnes is thanked for his liberality in lending Welsh manuscripts.

According to *The Myrvian Archailogy*, the ancient Bards 'were not barbarians amongst barbarians; they were men of letters'.[1] They were, furthermore, religious teachers, including Druids who wore white to distinguish them from other Bards, who wore blue. Their principles were 'immediately derived from the Patriarchs'; their motto was 'The Truth in Opposition to the World'.[2] They preserved true Christianity 'through the long and dark ages of Popish superstition', and the groundwork of their system was 'universal peace, and perfect equality'. Their poetry derived from 'Awen', which Pugh defines as 'genius, in the general sense, though more appropriately a poetical genius or the Muse; but often, in the language of the Bards . . . inspiration, or the Holy Ghost'.[3] The resemblance of these ideas to some of Blake's in *Jerusalem* is striking, particularly in their application to Los, the prophetic voice of visionary freedom. Blake had of course always been interested in the antiquities of Britain as conveyed through Gough's *Sepulchral Monuments,*[4] Gray's poems (especially 'The Bard'[5]), and Chatterton's *Poems of Rowley.*[6] What Owen Pugh's essays and translations did for Blake's primitivist notions was to give them a more extensive historical setting in which to exist and to provide enabling documentation for the myth of the prophetic Bard.

Yet another of Los's identities is that of etcher and engraver. As is widely recognized, Los's metalworking is in part a symbolism of the creative process as manifested in the arts of etching and engraving.[7] Thus there is a double meaning to

[1] I. xviii.

[2] *Heroic Elegies*, p. xxiv. It is possible that Blake also got his idea that there were Welsh Indians from this book. According to Owen Pugh (p. xxv), there is a nation 'known also to Indian traders by the name of the *Civilized Indians*, and the *Welsh Indians* . . . they do now actually speak the WELSH language'. Their ancestors emigrated to America 'under the conduct of Madog ab Orvaine Gwynned, in the year 1170'. In *83*: 59 Los declares 'Place the tribes of Llewellyn in America for a hiding place!' I owe this suggestion to Ms Patricia Pelfrey.

[3] *Heroic Elegies*, pp. xxvi, lxiii, 32.

[4] See Keynes, 'The Engraver's Apprentice', *Blake Studies*, pp. 14–30.

[5] One of Blake's earliest exhibited pictures, shown at the Royal Academy in 1785 and now lost, was on this subject. Among the 116 water-colour designs to Gray's poems that Blake produced for Nancy Flaxman in 1797–8 were fourteen for 'The Bard'. *The Bard, from Gray* (tempera) was exhibited by Blake in 1809 and probably dates from that year. See Butlin, *William Blake* (1971), p. 57.

[6] Blake's copy is in the collection of Sir Geoffrey Keynes.

[7] See Erdman, *Blake: Prophet*, pp. 330–1.

Los's work. It reaches in one direction to the industrial methods of Coalbrookdale and other sites of the Industrial Revolution, in the other to the artist/artisan working with his tools on the copperplate. These meanings reverberate further to Prophetic and alchemical images of metalworking, in which the material worked upon is humanity itself. We can see such multiple references in passages like *10*: 62–5, *11*: 1–4:

Yet ceasd he not from labouring at the roarings of his Forge
With iron & brass Building Golgonooza in great contendings
Till his Sons & Daughters came forth from the Furnaces
At the sublime Labours for Los. compelld the invisible Spectre

To labours mighty, with vast strength, with his mighty chains,
In pulsations of time, & extensions of space, like Urns of Beulah
With great labour upon his anvils[;] & in his ladles the Ore
He lifted, pouring it into the clay ground prepar'd with art

Here the Sons and Daughters are Blake's own illuminated books. The clay ground suggests the ground with which the copperplate is prepared, the ore the printing ink, the fiery furnace the aqua fortis. The 'iron rollers' which appear in *73*: 9 are probably not inking rollers (not yet in general use by engravers[1]) but the rollers of the printing-press that the Blakes owned.[2] Even the globe of light which Los carries in the designs of *1* and *97* may be a reference to engraving: in Blake's time engravers placed a globe of water between a candle and the copperplate, illuminating their work.

[1] According to Essick, the first composition roller was made *c.* 1813 and did not come into general use until the 1820s (*William Blake, Printmaker*, p. 100), while Los's 'thundering roller' is mentioned in *Milton* 25: 11, and *Milton* was probably published in 1810.

[2] This is no doubt 'the Printing-Press / Of Los' in *Milton* 27: 8–9. On the Blakes' rolling press, see *BR*, pp. 29, 97; Keynes, *Blake Studies*, pp. 125–9; Essick, *William Blake, Printmaker*, pp. 215, 232.

Spectre and Emanation

While the identities of Los are separable for the purposes of discussion, they do not establish discrete significances on several levels of allegory but are rather fused into a single figure which has a palpable identity unified by its reference to Blake himself. The Los who struggles at his Furnaces to save Albion is Blake, labouring at *Jerusalem*, passionately addressing an England that will not hear, driven close to despair, yet hopeful of that signal of the morning when sleepers awake. The Los who struggles with his Spectre is Blake, too, the visionary artist in conflict with his workaday self. This conflict expands inward in reference to a deep psychic division at times; at other times it expands outward to take an ideological form. Enitharmon also exists in both quotidian and mythical aspects. 'Enitharmon is a vegetated mortal Wife of Los: / His Emanation, yet his Wife till the sleep of Death is past' (*14*: 13–14). She is at the same time Catherine Blake and the idealized counterpart that Jung calls the anima. Potentially, she embodies the fulfilment of creative impulse, but in the fallen world, divided from Los, she struggles with him for dominion. Los's endeavour to save Albion by visionary work is at the same time a quest to reintegrate his own Spectre and Emanation. This double enterprise refers to Blake both as an artist/poet and as a man.

Los's conflict with his Spectre begins on *6* and carries through the next four plates (including inserted *10*) until Los compels the Spectre to labours mighty in *11*. The conflict resumes intermittently until *91*, where Los divides the Spectre into a separate space, but the Spectre also has a benign aspect, as in *43/29–44/30* when he and Enitharmon appear as fugitives from Albion's fall and in *83* where he labours co-operatively with Los at the furnaces. In the end, *100*, only that positive aspect remains. So most of the content of the Urthona myth involves a war within the self, a war which is waged both for the emanation Enitharmon and between Los and Enitharmon. Like the Spectre, Enitharmon attempts to assert dominion over Los; and like him, too, she is integrated into the harmony of *100*.

In addition to the Spectre's personal meaning as an aspect

of Blake, he also has a more general meaning, one which is nevertheless appropriate to Los—and therefore to Blake himself. It is difficult to separate these two levels of significance here, as elsewhere in *Jerusalem*, but to the extent that we can do so, we can understand the Spectre's power as alternatively projected outwards into ideology and inward into paranoia and self-hatred. In both senses the meanings particularly concern William Blake as distinguished from the meaning of the more generalized Spectre of Albion.

'The Spectre is, in Giant Man; insane, and most deform'd', says Los when he feels his own Spectre rising upon him.[1] In Albion's Spectre that insanity takes the ideological form of the worship of authoritarian Reason; in Los's it manifests itself as an obsession with a God who damns His subject creatures irrevocably and without reason. The Spectre's God is thus precisely the contrary—or, rather, the Negation—of Blake's 'brother and friend' (*4*: 18). The Spectre's great speech of *10* is an almost unbearably moving expression of the conviction of damnation:

> I said: now is my grief at worst: incapable of being
> Surpassed: but every moment it accumulates more & more
> It continues accumulating to eternity! the joys of God advance
> For he is Righteous: he is not a Being of Pity & Compassion
> He cannot feel Distress: he feeds on Sacrifice & Offering:
> Delighting in cries & tears & clothed in holiness & solitude
> But my griefs advance also, for ever & ever without end
> O that I could cease to be! Despair! I am Despair
> Created to be the great example of horror & agony: also my
> Prayer is vain I called for compassion: compassion mockd[,]
> Mercy & pity threw the grave stone over me & with lead
> And iron, bound it over me for ever: Life lives on my
> Consuming: & the Almighty hath made me his Contrary

[1] *33/37*: 4. This line occurs twice in *FZ*—5: 38–9, 84: 36–7.

To be all evil, all reversed & for ever dead: knowing
And seeing life, yet living not; how can I then behold
And not tremble; how can I be beheld & not abhorrd
(*10*: 44–59)

As I have suggested elsewhere, there is a model for this speech in the tragic life of William Cowper, a poet whose work Blake admired and whose example he had reason to dread.[1]

Blake's interest in Cowper was extraordinary. Cowper's letters were, wrote Blake to Thomas Butts, 'Perhaps, or rather Certainly, the very best letters that ever were published.'[2] He executed at least a dozen finished pictures on Cowperian subjects in various media, including six engravings for William Hayley's *Life and Posthumous Writings of William Cowper*,[3] two miniatures in water-colour and one larger pen, ink, and wash portrait after Romney, an idealized tempera portrait, two tempera illustrations to *The Task* (*Winter* and *Evening*), and a frieze of the bridge at Olney.[4] In his *Notebook* Blake wrote an epitaph for Cowper (E. 498) in which he accused Hayley of ignoring Cowper's inspiration:

You see him spend his Soul in Prophecy
Do you believe it a confounded lie

And he had a vision of the insane Cowper which he recorded in a copy of Dr J. G. Spurzheim's *Observations on the Deranged Manifestations of the Mind, or Insanity* (London, 1817).

Cowper came to me and said, 'O that I were insane, always. I will never rest. Cannot you make me truly insane? I will never rest till I am so. Oh! that in the bosom of God I was hid. You retain health and yet are as mad as any of us all—over us all—mad as a refuge from unbelief—from Bacon Newton & Locke.'[5]

[1] 'Cowper As Blake's Spectre', *Eighteenth-Century Studies*, I (1968), 236–52.

[2] 11 September 1801, *Letters*, p. 52.

[3] London: Joseph Johnson, vols. I and II, 1803; vol. III, 1804.

[4] One of the two miniatures is in the Ashmolean Museum, the other in the collection of Mrs Cowper Johnson; the pen, ink, and wash portrait is in the National Gallery of Art, Washington, DC; the tempera is in the Manchester City Art Gallery; *Winter* is in the Tate Gallery and *Evening* in a private collection; the picture of Olney Bridge was destroyed by fire.

[5] *The Works of William Blake*, ed. Ellis and Yeats, I. 155. Some time after the editors saw this note 'among the sheets of the Vala MS', the fragment of paper on which it had been written was lost.

In having Cowper call him 'mad as any of us all', Blake is ironically acknowledging the views of spiritual enemies like Hayley, who wrote of Blake to Lady Hesketh: 'I have ever wished to befriend Him from a Motive, that, I know, our dear angelic friend Cowper *would approve*, because this poor man with an admirable quickness of apprehension, & with uncommon powers of mind, has *often appeared to me on the verge of Insanity*.'[1] Cowper's words to Blake might be termed a visionary corrective of the conventional idea of madness. For Blake, Cowper had been mad in the wrong sense: his 'madness' lay not in his Evangelical Christianity but in the beliefs expressed in his 'Lines Written on a Window Shutter', first published in 1801:

> Me miserable! how could I escape
> Infinite wrath and infinite despair!
> Whom Death, Earth, Heaven, and Hell consigned to ruin.
> Whose friend was God, but God swore not to aid me![2]

Therefore Blake imagines Cowper as asking plaintively 'Can you not make me truly insane?'—insane enough to believe, with Blake, that all could be saved. Blake's vision of Cowper was probably prompted by a flurry of controversy about Cowper's insanity that occurred after the publication of Cowper's account of his first period of madness, including his attempts at suicide, as *Memoir of the Early Life of William Cowper, Esq.*[3] in 1816. Some of the details of Cowper's insanity had, however, been known earlier. *The Examiner* used Cowper as an example of 'The Folly and Danger of Methodism' in 1808—a year before it attacked

[1] 3 August 1805; *BR*, p. 164.

[2] *Memoirs of the Life and Writings of W. Cowper, Esq*r., ed. Samuel Greatheed (n.p., 1801), p. 33. Greatheed altered 'Hell' to 'all' and also made some less consequential emendations; I have rendered the text as it appears in *Complete Poetical Works*, p. 428.

[3] Two editions were published in 1816: by E. Cox and by R. Edwards; the Edwards edition was reprinted with the corrections that same year, and it went into third and fourth printings in 1817 and 1818. There were also a Birmingham edition and three American editions during those three years. See Norma Russell, *A Bibliography of William Cowper to 1837* (Oxford: The Clarendon Press, 1963), p. 195.

Blake as 'an unfortunate lunatic'.[1] In any event, Blake would already have been familiar with the *Memoir* and with other suppressed writings concerning Cowper's madness. When Blake was working with Hayley on the *Life and Posthumous Writings*, he had ample opportunity to see these manuscript materials. This is evident in Hayley's letter to Cowper's nephew John Johnson ('Johnny of Norfolk')[2] dated 1 October 1801: 'We want you as a faithful Coadjutor in the Turret more than I can express. / I say *we*; for the warmhearted indefatigable Blake works daily by my side, on the intended decorations of our Biography.'[3] Johnny of Norfolk came twice to Sussex to give Hayley materials for the *Life*.[4] Evidently these included Johnny's transcripts of the *Memoir* and of a diary of 1796 in which Cowper had recorded his certainty of damnation; Johnny had, moreover, kept one notebook in which he had recorded Cowper's visions and voices and another in which he recounted his life with Cowper.[5] Hayley must have seen all or most of this material, for he quotes from the manuscript of the *Memoir* in the *Life* (I. 24–5) and shows familiarity with the two notebooks elsewhere. Blake himself became at least a friendly acquaintance of John Johnson, painting his portrait in miniature as well as executing for him the two *Task* temperas and the frieze of Olney Bridge.[6] There was probably ample opportunity for Blake to learn about Cowper directly from Johnson as well as through Hayley, and there is much to suggest that Blake

[1] *Examiner*, 17 July 1808, 461; 17 September 1809, 605. Both articles are signed with a pointing hand.

[2] On Johnson, see Morchard Bishop, *Blake's Hayley* (London: Victor Gollancz, 1951), pp. 217–24; and Gerald E. Bentley, Jr., 'William Blake and Johnny of Norfolk', *Studies in Philology*, LIII (1956), 60–74.

[3] Bentley, 'Johnny of Norfolk', 64; *BR*, p. 82.

[4] In spring 1801 and January 1802. See Maurice J. Quinlan, 'Memoir of William Cowper', *Proceedings of the American Philosophical Society*, XCVII (1953), 363. Johnson wrote to Hayley disclaiming knowledge of the whereabouts of this manuscript (see Russell, *Bibliography*, p. 245n.), but even if he did not find it, another copy was in the possession of the Revd Samuel Greatheed, who visited Felpham in 1803.

[5] See Anon., 'Cowper's Spiritual Diary', *The London Mercury*, XV (1927), 493–6; Hoxie Neale Fairchild, 'Additional Notes on John Johnson's Diary', *PMLA*, XLIII (1928), 571–2; Robert E. Spiller, 'A New Biographical source for William Cowper', *PMLA*, XLII (1927), 946–62.

[6] Butlin (*Catalogue*, 1978, pp. 142–3) dates the miniature 1802 and the *Task* pictures *c.* 1821.

drew upon this knowledge in creating the speech of the Spectre in *Jerusalem 10*.

'O that I could cease to be!' cries the Spectre. 'Despair! I am Despair . . .'. In Cowper's *Memoir*, his despair is a reiterated theme.

Being assured of this [having sinned against the Holy Ghost], with the most rooted conviction, I gave myself to despair.[1]

After five months' continual expectation, that the divine vengeance would plunge me into the bottomless pit, I became so familiar with despair, as to have contracted a sort of hardiness and indifference as to the event.[2]

The 'speaker' of Cowper's great poem 'The Castaway' (first published in Hayley's *Life*) 'wag'd with death a lasting strife, / Supported by despair of life'.[3] Cowper wrote in his diary 'My Despair is infinite, my entanglements are infinite, my doom is sure'; and, in a letter to Hayley, 'Perfect Despair, the most perfect, that ever possess'd any Mind, has had possession of mine, you know how long.'[4]—'O that I could cease to be! Despair! I am Despair . . .'. Furthermore, the Spectre resembles Cowper in viewing his destruction as predestined. The Spectre says, 'The Almighty hath made me his contrary / To be all evil, all reversed & for ever dead . . .'. The Castaway is a 'Destined wretch'; 'Hatred and vengeance' are Cowper's 'eternal portion'; he is 'Pre-ordained to fall'.[5] Cowper compares himself to Abiram, one of the Levite leaders who was swallowed by the earth for rebelling against Moses:

> *Him* the vindictive rod of angry justice
> Sent quick and howling to the centre headlong;
> *I*, fed with judgment, in a fleshly tomb, am
> Buried above ground.[6]

[1] *Memoir* (London: R. Edwards, 2nd printing, 1816), p. 66.

[2] Ibid., p. 72.

[3] *Complete Poetical Works*, p. 431. Cf. *Memoir*: 'Already overwhelmed with despair, I was not yet sunk into the bottom of the gulf' (p. 63).

[4] 20 June 1797. *The Unpublished and Uncollected Letters of William Cowper*, ed. Thomas Wright (London: C. J. Farncombe, 1925), p. 82.

[5] *Complete Poetical Works*, pp. 431, 290; John Johnson's diary entry for 5 August 1798 (Cambridge University Library, Add. MSS 5993).

[6] 'Lines Written During a Period of Insanity', *Complete Poetical Works*, p. 290. Cowper may have recognized the irony of Abiram's name, which in Hebrew means

And like Cowper, the Spectre expresses his condition by an image of immolation, saying 'Mercy & pity threw the grave stone over me & with lead / And iron, bound it over me for ever . . .'. The Spectre appropriates not only Cowper's belief that he had been condemned by a God without mercy but also the terrible pathos of his tone, the same sense of desolation and abandonment.

Such was not the mercy I expected from Thee, nor that horror and overwhelming misery should be the only means of deliverance left me in a moment so important! Farewell to the remembrance of Thee. For ever, I must now suffer thy wrath, but forget that I ever heard thy name.[1]

So spoke the Spectre shuddring, & dark tears ran down
his shadowy face
Which Los wiped off, but comfort none could give! or
beam of hope (*10*: 60–1)

To create the suffering Spectre of *Jerusalem 10*, Blake must have drawn upon deep-rooted fears of his own that were dramatically opposed to his conscious beliefs. Blake believed in a God of infinite mercy and explicitly repudiated predestination,[2] but he too experienced despair, as he recorded in his Notebook: 'Tuesday Jan^ry. 20. 1807 between Two & Seven in the Evening—Despair' (E. 672). Although Blake was not tempted to believe in Cowper's God, his own despair enabled him to conceive of what such a God might be. Other personal characteristics of Blake's also go to make up the Spectre in different parts of *Jerusalem*. If we consider some of these characteristics as Blake himself described them, we will appreciate the extent to which Los's Spectre is built of aspects of Blake himself.

And my Angels have told me that seeing such visions I
could not subsist on the Earth,
But by my conjunction with Flaxman, who knows how to
forgive Nervous Fear.[3]

'My father is the Exalted One'. See Num. 16: 31; *Dictionary of the Bible*, ed. James Hastings (New York: Scribner, 1963), I. 46.

1 'Spiritual Diary', p. 496.
2 See Blake's annotations to Swedenborg's *Divine Providence*, E. 599–600.
3 Letter to John Flaxman, 12 September 1800, *Letters*, p. 38.

. . . My Abstract folly hurries me often away while I am at work, carrying me over Mountains & Valleys . . . in a Land of Abstraction where Spectres of the Dead wander.[1]

> When I look, each one starts! when I speak, I offend;
> Then I'm silent & passive & lose every Friend.[2]

. . . It affronted my foolish Pride [of his encounter with Schofield][3]

These Verses were written by a very Envious Man[4]

I have entirely reduced that Spectrous Fiend to his station, whose annoyance has been the ruin of my labours for the last passed twenty years of my life. He is the enemy of conjugal love and is the Jupiter of the Greeks, an iron-hearted tyrant, the ruiner of ancient Greece.[5]

Drawing upon these qualities which he feared and disliked in himself, Blake created a Spectre whose characteristics include anxiety, hostility—both passive and active—envy, pride, and black melancholy. Of another Spectral emotion, sexual jealousy, Blake says nothing with reference to himself; but it is often a theme in his other poetry and particularly in some of the very personal *Notebook* poems, to a degree that makes one suspect that Blake too had experienced the jealous rage that sometimes characterizes the Spectre of Los. In projecting these fearsome qualities into a *doppelgänger*, Blake achieves the goal of giving Los—in this respect his ego—the possibility of controlling them, and consequently of freeing his own artistic energies.

At the very end of *5* the Spectre begins to divide from Los,[6] and this division with its attendant conflict is in Chapter 1 the main subject of *6–10*; it is then taken up once more on *17*. Descending upon Los in the *6* design in the form of a bat,[7]

[1] Letter to Thomas Butts, 11 September 1801, *Letters*, p. 51.

[2] Letter to Thomas Butts, 16 August 1803, *Letters*, p. 74.

[3] Ibid., p. 73.

[4] 'Florentine Ingratitude', E. 504.

[5] Letter to William Hayley, 23 October 1804, *Letters*, p. 106.

[6] But this may not be the first reference to the Spectre of Los in *Jerusalem*. Among the inscriptions on the proof of *1* in the collection of Sir Geoffrey Keynes, occurs the reversed writing: 'Every Thing has its Vermin O Spectre of the Sleeping Dead!' (E. 143). Of course the line may apply to the Spectre of Albion as well.

[7] David V. Erdman points out that in John Gabriel Stedman's *Narrative of a Five Years' Expedition against the Revolted Negroes at Surinam*, for which Blake executed sixteen engravings, there is an engraving of a bat by A. Smith entitled *The Vampire or Spectre of Guiana*. (See *Blake: Prophet*, p. 234n.). Among meanings of 'Spectre' found in the *OED* are: 'an apparition, phantasm, or ghost, esp.

the Spectre goes on in the text of *7* to tempt Los to suspect Albion:

He drinks thee up like water! like wine he pours thee
Into his tuns: thy Daughters are trodden in his vintage
He makes thy Sons the trampling of his bulls, they are plow'd
And harrowd for his profit, lo! thy stolen Emanation
Is his garden of pleasure! all the Spectres of his Sons mock thee
Look how they scorn thy once admired palaces! now in ruins
Because of Albion! because of deceit and friendship! . . .
(11–17)

This is a paranoid fantasy on the level of some of those that Blake himself experienced in the bitter years following the *Grave* disaster of 1805–6; compare Blake's *Notebook* accusation of Hayley, who 'when he could not act upon my wife / Hired a Villain to bereave my Life'.[1] The Spectre displays the cleverness of a psychopath, trying 'To lure Los: by tears, by arguments of science & by terrors' (*7*: 6), but unlike the double in Poe's 'William Wilson', this *doppelgänger*[2] does not succeed in its destructive intent. The construction of Blake's myth tends towards integration not schizoid bifurcation. The Los in Blake declares to his Spectre: 'I know thy deceit & thy revenges. . . . I will compell thee to assist me in my terrible labours' (*8*: 7, 15). He also recognizes that the Spectre is indeed part of himself—'Thou art my Pride & Self-righteousness'—much as Prospero recognizes Caliban ('This thing of darkness I / Acknowledge mine').[3] Now the Spectre becomes

one of a terrifying nature or aspect'; 'an unreal object of thought; a phantasm of the brain'; 'an object or source of dread or terror, imagined as an apparition', 'one whose appearance is suggestive of an apparition or ghost', 'a faint shadow or imitation *of* something', and 'one of the images or semblances supposed by the Epicurean school to emanate from corporal things' (with an example from Reid, 1785). In creating his symbolic names and terms, Blake liked to play along a wide scale of meanings, and I suspect that all those I have selected here are relevant conceptually.

[1] 'On H----ys Friendship', E. 497. On the psychological consequences of Blake's betrayal by Cromek, see Essick and Paley, *The Grave*, pp. 18–35.

[2] For some other literary comparisons, see E. J. Rose, 'Blake and the Double: the Spectre as Doppelgänger', *Colby Library Quarterly*, XIII (1977), 127–39.

[3] *The Tempest*, V. i. 275–6.

Blake as working engraver, guided by Imagination, labouring with Los at the Furnaces to perfect the Spaces of Erin, in response to Los's magnificent command:

> Take thou this Hammer & in patience heave the thundering Bellows
> Take thou these Tongs: strike thou alternate with me: labour obedient[.] (*8*: 39–40)

Throughout most of the rest of *Jerusalem* the Spectre of Urthona is under Los's control but remains always incipiently a threat. In *17* the emphasis is on the Spectre's division; however, he does Los's bidding. In *33/37* Los feels his Spectre rising within him, though the later appearance of the Spectre in Chapter 2 is in a benign aspect, in *43/29*: 28–83 to *44/30*: 1–15. But as *Jerusalem* begins to approach its apocalyptic climax, the Spectre makes one more attempt to usurp Los's personality and function. In *88* the Spectre creates division between Los and Enitharmon. Then in *91* he asserts his power over the natural universe:

> The Spectre builded stupendous Works, taking the Starry Heavens
> Like to a curtain & folding them according to his will (32–3)

The reference here is to the God of Psalm 104: 2 'Who coverest thyself with light as with a garment: who stretchest out the heavens like a curtain . . .'. Blake is not impressed by such prestidigitation, any more than he is by the act that follows:

> . . . forming Leviathan
> And Behemoth: the War by Sea enormous & the War
> By Land astounding . . . (38–40)

Now the Spectre is the God of Job, trying to impress his audience with his ability to create monsters. Blake's satirical view of such endeavour may be found in *Job* design 15 and in the Spiritual Portraits of Pitt and Nelson.[1] Los's response is to show up the emptiness of Spectral power by destroying its illusory achievements. The topos for this confrontation is the battle of sacred and profane magicians—Moses vs. Pharaoh's

[1] See *Energy and the Imagination*, pp. 171–99.

sorcerers, Paul vs. Simon Magus. 'Los reads the Stars of Albion' for the same reason that the wise characters in Shakespeare accept natural (but not judicial) astrology: the stars and their influences relate us to a larger order of things.[1] 'The Spectre reads the Voids / Between the Stars' in a vain attempt to measure quantitatively distances that Blake regards as unreal. So the Hammer of Los destroys the Spectre's works, including 'the Smaragdine Table of Hermes'. 'Blake rejected this document', as Damon says, 'and with it all occultism' because 'it was the magician trying to be the mystic'.[2] After beating down the Spectre's works, Los beats down the Spectre himself, until it becomes evident that it is his own Faustian will that he is hammering, 'with many blows, / Of strict severity self-subduing'.

In consequence of this last victory over the Spectre, Nature assumes a frail, evanescent, Shelleyan beauty:

> Then he sent forth the Spectre all his pyramids were grains
> Of sand & his pillars: dust on the flys wing: & his starry
> Heavens; a moth of gold & silver mocking his anxious
>   grasp (47–9)

The Spectre, being part of Los's identity, is not to be destroyed; he is 'divided . . . into a separate space' where his powers contribute to the workings of that composite being whom Blake sometimes calls Urthona. When Albion awakens in *95*, he compels the Zoas Urizen, Tharmas, and Luvah to their tasks; but one he does not need to compel: 'Urthona he beheld mighty labouring at / His Anvil, in the Great Spectre Los unwearied labouring & weeping' (17–18). The integration of his Spectre with his imaginative self enables Los/Blake to actualize his powers in redemptive work.

The other division of Los is from his emanation[3] Enithar-

[1] Cf. Blake's spirited defence of an imprisoned astrologer: 'The Man who can Read the Stars often is oppressed by their Influence, no less than the Newtonian who reads Not & cannot Read is oppressed by his own Reasonings & Experiments.' Letter to Richard Phillips, 14 October 1807, *Letters*, p. 128.

[2] *Blake Dictionary*, p. 183.

[3] Sloss and Wallis point out that the term 'emanation' occurs nowhere earlier than in late passages of *The Four Zoas*. They suggest that 'Blake first met the term and its equivalent "Eon" in Jacob Bryant's *New System, or An Analysis of Ancient Mythology* (1774–6, vol. i, p. 18).' See *William Blake's Prophetic Writings*, II. 153.

mon, who divides from him in *6* and continues divided and divisive through *93*, to become part of a harmonious existence only in *100*. In part, this is a more personal particularization of the sexual myth of Vala–Albion–Jerusalem. It too is triadic but involves two males and a female, with the Spectre representing the unfulfilled sexual drive that Los fears and that he feels he must control. This triadic situation is also the subject of the *Notebook* poem 'My Spectre around me night & day',[1] in which the first person speaker would correspond to Los divided from his Spectre and from Enitharmon. In 'My Spectre around me', which Damon describes as 'a poem analyzing an unhappy marriage',[2] it is the Emanation and not the Spectre who plays the adversary role, burning for victory while savagely envisaging the death of the male speaker. The Spectre is the speaker's unleashed desire, tracking the Emanation 'On the hungry craving wind', leaving the remainder of the divided self protected from entrapment by the female. This ambivalent view of sexuality is also found in *Jerusalem 17*, where once more the Spectre is the vehicle of aggressive male desire. Here Los 'Dare not approach the Daughters [of Albion] openly lest he be consumed / In the fires of their beauty & perfection' (7–8). The Daughters are Siren figures who 'wooe Los continually to subdue his strength'; instead of yielding, 'he continually / Shews them his Spectre'. As in the *Notebook* poems where the unabashed display of desire frightens away the love object,[3] 'Shuddring they flee . . . / Subdued by the Spectre of the Living & terrified by undisguised desire' (14–15). Thus Los achieves an immunity from seduction but only at the cost of delegating his sexuality to the Spectre. At the same time he attempts through most of *Jerusalem* to regain his lost Emanation, an enterprise which the jealous Spectre opposes.

The separation of Los and Enitharmon is a theme in several parts of *Jerusalem*; it begins in *5* and persists unresolved throughout, until the great synthesis of *100*. As previously in *The Book of Urizen* and *The Four Zoas*, Los

[1] E. 467–8.

[2] *Blake Dictionary*, p. 381.

[3] Such as 'Never pain to tell thy love' (E. 458), and 'I askéd a thief to steal me a peach' (E. 459).

in effect gives birth to Enitharmon in a travesty of the creation of Eve:

And Enitharmon like a faint rainbow waved before him
Filling with Fibres from his loins which reddend with
desire
Into a Globe of blood beneath his bosom trembling in
darkness
Of Albions clouds. he fed it, with his tears & bitter groans
Hiding his Spectre in invisibility from the timorous Shade
Till it became a separated cloud of beauty grace & love
Among the darkness of his Furnaces dividing asunder till
She separated stood before him a lovely Female weeping
Even Enitharmon separated outside, & his Loins closed
And heal'd after the separation: his pains he soon forgot:
Lured by her beauty outside of himself in shadowy grief.
Two Wills they had; Two Intellects: & not as in times of
old. (*86*: 50–61)

This male fantasy of giving birth is painful yet reassuring, at least from the perspective of Los's creator. Although the unfallen Urthona may be thought of as androgynous, like the beings of Aristophanes' myth in Plato's *Symposium*, unlike them he is an androgynous *male*. His 'Vehicular form', Los, is scarcely distinguishable from him—even their names become interchanged at times—but the manifestation of his Emanation is a lapse from a higher state of being. She is 'like a faint rainbow' because she embodies the delusive beauty of the phenomenal world, once more a lapse from unity, as in the refraction of light.

There are passages concerned with the division of Enitharmon from Los in *6, 14, 17,* and *22*, but their longest conflict occurs in *86–8*, where they contend about how to weave the 'wild fibres' that emanate from him, fibres of which she herself is made. The fibres are ambivalent: positive, they are woven in 'the golden Looms of Cathedron sending fibres of love / From Golgonooza with sweet visions for Jerusalem, wanderer' (*86*: 40–1). Negative, they 'shoot in veins / Of blood thro all my [Los's] nervous limbs. soon overgrown in roots / I shall be closed from thy sight' (*87*: 5–7). Fibres are basic life-stuff which can be used for regenerative purposes, as in the new ending which Blake wrote for Night VIIa of *The Four Zoas*. There Enitharmon asks Los to 'fabricate forms sublime'[1] for the ravening, bodiless spectres, and he agrees. Working together, Los and Enitharmon become the powers of generation in a benign sense, creating bodies which sense may reach and apprehend, vehicles of joy. More particularly, they are William and Catherine Blake making the illuminated books. It is such happily productive activity that Los proposes to Enitharmon in *87*:

> sieze therefore in thy hand
> The small fibres as they shoot around me draw out in pity
> And let them run on the winds of thy bosom: I will fix them
> With pulsations. we will divide them into Sons & Daughters
> To live in thy Bosoms translucence as in an eternal morning (7-11)

Behind this conception is a view of material existence that is also characteristic of *Milton* in contrast to the more pessimistic Lambeth books, and which is expressed in *86*:

> Nor can any consummate bliss without being Generated
> On Earth; of those whose Emanations weave the loves
> Of Beulah for Jerusalem & Shiloh, in immortal Golgonooza (42-4)

The achievement of such bliss, however, depends upon the harmonious collaboration of the powers embodied in Los and Enitharmon. This is not what happens in most of *Jerusalem*, with the exception of one very short section in *83*: 71-4, where

> his Emanation
> Joy'd in the many weaving threads in bright Cathedrons Dome
> Weaving the Web of life for Jerusalem. the Web of life

[1] 98: 22, E. 356. On this section of VIIa, see *Energy and the Imagination*, pp. 157-61; and Mary Lynn Johnson and Brian Wilkie, 'The Spectrous Embrace in *The Four Zoas*, VIIa', *Blake*, XII (1978), 100-5.

Down flowing into Entuthons Vales glistens with soft affections.

This magnificent image shows the positive valence of Enitharmon's weaving, but it is compressed into less than four lines. For the most part the situation is as in *87*: 12–24, where Enitharmon opposes Los, declaring her intention to seize his Fibres and weave them as she wills, to create a body for Albion's Spectre. In the design on *85* we see her drawing the Fibres out of Los in the form of grape-vines emanating from his head, bowels, and loins.[1] In the text of *88* she weaves these Fibres into a husk of Moral Law for the natural man. Her goal is to create a religion in which God is a dependent child:

That he who loves Jesus may loathe terrified Female love
Till God himself become a Male subservient to the Female. (20–1)

In that 'Womans World' there is no place for Los, and without her 'His rage or his mildness were vain, she scattered his love on the wind' (*88*: 51).

The power struggle between Los and Enitharmon continues for the most part until *100*, the design which stands as an epitome of the regenerate world. In the *87* design they are shown as a pair of wilful children, evading the groping of their mother, the blind earth goddess Enion. In *92–3* occurs the last verbal exchange of this contentious pair. Enitharmon foresees her imminent disappearance as a separate identity when Albion awakens, for 'My Looms will be no more & I annihilate vanish for ever' (*92*: 11). This is indeed a partial truth, but it is because, Los answers, 'Sexes must vanish & cease / To be, when Albion arises from his dread repose' (13–14)—part of the larger conception whereby in the regenerate world embracings will be comminglings from head to foot. Not comprehending this impending transformation, Enitharmon desperately clings to her individual existence. Her last

[1] The beauty of this design in copy E can be misleading. Damon sees it as depicting the work of the male and female, weaving the Vine of Friendship in Beulah, but his own observation that 'they are separated and their faces turned from each other' (*William Blake*, p. 474) should guide us to the true meaning.

speech is a complaint to her sons that 'you forget all my Love! / The Mothers love of obedience is forgotten' (*93*: 3–4). She speaks no more after *93*: 16.

If it is the Los in Blake who urges Enitharmon/Catherine to collaborate in creative activity, it is the Spectre in him that continually interferes with such co-operation. The Spectre self is driven by an irresistible compulsion to absorb Enitharmon and at the same time to involve Los in paranoid delusion. In his very first speech, in *7*, like Iago at Othello's ear, he urges Los to suspect Albion. In *10* he demands 'Where is my lovely Enitharmon / O thou my enemy, where is my Great Sin?' (42–3). All appetite and dependence, the Spectre hates both himself and the object of his appetite and dependence. Los/Blake dreads this aspect of his own identity and he tries to guard Enitharmon from it: 'he infolded her in his garments / Of wool: he hid her from the Spectre, in shame & confusion of / Face' (*17*: 52–4). He exercises enormous psychic force to make the Spectre obey his conscious intention:

> that Enitharmon may not
> Be lost: & lest he should devour Enitharmon: Ah me!
> Piteous image of my soft desires & loves: O Enitharmon!
> I will compell my Spectre to obey: I will restore to thee
> thy Children. (*17*: 17–20)

Conversely, in *86*: 54 it is the Spectre that Los hides from Enitharmon, but the meaning is similar: the ego's control is ensured by the separation of desire from the object of desire. However, the ever-threatening Spectre succeeds in precipitating a crisis between Los and Enitharmon in *88*. As their bickering continues, 'A sullen smile broke from the Spectre in mockery & scorn / Knowing himself the author of their divisions & shrinkings . . .' (34–5). In this fine personal touch, we can sense Blake's satirical self-observation. As Blake wrote to Hayley, the Spectre is the enemy of conjugal love.

He is also the enemy of sexual joy. Guilt-obsessed, regarding Enitharmon as 'my Great Sin', he engages in a demonic parody of Los's continual building of Golgonooza—'Continually building, continually destroying in Family feuds'. He regards sexual love as a filthy, Yahoo activity: 'For I will make their places of joy & love, excrementitious' (*88*: 39).

This sentence has been traced to Augustine's 'Inter faeces et urinam nascimur'.[1] Elaborating that statement in another way, Yeats, who may also have had Blake's words in mind, makes his Crazy Jane say that although Love's mansion is pitched in 'The place of excrement', it is that very rending that makes a woman's love 'sole or whole'.[2] Crazy Jane's tragic sensibility unites what the Spectral self divides. Something like this happens—or almost happens—in *The Four Zoas* VIIa when Los embraces Enitharmon and the Spectre, and 'Clouds would have folded round in Extacy & Love uniting';[3] but at this point in *Jerusalem* Los himself is affected by the Spectre's sexual fantasies and becomes like Urizen, segregating sexual love from the rest of human existence, 'dividing the Space of Love with brazen Compasses' (*88*: 47).

An exception to the disharmony of Los, Enitharmon, and Spectre in *Jerusalem* occurs in *43/29* and *44/30*, beginning when 'two Immortal forms' tell the story of Albion's fall, rewritten from Night III of *The Four Zoas* (see above, pp. 78–9). In *44*: 1–2 these messengers are identified as 'the Emanation of Los & his Spectre'; here 'his Spectre is named Urthona' (4). In this benign aspect the Spectre and Emanation are suggestive of the Blakes' view of themselves amid the Hayley circle in Sussex, 'Being not irritated by insult bearing insulting benevolences' (9). The Divine Hand bears them safely back to their humanity, '& Los put forth his hand & took them in / Into his Bosom' (16–17). This is also the subject of the *44* design, where Los extends his downturned palms to receive two figures which we last saw flying towards the upper right margin of *23*. Enitharmon has lepidopterous wings like those of the fairy mimes of the title-page; the Spectre's wings are once more batlike, but their effect is comical rather than threatening—a Fledermaus, not a Dracula. So positive is the view of the Spectre in *44/30* that we are told

> Therefore the Sons of Eden praise Urthona's Spectre in
> Songs
> Because he kept the Divine Vision in time of trouble.
> (14–15)

[1] See Raymond Lister, *William Blake* (New York: F. Unger, 1969), p. 154.

[2] 'Crazy Jane Talks with the Bishop', *Collected Poems* (London: Macmillan, 1958), p. 295.

[3] 86: 14, E. 354.

This high praise of the Spectre is repeated verbatim after Albion awakens in *95* and beholds 'in the Great Spectre Los unwearied labouring & weeping' (18). There Los and the Spectre seem to have fused their identities. The Spectre is, then, capable of embodying positive value; although Los and his Spectre battle throughout much of *Jerusalem*, they are in harmonious relationship in *44/30*, in *95*, and in *100*.

'My Great Task'

Los is subject to great vicissitudes in the course of *Jerusalem*. Divided from his Spectre and from his Emanation, attacked by Albion's sons and lured by his daughters, shunned as 'the abhorred friend' by Albion himself, Los must struggle continually to maintain the integrity of his vision. In *35/39* he is characterized as 'not yet infected with the Error & Illusion', (27) indicating that there are points at which he is so infected. Among these are *53*: 4–5:

> And the roots of Albions Tree enterd the Soul of Los
> As he sat before his Furnaces clothed in sackcloth of hair

Here Los is a Job figure who reduces himself (temporarily) to passive mourning and so becomes infected with the errors of repressive morality and retributive justice implicit in Albion's fatal tree. The weakened Los is reduced to 'rearing his hands to heaven for aid Divine!' (*71*: 57) instead of heeding his own admonition: 'Why stand we here trembling around / Calling on God for help; and not ourselves in whom God dwells' (*38/43*: 12–13). Consequently he is forced to recede before Albion and Vala. A further deterioration occurs when

> . . . Hyle roofd Los in Albions Cliffs by the Affections rent
> Asunder & opposed to Thought, to draw Jerusalems Sons
> Into the Vortex of his Wheels. therefore Hyle is called Gog
> Age after age drawing them away towards Babylon
> (*74*: 28–31)

Here Los is Blake in Sussex, drawn into a friendship with William Hayley in which Blake feels the Los in himself is betrayed.[1] Hayley/Hyle's real motive in diverting Blake to miniature painting and other potentially remunerative activities 'opposed to Thought' was to neutralize Blake/Los's prophetic vision, diverting him from that function to the Babylon of commercial success, or at least of workaday survival. Since the action in *Jerusalem* is not temporal, this situation can be referred to in *11* as having previously occurred: when Los draws his Sons and Daughters from the Furnaces in *11*,

> Los wept with exceeding joy & all wept with joy together!
> They feard they never more should see their Father, who
> Was built in from Eternity, in the Cliffs of Albion.
> (13–15)

Here Blake expresses the anxiety of the creative artist who, after his three years' slumber on the banks of ocean, fears that he may never produce works of genuine vision again. But the works are produced, and produced in joy; Los continually triumphs over his intermittent weakness to go on with his redemptive activities. These are manifest in two forms: hortatory and creative.

Los is, in his capacity as the poetic imagination, an embodiment of the Logos or primordial word. It is he who creates the English language so that an intellectual structure may exist to contain the results of the Fall—'Los built the stubborn structure of the Language, acting against / Albions melancholy, who must else have been a Dumb despair' (*36/40*: 59–60). Attempting to stimulate the process of regeneration in Albion, Los constructs speeches of magnificent power:

> Thou wast the Image of God surrounded by the Four
> Zoa's
> Three thou hast slain! I am the Fourth: thou canst not
> destroy me.

[1] In his highly interesting essay, 'Blake and the Gnostic Hyle: a Double Negative', Stuart Curran points out that the Gnostics call the devil Hyle, a word derived from the Greek word for matter, and maintains that this is its primary meaning in Blake's symbolism. Considering the tendency of Blake's symbolism to operate on more than one level, there is no reason why both meanings cannot be present. Curran writes that 'Hayley is merely a sympathetic liberal . . . not a Fascist menace' (121). But Blake makes the mild Hayley the mighty Hyle of *Jerusalem* for the same ironical reason that he makes him the Satan of *Milton*.

> Thou art in Error; trouble me not with thy righteousness.
> (*42*: 23–5)

In Los's great speech of *82*: 81–*83*: 64 there is an extraordinary combination of myth and personal pathos. Addressing the sleeper as 'O Albion! my brother!' Los recognizes that his own powers are severely compromised by his service to humanity. He could 'at will expatiate in the Gardens of bliss', creating a far different kind of poetry and art, were it not for his mission to save Albion his brother. The theme of this speech is the preservation of love from the world's forces of destruction. Its dominant figure is the labyrinth, imaging how the senses are self-enfolded. This address ends on a note of heroic resolution, expressed in short clauses separated by emphatic pauses:

> The night falls thick: I go upon my watch: be attentive:
> The sons of Albion go forth: I follow from my Furnaces:
> That they return no more: that a place be prepared on
>   Euphrates
> Listen to your Watchmans voice: sleep not before the
>   Furnaces
> Eternal Death stands at the door. O God pity our
>   labours.[1]

Despite the powerful determination embedded in these and other speeches, Los's words fail to revive Albion, for humanity closes itself off from the Prophetic voice:

> . . . Albion fled more indignant! revengeful covering
> His face and bosom with petrific hardness, and his hands
> And feet, lest any should enter his bosom & embrace
> His hidden heart . . . (*33/37*: 12–*34/38*: 1–3)

Albion's inner state is projected outwardly in England's long wars with France. Recognizing Albion's obduracy of heart, Los agonizes over how to prevent England from revenging itself on defeated France:

> O Albion, if thou takest vengeance; if thou revengest thy
>   wrongs

[1] *83*: 61–5. The beginning of Los's long speech is, as mentioned, addressed to the sleeping Albion. After *83*: 3, the audience shifts several times; this last part is spoken to the Daughters of Beulah.

Thou art for ever lost! What can I do to hinder the
Sons
Of Albion from taking vengeance? or how shall I them
perswade. (*45/31*: 36–8)

Nevertheless, Luvah as France is subjected to a rapacious and humiliating peace: 'Albion brought him / To Justice in his own City of Paris, denying the Resurrection' (*63*: 5–6).[1] Once more, Los's most heartfelt expressions of concern fail to achieve their purpose.

Although Los is the creator of language, his words do not influence the figures he addresses (with the exception of his own Spectre) any more than they do Albion. In *56* Los 'chaunts' his Song to the Daughters of Albion, declaring 'You must my dictate obey from your gold-beam'd Looms' (31); and his message is amplified by the Great Voice of the Atlantic in *57*, but nevertheless *58* begins with the Daughters celebrating war in a sadistic orgy. When Vala proclaims the dominion of Woman in *64*, Los denounces her, but the Spectre of Albion draws her into his bosom, and in hermaphroditic union they preside over the execution of Luvah in *65*. To encourage the Friends of Albion to save him from falling into Non-Entity, Los exhorts the Friends in *38/43*. His message begins with enormous urgency and goes on to range powerfully over the world of fallen Albion, reaching an impassioned climax in 71–2: 'I will not endure this thing! I alone withstand to death, / This outrage!' Then, suddenly, as if struck by the words 'I alone', Los recognizes the difference between himself and the Friends. These embodiments of Cathedral Cities, their original force sapped by centuries of institutional Christianity, are in no condition to help Los save Albion. 'Ah me! how sick & pale you all stand round me!' Los says. 'Ah me! pitiable ones! do you also go to deaths vale?' And the passage ends with Los's recognition of the pathos of his isolation:

All you my Friends & Brothers! all you my beloved
Companions!

[1] Erdman, *Blake: Prophet*, pp. 463, 466, 467, relates this passage and *66*: 15 ('For Luvah is France: the Victim of the Spectres of Albion') to the two Treaties of Paris of 1814 and 1815.

Have you also caught the infection of Sin & stern Repentance?
I see Disease arise upon you! yet speak to me and give
Me some comfort: why do you all stand silent? I alone
Remain in permanent strength. Or is all this goodness & pity, only
That you may take the greater vengeance in your Sepulcher. (*38/43*: 74–9)

Although the Friends do try to bear Albion back 'thro Los's Gate to Eden' (*39/44*: 3), they fail. And in general it is true to say that Los's 'terrific' speeches, no matter how grand their poetry or how profound their doctrinal content, produce little change in the desperate situation of Albion—just as, it could be said, Blake's own words had no immediate effect on Britain.

A partial exception may be made for Los's words to his Spectre, if we allow two qualifications. First, the dialogue with the Spectre is primarily a dialogue with the self, and such intrapsychic activity means much the same thing whether projected in terms of language or of action. Second, the Spectre is affected not only by Los's words but also by the threat of action: 'unless / Thou abstain ravening I will create an eternal Hell for thee' (*8*: 37–8). The Spectre is not entirely subdued until Los with his hammer 'completely divided him into a separate space' (*91*: 52). Of course this is not to say that because they do not alter events, Los's speeches are wasted. Los is a Prophetic witness whose doctrinal statements, embodied in passages of great poetic intensity, carry much of the meaning of *Jerusalem*. This is exemplified throughout the book, but nowhere more than in the grand Watch Song of *85*: 22–*86*: 32, where Los eloquently describes his vision of Jerusalem (see above, pp. 141, 239). Here Los's imaginative perception is itself an act. Elsewhere, in his dramatic confrontations of Albion, the Daughters, Vala, the Friends, and Enitharmon, Los's language gives meaning and value to events though it does not change their course. At the same time it is his action, his incessant labour, that changes the course of events by initiating the processes of regeneration.

Los's first redemptive work in *Jerusalem* is the perfection of the Spaces of Erin in his furnaces, and with these his own sons and daughters. This is only possible after Los has achieved mastery of his Spectre in *9*, so that his workaday self becomes an adjunct of his imaginative powers.

> Groaning the Spectre heavd the bellows, obeying Los's frowns;
> Till the Spaces of Erin were perfected in the furnaces
> Of affliction, and Los drew them forth, compelling the harsh Spectre. (*9*: 33–5)

What they create is the vision of freedom implicit in *Jerusalem* itself. The failed revolution of the United Irishmen in 1798 was a recent memory when Blake began *Jerusalem*, and the perfection of the Spaces of Erin may be Blake's response to the Act of Union debate or its aftermath.[1] In the Spaces of Erin are preserved the possibility of freedom for England as well as for Ireland. When Los draws Erin from the furnaces, he creates the vision of such freedom in Blake's art—appropriately, Erin is accompanied in *11* by the Daughters of Beulah (Blake's Muses) and by the Sons and Daughters of Los, which are Blake's own works 'in perfection lovely!' (11). After all these come from the Furnaces, Los contemplates his sons and daughters, each of whom has three gates:

> . . . and they every one in their bright loins:
> Have a beautiful golden gate which opens into the vegetative world:
> And every one a gate of rubies & all sorts of precious stones
> In their translucent hearts, which opens into the vegetative world:
> And every one a gate of iron dreadful and wonderful,
> In their translucent heads, which opens into the vegetative world (*14*: 19–24)

These gates are the three planes of accessible meaning in Blake's imaginative creations: sensual, emotional, and intellectual. The level of explicit statement, the western gate of the tongue, is closed: like Jesus, Los/Blake must speak in parables. In this respect, the Sons and Daughters of Los are

[1] See Erdman, *Blake: Prophet*, pp. 482–4; and Chapter IV above, p. 185.

analogues of the great city of Golgonooza, as is made explicit in *12*: 45–6.

Golgonooza, built and contemplated by Los in *12–13* was our subject in Chapter III as the continuing city, the Spiritual Fourfold London that is Blake's version of the New Jerusalem. Now I am concerned with Golgonooza as the greatest of Los's creative works.

> Here on the banks of the Thames, Los builded Golgonooza,
> Outside of the Gates of the Human Heart, beneath Beulah
> In the midst of the rocks of the Altars of Albion. In fears
> He builded it, in rage & in fury. It is the Spiritual Fourfold
> London: continually building & continually decaying desolate! (*53*: 15–19)

Here in addition to being like his prototypes Ezekiel and John of Patmos, Los resembles the Shaddai of Bunyan's *Holy War*, the builder of a city between Time and Eternity: 'As to the Situation of this Town, it lieth just between the two worlds, and the first founder, and builder of it, so far as by the best, and most Authentick records I can gather, was one *Shaddai*; and he built it for his own delight.'[1] This city is built throughout *Jerusalem* by Los, for it is by definition a work in progress. In this respect, Golgonooza may be contrasted with the city of Yeats's 'Byzantium', whose icon is represented 'in glory of changeless metal'.[2] The two have in common their creation by the artistic imagination, but Byzantium, presented in tension with the forces of the natural world, is beyond Time, while Blake's continuing city is the fulfilment of Time. Golgonooza is both the city of art and the city of millennial freedom; it is therefore built in conjunction with the emergence of Los's Sons and Daughters and of Erin from Los's furnaces.

Los's building activities are also directed toward ends which are not always charged with positive value (as is Golgonooza),

[1] Bunyan, *The Holy War* (London: 1682), pp. 2–3. Shaddai is of course one of the names of God in Genesis, as is Elohim, the creator of Adam. In *73*: 24 'Los . . . is of the Elohim.'

[2] *Collected Poems*, p. 281.

but which are positive within certain contexts. Thus he is the creator of the Mundane Shell, the rim of the Mundane Egg which is the natural world in which we live. Viewed pessimistically, the Shell can be seen as constricting and illusory,[1] but in *Jerusalem* it can be a protection against the indefinite. Los forms it from the Veil of Vala, the illusion of nature that would become a prison if not transformed into an avenue of regeneration:

> For the Veil of Vala which Albion cast into the Atlantic Deep
> To catch the Souls of the Dead: began to Vegetate & Petrify
> Around the Earth of Albion. among the Roots of his Tree
> This Los formed into the Gates & mighty Wall, between the Oak
> Of Weeping & the Palm of Suffering beneath Albions Tomb. (*59*: 2–6)

Thus what would otherwise be perceived as a vale of tears becomes, to use Keats's term, a vale of Soul-making. The Gates that Los builds allow the ravening Spectres entrance to the generated world, where they are given bodies and individual identities:

> The Spectres of the Dead howl round the porches of Los
> In the terrible Family feuds of Albions cities & villages
> To devour the Body of Albion, hungring & thirsting & ravning
> The Sons of Los clothe them & feed, & provide houses & gardens[.]
> And every Human Vegetated Form in its inward recesses
> Is a house of ple[as]antness & a garden of delight Built by the
> Sons & Daughters of Los in Bowlahoola & in Cathedron
> (*73*: 46–52)

The Gates also provide access back to the world of Eternity, but only after the work of regeneration has been accomplished. As one of the Elohim, Los also populates the natural world with animals, vegetables, and minerals—a process

[1] In *13*: 52–4 the darker aspect of the Mundane Shell is presented.

viewed pessimistically in *The Book of Urizen* but optimistically here—and with the seasons and heavenly bodies. In the designs to *32* and *73* we see him hard at work at his anvil, forging the sun as in *The Book of Los*. He also creates the moon, 'Building the Moon of Ulro, plank by plank & rib by rib' (*32/36*: 4) as a Noah's ark in which humanity may safely travel over the sea of Time and Space.[1] In *39* the ark is pictured as a sublime houseboat, radiant and winged. In performing these constructive activities, Los is the architect of the natural world, now viewed as a vessel travelling on a voyage of redemption, like the moon-boat itself.

Another aspect of Los's activity is expressed in terms of 'dividing' and 'fixing'. These actions are elaborations of Los's binding of Urizen in *The Book of Urizen*, a task which, though necessary for the prevention of a further fall into chaos, there had the effect of reducing Los's visionary power as well. In *Jerusalem*, such work is more integrated with Los's prophetic identity, and he is in control of its consequences. He must, for example, fix the warring contraries of the generated world on his anvil, preventing premature and specious unity from taking place and making possible the true unity that can only occur after a painful process of definition (see *58*: 13–20). This necessarily involves 'Dividing the Masculine & Feminine', for however pessimistically Blake may view the division of the androgynous Adam, the being who James Joyce said 'rode and not rutted', it is only through Generation that the divided Spectres can become united once more. Therefore Los must break the 'rocky Spectres' of Albion's Sons with his mace of iron, 'as the Potter breaks the potsherds'—an image derived from Isaiah 30: 14—in order to divide the Spectres into male and female (*78*: 1–9). Los divides and 'fixes' in order to establish a structure of meaning in the fallen world. His 'fixing' of the counties of Britain and Ireland in relation to the Gates of the twelve tribes of Israel creates meaning in a topographical framework (*16*: 28–60). The field of action on which the typological events recorded in biblical history will be enacted in Britain needs to be defined by analogy. In a sense what the specific analogies are

[1] Damon, *Blake Dictionary*, p. 346. On Blake's various moon-arks, see Nicholas O. Warner, 'Blake's Moon-Ark Symbolism', *Blake*, XIV (1980), 44–59.

is less important than the fact that a general analogical relationship can be envisaged.[1] Therefore

> Here Los fixd down the Fifty-two Counties of England & Wales
> The Thirty-six of Scotland, & the Thirty-four of Ireland
> With mighty power . . . (*16*: 28–30)

Perhaps the most singular example of Los's 'fixing' is the episode of the bending of the senses of Reuben. Reuben is the mother-fixated man, who would rather sleep in the womb of Nature than awaken to life in order to realize his own form. In Genesis, Reuben found mandrakes in the wheat field and gave them to his mother Leah, an action which Enitharmon finds exemplary in her speech on maternal power (*93*: 1–16). By giving Leah the foetus-shaped plants, Reuben dramatized his Oedipal fantasy, which he enacted even more explicitly in lying with his father's concubine. Intoxicated by female beauty, Reuben is perpetually victimized by it. While he sleeps on London Stone, the Daughters of Albion send him 'over Europe in streams of gore' until he takes root in Bashan (*74*: 34–43). Bashan, the land once ruled by the giant Og, is on the east side of the Jordan from the Holy Land. Los's effort is to get Reuben to cross the river and stay on the other side, which would mean deliverance from the illusion of materiality that makes Reuben say 'Doubt is my food day & night' (*32/36*: 7). But the recidivist Reuben keeps returning to the wrong side of the river, enrooting himself, and falling asleep.[2] Nevertheless, Reuben has a potentially imaginative self.

> Hand stood between Reuben & Merlin, as the Reasoning Spectre
> Stands between the Vegetative Man & his Immortal Imagination[3]

[1] For a discussion of the particulars, see Damon, *William Blake*, pp. 442–3, 460. Damon argues that in the verbal map of *72*, where the Irish counties are given, the analogies are correct according to the points of the compass, because Ireland represents the state of salvation; while the rest (*62*) is in confusion because of the Fall.

[2] Reuben is shown enrooting himself in the design on *15* (cf. text *15*: 25); he is also facing the wrong direction—*towards* Chaldea, from which Abraham is shown fleeing.

[3] *32/36*: 23–4; see Frye, *Fearful Symmetry*, p. 376. Merlin is an appropriate

Los's task is to enable Reuben to realize his Imaginative potentiality and to cast off the selfhood, but because Reuben's identity is so amorphous—'Unstable as water, thou shalt not excel' was his father Jacob's curse on him (Gen. 49: 4)—Los must first organize Reuben's senses. At first this appears paradoxical and even cruel, since the life of the senses is presented in *Jerusalem* as an imprisonment. But the wandering Reuben is a mass of chaotic appetite; this must be given a structure, just as the ravening spectres must be clothed in body-garments, before generation can begin.

Los's method is to 'bend' each of Reuben's senses, working on the human raw material with formidable purposefulness. 'Los bended his Nostrils down to the Earth . . . Los rolled, his Eyes into two narrow circles . . . Los folded his Tongue / Between Lips of mire & clay. . . . Los bended / His Ear in a spiral circle outward. . . .'[1] The process seems a deliberate parody of the punishment of criminals in the eighteenth century and earlier, as related in contemporary accounts:

> The Time being then expired, he was set on a Chair on the Pillory, when the Hangman dressed like a Butcher, came to him, attended by two Surgeons, and with a Knife, made like a Gardener's Pruning Knife, cut off both his Ears, and with a pair of Scissors slit both his Nostrils, which were afterwards seared with a hot iron. Afterwards he was carried to the Ship Tavern in Charing Cross.[2]

If we recall that boring through the tongue, as was done to the Quaker Messiah James Nayler, was also a public punishment, we can see that Los's operations on Reuben parody the mutilation once visited on criminals. Los's purpose, however, is merciful; he must equip Reuben for existence in a fallen world as a prerequisite for the attainment of vision: 'As Los bended the Senses of Reuben Reuben is Merlin / Exploring the Three States of Ulro; Creation; Redemption. & Judgment'

but ambiguous prophetic identity for the woman-dominated Reuben; as Damon (*William Blake*, p. 449) points out, the Lady of the Lake sealed Merlin in a rocky tomb.

[1] *30/34*: 47, 53; *32/36*: 5–6, 12–13.

[2] Account of the execution of a convicted forger named Japhet Crooke, 1731, quoted in Peter Quennell, *Hogarth's Progress* (London: Collins, 1955), pp. 81–2 (no source given).

(*32/36*: 41–2). To emphasize the redemptive nature of Los's seemingly cruel activity, Blake inserted plate *31/35* between the two plates in which the bending of Reuben's senses is recounted, thereby reminding us that Los's purpose is 'to Create / States: to deliver Individuals evermore!' Reuben is not delivered until Chapter 4 where, after becoming the Wandering Jew in *84*, he is conducted by Los to the Promised Land, '& he brought / Reuben from his twelvefold wandrings & led him into it' (*85*: 3–4).[1]

Los also works upon human raw material in the episode of Gwendolen, Cambel, and their male counterparts, Hyle and Hand. In what may be a parody of Joanna Southcott's false pregnancy of 1814,[2] Gwendolen declares: 'Hyle is become an infant Love: look! behold! see him lie! / Upon my bosom' (*82*: 37–8). But when she draws aside her veil 'from Mam-Tor to Dovedale'—that is, from breasts to vagina[3]—Hyle is revealed to be no more an infant than Joanna Southcott's Shiloh—he is 'a winding worm', the worm of mortality. Envious Cambel is drawn by Los into his Furnaces, where, purged by Los's transforming fires, she learns to sacrifice her Selfhood in genuine love. Labouring to humanize Hand, 'she minded not / The raging flames . . . / she gave her beauty to another' (*82*: 66–7, 69). Gwendolen learns from the example of her sister. She too works 'in the eddying wind of Los's Bellows'—a wind that has numerous Romantic analogues as a symbol of the imaginative power that can transform reality.[4] The once fiercely wilful Gwendolen now struggles 'To form the Worm into a form of love by tears & pain'. Los is comforted by this confirmation of the doctrine of Individuals and States, and he is moved to make his powerful statement 'I know I am Urthona keeper of the Gates of Heaven.' From this point on, Los, who has at times been close to despair at his seeming inability

[1] But in *90* Hand and double Boadicea 'In cruel pride cut Reuben apart from the Hills of Surrey', and the Daughters of Albion 'drink Reuben & Benjamin as the iron drinks the fire' (lines 25, 46).

[2] See 'William Blake, the Prince of the Hebrews, and the Woman Clothed with the Sun', pp. 285–92.

[3] Mam-Tor is part of a double peak in Derbyshire; nearby Dovedale is a narrow limestone valley—see Damon, *Blake Dictionary*, pp. 260, 107.

[4] See M. H. Abrams, 'The Correspondent Breeze: A Romantic Metaphor', *Kenyon Review*, XIX (1957), 113–30.

to shape events, labours with renewed potency to save Albion.

Urthona

The end of *Jerusalem* necessarily involves the reconstitution of Urthona, the unfallen form of the imagination, who after the Fall became divided into Los (his 'Vehicular Form' (*53*: 1)), Enitharmon (Los's emanation), and the Spectre. The last is sometimes called the Spectre of Los, sometimes the Spectre of Urthona, and once merely 'Urthona' (*44/30*: 4). Blake may at some point have intended a substantive distinction by these names, but in *Jerusalem* the only difference is one of nomenclature; there is only one Spectre.[1] Throughout *Jerusalem*, Los, the operative human imagination in the fallen world, labours, as we have seen, to prevent the utter destruction of Albion. He engages in terrible conflicts with his Spectre and with his Emanation, striving for but not permanently attaining unity of being. Subjected to the vicissitudes of the world of Generation, he is at various points roofed into Albion's cliffs by Hyle, drawn into his own loins by pangs of love, and infected with error and illusion. Even his positive activities—building Golgonooza, keeping the Divine Vision, protecting the 'dead' body of Albion—are in effect holding actions against the dominant powers of destructiveness. All this changes in the final plates of *Jerusalem*, where Los's activities are brought to fruition and he regains his complete identity.

When Albion awakens in *95*, he compels three of the Zoas to their tasks, but the fourth, Urthona, 'he beheld mighty labouring at / His Anvil, in the Great Spectre Los unwearied labouring & weeping' (17–18). This perception of the unfallen state existing within the fallen gives way in *96* to a vision of the unfallen state alone: 'And the Divine Appearance was the likeness & similitude of Los' (7). The identification of the indwelling human imagination with Jesus, a major

[1] Los is the Spectre of Urthona in *95*: 18, but in *82*: 81 he says, 'I know I am Urthona . . .'. However inconsistent Blake's terms may appear here, what they refer to remains clear: the prelapsarian imagination is Urthona; its fallen form is Los, whose Spectre is in turn divided from him. There is in *Jerusalem* no 'Spectre of Urthona' other than Los.

theme throughout *Jerusalem*, is reiterated when Albion imitates Jesus's sacrifice,

> . . . & Self was lost in the contemplation of faith
> And wonder at the Divine Mercy & at Los's sublime
> honour (31–2)

The words 'sublime honour' introduce a note of heroism which is entirely apposite for Los at this point. Indeed, the final plates provide an *aristeia* for Los/Urthona, a manifestation of value which is also the subject of the *97* design. Here the figure who entered the Door of Death in *1* reappears, having gone through the intervening plates and become transformed.[1] He holds his globe of radiance in such a way as to remind us of Edward Taylor's audacious question 'Who in this Bowling Alley bowld the Sun?'[2] Displaying the nakedness of the divine human form, he dances in a sunburst of Eternal Day.[3]

The mode of sublime heroism is continued in plate *100* (Fig. 18 and Plate II), the subject of which is life in a millennial state, after all Human forms have been identified. Los rightly occupies the central position. An Apollo Belvedere figure turned slightly to the left, he holds in one hand his hammer and in the other his tongs. Both these tools appeared unused in *6*; here Los handles them with nonchalance, his Great Task accomplished. The tongs by their shape recall the enormous carpenter's compasses held by Christ in *Christ in the Carpenter's Shop,*[4] those in the background of *The Christ*

[1] See Wicksteed, *Blake's Jerusalem*, p. 245. Damon identifies this figure as 'The Poet advancing inwards towards Eternity' (*William Blake*, p. 474). For Erdman the subject is 'Albion as Los . . . taking in his left hand the sun' (*Ill. Bl.*, p. 376).

[2] *The Poems of Edward Taylor*, ed. Donald E. Stanford (New Haven: Yale University Press, 1960), p. 263.

[3] Blake based this design upon his *Night Thoughts* illustration 11, which he later redrew in pencil (British Museum) with the title 'The Journey of Life'. The *Jerusalem* design reverses the two previous ones, and substitutes the globe of light in the figure's left hand for the stick which in the previous drawings he held in his right. The final version may be indebted to Dürer's engraving of Apollo as a naked man holding the sun as a globe of radiance in his left hand (reproduced in John Beer, *Blake's Humanism* (Manchester: Manchester University Press, 1968), pl. 42).

[4] Coll. Lady Epstein; repr. Anthony Blunt, 'Blake's *Glad Day*', *Journal of the Warburg Institute*, II (1938), pl. 10d.

Child Asleep on the Cross,[1] and those wielded by the Ancient of Days in the frontispiece to *Europe*. The last of these is a tool of fallen Reason, while the first two suggest, as Blunt puts it, 'that in the new dispensation reason, symbolised by the mathematical instrument, will be synthesized with imagination'.[2] Just so Los's tongs, placed almost at the centre of the picture, indicate the full integration of reason and the imagination. A further integration is shown by the Spectre, now depicted not as a bat but as the back view of Los himself, even to the point of having a rich head of hair. Having learned to 'labour obedient', the Spectre has taken up Los's radiant globe from *97*, and is carrying it through the air on its diurnal round.

The dark[3] figure of Enitharmon on the right completes the triad that constitutes the unfallen Urthona. As a spinner, she has numerous prototypes. She superficially resembles the Parcae-like figures of *25*, but the relation here is contrastive, for her spinning in *100* is benevolent; the thread it provides will go into weaving bodies for Spectres in the Looms of Cathedron.[4] (Another such positive image of spinning is the distaff in the fourth *Paradise Regained* water-colour, *Mary's Lamentation for Christ.*[5]) Behind this representation of Enitharmon may be, as Nelson Hilton argues,[6] portrayals of Venus *genetrix* as the Spinning Aphrodite.[7] Closer to home, there may be something in Enitharmon of George Romney's painting of *Emma Hart as The Spinstress* (Kenwood House). Blake was much occupied with Romney's art in the years

[1] Victoria and Albert Museum, rep. Blunt, *The Art of William Blake*, pl. 35a.

[2] Blunt, op. cit., p. 72.

[3] In copy E. In the monochrome copies her body is white, as are those of Los and the Spectre. (Note that of the five full-page designs, this is the only one that is a relief etching rather than a white-line engraving. See Essick, *William Blake, Printmaker*, p. 158.)

[4] The most extensive description of this is in the long passage Blake added to Night VIIa of *The Four Zoas*; for discussion, see *Energy and the Imagination*, pp. 157–61.

[5] Fitzwilliam Museum. Repr. David Bindman, *William Blake: an Illustrated Catalogue of the Works in the Fitzwilliam Museum* (Cambridge, 1970), pl. 26.

[6] *Literal Imagination*, p. 116.

[7] See Elmer G. Suhr, *The Spinning Aphrodite: The Evolution of the Goddess from Earliest Pre-Hellenic Symbolism Through Late Classical Times* (New York: Helios Books, 1969).

1803–6,[1] and it seems likely that he would have seen this striking picture at some point. And while there may seem a great distance between Venus *genetrix* and Emma Hamilton, it was precisely the nature of Blake's imaginings to syncretize such apparently disparate images, bringing out their archetypal identity.

The specific nature of Enitharmon's spinning may be viewed in two ways, depending on what object she is holding in her left hand. If it is a spindle,[2] which is suggested by the fact that she is looking at it, the motion of the fibres is counterclockwise, up to the moon and then from the moon through her right hand and then across to her left. If it is a distaff,[3] as the fact that it is held high would indicate, the motion is clockwise, with fibres being guided across to her right hand, falling down to the moon, and showering from the moon to the earth. Either interpretation is possible,[4] but the whole visual scene of the design demands the second one, in which case the moon itself could be regarded as doing the weaving of fibres of life with which new bodies will be created. In this sense, the design is the Contrary of *25*, where the human body is horribly unwoven. Seen in another way, it is also, as Robert Essick argues,[5] a counter to *51*, where three other figures preside over the world. The benevolent workers of *100* have the last word, overpowering the blindness and despair of Vala, Hyle, and Skofeld.

Behind and below the human forms is a visionary reconstruction of the Serpent Temple at Avebury, based on an engraving in William Stukeley's *Abury: A Temple of the British Druids* (London, 1743).[6] Such 'Druid' architecture is usually charged with negative meaning, as in *66*:

[1] While the impetus for this was running errands in connection with Hayley's biography of Romney, Blake's interest in Romney seems genuine enough. For some pertinent comparisons, see Jean H. Hagstrum, 'Romney and Blake: Gifts of Grace and Terror', *Blake in His Time*, pp. 201–13.

[2] This is the view of Anne K. Mellor, *Blake's Human Form Divine*, p. 331.

[3] This is the view of Wicksteed, *Blake's Jerusalem*, p. 251. The object cannot be a shuttle (which is not used in hand spinning), although this is the view of Henry Lesnick, 'The Antithetical Vision of *Jerusalem*', *Blake's Visionary Forms Dramatic*, pp. 410–11n.; and of Erdman, *The Illuminated Blake*, p. 379.

[4] Hilton (*Literal Imagination*, pp. 116–17) suggests that both this and the alternative clockwise motion may be perceived at the same time.

[5] *William Blake, Printmaker*, p. 158.

[6] As pointed out by Ruthven Todd, *Tracks in the Snow*, pp. 48–9.

1–9.[1] However, according to Stukeley, the builders of Avebury intended it as a symbol of the Godhead:

> The whole figure is the circle, snake, and wings. By this they meant to picture out, as well as they could, the nature of the divinity. The circle meant the supreme fountain of all being, the father; the serpent that divine emanation from him which was called the son; the wings imported that other divine emanation from them which was called the spirit, the *anima mundi.*[2]

At the millennial conclusion of *Jerusalem*, all unfallen forms are recovered, including 'the all wondrous Serpent clothed in gems & rich array' (*98*: 44; see also the design at the top of this plate); and the unfallen form of the Serpent Temple turns out to be a version of Golgonooza itself.[3] Characteristically, Blake's millennial world is a world of work and of naked beauty displayed. It is fitting that the Giant forms of *100* are seen before the gleaming white structure of the continuing city.

[1] For a discussion of 'Druid' architecture in Blake's works, see 'The Fourth Face of Man'.

[2] *Abury, a Temple of the British Druids, with Some Others, Described* (London, 1743), p. 54.

[3] See Wicksteed, *Blake's Jerusalem*, p. 251; and Kenneth R. Johnston, 'Blake's Cities: Romantic Forms of Urban Renewal', *Blake's Visionary Forms Dramatic*, pp. 436–9. Johnston observes that elsewhere Blake represents trilithons as imperfect, separate, or fallen, but never in a complete circle as in *100*; and he suggests that the *69, 70, 92,* and *94* designs 'can be seen as preparations for plate *100*, which represents their fulfillment' (p. 436). It should also be noted that it is Blake who supplies the trilithons of *100* in the first place; Stukeley's design, very close in all other respects, shows the structural units as megaliths. (See *Abury*, plate VIII.) Blake's rendering turns the structure into a more highly developed work of architecture.

Chapter VI

Form

Critical Views

It was Ellis and Yeats who first postulated that *Jerusalem* had a comprehensible form, a form which in their view consisted of a progression of states—Creation, Redemption, Judgement, and Regeneration—each corresponding to a chapter of the work.[1] This approach was carried further by S. Foster Damon:

> The first chapter pictures Man already below Eternity, falling into Beulah. The second chapter continues the Fall, bringing him into Generation. The third chapter contains the triumph of Error, the Conception of Christ, the Nativity and the Crucifixion. The fourth chapter describes the first perceptions of Truth, the appearance of Antichrist, and the ultimate resurrection of Man.[2]

The assumption that if *Jerusalem* has a form, that form must consist of a sequence of events, has dominated the discussion of the subject since the work of these great early critics. But one problem with such an analysis is that it must be selective. It is true, for example, that the traumatic sexual event that precipitates Albion's fall takes place in Beulah, that Albion 'sunk / Down' on the edges of Beulah in *23*: 25–6, and that 'a great lamenting in Beulah' takes place in *25*. Nevertheless, the events of Chapter 1 begin in Generation and much of the rest occurs there, including the terrible struggle of Los with his Spectre and the agonized dialogue of Jerusalem, Albion, and Vala. In *12*: 6 Los can say, 'Albion is dead! his Emanation is divided from him!' The rage, conflict, and 'death' which predominate in Chapter 1 are hardly characteristic of Beulah, that sweet and pleasant rest from the labours of Eternity. Furthermore, Beulah references abound throughout *Jerusalem*, and in fact events occur on all four levels in all four chapters, though mostly on the plane of Generation with

[1] See Introduction, p. 20.

[2] *William Blake*, p. 187.

perspectives opening 'upward' to Beulah and Eden, and 'downward' to Ulro.

When viewed in a linear perspective, *Jerusalem* can only be judged an unsuccessful, patchwork narrative; and this is indeed what Damon concludes.

> It is perfectly evident from this synopsis that Blake had not developed his narrative powers. There are many incoherences, and even some contradictions. For example, Albion utters twice his last words in Eternity (*23*: 26 and *47*: 17). The surmise is that Blake did not view the Fall as one steady act, but as a spiral alternating upward and downward; sometimes gleaming with the old light, sometimes passing a point already passed before.[1]

It is a pity that Damon did not apply the spiral image to *Jerusalem* itself, for such a model could suggest much more about the form of the work than the assumed linear one. Instead, Damon's view is that *Jerusalem* is great *despite* its 'broad and vague' plot; that it is a 'storehouse' rather than a 'vehicle' of thought, 'decorated with splendid passages of poetry'.[2] The difficulty, Damon suggests, may be due to Blake's 'inspirational' method of writing. 'He would insert invocations and choral passages, jotting them down as they came within the broad outline of each chapter.'[3] The implications of such a view have been discussed in Chapter I and need not be repeated here. As Damon recognizes, plates were moved from one point to another in *Jerusalem*, passages from *The Four Zoas* were revised for inclusion, and the work took at least sixteen years to complete. These facts do not accord well with purely inspirational composition. And if *Jerusalem* has a firm intellectual consistency, as Damon was the first to insist, it may also have a form that can accommodate, for example, the two utterances of Albion's last words.

That *Jerusalem* is a patchwork construction is also the view of Sloss and Wallis. They too find that whatever consistency *Jerusalem* may have consists of ideas, and they too ascribe its alleged disorganization to Blake's supposed method of composition. At the same time, since their understanding of *Jerusalem* is far less comprehensive than Damon's, their

[1] *William Blake*, p. 193.
[2] Ibid., pp. 185, 195. [3] Ibid., p. 193.

critical judgement of it is less positive, especially in respect of the matter of form:

It is . . . to be read not as an ordered whole, nor even as a series of visions, but as a congeries of episodes bearing upon the conflict between the Everlasting Gospel and Natural Religion, between Forgiveness and Punishment. As in *The Four Zoas*, revision appears never to have been systematic: the work was probably altered by additions and possibly also by eliminations, made without regard to the balance of the poem. What mattered to Blake was obviously the vision that possessed him at the moment: and his unwillingness to do more than merely transcribe it produces frequently the effect of inconsistency.[1]

It is odd that Sloss and Wallis, the first editors to publish a text and analysis of *The Four Zoas* revisions, should take Blake's statements about Spiritual Dictation so literally, in addition to overlooking the difference between an abandoned manuscript and a finished work. Nevertheless, their judgement cannot be dismissed lightly. It persists among a minority of Blake scholars and, what is more important, it is the received idea of many other students of literature, most of whom would be likely to endorse F. R. Leavis's view that Blake was a great writer of lyrics but failed in his attempt to create successful long poems.[2]

Northrop Frye's great contribution to the study of *Jerusalem* is his demonstration, anticipating the concerns of some later critics, of its mythical structure. At times Frye brilliantly bridges the two aspects of the subject: the coherence of the work and the coherence of the myth, as when he observes that the numbers three and four 'are respectively those of infinite extension and cyclic recurrence', and that '*Jerusalem* has four parts, and the end of the third part brings us back to where we started'.[3] For the most part, however, perhaps owing to the necessities of a book that treats of the entire canon of Blake's written work, *Fearful Symmetry* states rather than demonstrates the formal cohesion of the work itself.

Each part of *Jerusalem* [writes Frye] presents a phrase of imaginative vision simultaneously with the body of error it clarifies. Part One,

[1] *Prophetic Writings*, I. 439.

[2] 'Justifying One's Valuation of Blake', in *William Blake: Essays in Honour of Sir Geoffrey Keynes*, pp. 82–3.

[3] *Fearful Symmetry*, p. 368.

> addressed to the public, sets the Fall over against Golgonooza, the individual palace or watchtower of art from which the visionary may see nature in its true form as a sleeping giant. . . . Part Two, addressed to the Jews, sets the vision of the world under the law over against the evolution of the Bible out of history. Part Three, addressed to the Deists, contrasts the coming of Jesus with the resistance to his teachings which Deism expresses. Part Four, addressed to the Christians, deals at once with the apocalypse and the final epiphany of Antichrist.[1]

While this analysis goes beyond any hitherto advanced, it does not attempt to account for the seeming disunity which all readers notice in *Jerusalem*. Furthermore, Frye does not distinguish between the type of structure manifested in *The Four Zoas* and that of *Milton* and *Jerusalem*. Yet the skeletal structure of *The Four Zoas* is cumulative and progressive—a series of actions leading to other actions. The structure of *Jerusalem* is radically different, as can be seen from attempts to summarize the respective plots of both works. Such a summary is feasible for *The Four Zoas,*[2] but it is not at all helpful for *Jerusalem*. Wicksteed's *William Blake's Jerusalem* provides a synopsis of approximately 5,000 words which devotes a sentence to every action or speech, but which, paradoxically, creates an impression of disjointedness and fragmentation.[3] The form of *Jerusalem* must be distinguished from the sequential narrative of *The Four Zoas* as a prelude to further discussion of the subject.

In the years following the publication of *Fearful Symmetry*, there developed a view among Blake critics that *Jerusalem*, if subjected to the kind of scrutiny that the New Critics had promulgated, could be shown to possess unity in a thematic sense. Support for this assumption came from Blake himself, for the arrangement of the work into four chapters and 100 plates suggested that *Jerusalem* could be explained by schematic analysis. One such attempt is that of Karl Kiralis.[4] Kiralis cites the magnificent passage in *98*: 28–40 as a key to the

[1] *Fearful Symmetry*, p. 359.

[2] See Damon, *William Blake*, pp. 154–67; and Brian Wilkie and Mary Lynn Johnson, *Blake's* Four Zoas: *the Design of a Dream* (Cambridge, Mass.: Harvard University Press, 1978). Of course no summary can hope to do justice to the status of *FZ* as a palimpsest manuscript.

[3] pp. 93–102.

[4] 'The Theme and Structure of William Blake's *Jerusalem*', in *The Divine Vision*, ed. V. de Sola Pinto (London: Gollancz, 1957), pp. 141–62.

form of the entire work. In particular he takes 'the Three Regions immense / Of Childhood, Manhood, & Old Age' (*98*: 32–3) as indicating 'the groups addressed in chapters 2, 3, and 4', chapter 1 being 'the general introduction' (pp. 147–8). Like Damon, Kiralis sees the events of the poem as progressive, a 'structure of growth' by which 'the chapters of *Jerusalem* reflect one another but at the same time remain a unit as the child, youth, and mature man are "One Man" ' (p. 158). However, there seems no reason to regard Chapter 1 as a 'general introduction'; that purpose is served by the first Preface, while after a brief statement of the epic theme on plate *4*, and an invocation on plate *5*, Chapter 1 goes directly into Los's conflict with his Spectre and then into the condition and circumstances of Albion's fall. Nor does Albion mature progressively through the course of the poem: he is already in a fallen state when he is first extensively described in *18*, and he remains in that state throughout Chapters 2 and 3, and most of Chapter 4, until his resurrection in *95*. If, however, it is Los who is supposed to reflect a progression through three phases, the application is equally difficult, for Los's struggle to integrate his prophetic powers and to rescue Albion is likewise a major theme of all four chapters until its successful resolution in *91–2*. Yet there seems no other sense in which the tripartite ages of Man can be applied to the audience, and the notion of a 'reflective pattern' (p. 158) by which elements of each chapter reappear in the others complicates this dilemma but does not resolve it: as Kiralis admits, 'The pattern of reflection cannot be consistently applied' (p. 161). Most persuasive is Kiralis's observation that 'in this respect Blake is walking up and down in man's history and "to and fro" in eternity'—but this should indicate the need for a different approach to the entire poem.

Kiralis's thematic analysis has been rebutted by E. J. Rose,[1] who posits an alternative schema. 'The four parts', according to Rose, 'are a series of states dominated by an appropriate Zoa, and marked by the attributes and imagery associated with that Zoa. Thus, each part is controlled structurally (as indicated by the imagery and thematic patterns) by a major aspect of fallen man represented in turn by Tharmas, Luvah,

[1] 'The Structure of Blake's *Jerusalem*', *Bucknell Review*, XI (1963), 35–54.

Urizen, and Los' (pp. 48–9). Yet what is most striking about the Zoas' role in *Jerusalem* is its reduction: three of them have been relegated to a largely passive state. Their role as agents has been superseded by Albion and his sons and daughters in one myth, and by Los, his Spectre, and Enitharmon in the other. And although Los may rightly be said to dominate the final chapter, he is far more important than the other Zoas in the other three chapters as well; he is a Zoa and yet much more than a Zoa. 'The Imagination', as Blake's Milton says, 'is not a State: it is the Human Existence itself' (*M* 32: 32, E. 131). No comprehensive view of *Jerusalem* can be based on a system that Blake had left behind in *The Four Zoas*. Rose correctly contrasts the structure of *Milton* and of *Jerusalem* with that of *The Four Zoas*, but the nature of *Jerusalem*'s structure remains to be elucidated.

There is, of course, yet another alternative conclusion: that Blake was simply wrong in his belief that everything in *Jerusalem* 'is studied and put into its fit place', that it really is formless after all. Such was the judgement of Swinburne, and such is that of W. H. Stevenson. 'The first impression of *Jerusalem*', Stevenson asserts, 'is of a vast idea lost in confusion, and it is also the abiding impression.'[1] Stevenson complains that on *92* 'suddenly, everything happens at once' and that after *94*: 5 'the rest is coda' (p. 257). He deplores the 'pseudo-Biblical genealogies and geography', and as for the form, 'it is not a narrative, but a series of pageants' (p. 259). These observations are valid at least in part, but the judgements associated with them may not be. The question is whether such aspects of *Jerusalem* are deep flaws or whether the work possesses a form other than that which the critic seeks in vain.

Models

Henry James, in speaking of certain novels, including *War and Peace*, asks: 'What do such large loose baggy monsters, with their queer elements of the accidental and the arbitrary, artistically *mean*?'[2] And what are we to do with our own large

[1] 'Blake's *Jerusalem*', *Essays in Criticism*, IX (1959), 254–64.

[2] Preface to *The Tragic Muse*, in Henry James, *The Art of the Novel*, ed. R. P. Blackmur (New York: Charles Scribner's Sons, 1962), p. 85.

loose baggy monster, *Jerusalem*? Schematic analyses of *Jerusalem* fail because none of them account for the Minute Particulars of the work. They are Procrustean beds upon which critics can accommodate Blake's Giant Forms only by lopping off their limbs.[1] *Jerusalem* is not essentially a narrative poem,[2] and if we are to find models that help us understand its structure, those models will not be literary epics. Blake specifically rejects epic models in the Preface to *Milton* when he includes Homer among the authors of 'Stolen and Perverted Writings' and Milton among those who were 'curbd by the general malady & infection from the silly Greek & Latin slaves of the Sword' (E. 94). However, alternative models do exist, and recent critics have put forward the examples of Ezekiel,[3] the Synoptic Gospels,[4] Revelation,[5] *Paradise Regained,*[6] and the 'encyclopedic anatomy'.[7] To these I would add a seventeenth-century tradition of the structural analysis of Revelation, Handel's *Messiah*, and possibly Smart's *Jubilate Agno*. The adducing of such models is no substitute for a close discussion of *Jerusalem* itself, but by helping us to envisage the sort of work *Jerusalem* is, it can provide a framework for such a discussion.

As we have seen, Blake drew in *Jerusalem* upon the language

[1] Some discussions recognize the problem only to advance new theories of linear progression. For Jane McClellan the unity of the work is provided by the dramatic activity of Los ('Dramatic Movement as a Structuring Device in Blake's *Jerusalem*', *Colby Library Quarterly*, XIII (1977), 195–208), and the reader's interest is seen as maintained by the building of suspense. Even Mitchell, after thoroughly demonstrating the unsatisfactory nature of linear readings of the work, substitutes one of his own: the succession of patriarchy by matriarchy (*Blake's Composite Art*, pp. 189–91).

[2] Mitchell posits 'a structure of antiform' for *Jerusalem*, meaning that 'the poem's structure undercuts the whole notion of predictable linear chronology by embodying it as chaos' (pp. 169–70).

[3] See Harold Bloom, E. 243, and 'Blake's *Jerusalem*: The Bard of Sensibility and the Form of Prophecy', *The Ringers in the Tower*, pp. 65–9.

[4] See Joanne Witke, '*Jerusalem*: a Synoptic Poem', *Comparative Literature* XXII (1970), 265–78.

[5] See Joseph A. Wittreich, Jr., 'Opening the Seals: Blake's Epics and the Milton Tradition', *Blake's Sublime Allegory*, pp. 48–50.

[6] Stuart Curran argues interestingly that *Jerusalem* involves a modification of the form of *Paradise Regained*: 'The Mental Pinnacle: *Paradise Regained* and the Romantic Four-Book Epic', in *Calm of Mind*, ed. Joseph Anthony Wittreich, Jr. (Cleveland and London: Case Western Reserve University, 1971), pp. 133–62.

[7] See below, page 290 and nn. 2, 3, and 4.

and conceptions of Old Testament Prophecy; he is also indebted to it, and particularly to Ezekiel for a notion of form that provides an alternative to epic narrative. Ezekiel, as Bloom points out, is divided into two parts of twenty-four chapters each. Moreover, its purpose is not primarily to tell a story—although, like *Jerusalem*, it does have narrative elements—but to transmit Prophecy in an appropriate form, a form which Bloom likens to 'a series of fire-bursts, one wave of flame after another'.[1] The synoptic Gospels provide a model of another kind. Although each Gospel is a narrative, the four together may be considered, as Joanne Witke suggests, as corresponding to the chapters of *Jerusalem*, particularly as, according to the tradition of the 'fourfold Gospel', each one was addressed (like the chapters of *Jerusalem*) to a different audience.[2] Most compelling of all is the analogy of Revelation, a non-narrative visionary work that was of lifelong interest to Blake, and that was, furthermore, the subject of a body of structural interpretation that in turn sheds light on *Jerusalem*.

In speaking of the tradition of interpreting Revelation as 'visionary theatre',[3] we return to some of the writers who occupied us in Chapter III—namely David Pareus, Joseph Mede, and John Lightfoot.[4] Here, however, doctrinal differences do not concern us. Mede and Lightfoot were millenarians, Pareus was not, but all three agree on how the images of Revelation were envisaged and how they were ordered in a non-chronological structure. They are, furthermore, in agreement with Blake in *Jerusalem* in emphasizing

[1] 'Blake's *Jerusalem*', p. 65.

[2] Matthew: Jews of Palestine; Mark: Jews of Alexandria; Luke: Colossians, John: spiritual members of the Church. Witke remarks: 'The digressions and repetitions that first appear to be obtrusions in *Jerusalem*'s narrative are, then, intrinsic to the poem's structure according to the synoptic form, which unites divers elements of the varied yet harmonious parts.' ('*Jerusalem*: A Synoptic Poem', pp. 277–8.)

[3] The expression is Lightfoot's; see below, p. 286, n. 1.

[4] Joseph Anthony Wittreich, Jr. has persuasively argued the affinity between *Milton* and *Jerusalem* and Pareus' reading of Revelation; see 'Opening the Seals: Blake's Epics and the Milton Tradition', *Blake's Sublime Allegory*, pp. 33–49. In *Visionary Poetics* (San Marino, California: Huntington Library, 1979), Wittreich applies some ideas of Pareus and of Joseph Mede about Revelation to the poetry of Milton.

that the visions are both actually seen and figures to be interpreted. Blake writes:

> I see Albion sitting upon his Rock in the first Winter
> And thence I see the Chaos of Satan and the World of
>   Adam (*15*: 30–1)
>
> I write in South Molton Street, what I both see and hear
> In regions of Humanity, in Londons opening streets.
>
> I see thee awful Parent Land in light, behold I see!
> (*34/38*: 42–4)

This insistence upon things 'Heard and Seen', to use the Swedenborgian formula of which Blake was aware,[1] puts Blake into direct relationship not only with Swedenborg but also with Ezekiel and John of Patmos. Furthermore, the visions of *Jerusalem* are also symbols which must be read in relation to one another in the context of the work. The same may be said of the visions of Revelation—and, indeed, was said of them by the writers employing what I shall call the synchronous method of interpretation.[2]

Writing of Revelation 4: 6, John Lightfoot remarks that 'these living *Creatures* or *Cherubims* are never mentioned but in vision or Hieroglyphick', and continues: 'They are to be expounded to such a doctrinall and figurative sense, and so is the whole body of glory, as I may call it, the whole visionary theatre or spectacle that is before us to be taken.'[3] David Pareus also employs this striking conception of a theatre of the mind, elaborating the idea so as to comprehend the structural components of drama as experienced by an audience:

> For as in humane Tragedies, diverse persons one after another come upon the Theater to represent things done, and so again depart: diverse Chores also or Companies of Musicians and Harpers distinguish the diversity of the *Acts*, and while the *Actors* hold up, do with musicall accord sweeten the wearinesse of the Spectators, and keepe them in

[1] It forms, for example, part of the full title of the copy of *Heaven and Hell* that Blake annotated. Of course in using this expression, Swedenborg must have wanted to establish a parallel between himself and biblical seers of visions.

[2] I use 'synchronous' in referring to the writers of the period, as the word is used by Mede (see below); in discussing the structure of *Jerusalem*, however, I employ the word interchangeably with 'synchronic'.

[3] *The Temple*, p. 253.

attention: so verily the thing it selfe speaketh that in this Heavenly Interlude, by diverse *shewes* and *apparitions* are represented diverse, or rather (as we shall see) the same things touching the Church, not past, but to come, and that their diverse *Acts* are renewed by divers *Chores* or Companies, one while of 24. *Elders* and four *Beast* [*sic*], another while of *Angels*, sometimes of *Sealed ones in their foreheads*, and sometimes of Harpers, &c. with *new Songs*, and worthy *Hymmes*, not so much to lessen the wearisomnesse of the Spectators, as to infuse holy meditation into the minds of the Readers, and so to lift them up to Heavenly matters.[1]

Joseph Mede, too, employs the analogy of a drama, observing that John beheld his visions as 'upon a Stage' and terming Revelation 'The Apocalyptick Theatre'.[2] Across its stage parade figures of symbolic import. 'Angels are put for the nations which they were thought to govern'[3] (cf. Albion's Angel in *America* and 'Tharmas the Angel of the Tongue' in *63*: 5). Women are 'not such as are commonly called so, but Cities'[4] ('Am I Jerusalem the lost Adultress? or am I / Babylon come up to Jerusalem?' (*61*: 34–5)). Such views make it possible to regard the book of Revelation as simultaneously vision and artefact. The concept of a visionary or apocalyptic theatre is closely linked to the notion of the representation of events in a non-chronological form.

David Pareus recognizes of Revelation what we must recognize of *Jerusalem*: that its development cannot be explained according to a linear model. Pareus quotes Augustine to this effect: 'It so repeateth the same things after a diverse manner, as if it seemed to speake of different things, whereas we shall find that it speakes of the very same things, after a diverse manner.'[5] So, observes Pareus, each of the seven visions of Revelation ends with a last judgement, even though there is

[1] *The Authors Preface Upon the Revelation* (Amsterdam, 1644), p. 20. Pareus takes as a precedent Origen's description of the Song of Solomon as 'a Fable acted on the Theater . . . a Spirituall Interlude of foure Personages'; and goes on to characterize Revelation as 'An Heavenly *Dramma* or Interlude, not only of *foure* but of diverse persons and things, by Typicall Speeches and Actions, exhibiting to John's sight or hearing those things in the Heavenly Theater, which God would have him to understand' (p. 20).

[2] *The Key of the Revelation*, p. 30.

[3] Ibid., p. 109.

[4] Ibid., p. 83.

[5] *The Authors Preface Upon Revelation*, p. 21; from *Civitatis Dei*, Lib. 20, cap. 17.

only one Last Judgement, and the same is true of other repetitions of events.

By the seven Seales and seven Trumpets different things seem to be signified, whereas the same things are treated of after a different manner. Thus the *Beasts* appear to be diverse, whereas notwithstanding they are one. The rupture and ruine of Babylon is diversely set forth: and yet it always comes but to one thing.[1]

These corresponding visions are termed 'Parallel-Acts' by Pareus, and are described as 'not alwayes divided by whole Chapters (like as Tragedie-writers use to do) but sometimes are joyned together, and as it were mingled in the same Chapters, because they shadow out Histories or things by the same periods, and walking (as the saying is) with equall steps'.[2] In this manner Pareus hopes he can realize his aim 'to shew the Harmonie and consent of the foregoing and following Types, and of the darker and more clear with each other, and with the Types and Phrases of the ancient Prophets, that so I might illustrate the Revelation by the Revelation'.[3]

Joseph Mede's brilliant analysis of Revelation starts from premisses similar to those of Pareus. In order to develop an interpretation that is not based upon succession in time, Mede proposes to demonstrate 'The Synchronism and order of the Prophecies of the Revelation'.[4] Mede is careful to define his meaning: 'By a *Synchronisme* of prophecies, I mean when the things therein designed, run along in the same time; as if thou shouldest call it *an agreement in time or age*: because prophecies of things falling out in the same time, run on in time together, or Synchronize.'[5] The notion of Synchronism allows Mede to go from one part of Revelation to another, joining 'into one time as it were visions of the same time, and altogether of the same thing, and which there was no need to sever in this matter'.[6] Spatial relations may be

[1] *The Authors Preface Upon Revelation*, p. 27.

[2] Ibid., pp. 22, 24.

[3] Ibid., p. 28. Pareus divides Revelation into three major parts: a Preface, consisting of title and dedication (i. 1–8); a Prophecy comprising seven visions (i. 9–xxii. 52), and a Conclusion and Anathema (xx. 53 to the end). Thus the great bulk of the work is the middle, divided as follows according to the seven visions: from i. 9 to the end of iii, iv–vii, viii–xi, xii–xiv, xv–xvi, xvii–xix, xx–xxii. 52 (p. 19).

[4] *The Key of the Revelation*, subtitle on p. 1.

[5] Ibid., p. 1.

[6] Ibid., p. 10.

regarded as temporal relations, for 'It is no new thing, that the order of situation should express the order of time, as it is to be seen in the *Statue* of Nebuchadnezzar's dream.'[1] So according to Mede's analysis, Revelation displays a coherent structure but one which must be explained according to synchronic rather than diachronic principles.

We can see how such ideas may be applied to the structure of *Jerusalem. Jerusalem* is a work virtually all middle. It begins as if it were an epic, with an invocation and a statement of theme, and then moves rapidly to the agon of Los and his Spectre beginning on plate *6*. Instead of going on to create a sequence of strongly plotted actions, each leading to another until a climax is inevitably generated (as in *The Four Zoas*), Blake allows the poem to develop in another way. As Hazard Adams has put it:

> One fable grows into another, one set of images begets another. The fable of Los and the Spectre begets the story of Los and Enitharmon or the fable of the Emanation. Albion's sleep generates a parallel situation between Albion and Jerusalem. The logic of the appearance of these new situations is the logic of metaphor, not cause and effect, not plot.[2]

The extended middle of *Jerusalem* continues (with intermittent evocations of the pre-lapsarian world and occasional foreshadowings of the millennium) until the Covering Cherub is revealed in *89*. Events then lead rapidly to an ending: the resurrection of Albion in *95*, the sacrifice of Jesus and the consequent self-sacrifice of Albion in *96*, and the millennial realization of the last four pages of text and designs. This structure generally resembles that of Revelation as described by David Pareus—plates *1–5* corresponding to the title and dedication, *6–88* to the successive prophetic visions, and *88–100* to the Conclusion and Anathema. The body of *Jerusalem* does not consist of a cumulatively developing story any more than do the seven visions of Revelation. 'In these prophecies and visions of things done', writes Mede, '. . . it falleth out, that they labour in vain, that so go about to interpret the Revelation, as if the events every where should succeed one after another, in the same order and course, as the visions are

[1] *The Key of the Revelation*, p. 11.
[2] 'Blake, *Jerusalem* and Symbolic Form', *Blake Studies*, VII (1975), 163.

revealed.'[1] The same admonition could be addressed to critics of *Jerusalem*. If we are to understand the form of that work, we must discover the interrelationships of its parallel acts, its synchrony, in order to illustrate *Jerusalem* by *Jerusalem*.

In addition to exemplars provided in the Bible and by the synchronous interpretation of Revelation, some literary works of the seventeenth and eighteenth centuries present analogies of form with *Jerusalem*. Mitchell, drawing upon Northrop Frye's theory of genres,[2] terms these 'encyclopedic anatomies'.[3] Among the works Mitchell includes with *Jerusalem* under this rubric are *The Anatomy of Melancholy, Tale of a Tub*, and *Tristram Shandy*. This classification does much to show us that *Jerusalem* belongs to a genre characterized by digressiveness, catalogues, and 'the constant tendency to be encyclopaedic and exhaustive both in technique and in subject matter, and to see both in highly intellectualized terms'.[4] These anatomies are not the only examples previous to *Jerusalem* of non-chronological, non-linear modes of development. Two works of the mid-eighteenth century demand notice in this regard. One, Handel's *Messiah*, was so well known that we may assume Blake's familiarity with it. The other, Smart's *Jubilate Agno*, then only in manuscript, could have been known to Blake through William Hayley. Each in its own way provides an alternative to epic narrative in organizing the treatment of a profound and exalted subject.

In Chapter I, I compared *Jerusalem* with Smart's *Jubilate Agno* with respect to certain aspects of the verse of each. Some interesting parallels in form can also be found between the two. Both poets sought models for the non-narrative structuring of a long poem in sacred texts; Smart discovered his not in the Bible but in the Anglican liturgy. As W. H. Bond observes, 'The title and peroration of *Jubilate Agno* are . . . closely parallel to portions of the Order for Morning Prayer and the Psalter.'[5] In adopting this arrangement, Smart was strongly influenced by Lowth's emphasis on the antiphonal or responsive nature of Hebrew poetry. Indeed, the

[1] *The Key of the Revelation*, p. 27.

[2] See *Anatomy of Criticism* (Princeton: Princeton University Press, 1957), pp. 311-15.

[3] *Blake's Composite Art*, pp. 174-6.

[4] Frye, *Anatomy of Criticism*, p. 313.

[5] *Jubilate Agno*, p. 20.

entire poem was meant to parallel the liturgy. As W. H. Bond demonstrates, the *For* verses were intended as responses to the *Let* verses, something that would have been more apparent to those who saw the manuscript before its leaves became disordered, especially as in the earlier part a line-for-line relationship is maintained. Presumably Smart's mental illness prevented him from adhering to his scheme throughout, and the fact that some leaves were lost further obscures his original intention. Blake of course did not choose Smart's particular form for *Jerusalem*, but if he knew *Jubilate Agno*, or if, as seems likely, he at least knew something about it, he would have recognized in it an attempt akin to his own to find an alternative structure for a long poem.

Blake's probable attitude towards Handel's oratorios has been discussed by Martha W. England, who wittily observes:

> George Bernard Shaw once remarked on the conviction prevalent among English-speaking people that Milton wrote the Bible. . . . Surely Shaw must have been aware that, for the English, Handel wrote a good deal of the Bible. Once the sound of Milton gets into the human frame, it is likely to be there to stay. The same is true of Handel. Blake had the opportunity to be thus affected.[1]

Professor England goes on to draw some parallels between the Handel/Milton–Hamilton *Samson* and Blake's works, early and late. Although she does not consider *Messiah* in relation to *Jerusalem*, she lays the ground for such a discussion by extrapolating from Blake's works the probability of his knowledge of Handel, and by showing that the Handelian parodies in *An Island in the Moon* indicate a complex attitude towards Handel on Blake's part, not dissimilar to Blake's attitude towards Milton.[2] Having the perception to reject an orthodox representation of Milton still common in his time,[3] Blake, we may hope, could have appreciated *Messiah* even though George II had admired it.

[1] 'The Satiric Blake: Apprenticeship at the Haymarket?' Part II, *Bulletin of the New York Public Library*, LXXIII (1969), 541.

[2] It is worth noting that one could admire Handel and yet condemn the gigantic Handel Commemorations in Westminster Abbey, as did William Cowper, who praised Handel as 'the Homer of the Age' in *The Task* and who subscribed to the first edition of the score of *Messiah*. See Robert Manson Meyers, *Handel's Messiah: A Touchstone of Taste* (New York: Macmillan, 1948), p. 185.

[3] See the valuable discussion on this subject in *Angel of Apocalypse* by Joseph Anthony Wittreich, Jr. (Madison: University of Wisconsin Press, 1975).

The appositeness of *Samson* to *Jerusalem* can easily be seen. One could draw analogies between Samson and the fallen Albion, Dalila and Vala, Micah and Los, the chorus of Philistines and the Sons of Albion, and the Chorus of Israelites and the Daughters of Beulah. Of course Blake would have found most of these elements, though not Micah or the chorus of Philistines, in Milton's original before Newburgh Hamilton adapted it. More important than any single comparison, however, is the general sense of a grand lyric drama for voices. This would of course be even more true of *Messiah*, and in addition the latter eschews telling a story in order to develop its meaning in another manner.

Such is the artistry of Charles Jennens's *Messiah* libretto, that in performance one is scarcely aware that it is an arrangement of fifty-six passages from the Prophets, the Psalms, Job, the Gospels, the Epistles, and Revelation. Yet, as Paul Henry Lang remarks, 'the libretto was more than a compilation, for it had a subtle plan behind it: the sequence of Promise, Incarnation, Passion, and Resurrection provides an epic unity that dispenses with a dramatic plot'.[1] In part I, the subject is first the prophecies of a Messiah and then the miraculous birth that fulfils those prophecies. It is therefore appropriate that sections 2–12 are taken from the Old Testament Prophets, beginning with Isaiah 40: 1–3:

> Comfort ye, comfort ye my people saith your God. Speak ye comfortably to Jerusalem, and cry unto her that her warfare is accomplished, that her iniquity is pardoned. The voice of him that crieth in the wilderness, Prepare ye the way of the Lord, make straight in the desert a highway for our God.[2]

After the pastoral symphony, sections 14–18 from Luke recount the revelation to the shepherds; of the remainder of part I, three sections are from Isaiah and Zachariah, and two are from Matthew, these last embodying the realization of the prophecy of the others. Part II concerns Christ's mission

[1] *George Frideric Handel* (London: Faber and Faber, 1967), p. 342.

[2] I quote the *Messiah* libretto from the text printed in Myers, *Handel's Messiah*, pp. 291–8. There are some differences in wording between Jennens and the Authorized Version. The libretto, it is worth noting, was easily available: a printed wordbook was issued for every performance of *Messiah* conducted by Handel, and frequently thereafter (see Myers, p. 148).

and sacrifice, beginning with John's 'Behold the Lamb of God, that taketh away the sins of the world' (1: 29) and culminating in the great Hallelujah Chorus from Revelation. The majority of the intervening passages are from the Old Testament, emphasizing once more the continuity and fruition of the Messianic tradition. Part III explores the consequences of the Crucifixion: victory over death in the resurrection of the flesh. Here all the texts are from the New Testament, with the exception of part of the first, in which are combined Job 19: 25-6 and 1 Corinthians 15: 20:

I know that my Redeemer liveth, and that He shall stand at the latter day upon the earth. And though worms destroy this body, yet in my flesh shall I see God. For now is Christ risen from the dead, the first-fruits of them that sleep.

Like *Jerusalem*, Handel's Sacred Oratorio has narrative elements, and as in *Jerusalem* these elements are less important in themselves, in the sense of telling a story, than they are as a vehicle for the major themes of the work. Furthermore, *Jerusalem* too is a song for many voices, and a number of different types of music are indicated in it. Many passages spoken by the narrator introducing speeches by the dramatis personae are reminiscent of the Handelian dry recitative, consisting of statements like 'Then Albion broke silence and with groans reply'd' (*20*: 42), 'Los answered sighing like the Bellows of his Furnaces' (*88*: 1), or 'And One stood forth from the Divine Family & said' (*33/37*: 1). Other passages are identified as specific types of song. When we read that Los 'chaunted his song' (*6*: 11 and *56*: 2), for example, the archaic word 'chaunt'[1] is appropriate to his vatic nature. We may well imagine him as a mighty bass when we are told 'And this is the Song of Los, the Song that he sings on his Watch' (*85*: 21) before his long, powerful address to Jerusalem, a passage closed by 'Thus Los sings upon his Watch walking from Furnace to Furnace' (*86*: 33). A very different type of singing is indicated for Mary's lyrical outburst in *61*, when in her exchange with Joseph 'Mary burst forth into a Song!' (28). Vala is given music consistent with her bad intentions—'So

[1] The *OED* gives examples from Carlyle and from Ruskin, but both are obviously deliberately archaic.

sang she: and the Spindle turnd furious as she sang' (*80*: 32); and in *88*: 23–4 Enitharmon's duplicity is indicated musically: 'So speaking she sat down on Sussex shore singing lulling / Cadences'. These are some of the many examples of the ways in which individual characters are presented as singers and assigned appropriate songs.

Oratorio-like, *Jerusalem* also contains parts for groups of voices and for massed voices. The marvellously sinister passage beginning 'Cast! Cast ye Jerusalem forth!' (*18*: 11) is a duet for Hand and Hyle. Beautiful open vowels characterize the very different duet for Los's Emanation and Spectre, opening 'We alone are escaped. O merciful Lord and Saviour' (*43/29*: 29). In *57*: 1 a quartet for four Cathedral Cities is indicated. Elsewhere larger forces are called for. The beautiful lyric address to Jerusalem on *60* is 'the Song of the Lamb, sung by Slaves in evening time' (38); while the savage, frenzied chorus of *68* is introduced 'And thus the Warriors cry, in the hot day of Victory, in Songs' (10). The deeply moving chorus of impressed seamen in *65*: 33–6 is actually embedded in a larger chorus for the Spectre Sons of Albion. A mixed group of Los's Sons and Daughters 'lament' from *11*: 17 to *12*: 4, and there are chorales for women as well. An elegiac passage (*83*: 85–*84*: 28) is sung by the Daughters of Albion 'in lamentation'; Chapter 2 ends with the invocation 'Come O thou Lamb of God and take away the remembrance of Sin' sung 'in sweet response' by the Daughters of Beulah (*50*: 23–4). There are even orchestral interludes, as the warlike one of *80*: 37–9:

> . . . loud sound the trumpets
> Of war: the cymbals play loud before the Captains
> With Cambel & Gwendolyn in dance and solemn song

Finally, the whole of *Jerusalem* is referred to as a musical work in Enitharmon's words 'The Poets Song draws to its period' (*92*: 8) and again in *99* at the very end of the text: 'The End of the Song / of Jerusalem'.

The Form of *Jerusalem*

From Aristotle on, certain types of literary works have been sustained by the notion of organicism, the idea that the work is like an animal or a plant, every minute part of which, encoded in it from the beginning, has its function. Coleridge's famous distinction between shape and form posits the latter as a 'self-witnessing and self-effected sphere of agency' in contradistinction to 'The death or imprisonment of the thing', which is shape.[1] Blake too asserts a belief in the inevitable relationship of parts to the whole, in 'To the Public': 'all [the parts] are necessary to each other' (E. 144). Yet when we come to examine *Jerusalem*, we find that in numerous instances, some of which have already been mentioned, plates were moved from one position to another. This is what suggests to some that *Jerusalem* has the form of a scrap-book and seems to legitimize its use as a quarry for selections in anthologies and textbooks[2] and presenting it in a simplified version for those who do not want to take the trouble to read it as Blake wrote it.[3] The lack of inevitability of sequence is remarked on by John Beer, who plausibly suggests that *16, 72, 59*, and *73* may originally have formed a group which was later dispersed, which leads him to conclude that 'the general order of the poem is not absolutely determined or sacrosanct' in Blake's mind.[4] That this is so is best illustrated by Chapter 2, in which there are two extant orders of plates. What kind of a form is it, we may ask, in which more than one arrangement of pages is possible? If we can answer this question satisfactorily with respect to Chapter 2, we shall be well on the way to demonstrating what kind of form characterizes the work as a whole.

Of the five copies of Chapter 2 which Blake himself produced—and no other copies can have authority in this matter—three follow a certain sequence in Chapter 2, while the two others follow a different sequence. As if to baffle his critics further, Blake foliated copies A, C, and F according to the majority sequence and copies D and E according to the minority one. Moreover, if we are tempted to follow a simple

[1] 'On Poesy or Art', *Biographia Literaria*, ed. J. Shawcross (London: Oxford University Press, 1958), II. 262.

[2] Among books specifically intended for student use, an exception is *William Blake / Selected Poems and Prose*, ed. Hazard Adams (New York: Holt, Rinehart, and Winston, 1970), in which *Jerusalem* is printed entire.

[3] *Jerusalem: A Simplified Version*, ed. William R. Hughes.

[4] *Blake's Visionary Universe*, p. 173.

rule by majority here, we must somehow account for the fact that the magnificently coloured Tatham–Stirling–Mellon copy is paginated according to the minority sequence.[1] The position is summarized by David V. Erdman, 'The supposedly "standard" order is neither the latest nor the earliest order established by Blake. It is found in the Harvard and the Mellon, but in his latest copy, the Morgan, Blake returned to the order of his first two copies.'[2] There are strong arguments in favour of either sequence of plates. 'Perhaps', says Erdman, 'the soundest conclusion is that Blake found both sequences attractive but considered neither definitive'. In the editions of Sir Geoffrey Keynes, the order of copies D and E is observed; Erdman follows the A C F order; Bentley reverts to the D E order. Rather than argue in support of one or the other,[3] my concern here is to discuss the implications of their very existence as far as the form of *Jerusalem* is concerned.

First I shall indicate by means of the table below the actual sequence of plates in the two arrangements, and at the same time I shall indicate by italicized capitals the segments or blocs of plates that remain together in each sequence. At first this may look confusing, as if Blake had been arbitrarily experimenting with the pagination of the chapter, but if we study the numeration for a few moments it is clear that the deviations are simpler than they seem. In fact, before even considering the content and poetic structure of Chapter 2, we can find by the evidence of the foliation alone that the changes Blake made were few and simple. The prefatory plates *25, 26,* and *27* were of course unaffected by the reordering. The first plate of Chapter 2 proper, *28*, is the same in both sequences. So are the last four plates, *47–50*, but of the intermediate plates, *42* alone holds its place. As can be

[1] Copy B does not, of course, concern us, because it consists only of Chapter 1. Copy G, the Isman copy, remains unlocated and its foliation has never been described.

[2] 'The Suppressed and Altered Passages of Blake's *Jerusalem*', p. 40. Of course it may be hypothesized that copy E could have been foliated after the others.

[3] Clearly the fact that the majority order is also the order of the first and last copies ought to bear considerable weight, and I have expressed my own preference for this order in my review of *Blake Books*. (*Papers of the Bibliographical Society of America*, LXXII (1978), 397–8.) Bentley, on the other hand, regards the minority order as 'the later of the two', because Blake worked on its colouring 'perhaps . . . in the last months of his life' (*William Blake's Writings*, I. 735).

Copies A, C, F (British Museum, Harvey, Morgan)		Copies D, E (Harvard, Mellon)	
28	*A*	*A*	28
29			43
30		*E*	44
31			45
32			46
33	*B*		29
34			30
35			31
36		*B*	32
37			33
38			34
39			35
40	*C*		36
41			37
42	*D*	*D*	42
43			38
44		*C*	39
45	*E*		40
46			41
47			47
48		*F*	48
49	*F*		49
50			50

seen from the columnar display, the plates that change position comprise three groups: *29–37* (*B*), *38–41* (*C*), and *43–6* (*E*). What appears to have happened is that after printing the British Museum and Harvey copies, or at least after completing the second chapters of these copies, Blake adopted an alternate order. He moved one bloc of four plates from its position immediately after *37* to the location previously occupied by *43–6* (*E*), which in turn were moved so as to follow *28*. Therefore, of the six blocs, three did not move at all, though in the shift the single-plate bloc *D* acquired new neighbours on either side. The bloc sequences changed from *ABCDEF* to *AEBDCF*. New linkages between plates now appeared as follows: *28–43, 46–29, 37–42, 42–38, 41–7*. By discussing these new connections in relation to those of the original order, we may gain a clearer idea of the differences between the minority order of plates and the majority order. In envisaging these differences, a diagram will be helpful.

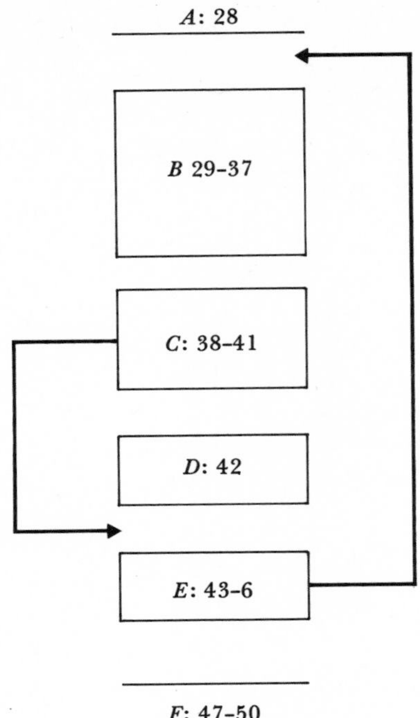

The link between *28* and *29* is not a strong one.[1] Plate *28*, with its intriguing design, begins its text with the speech and actions of Albion as punisher and judge. The first word of *29* is apparently a dangling participle: it is presumably *Albion* (not the Spectrous Chaos) who is 'Turning his back to the Divine Vision' when 'his Spectrous / Chaos before his face appeard' (1–2). This plate, in a wider and more flowery script than *28*, contains speeches by the Spectre, Albion, and Vala; none of these are closely related to the contents of *28*. However, *30* continues the speech of Vala from *29* and is, moreover, etched in a flowery script similar to that of *29*. The binding of the senses of Reuben begins at *30*: 51, but this episode is interrupted by *31*, with its introduction of limits to the Fall and the creation of States, and with its memorable white-line etching of the creation of Eve by Jesus. Plate *32*

[1] For obvious reasons, I use only single numerals in referring to the plates in this part of the discussion.

then returns in both text and design to the Los–Reuben episode, but in turn is followed by an obviously interpolated plate; *33*, with its beautiful white-line designs, begins with a first line that was evidently engraved on the plate after the rest of the text had been etched. Presumably this was done to create a jointure, but actually the 'And One stood forth from the Divine family & said' could follow any number of other plates. In contrast, *34* is closely linked with *33*, with Albion 'revengeful covering / His face and bosom with petrific hardness' in the transition from the one to the other. Another tight connection exists between *34* and *35*, for the description of the Gate of Los straddles these; and Los's efforts to save Albion, beginning at *35*: 12, are carried over to *36*. Although *37* joins with *36* by taking up the last word of that plate ('and benevolent Bath / Bath who is Legions'), it seems to have been introduced later in order to amplify the negative side of Bath and to stress the weakness of the Friends.

Segment *B*, then, consisting of nine plates, begins with the loose fit of 28–9, follows with two closely related plates, then an interpolated plate, then a plate closely following the two that precede the interpolation; another interpolation follows *32*, but the next three plates are closely linked; the last plate of the bloc is a 'later' addition. (We must remember, however, that a late addition to a sequence does not necessarily imply a later date of composition or of etching, since existing plates can be moved from one point to another.)

The concluding line of *37* is linked by parallel structure referring to the Friends, and so segment *C* is made to follow closely on *B*:

> They saw Albion endeavouring to destroy their Emanations.
> They saw their Wheels rising up poisonous against Albion

While *37* seems to have been created in order to fit into place, *38–40* were evidently conceived as a unit. The action of the Friends straddles the juncture of *38–9*:

> . . . at length they rose
> With one accord in love sublime, & as on Cherubs wings
> They Albion surround with kindest violence . . .

The speech of Bath, introduced at the end of *39*, begins at the third line of *40*—not quite so close a joining, but necessary because Blake had decided to have Bath speak in his own person, as well as through Oxford in *41*. Plate *40* is then made to connect with *41* by the addition of one engraved line: 'And these the names of the Eighteen combining with those Ten'. Of the twenty-four Friends of Albion, six had been named in *36*, with the remaining eighteen following in what is now *41*. The new line at the end of *40* provides a new, plausible fit, although we have the evidence of the Morgan Library proof lacking this line to show how the link was accomplished.[1] Segment *C*'s four plates therefore comprise two that were always closely associated and two that were individually adapted so as to relate more or less closely to their neighbours.

Plate *42*, the one interior plate of Chapter 2 that has the same number in both sequences, is nevertheless not inevitably connected with either *41* or *43* in the majority sequence. In our diagram, it could equally have been represented as moving upward in front of *C*, but this would blur the fact that the single-plate *D* is always *42*. *E*, though only loosely connected to it, consists internally of two pairs of closely related plates. *44* must follow *43* because the 'two Immortal forms' who in *43* relate the anterior myth are in *44* discussed as already having done so. The line that ends *44* may have been an afterthought providing a transition to *45*:

> So Los in lamentation followd Albion. Albion coverd,
> His western heaven with rocky clouds of death & despair.

The last transition in segment *E*, from *45* to *46*, is very tight:

> . . . pale stood Albion at his eastern gate,
> Leaning against the pillars . . .

More than two-thirds of the lower part of *46* is taken up by the design showing the confrontation of Jerusalem and Vala, and this effectively closes the bloc. *47*, which begins segment *F*, is not closely related to the text of *46*.

If we now consider the minority order AEBDCF with respect to the jointures of the segments, we find that the *A–E*

[1] See E. 786.

transition is abrupt, though in itself not less convincing than the loose fit of *A–B*. The transition from *E* to *B* is very abrupt, but that from *B* to *C* seems to have been contrived for the purpose. However, *42* or *D* is markedly less related to its immediate neighbours in the minority sequence, where it interrupts the juncture by parallelism of the majority sequence and also breaks into a group of plates about the Friends of Albion with a text largely devoted to the conflict of Albion and Los. In the minority order, we then return to the episode of the Friends with *C*. The minority sequence lacks even the semblance of a fit between *C* and *F*, while in the majority order the first line of *47* was evidently deleted to afford a more plausible transition, albeit a very loose one, from *E* to *F*. On the basis of the jointures alone, neither sequence displays a dramatic advantage with respect to how closely the six segments are joined, although Blake seems to have tinkered more successfully with the connections of the blocs in the majority order. When the two sequences are considered with respect to the development of their content, however, the differences between them are very striking.

In the minority order the episode of the Friends of Albion is not merely broken up by the change from *BCD* to *EBD*. Now the Friends are made to reach their lowest point in *42* *before* they attempt to save Albion:

> . . . Oxford groans in his iron furnace
> Winchester in his den & cavern; they lament against
> Albion; they curse their human kindness & affection
> (*42*: 58–60)

After this it is scarcely credible that the Friends should try to bear Albion back through Los's gate to Eden or that Oxford should take Bath's leaves from the Tree of Life, while it makes sense for them to curse their human kindness after these efforts have failed. The dramatic appearance of the Divine Vision like a silent sun at the beginning of *E* is also more appropriate after the collapse of the Friends' efforts than it is following *28* in the minority arrangement. Most important, perhaps, moving *E* to second place among the segments puts Albion *hors de combat* before he makes major speeches on *29, 30, 35,* and *42*; as a corollary, it is appropriate for Albion to be carried off the bloody field in the last plate of *E* and then to speak his last words in the first plate of *F*.[1] These and other differences make it evident that what narrative line there is is distinct in the majority order and broken up in the minority order.[2] Yet both orders are authentically Blake's, and in their joint existence there must then be implications about the form of both Chapter 2 and, by extension, of *Jerusalem* as a whole.

Jerusalem begins after the Fall and affords only sporadic glimpses of a prelapsarian state; it begins to end only late in Chapter 4. Its two great central myths carry with them a sense of plot, but that plot is a relatively simple one underlying complexly elaborated episodes. The episodes are developed in blocs or segments. Their thematic connection with the controlling myths is usually evident, but their narrative connection with one another is often less so, and quite rightly, since the plot moves as a submarine current producing episodic surface movements. In this regard the extraordinarily regular (for Blake[3]), organization of the work is misleading. One hundred pages, four equal chapters separated by full-page designs, four half-page headpieces and tailpieces likewise —all this suggests a degree of control that is hardly characteristic of other aspects of the work, and in this sense the organization of *Jerusalem* may usefully be distinguished from its form. This is especially evident with regard to Chapter 2 because it exists in two different orders, but it is equally true of the other chapters; what we learn about the form of Chapter 2 is pertinent to Chapters 1, 3, and 4.

One striking fact concerning the two orders of plates is how little difference their existence has made to criticism. The order of plates in the editions used by Damon and Frye, for example, is the minority order (then thought to be the

[1] He originally did so in *47*: 1; this was deleted, but the last words still appear in *47*: 18.

[2] The narrative transition is, as Bentley says, 'at every junction . . . dislocated' in the alternative sequence (*Writings*, I. 735); but it is not merely the transition that is dislocated.

[3] Compare *Milton*, conceived as a poem in twelve books, but executed in two very unequal ones. The facts that the first book is about twice the size of the second, and that none of the four copies contains the full complement of fifty plates, prepares the reader for a work that will be irregular in other senses as well.

majority one[1]), yet their discussions of this chapter remain coherent and pertinent. When the true majority order was established,[2] it was regarded as of editorial and bibliographical importance but had little effect on critical discussion. One need only imagine the effect on Wordsworth criticism were it discovered that an alternative pagination of one-quarter of *The Prelude* were possible. Does this suggest that critics of *Jerusalem* have been obtuse or inattentive? I think not. It reflects a correct intuition that the story line is not of paramount importance, not even when it is construed as in the majority order so that causes and effects are more credibly related to one another. There *is* a story in *Jerusalem*, consisting of many episodes, but this diachronic aspect of the work is for the most part subordinated to its synchronic aspect: the interrelationship of themes as manifested in its 'spatial form'. The organizational container reinforces the expectation of a strong narrative line, an expectation which is subverted time after time in the work itself.

In *Jerusalem* the unit of thought is neither the individual plate nor the chapter. Attempts to view the chapters as discrete units depend upon rationalizing after the fact, and quite different chapter constructions could be so rationalized. Blake develops *Jerusalem* in what may best be called, following Mede, a series of synchronisms. Just as Revelation is in Mede's view not a diachronic structure but a synchronous one, so *Jerusalem* is primarily to be read not for its relatively subordinated story line but for the way in which its interrelated parts explain one another. As Joseph Wittreich says, 'What poets like Spenser, Milton, and the Romantics borrow from the Book of Revelation is not a structural mechanism that lends to their poetry a visible external design; instead, they borrow structural principles that by each poet are suited to his own special subject matter.'[3] In the case of Blake's *Jerusalem* this means specifically the subject-matter of the

[1] As Erdman (E. 730) points out, for some time the majority order was considered the minority one and vice versa; this is the case as late as *The Complete Writings of William Blake*, ed. Geoffrey Keynes (London: Oxford University Press, 1966), p. 918.

[2] By Erdman, in 'The Suppressed and Altered Passages', pp. 39–41.

[3] *Visionary Poetics: Milton's Tradition and Its Legacy* (San Marino, California: The Huntington Library, 1979), p. 44.

two great intertwined myths: the sexual myth of humanity culminating in regeneration, the imaginative myth of the poet culminating in prophetic potency. 'It may be', Susan Fox suggests, 'that what is now considered progressive may ultimately prove circular, that the events of *Jerusalem*, like those of *Milton*, are all the same event witnessed through various perspectives.'[1] That this is indeed so may be demonstrated only by describing a form for *Jerusalem* that has as its basis some model other than the long narrative poem.

There are various ways in which we might try to describe *Jerusalem* according to an alternative structural model. One would be to regard the work as simultaneously possessing several structures, as does Stuart Curran in 'The Structures of *Jerusalem*'.[2] Another is to concentrate upon variations on a single paradigmatic situation, which Richard Herrstrom finds in the constellation of a human form, a rock, a city, a furnace, and wheels.[3] The prototype of this situation is of course 'Ezekiel . . . by Chebars flood' (*12*: 58), and, as Professor Herrstrom shows, Blake freely adapts both figure and vision in different contexts of *Jerusalem*. These recurrent adaptations are one example of synchronism in Mede's sense, and so are some of the structures discussed by Curran, particularly 'climactic symbols of the fallen state' and 'the antithesis of Christ and Satan'.[4] By enlarging the scope of enquiry, we may describe *Jerusalem* as structured according to events that, to use Joseph Mede's words, 'run on in time together, or Synchronize'.

Let us begin with a single example, by representing synchronously with the events concerning a single figure—Reuben.[5] Reuben is in many ways a microcosm of Albion. His role in *Jerusalem* has already been discussed, but it is useful

[1] Fox then rejects this excellent suggestion, limiting the principle of simultaneity to *Milton*. See *Poetic Form in Blake's Milton* (Princeton: Princeton University Press), p. 14. But Fox's observation that 'within the poem's apparent progression certain major elements are repeated unexpectedly and insistently' should lead to a different conclusion.

[2] *Blake's Sublime Allegory*, pp. 329–46.

[3] See 'Blake's Transformation of Ezekiel's Cherubim Vision', *Blake*, XV (1981), 64–77.

[4] 'The Structures of *Jerusalem*', pp. 334, 336.

[5] I omit those contexts in which Reuben is named merely as one of the twelve tribes of Israel.

to see by means of the table below what parts of his myth can be represented synchronously.

Chapter	1	2	3	4
Reuben				
sleeps/is divided/ enroots/ fibres cut/destroyed	15*, *15*: 25–8	*30*: 43–5, 51 *32*: 5	*63*: 12, 23 *74*: 33–4 *74*: 41–2	*81*: 10 *90*: 24–5, 46
flees/wanders		*30*: 47–51 *32*: 1, 6–10, 41–2	*63*: 44 *68*: 47 *72*: 36 *74*: 36–7	*84*: 13
subject of redemptive action by Los		*30*: 47–8 53–4 **32*, *32*: 3–6 12–13 41		*85*: 3–4

It can be seen that the components of this myth can be rearranged as a story. In such a linear narrative Reuben would first sleep on a stone and enroot himself, then have his fibres cut and be divided, and next be subjected to Los's cruel kindness in the binding of his senses. Last, he would be led into Canaan, restored by Los from his twelve-fold wanderings. A more complex narrative arrangement might arrange the components of the story differently, beginning *in medias res* and telling part of the tale in flashback; but in no such arrangement would the last appearance of Reuben be that of *90*.[1] Regarded as a temporal sequence, this would make Reuben again the victim of the Sons and Daughters of Albion *after* the happy ending of *85*: 3–4. However, our sense of the Reuben myth is that it follows the structure of the larger, encompassing myth of Albion. As Frye puts it, 'Reuben purified of his Selfhood would become a prophetic imagination.'[2] In

[1] I have not included the last *mention* of Reuben, which is in Enitharmon's speech on *93*: 'Could you love me Rintrah, if you Pride not in my Love / As Reuben found Mandrakes in the field & gave them to his Mother' (7–8). This could, however, be placed with Reuben's enrooting, as both are manifestations of his Oedipal wish to enwomb himself.

[2] *Fearful Symmetry*, p. 376. Frye cites *32*: 41–2: 'Reuben is Merlin / Exploring the Three States of Ulro; Creation; Redemption. & Judgment.'

order to imagine this, we must think of it in terms of synchronous events.

Having shown the synchronisms of a relatively minor figure, we are ready to consider one of Blake's Giant Forms. The active labour of Los with his tools at his furnaces is one of the great themes of *Jerusalem*. These are distributed as follows when viewed synchronously.

Chapter 1	Chapter 2	Chapter 3	Chapter 4
9; *10*; *12*: 21–4, 45–66; *13*; *16*	*30*: 17; *32**; *42*: 77–81	*53*: 15–20; *56*: 1; *58*: 13–20; *59*: 1–9; *62*: 41–2; *66*: 16; *73*: 2–54; 73*	*78*: 10–11; *82*: 56–9; *83*: 79–80; *85*: 10–13, 20; *86*: 33–41

These labours of Los are synchronic in that they do not necessarily follow or produce one another but may be imagined as taking place simultaneously in the extended middle which constitutes most of *Jerusalem*. Similarly, Los's conflict with the Sons and Daughters of Albion may be represented as in the table below.

Chapter 1	Chapter 2	Chapter 3	Chapter 4
With Sons:			
5: 26–33; *7*: 71–3 *8*: 1–6; *17*: 6, 59–63		*58*: 29–33 *74*: 23–9	*78*: 1–9; *90*: 49–50
With Daughters, Rahab, Tirzah, and Vala:[a]			
17: 10	*30*: 19	*56*	*80*: 41–5; *82*: 56–79 *83*: 33–48; *90*: 40–5

[a]Daughters at various points combine into Vala and/or Rahab and Tirzah, so all must be considered together.

This distribution, as can be seen, is skewed, with the most important conflicts occurring in the first chapter (with the Sons) and in the last (with the daughters). Indeed, one of the many things we can learn from a schematization of these synchronous events is that their distribution is anything but regular. Regularity is an aspect of what I have called the 'container'; the poem and the designs build up a tension with that regular order. The container is supportive of our sense of narrative line—which, as we have seen in relation to Los, does exist, though in a much weaker form than one might otherwise suppose.

To some extent the choice of events that recur in *Jerusalem* and that may be called synchronous is determined by the interest of the reader, but there are a number of events that would probably be part of any serious discussion of the work. In giving a list of such events as examples of synchronism, I am far from wishing to suppose any Mathematical Form as governing the work. On the contrary, such a list will show that *Jerusalem* cannot be reduced to a diagram but follows its own internally generated course of development. In the list I give here, it can be seen that certain events recur in *Jerusalem* in such a way as to create areas of emphasis but no inexorable sense of plot. Admittedly any such selection of events must be to some degree arbitrary, and another reader might produce some different rubrics—just as the synchronous visions of Revelation might be classified and described somewhat differently by different commentators. What is important is not so much particular rubrics and instances, although the rubrics presented here describe essential actions in the poem, and I have been conservative in choosing the instances that each can accommodate; it is our overall sense of a synchronous work that matters. It is only by appreciating the difference between such a structure and that of *Paradise Lost* or that of *The Four Zoas*, that we can avoid judging *Jerusalem* by the inapplicable criteria that have so often been applied to it.

Certain events in *Jerusalem*—apart from those in the last plates—either occur only once or for other reasons should not be considered as synchronous. Among the former are the Joseph and Mary episode *61*, the extension of Time and Space by Erin (*48*: 30-41), and the election of the Seven Eyes of God (*55*: 30-3). Such events can nevertheless be related to the major synchronic ones. Joseph and Mary, as we have seen, are thematically related to the myth of Jerusalem. Erin is a Jerusalem-surrogate, but her activity in *48* is related to that of Los throughout the poem. The Seven Eyes of God

THE SYNCHRONOUS EVENTS OF *JERUSALEM*

	Chapter 1	Chapter 2	Chapter 3	Chapter 4
LOS				
Division	*6*, *17*: 1 ff.[a]			*87*: 34–8
and his Spectre Conflict/ Reconciliation[b]	*6**, { *7*: 7–43 *8*: 1–44 *9*: 1–35 }	*33*: 2–9 *43*: 28–32 *44**, *44*: 1–15		*83*: 78–80
and his Emanation	*3*: 4–7 *5*: 66–8, *6*: 1			
are divided	*12*: 7–9, *17*: 48–58		*62*: 37–8	*86*: 39–41
contend				*85** { *86*: 50–67 *87*: 1–24; *87** *88*: 1–33 } *88*: 51–2 *92*: 7–11
tries to save Albion	*1** *1*: 8–10[c]	*30*: 21–40 *35*: 15, 24–7 *42*: 2–6, 19 ff. { *44*: 41–4 *45*: 1–39 *46*: 1–9 }	*53*: 1 ff. *56*: 32–6	*71*: 56–63
LUVAH				
murdered in the anterior myth	*21*: 15–16, 57–8 *22*: 31 *24*: 51–2	*43*: 33–82	*59*: 10–26	*80*: 16–30
sacrificed by the Sons & Daughters			*65*: 5–11, 56–79 *66*: 18–64 *67*: 24–34, 44–62 *69**	

ALBION				
in his Spectre's power	*1*: 5[C]	*27* (verse): 37–40 *29*: 1–24	*54*: 6–8, 15–26 *57*: 15	
flees Divine Vision	*4*: 22–32	*29*: 1 { *33*: 12–13 *34*: 1–13 *34*: 11 }	*57*: 1–16	
speaks last words	*23*: 26–40 *24*: 60	*47*: 1[C] { *47*: 18 *48*: 1 }		
described in his fallen state	*1*: 1–5[C] *9**, *14** *15*: 29–30 { *18*: 44–6 *19*: 16, *19** } *20*: 1–2 *23*: 24–6 *25**	*28*: 13–19 *33** *36*: 11–20 *37**, *40** *41**, *47**	*54*: 9–14	*91** *94*: 1–17 *94**
SONS OF ALBION				
combine	*18*: 1–10, 36–45	*50**	*69*: 1–5 *70*: 1–16	*90*: 40–3 *93**, *94**
DAUGHTERS OF ALBION				
combine	*5*: 40–5		*58*: 1–2 *64*: 6 *67*: 2–23	*82*: 10–11 *84*: 29–30

Notes to Table on p. 311.

(cont. on next page)

THE SYNCHRONOUS EVENTS OF *JERUSALEM* (*cont.*)

	Chapter 1	Chapter 2	Chapter 3	Chapter 4
FEMALES (VALA, RAHAB, TIRZAH, DAUGHTERS)				
assert/manifest power	*4**, *25**	*40** *45*: 50–66 *45**, *46** *47**	*53** *60*: 45–9 *63*: 7–12, 39–41 *64*: 7–17 *67**, *69** *70*: 17–31 *75*: 1–6 *75**	*78*: 15–20 *80*: 31–6, 52–85 *80**, *81** { *81*: 1–14 { *82*: 1–50
JERUSALEM				
in illo tempore	*18** *19*: 40–7 *20*: 32–41 *24*: 17–22, 36–50	*27* (verse): 1–24 *28**	*60*: 10–21	*77* (verse²): 1–12 *79*: 21–55
falling or fallen	*1*: 6ᶜ *5*: 13, 47 ff. *12*: 43–4 *14*: 31–2 *20*: 5–9, 22–8 *22*: 19–24 *23*: 8–12 *23**	*27* (verse): 41–4 *45** *47**	*57** *60*: 23–37, 39–41 *62*: 2–7	{ *78*: 21–33 { *79*: 55–80 { *80*: 1–5 *88*: 56–8 *89*: 43–5 *92**
ZOAS				
Fallen Zoas described	*14*: 1–8	*32*: 25–26 *37*: 26–30 *42*: 23–4	*54** *58*: 47–51 *59*: 10–21 *63*: 4 *74*: 1–9	*87** *88*: 55–6 *92**

STATES				
distinguished from individuals	*25*: 12–13, 14–16	*31*: 9–18 *49*: 70–5	*61*: 52 *71*: 9 *73*: 44–5	
SATAN				
becomes manifest		*27* (verse): 27–8 39–40 45–55 *29*: 17–24 *49*: 29–30 67–70	*52* (verse): 17–21	*90*: 40–3
JESUS / THE SAVIOUR DIVINE VISION				
incarnated		*27* (verse): 57–63 *42*: 34	*61*: 47–8 *63*: 16–17	(*90*: 34–8)[d]
crucified		*27* (verse): 57–63	*61*: 49	*76** *77* (verse[1]): 16–17
appears/speaks	*4*: 6–21	*31** *33** *43*: 1–26	*60*: 10–37, 65–9 *61*: 1–2 *62*: 18–29	*77* (verse[1]): 11–12 *79*: 41–4, 51–2

NOTES:
This schema covers plates *1–94*. Asterisks indicate designs. When a passage runs from one plate to another, the numerals are yoked. Superscript numerals refer to portions of verse on pages featuring both verse and prose; thus '*77* (verse[1])' indicates the first passage of verse on plate *77*.

[a]At some points it is difficult to tell whether an episode should be imagined as ending at a certain line or as continuing. In such instances, I have (sparingly) used ff.

[b]The conflict and reconcilation of Los and his Spectre are at times so intermingled that the two are in effect one; but *43* and *44* concern reconciliation only.

[c]Line(s) deleted.

[d]This passage is really a parody of the Incarnation; hence parentheses.

is one of a number of conceptions which create a structure for the fallen world in order to make redemption possible; others are the creation of the Mundane Shell by Los and the establishment of Individuals and States. Associated with these is the finding of the limits of Opakeness and of Contraction in Albion's bosom. As there are only two instances of this, both in Chapter 2,[1] I have not listed it, but there could be an argument for a somewhat broader rubric such as 'positive acts of limitation' to include all such events. This is only one of numerous possible instances where the rubrics could be redefined; but what matters most are the overall implications of the repetition of events as far as the form of *Jerusalem* is concerned.

There are some repetitions which do not belong on our list for other reasons. Perhaps the most evident of these is Blake's speaking in his own person—an event which, though repeated, occurs outside the mythological frame of the work and which has the effect of a sudden change of perspective.[2] Apart from the *Preface*, in which we expect to hear the author's voice, this occurs at the following points:

Chapter 1	Chapter 2	Chapter 3	Chapter 4
4: 3–5	*34*: 28 ff.	*74*: 14 ff.	*97*: 5–6
5: 16 ff.	*47*: 17–18		*98*: 40–3
15: 5–34			*99*: 5

The first two examples are part of Blake's invocation and statement of theme, introducing the poet as Prophetic visionary:

. . . I rest not from my great task!
To open the Eternal Worlds, to open the immortal Eyes
Of Man inwards into the Worlds of Thought: into Eternity
Ever expanding in the Bosom of God. The Human Imagination (*5*: 17–20)

[1] *31*: 1–8 and *42*: 29–31. The latter instance, recounted by Los, is followed by Los's account of how the Saviour forms Woman from Contractions Limit.

[2] Hazard Adams goes so far as to speak of 'the presentness established by Blake's dominating and circumferential intrusiveness' ('Blake, *Jerusalem*, and Symbolic Form', p. 158).

As Blake goes into the myth of Albion, we lose sight of the poet who is telling the tale, much as in *Milton* 2: 25–13: 44 we are for the most part unconscious of the Bard reciting his 'prophetic Song'. As in *Milton* we are suddenly reminded of the Bardic speaker with 'The Bard ceas'd' at 13: 45,[1] so at *15*: 5 Blake suddenly breaks in at mid-line with 'such is my awful Vision'. He then goes on to develop his own Bardic-Prophetic presence for the rest of *15*. The language and imagery are worthy of a modern Ezekiel:

> I turn my eyes to the Schools & Universities of Europe
> And there behold the Loom of Locke whose Woof rages dire
> Washd by the Water-wheels of Newton. (14–16)

The powerful sense of the speaker's presence here does not, however, continue into *16*, and the rest of Chapter 2 is narrated without Blake's first-person intervention.

Each of Blake's interventions opens up a dimension of meaning in which we are aware of the visionary speaker who records but does not arbitrarily control the meaning of events:

> I heard in Lambeths shades:
> In Felpham I heard and saw the Visions of Albion
> I write in South Molton Street, what I both see and hear
> In regions of Humanity, in Londons opening streets.
> (*34*: 40–3)

In part, these first-person passages also make us aware of the personal struggle of a man who sits trembling night and day, whose friends are astonished at him but who forgive his wanderings as he labours to communicate the Divine Vision. Yet this is also associated with one of the central themes in *Jerusalem*, the actualization of Los's powers; and in *74* Blake the speaker virtually becomes Los the protagonist: 'I walk up and down in Six Thousand Years: their Events are present before me' (19) he writes, while in *75*: 7 'Los in Six Thousand Years walks up & down continually'. Thus Blake becomes

[1] But in *Milton* the reader is reminded of the Bard's Song in another way: by the reiteration of the Bard's first line—'Mark well my words! they are of your eternal salvation!' (2: 25) at 3: 5, 4: 20 (with a variant at 4: 26), 7: 18, 7: 50, 9: 7, and 11: 31. This refrain keeps the reader at least sporadically aware of the Bard's voice, while of course there is no such device in *Jerusalem*.

present in his own myth as well as inserting himself as the narrator of that myth. These interventions are in a sense synchronous, since they can be thought of as occurring at any point in the work; but they are different from the passages in which parallel episodes are presented. The points at which Blake is both the subject and object of exposition have a peculiar status in that they make us suddenly aware of a major figure who is at the same time part of the work and its creator.

In Chapter 4, Blake's first-person appearances are limited to the last few pages, to that part of *Jerusalem* which is not middle but end. As in several other places, he reminds us of the perceptual quality of his vision. '. . . So spake in my hearing / The Universal Father' (*97*: 5-6). 'And I heard Jehovah speak / Terrific from his Holy Place & saw the Words of the Mutual Covenant Divine . . .' (*98*: 40-1). This seer and listener is given a prominent place in the last line of the poem, sharing a place of extraordinary importance with Jerusalem herself. We are brought full circle to the opening passage of the poem, in which the first-person speaker sees the Saviour 'dictating the words of this mild song' (*4*: 5). Blake's 'I' is thus presented synchronously as the narrator of synchronous events, and at the same time as a figure who, with his subject, finds fulfilment at the end of the poem: 'And I heard the Name of their Emanations they are named Jerusalem' (*99*: 5).[1]

[1] Erdman, p. 256, prints the seventh word as 'Emnations'; Bentley, p. 638, has the correct reading, which I follow. Presumably the misprint will be corrected in the fifth printing of E, to be published as *The Complete Poetry and Prose of William Blake* in 1982.

Index of Works by William Blake

Albion kneeling, pencil drawing of, 230
Albion rose, 114, 116, 231
All Religions are One, 94, 104
America, 14, 28, 84, 131, 181, 203
Ancient of Days, The, 275
Angel of the Revelation, The, 141, 158
Angels Hovering Over the Body of Jesus, The, 155
Archangel Raphael with Adam and Eve, The, 153
Auguries of Innocence, 171

Bard, The (exhib. 1785), 242
Bard, The (exhib. 1809), 197
Blair, Robert, *The Grave*, illustrations to, 4, 5, 74, 184, 218, 252
Blasphemer, The, 99–100
Body of Christ Borne to the Tomb, The, 151
Book of Ahania, The, 94, 199, 213
Book of Los, The, 94, 269
Book of Thel, The, 52
Book of Urizen, The, 105, 171, 235, 237, 255, 269

Caritas-figure, untitled print of, 111
Chaucer's Canterbury Pilgrims, 5, 86
Chaining of Orc, The, 112
Christ in the Carpenter's Shop, 274
Cowper, William, pictures associated with:
- engravings for Hayley's *Life of Cowper*, 246
- *Evening* (*The Task*), 246, 248
- frieze of bridge at Olney, 246, 248
- miniatures of Cowper, 246
- portrait after Romney, 246
- *Winter* (*The Task*), 246

Dante Alighieri, *The Divine Comedy*, illustrations to, 84; *Beatrice Addressing Dante from the Car*, 181; *The Queen of Heaven in Glory*, 191

Death Chamber, The, 100–1
Descriptive Catalogue, A, 4, 34, 59, 60, 86, 154–5, 161, 196, 197, 241

Europe, 14, 28, 109, 131, 183, 187, 190, 201, 204, 219, 235, 275
Everlasting Gospel, The, 73, 188
'Exhibition of *Paintings in Fresco*', 54–5
Ezekiel's Wheels, 140, 141, 154

Fall of Fair Rosamund, The (drawing), 187
Fall of Rosamond, The (engraving after Stothard), 187
'Florentine Ingratitude', 251
Four Zoas, The, 1, 3, 35–41, 54, 78–82, 95–6, 105–6, 109, 111, 122, 173, 176, 179, 185, 192, 197, 199, 202, 213, 234–5, 245–6, 255, 257, 260, 275, 279–81, 283, 289, 307
French Revolution, The, 52

Gates of Paradise, The, 14, 94, 171, 181, 213, 219
'Glad Day', see *Albion rose*
God Judging Adam, 108–9, 198
Gray, Thomas, illustrations to the poems of, 65, 193, 197, 242
'Grey Monk, The', 71–2

Hesiod, engravings after Flaxman's illustrations to, 213
House of Death, The, 217

'I askéd a thief to steal me a peach', 255
Island in the Moon, An, 203, 291

Jerusalem:
- calligraphy, 228, 298
- colour, 90–1
- colour symbolism, 75
- copy A, 4, 7, 8, 88, 90, 181, 204, 210, 238–9, 295, 296, 297

Jerusalem (*cont.*)
copy B, 2, 4, 7, 8, 10, 90, 92, 94, 238–9, 296
copy C, 4, 7, 8, 10, 90, 181, 210, 238–9, 295–7
copy D, 8, 9, 90, 181, 210, 238–9, 295–6
copy E, 3, 7, 10, 14, 17, 84, 90, 92–4, 102, 104, 110, 112, 117, 169, 181, 219, 231, 238–9, 258, 275, 295–6
copy F, 8, 90, 181, 238–9, 295–6
copy G (supposed), 8, 296
copy H, 8
copy I, 8
copy J, 8
editions, 10–12
facsimiles, 9, 19
pencil drawings, *25*, 100; *26*, 219; *51*, 219; *46/32*, 112, 181–2; *76*, 116–17; *95*, 230
proofs, 8; *1*, 10, 60; *28*, 170; *33/37*, 204; *40*, 300; *46/32*, 181; *51*, 190
punctuation, 11–12
text and designs:
designs, *1*, 238–9, 243, 274; *2*, 182; *4*, 109, 181, 184; *6*, 237–8, 251; *7*, 92; *9*, 202–3; *11*, 104; *14*, 92, 94, 210; *15*, 93, 270; *19*, 202, 223; *21*, 72, 155; *22*, 92; *23*, 182–3; *24*, 182, 223; *25*, 15, 99–104, 200, 275–6; *26*, 117–18, 183; *28*, 119, 167, 169, 171–2, 180; *29/33*, 92; *31/35*, 15, 92, 99, 104–7; *32/36*, 237; *33/37*, 15, 92, 104, 182–3, 208; *34/38*, 93; *35/39*, 72, 92, 104; *36/40*, 93; *37/41*, 72, 93; *38/43*, 92; *39/44*, 183, 223, 269; *41/46*, 89, 107–10, 113, 198, 232; *42*, 152; *43/29*, 92; *44/30*, 90, 260; *46/32*, 99, 109, 111–13, 181–2, 184, 194, 300; *47*, 93, 182, 200; *49*, 93; *50*, 218; *51*, 15, 190, 217, 221, 276; *52*, 93; *53*, 190; *57*, 112, 182; *59*, 224; *65*, 153; *66*, 225; *67*, 211; *69*, 100, 200, 225, 277; *70*, 90, 277; *72*, 135, 157, 270, 295; *73*, 237; *74*, 93; *76*, 15, 105, 113–18, 229; *78*, 89; *80*, 221; *81*, 226; *82*, 221; *84*, 112; *85*, 93, 258; *87*, 258; *91*, 103, 211; *92*, 92, 183, 277; *93*, 104; *94*, 15, 92, 104, 219, 232, 277; *95*, 230–1; *96*, 108, 232; *97*, 92, 243, 274–5; *99*, 183–4; *100*, 244, 255, 258, 261, 274–7

text, *1*, 60, 251; *3*, 4, 7, 22, 33, 42, 57, 71, 73, 295, 312; *5*, 100, 215, 224, 251, 255, 282, 312; *6*, 173, 215, 244, 251, 256, 274, 289, 293; *7*, 95–6, 217, 251, 252, 259; *8*, 251, 252–3, 265; *9*, 62, 232, 237, 251, 266; *10*, 46, 243–6, 249–51, 259; *11*, 28, 192, 217, 243–4, 262, 266, 294; *12*, 61, 66, 137, 142, 150, 153, 155–6, 164, 215, 267, 278, 294, 304; *13*, 51, 137, 142, 150, 153, 157, 164, 215, 267–8; *14*, 219, 244, 256, 266; *15*, 51–2, 92, 157, 214, 270, 286, 313; *16*, 59, 89, 159–60, 270, 295, 313; *17*, 192, 251, 253, 255–6, 259; *18*, 68, 134, 180, 215–16, 282, 294; *19*, 35, 56, 167, 171–2, 200, 202; *20*, 20, 22, 54, 67, 167–8, 171, 191–2, 194, 293; *21*, 20, 22, 155, 169, 195, 203–4, 219, 221–2; *22*, 20, 22, 79–80, 195, 200, 256; *23*, 20, 22, 80, 176, 195, 200, 209, 278; *24*, 9, 20, 22, 195; *25*, 8, 67–8, 278, 296; *26*, 296; *27*, 71, 73–8, 104, 296; *28*, 8, 28, 198–9, 212, 296–8, 301; *29/33*, 192, 200–1, 211, 298, 301; *30/34*, 46–7, 188, 192, 201, 271, 298, 301; *31/35*, 272, 298, 312; *32/36*, 178, 219, 270–2, 298–9, 305; *33/37*, 80, 159, 204, 245, 253, 293, 299; *34/38*, 35, 61, 165, 204–5, 231, 286, 299; *35/39*, 261, 299; *36/40*, 31, 80–1, 204, 206, 262, 264, 300; *37/41*, 8, 186, 206, 297, 299; *38/43*, 2, 204, 206–7, 261, 264–5, 299; *39/44*, 132, 185, 206–8, 214–15, 239, 265, 300; *40/45*, 28, 206–7, 300; *41/46*, 205, 306; *42*, 106, 195, 208, 232, 240, 262–3, 296, 300–1, 312; *43/29*, 78, 173, 175, 244, 253, 260, 300;

44/30, 201-2, 244, 253, 260-1, 300; *45/31*, 8, 111, 182, 193, 236, 263-4, 300; *46/32*, 8, 14, 213, 300; *47*, 8, 173-4, 208-9, 296, 300, 302; *48*, 36, 118, 185, 208-10, 296, 307; *49*, 181, 296; *50*, 81, 94, 185, 210, 215, 294, 296; *52*, 71-2, 129, 231; *53*, 72, 166, 200, 261, 267, 273; *54*, 199-200, 210; *55*, 30, 69-70; *56*, 8, 102, 188, 203, 223, 264, 293; *57*, 45-6, 182, 187, 210, 264; *58*, 61, 197, 224, 264, 269; *59*, 2, 153, 195-6, 224, 235, 268, 295; *60*, 135, 188, 215, 294; *61*, 46, 67, 105, 135, 188, 191, 201, 228, 287, 307; *62*, 135, 193, 270; *63*, 188, 287; *64*, 38-40, 49-50, 65, 100, 180, 190, 224-5, 264, 294; *65*, 38, 108, 204, 216, 264; *66*, 215-16, 226, 276-7; *67*, 39-41, 100-1, 214, 224, 226; *68*, 39-41, 216-17, 294; *69*, 82, 149, 156, 201, 215; *70*, 218; *71*, 68, 229, 261; *73*, 76, 243, 267-8, 295; *74*, 185, 215, 219, 261, 270, 313; *75*, 82, 126, 313; *77*, 51, 73-4, 93, 102; *78*, 180, 217, 269; *79*, 211; *80*, 35, 67, 173, 180, 219, 229, 294; *81*, 219, 227; *82*, 43-4, 135, 219, 228-9, 238, 263, 272-3; *83*, 48-9, 186-7, 219, 223, 237, 239, 244, 257-8, 263, 294; *84*, 187, 223-4, 272, 294; *85*, 228, 239, 265, 272, 293, 305; *86*, 66, 141, 179, 221, 239, 256-7; *87*, 256-8; *88*, 187, 256, 258-60, 293-4; *89*, 183, 289; *90*, 114, 218, 272, 305; *91*, 146, 244, 253-4, 265, 282; *92*, 38, 258, 282-3, 294; *93*, 255, 258-9, 270, 305; *94*, 185, 216, 219, 230, 283; *95*, 122, 197, 203, 211, 230-1, 240-1, 261, 273, 282, 289; *96*, 116, 122, 178, 229, 239, 273-4, 289; *97*, 63, 122, 208, 232, 314; *98*, 63-4, 122, 211, 233, 277, 281-2, 314; *99*, 9, 63-4, 122, 230, 233, 314

Job, Illustrations of The Book of, 14, 86-7, 98, 153, 203, 253

Johnson, John, portrait of, 248

Journey of Life, The, 274

Judgment of Paris, The, 229

Lambeth books, 1, 6, 234, 257

Laocoön, The, 98, 160-1

Large Book of Designs, A, 90

Last Judgment, The, 5, 155

Lear and Cordelia in Prison, 222

Letters:
- 23 Aug. 1799, to Revd. John Trusler, 29
- 2 Oct. 1800, to Thomas Butts, 166
- 11 Sept. 1801, to Thomas Butts, 251
- 25 April 1803, to Thomas Butts, 3
- 6 July 1803, to Thomas Butts, 4
- 11 August 1803, to Thomas Butts, 188
- 16 August 1803, to Thomas Butts, 217, 251
- 27 Jan. 1804, to William Hayley, 205, 207
- 4 May 1804, to William Hayley, 59
- 28 Sept. 1804, to William Hayley, 84
- 23 Oct. 1804, to William Hayley, 84, 251
- 14 Oct. 1807, to Richard Phillips, 254
- 18 Jan. 1808, to Ozias Humphry, 155
- 19 Dec. 1808, to George Cumberland, 5
- 9 June 1818, to Dawson Turner, 2, 90
- 1 Feb. 1826, to John Linnell, 218
- 12 April 1827, to George Cumberland, 3

Magdalen at the Sepulchre, The, 84

Marriage of Heaven and Hell, The, 1, 33, 59, 72, 162, 167-8, 175, 239

'Mary', 188-9

'Mental Traveller, The', 72

Milton, a Poem, 1, 3-6, 24, 27, 34, 63, 75, 81, 84, 90, 137, 149, 154, 179, 183, 206, 210, 216, 230, 235, 243, 257, 262, 281, 283-5, 302, 304, 313

Milton, head of, 203

Milton, John, illustrations to the poems of:
Comus, 184, 222
L'Allegro, 158
Paradise Lost, 5, 104, 117, 184
Paradise Regained, 151, 200, 275
Mirth, 87
'My Spectre around me night & day', 255

'Never pain to tell thy love', 255
New and Complete Universal History of the Holy Bible, A, engravings for, 142
Newton, 83
Notebook, 35, 71–2, 112, 115, 134, 181–2, 234, 246, 251–2

'On H----ys Friendship', 252
'On the Virginity of the Virgin Mary & Joanna Southcott', 134, 227

Pickering Manuscript, 171, 177, 188, 204
Poetical Sketches, 42
Public Address, 4, 87, 89

Reynolds' *Discourses on Art*, annotations to, 61, 107
River of Life, The, 128

Small Book of Designs, A, 90
Soldiers Casting Lots for Christ's Garments, The, 84
Song of Los, The, 169, 185
Songs of Innocence, 206
Songs of Innocence and of Experience, 14, 38, 182
Spiritual form of Nelson, 5
Spiritual form of Pitt, 5, 253

There is No Natural Religion, 94, 117
Thornton's *The Lord's Prayer*, annotations to, 106
Tiriel, 52, 213
'To English Connoisseurs', 115
'To Tirzah', 231

Virgin and Child, 115
Visions of the Daughters of Albion, 182
Vision of the Last Judgment, A, 150, 155, 199
Vision of the Last Judgment, The, 5, 155

Watson's *Apology for the Bible*, annotations to, 132, 208
'William Bond', 177, 210
'William Cowper, Esq[re]', 246

Young, Edward, *Night Thoughts*, illustrations to, 104, 140, 190, 274

Zacharias and the Angel, 152

General Index

Abdiel, 239–40
Abiram, 249
Abraham, 178, 270
Abrams, M. H., 272
Ackermann, Rudolph, 184
Act of Union, 133, 185, 266
Adam, 4, 92, 104, 106, 117, 153, 169, 203, 217, 267, 269
Adams, Hazard, 12, 19, 29, 127, 289, 295, 312
Africa, 128, 207
Agrippa, Cornelius, 30
Ahania, 79–82
Albion, 1, 13–14, 18, 20, 25, 27, 30, 35–6, 38, 50, 52, 56, 58, 60, 65–6, 75–6, 78–80, 92–3, 99–100, 102–3, 107–8, 110–11, 113–18, 125, 157, 167–9, 171–8, 180, 182, 185, 192–8, 199–204, 206–14, 216, 221–2, 229–32, 234–7, 239–40, 244, 250, 252, 254–5, 258, 260–5, 273–4, 278–9, 282, 289, 292–3, 298–9, 301–2, 305, 312–13
Albion's Angel, 287
Alchemy, 129, 234, 243
Aldegrever, Heinrich, 87
Allamanda, 81
Altick, Richard D., 165
Ancient Britons, 197, 241
Angel of the Tongue, 287
Angels, 283
Anglican liturgy, 290
Antamon, 186–7
Anvil, 238, 254, 269, 273
Anytus, 219
Apocalyptic, 236
Apollo, 274
Apollo Belvedere, 274
Apollo Gardens, 149
Ark, 146, 269
Ark of the Covenant, 146, 155, 223
Arnold, Matthew, 85
Arrows, 63, 231
Artegall, 172
Arthur, 190, 200
Asia, 77
Astrology, 254
Atlantic, Voice of, 264
Atonement, 189, 216
Augustine, 121–2, 260, 287
Aurenhammer, Hans, 158
Avebury, 276–7
Awen, 242
Axe, 238
Aztecs, 226

Babylon, 134, 146, 215, 223, 262, 287
Bachelard, Gaston, 149
Bacon, Francis, 214, 219
Baker, C. H. Collins, 103
Ballads, 221
Bard, 197, 234, 242, 313
Bard of Oxford, 205, 207
Bartsch, Adam, 105, 116
Bashan, 270
Basire, James, 109, 158, 166
Bat, 251, 260, 275
Battersea, 198
Bath, 28, 38, 205–7, 299–301
'Battle of Maldon, The', 76
Beatrice, 101, 191
Beautiful, the, 69
Beer, John, 29, 108, 191, 274, 295
Behemoth, 253
'Bellman's Song, The', 73–4
Bellows, 238, 272, 293
Benjamin, 272
Bentley, G. E., Jr., 2–3, 5–8, 12, 35, 52, 71, 90, 96, 142, 177, 182, 188, 201, 210, 213, 237, 248, 296, 302, 314
Beulah, 25, 81, 99, 167, 182, 191, 198, 258, 278–9
Beverley, Thomas, 125–6
Bible, 26, 30, 44–5, 49–50, 124, 127, 209–10
  Old Testament, 61, 136, 157, 175, 293; Prophets, 135, 234–7, 239, 285, 288, 292; Chronicles, 141; Daniel, 104, 237, 289; Exodus, 50, 153, 155, 203; Ezekiel, 9,

Bible (*cont.*)
Old Testament (*cont.*) 110, 121, 140, 142, 144, 146, 149, 151–6, 158, 162, 166, 179, 215, 237, 239, 284–6; Genesis, 121, 168, 186, 270–1; Isaiah, 30, 45, 120, 124, 152, 162, 178–9, 183, 237, 239, 269, 292; Job, 49, 108, 199, 219–20, 292–3; Jonah, 199; Joshua, 190, 212–3; I Kings, 30, 141, 152; Lamentations, 74; Numbers, 159, 250; Psalms, 49, 59, 74, 253, 292; Ruth, 59; Song of Solomon (Song of Songs), 171, 184, 193, 232, 287; Zachariah, 292; Apocrypha, 149–50
New Testament, 293; Gospels, 234, 284–5, 292; Epistles, 292; I Corinthians, 231, 293; Ephesians, 204; Galatians, 178; Hebrews, 136; John, 49, 106, 121, 210, 285, 293; Luke, 181, 288, 292; Mark, 181, 285; Matthew, 50, 181, 188–9, 200–1, 285, 292; Revelation, 9, 63, 120, 124, 128, 130, 141, 145, 148–9, 152–3, 155, 157, 162, 187, 207, 230, 284–90, 303, 307; Romans, 163
Biblia Pauperum, 88, 105–6
Bicheno, Joseph, 132–3
Bindman, David, 83, 85, 87–8, 113, 116, 151, 275
Bishop, Morchard, 205, 248
Blackmur, R. P., 23–4
Blacksmith, 234, 236–7
Blackwater, river, 76, 198
Blair, Hugh, 61
Blake, Catherine, 3, 31, 176–7, 234, 241, 244, 257, 259
Blake, William:
courtship and marriage, 176–7; trial for sedition, 71, 211, 217; exhibition, 218, 242; rolling press, 243
and Albion, 177; and Los, 235, 253–4, 259; and Spectre of Los, 245, 250–2, 259
handwriting, 94; calligraphy, 90, 94–7; copperplate hand, 95–7
in his own works: *Ezekiel's Wheels*, 141; 'William Bond', 177; *FZ*, 141; *J*, 31, 108, 177, 244, 257, 261–2, 266, 286, 312–14
Bloom, Harold, 11, 29, 90, 140, 284–5
Blunt, Anthony, 83, 89, 109, 145–6, 183, 191, 274–5
Boadicea, 76, 229, 272
Boaz, 152
Boden, James, 74
Boehme, Jacob, 98–9, 125, 147
followers of, 20, 126–7, 147
Bonasone, Julio, 87–8, 106, 116
Bonato, I., 106
Bond, W. H., 48, 290–1
Bow, 63, 72, 230–2
Bow ('Old Bow'), 76
Bower of Bliss, 172
Bowlahoola, 81, 183
Boydell, John, 238
Boyvin, René, 101
Bradley, A. C., 62
Bricard, Joanny, 128
Brittannia, 92, 108, 178, 189, 232
Brothers, Richard, 131–4, 163–4
Brown, Norman O., 199, 201, 214
Bryan, Michael, 103
Bryan, William, 130–1
Bryant, Jacob, 109, 254
Bunyan, John, 146, 267
Burford's Panorama, 165
Burke, Edmund, 61, 68, 194
Burke, Joseph, 89
Burton, Robert, 290
Butlin, Martin, 83, 102, 107, 117, 140, 141, 151, 158, 187, 204, 231, 242, 248
Butts, Thomas, 3–5, 141, 246
Byzantium, 136, 267

Caerlon, 206
Cagliostro, Count Alessandro, 162
Caliban, 252
Calvinism, 216
Cambel, 221, 228–9, 272
Cambridge, 229
Cambridge Platonists, 199
Camden, William, 166
Camp, the, 149, 156
Canaan, 305
Candlesticks, 152
Canterbury, 38, 204
Cardiganshire, 206
Caritas, 111, 182

Carlsson, Frans, 145
Carlyle, Thomas, 293
Carstens, Asmus Jacob, 85
Carwardine, Revd. Thomas, 47
Cary, Mary, 147
Caterpillar, 170-1
Cathedral Cities, 23, 197-8, 214, 264, 294
Cathedron, 141, 152, 256, 275
Caylus, comte de, 89
Ceres, 109
Chaldea, 270
Chapman, George, 43
Chariot, 108-9
Charlemaine, 71
Chastanier, Benedict, 129-30
Chatterton, Thomas, 52, 242
Chaucer, Geoffrey, 60
Chelsea, 198
'Cherry Tree Ballad, The', 188-9
Cherubim, 140, 150, 152-6, 161-2, 286
Cheviot Hills, 38, 197
Chiaroscuro, 200
Chichester, 166, 205
Child, Francis James, 221
Children of Albion, 192, 201-2, 223, 229 (*see also* Sons and Daughters)
Children of Los, 192-3
Churches, 82, 126
Clowes, John, 221
Coalbrookdale, 243
Cockerell, Samuel Pepys, 164
Cohn, Norman, 120, 122-3
Colchester, 76, 198
Coleridge, Samuel Taylor, 26, 42, 64, 208, 295
Colnaghi's, 86
Colossus of Rhodes, 158
Colour printing, 83
Commonwealth, 125, 147-8
Compasses, 274-5
Constantine, 71, 76
Cordelia, 222
Correggio, 85
Counties, 228, 269-70
Covenant, 185, 210-11, 314
Covering Cherub, 65, 110, 289
Cowper, William, 47, 246-50, 291
Crashaw, Richard, 226
Crooke, Japhet, 271
Crucifixion, 104, 113, 117, 189, 292-3
Cumberland, George, 2, 5-6, 87-8, 106, 116, 206
Cumberland, George, Jr., 6
Cummings, F., 231
Cunego, Domenico, 106
Cunningham, Allan, 7, 13-14, 90
Cup of abominations, 187
Curran, Stuart, 113, 219, 262, 284, 304

Dalila, 189, 292
Damon, S. Foster, 3, 20-1, 23-5, 28, 30, 49, 52, 53, 55, 73, 75, 81, 98, 100, 102, 107-8, 113, 116, 130, 137, 140, 169, 174, 180, 185, 187, 191, 195, 196, 197, 198, 203, 204, 205, 206, 208, 210, 211, 214, 219, 221, 228, 254, 255, 258, 270, 271, 274, 278, 279, 281, 282, 302
Danilewicz, M. L., 128, 162
Dante, 27, 123, 144, 153, 208, 218
Danube, River, 76
Darwin, Erasmus, 171, 214
Daughters of Albion, 18, 23, 65, 68, 79, 100-1, 167, 174, 197, 200, 202-3, 211, 217, 219, 221-6, 228-9, 235, 255-61, 264-5, 270, 272, 283, 294, 305-6
Daughters of Beulah, 37, 67, 263, 266, 292, 294
Daughters of Jerusalem, 93, 111, 181, 184
Daughters of Los, 153, 224-5, 262, 266-7, 294
David, 199, 223
Davies, Edward, 198
Day of Judgement, 124
Day of Wrath, 122
De l'Orme, Philibert, 145-6
Deck, Ray A., Jr., 13
Defoe, Daniel, 204
Deism, 199
Derbyshire, 198, 272
Dhinas-Bran, 198
Dinah, 186, 188
Diogenes, 239
Distaff, 276
Divine Family, 293
Divine Vision, 301, 313
Dobbs, Francis, 133, 162-3
Dockhorn, Klaus, 57
Dodgson, C, 121

Dog rose, 180–1
Dorfman, Deborah, 13, 16
Dovedale, 135, 228, 272
Drayton, Michael, 196
Druids, 39, 63, 160–1, 198, 204, 210, 216, 230, 233, 242, 276–7
Dublin, 136
Duché, Revd. Jacob, 128–9, 162
Duché, Thomas Spence, 130
Duessa, 191
Dürer, Albrecht, 84, 86–7, 274

Earlom, Richard, 238
Eaves, Morris, 23
Eckington C., 74
Edelinck, Gerard, 87
Eden, 35, 140, 167, 206, 265, 279
Edinburgh, 164, 198, 204
Egypt, 88–9, 203
Elder Edda, 189
Eleanor, Queen, 187
Eliade, Mircea, 121, 143, 150
Elijah, 107, 132
Eliot, T. S., 23, 69, 110
Ellis, Edwin J., 10, 18, 21
  and Yeats, William Butler, 9–10, 19, 21, 25, 212, 246, 278
Elohim, 287
Emanation, 18, 81, 175, 197, 215, 228, 254–5, 314
  of Albion, 198, 201–2, 278
  of Los, 79, 173, 234, 244, 254–6, 260–1, 273, 294, 300
Encyclopedic anatomy, 284, 290
England, Martha W., 73, 291
Engraving process, 242–3, 253
Enion, 35, 79–80, 192, 213, 258
Enitharmon, 31, 35, 66, 82, 93, 141, 177, 234, 244, 254–60, 265, 270, 273, 275–6, 283, 294, 305
Eno, 36, 185
Enochian period, 126
Eon, 81, 202, 254
Epstein, Lady, 274
Erbery, William, 147
Erdman, David V., 2, 4, 6, 7, 9, 11, 12, 27–8, 31, 71, 77, 100, 104, 108, 112, 114, 135, 149, 169, 170, 174, 177, 180, 181, 182, 183, 185, 203, 204, 205, 206, 211, 218, 221, 228, 229, 230, 231, 242, 251, 264, 274, 296, 303, 314
Eremitani frescoes, 239
Erin, 37–8, 94, 184–6, 188, 210, 266–7, 307
Essick, Robert N., 5, 74, 83, 86, 94, 111, 112, 116, 218, 231, 243, 252, 275, 276
Estrild, 227
Etching process, 243
Ethos, 58
Euphrates, 77
Eve, 92, 104–6, 186, 203, 256, 298
Everyman, 203
Examiner, 4, 218, 247–8
Eyes of God, 30, 122, 125, 307–8
Ezekiel, 140–1, 267, 286, 313

F. B. P., 73–4
Fairchild, H. N., 248
Fairies, 190, 260
Familists, 125, 146
Farrer, Austin, 142
Fates, 100–3, 189, 275
Faulkner, William, 186
Faustus, Dr., 209
Fécamp, Jean de, 73, 145
Felpham, 166, 177, 181, 219
Feuerbach, Ludwig, 175
Fibres, 66, 93–4, 101–3, 182, 211, 214, 256–8, 276, 305
Fiedler, Leslie, 176
Fifth Monarchy Men, 125
Fisch, Harold, 125
Fischer von Erlach, J. B., 152, 158–9
Fisher, Peter F., 29–30
Fitler, J., 154
Flaxman, Ann, 242
Flaxman, John, 85, 103, 134, 210, 213, 251
Flaxmer, Sarah, 130
Fletcher, Ian, 19
Fludd, Robert, 30
Fox, Susan, 304
France, 27, 174, 263–4
French Prophets (Camisards), 126
French Revolution, 27, 131–2
Freud, Sigmund, 199, 212
Friends of Albion, 67, 132, 198, 204–8, 264–5, 299–301
Frosch, Thomas, 232–3
Frye, Northrop, 1, 25–7, 29, 44, 64, 75, 80, 174, 189, 196, 203, 213, 270, 281, 290, 302, 305
Furnace(s), 217–18, 221, 229, 238,

244, 261, 262, 266, 267, 272, 304, 306
Fuseli, Henry, 74, 85, 102-3, 105-7, 182, 206

Galle, Phillip, 158
Gandhi, M. K., 186
Gardner, Stanley, 75
Garment, 101, 114, 141, 201, 210, 222, 224-5, 231, 271
Garrett, Clarke, 128, 130-1, 132, 162
Garuda, 110
Gate(s), 140, 215, 266, 268-0, 272, 299
Gegenheimer, Albert Frank, 130
Gentleman's Magazine, 206
Generation, 140, 269, 273, 278
Geoffrey of Monmouth, 206, 227
George II, 291
Georgi, Francesco, 145
Gibbon, Edward, 71-2, 77
Gilchrist, Anne, 16
Gilchrist, Alexander, 6-7, 16-18, 34, 87, 89, 109, 116, 120, 205, 217-18
Gilchrist, H. H., 16
Giotto, 88
Globe of light, 243, 274-5
Gnosticism, 219, 262
Godwin, William, 188
Golgonooza, 114, 127, 136-7, 140-3, 145, 152-3, 155-8, 160, 166, 215, 239, 256, 259, 267, 273, 277
Golgotha, 198
Goliath, 199
Goltzius, Hendrick, 87
Gombrich, E. H., 31
Gothic, 88, 112, 151-3, 161, 181
Gough, Richard, 166, 242
Goya, Francisco de, 26, 71-2
Goyder, George, 187
Grabianka, Thaddeus, 128-9, 162-3
Grant, John E., 167, 169-70, 180, 191
Grapevine, 258
Gray, Thomas, 65, 193, 225, 242
Great Tartary, 221
Greatheed, Samuel, 247-8
Green Man Inn, 75
Grotesque, the, 65
Gustav III, 132
Gwendolen, 135, 188, 219, 221, 226-9, 272
Hafod, 205-6
Hagar, 178
Hagstrum, Jean H., 58, 85, 90, 115, 276
Haines, William, 16
Halhed, Nathaniel Brassey, 133, 163
Hamilton, Emma Hart, 275-6
Hamilton, Newburgh, 291-2
Hammer, 237-8, 253-4, 265, 274
Hand, 4, 52, 68, 93, 117-18, 187, 208, 215, 217-19, 226, 228-9, 270, 294
Handel, George Frederick, 284, 290-3
Harper, G. M. 158
Harrison, J. C. F., 134
Hartley, Thomas, 124, 127, 162
Hartman, Geoffrey, 62-3
Hastings, James, 250
Havilah, 167-9
Haydon, Benjamin Robert, 88
Hayley, William, 47, 58-9, 204, 157, 219, 246-9, 252, 259-62, 276, 290
'Hearts of Oak', 222
Heath, James, 86
Hebrew poetry, 290
Hephaistos, 234, 237
Hereford, 205, 241
Herefordshire, 197
Hermes Trismegistus, 254
Herod, 136, 151-2
Herrstrom, Richard, 304
Hertz, John Daniel, 165
Hesiod, 213
Hesketh, Lady, 247
'Hierusalem my happy home', 73-4
Highland Society, 52
Hill, Christopher, 124-5, 147
Hilton, Nelson, 96, 198, 223, 275
Hind, Arthur M., 239
Hindmarsh, Robert, 128-9
Hindu art, 89, 110, 191
Hiram, 152
Hirsch-Reich, Beatrice, 123
Hirst, Désirée, 123
Hisben (Hans Sebald Beham), 87
Hobsbawm, E. J., 121
Hogarth, William, 217, 238
Homer, 43, 284
Hollander, John, 44
Hooper, E. W., 9
Hoover, Suzanne R., 12
Hopkins, Gerard Manley, 234

Horsley, Samuel, 157
Hotten, John Camden, 17
Hughes, William R., 71, 295
Hume, David, 165
Humphry Clinker, 207
Humphry, Ozias, 90
Hunt, John, 4, 218–19
Hunt, Leigh, 4, 218–19
Hunt, Robert, 4, 218–19
Hurlbut, Stephen A., 73, 145
Hyle, 219
Hyle, 52, 135, 208, 215, 217, 219, 221, 226, 228, 261–2, 272–3, 276

Iago, 259
Imagination, 234–5, 273, 275, 283, 305
In illo tempore, 169, 178–80, 182, 189, 196, 223
Incarnation, 104, 292
Indians, American, 242
Industrial Revolution, 243
Ingres, Jean-Auguste-Dominique, 85
International Style of 1800, 84–5, 88
Ireland, 28, 185–6, 266, 269–70
Irenaeus, 121, 127
Isaiah, 239
Islington, 75
Israel, Tribes of, 23, 304
Israelites, 292

Jack, Ian, 88
Jackson, Mary, 109
Jacob, 212–13, 271
James, Henry, 283
Janus, 219
Japan, 214
Jehovah, 105–6, 108, 211
Jennens, Charles, 292
Jericho, 190
Jerusalem, 18, 20, 25, 49–50, 66–7, 75–6, 79–80, 93, 99, 107–8, 111–12, 118, 120, 134–5, 167–70, 172, 175, 178–86, 189–90, 193–5, 200–1, 211, 215–17, 232, 235, 255–6, 278, 287, 293, 294, 300, 307, 314
Jerusalem (city), 120–1, 123–8, 132–3, 136–7, 140, 142–3, 145–7, 149–51, 155–6, 159, 162–3, 165–6, 190, 192, 223
Jerusalem lyrics, 73–4, 144–5, 232
Jesus, 36, 39, 41, 49–50, 66–7, 77, 104, 106, 111, 113–18, 121–2, 125–6, 130, 136, 149–50, 165, 169, 173, 181, 187–9, 191–2, 195, 199, 206–8, 210–11, 219, 228–9, 231, 239, 266, 273–4, 292–3, 298, 304, 312, 314
Jew's Harp House, 75
Joachim of Fiore, 123, 152
Job, 50, 169, 203, 261
John of Patmos, 141–4, 155, 267, 286–7
Johnes, Thomas (of Hafod), 205–6, 241
Johnson, Cowper, Mrs. 246
Johnson, John, 248–9
Johnson, Joseph, 45, 89, 246
Johnson, Mary Lynn, 257, 281
Johnson, Samuel, 58, 60
Johnston, Kenneth R., 277
Jones, H., 130
Jordan River, 270
Joseph (OT), 41, 217
Joseph (NT), 67, 135, 188–9, 293, 307
Josephus, Flavius, 142–3, 153, 159, 165, 194
Joshua, 185, 212
Joyce, James, 23, 136, 166, 186, 269
Julian, John, 74
Jung, C. G., 244
Justin Martyr, 121, 124, 127, 157

Kabbala, 30
Kazin, Alfred, 26
Keats, John, 62, 88, 155, 203, 268
Kermode, Frank, 230
Keynes, Geoffrey, 2–3, 5–7, 10–11, 13, 65, 87, 90, 100, 109, 190, 204, 211, 237, 242, 243, 251, 296, 303
Kimpton, Revd. Edward, 142
King's College Chapel, 151
Kiralis, Karl, 281–2
Knowles, John, 102–3, 106–7
Kox, 217
Kroeber, Karl, 64, 214
Kumbier, William, 34, 42

Labor, 237, 306
Lactantius, 121–2, 127
Lady of the Lake, 271
'Laily Worm and the Mackrel of the Sea, The', 221

Laing, Malcolm, 52
Lamb of God, 20, 40, 99, 168, 293-4
Lambeth, 76, 128, 149
Lang, Paul Henry, 292
Language, 231, 262, 264
Laodicean Period, 126
Last Judgment, 127, 288
Law, William, 127
'Law edition' of Boehme, 98
Lawrence, D. H., 177
Lazarus, 50, 210
Leade, Jane, 126
Leah, 270
Lear, 59, 221
Leavis, F. R., 280
Lediard, Thomas, 159
Legions, 206, 299
Lesnick, Henry, 114, 116, 276
Lessing, Doris, 166
Leviathan, 253
Lewis, C. S., 70
Lightfoot, John, 150-6, 194-5, 285-6
Lily, 93, 180, 188
of Calvary, 183
of Havilah, 171, 180
Limits, 298, 312
Lincoln, 198
Lindberg, Bo Ossian, 87
Lindenberger, Herbert, 57
Linnaeus, 214
Linnell, John, 2-3, 7, 43, 164
Lister, Raymond, 260
Liverpool, 198
Llandaff, Cathedral of, 161
Llywarc Hen, 55-6
Locke, John, 199
Locrine, The Lamentable Tragedy of, 227
Logos, 262
Loins, 202, 273
London, 39, 76-7, 136, 151, 164-6, 191, 218, 267
London Stone, 270
London University Magazine, 13
Longinus, 60
Loom, 141, 256, 258, 264, 275
Lopez-Rey, José, 225
Los, 18, 24, 31, 62, 66, 81-2, 85-6, 90, 92-3, 104, 108, 114, 126, 132, 136, 141, 143, 145-6, 177, 179, 186-7, 192, 195, 201, 203-4, 212-13, 216-19, 221, 223-4, 226, 229-30, 232, 234-45, 251-75, 278, 282-4, 289, 292-4, 299, 301, 305-7, 312-13
Children of, 66
Gate of, 265, 301
Halls of, 59, 89, 160
Printing Press of, 243
Loutherbourg, Philippe-Jacques de, 154
Lowry, Wilson, 164
Lowth, Robert, 45-7, 290
Lubac, Henri de, 144
Luban, 141
Luvah, 35-6, 39-40, 107, 109, 122, 173-5, 196, 200, 204, 216, 222, 225, 228, 254, 264, 282
Lycon, 219
Lyra, Nicolas de, 144

McClennan, Jane, 284
Mace, 238, 269
Mackenzie, Henry, 52
Macklin Bible, 154
Maclagan, E. R. D., and Russell, A. G. B., 10-11
Macpherson, James, 52
Maher, Ralph, 130
Maldon ('Malden'), 38, 76, 198
Malkin, Benjamin Heath, 86, 206
Mallarmé, Stephane, 172
Malvern Hills, 197
Mam-Tor, 135, 228, 272
Manchester, 198
Mandrakes, 305
Mantegna, Andrea, 87
Marcantonio Raimondi, 84, 87, 237
Marlowe, Christopher, 209
Marsh, Edward Garrard, 205, 207
Martha, 210
Marx, Karl, 175
Mary, 67, 134-5, 173, 180, 185, 187-8, 191, 227, 293, 307
Mary Magdalen, 193
Marylebone ('Marybone'), 39, 75
Masons, 129, 162
Maternal Line, 49, 180
Matham, J., 107
Maynard, Dr. George Henry, 142
Mede, Joseph, 124, 127, 148-9, 154-5, 285, 287-9, 303-4
Medici Venus, 229
Medway, River, 198
Melitus, 219
Mellon, Mr. and Mrs. Paul, 14, 197

Mellor, Anne K., 31, 113, 177, 276
Melville, Herman, 63
Merlin, 206, 270–1, 305
Metalworking, 226, 237, 242–3
Methodists, 73, 127, 247–8
Mexico, 28, 226
Michelangelo, 14, 84, 86, 89, 98–9, 106
Miles, Josephine, 34, 61
Millan, Pierre, 101
Mills, 215
Milnes, Richard Monckton, 16
Milton, John, 33, 41–2, 49–53, 58, 61, 69–70, 124, 166, 168, 186, 193, 196, 206, 208, 222, 234, 239–40, 284–5, 291–2, 303, 307
Miner, Paul, 65, 193, 201, 225
Mitchell, W. J. T., 32, 100, 108, 115, 170, 284, 290
Mitelli, Joseph Marie, 103
Monk, Samuel H., 60
Monmouth, 198
Montfaucon, Bernard de, 89, 109
Montgomery, James, 73–4
Montgomeryshire, 197
Moon, 269
Moon-arks, 181, 269, 276
Moor, Edward, 88, 110, 191
Moore, Donald K., 112
Moore, Sir John, 222
Morrison, Peter (of Liverpool), 134
Morton, A. L., 123, 125, 147
Moses, 249, 253
Mosheim, J. L., 122
Mountains, 185, 197–8
Muggletonians, 125
Munby, A. N. L., 157
Mundane Shell, 195, 268, 312
Myers, R. M., 291–2
Myrvian Archailogy, 55

Nanavutty, Piloo, 183
Napoleon, 77, 102
Napoleonic Wars, 27–8, 76–7, 133, 222, 263
Nash, John, 75
Nativity, 238
Natural Religion, 36
Nature, 254, 270
Nayler, James, 125, 271
Nebuchadnezzar, 289
Neoplatonism, 219
Nesbit, C., 184
New Critics, 281
New Jerusalem, 126–8, 131, 136, 141, 143–4, 146–8, 161–5, 207, 267
New Jerusalem Church, 128, 131
Newton, Isaac, 157, 159
Niclas, Henry, 146–7
Nicolson, Benedict, 238
Nicolson, Marjorie Hope, 197
Nietzsche, Friedrich Wilhelm, 175
Nineveh, 109
Noah, 269
Nordenskjöld, Augustus, 128
Norns, 189, 225
Norwich, 198
Novalis, 13
Number symbolism, 18, 280
Nuremberg Chronicle, 105–6

Oak, 208, 222
Oedipus complex, 270, 305
Og, 185, 270
Ololon, 210
Oothoon, 134, 185–8, 222
Orc, 109, 213, 234
Orcagna, 88
Origen, 144, 287
Osiris, 88
Ossian, 52–3, 60–1
Ostriker, Alicia, 12, 29, 34, 38, 52, 177, 206, 208, 232
Othello, 259
Ottley, William Young, 7, 88, 105
Owen, William, *see* Pugh, Owen
Oxford, 186–7, 205–7, 229, 300–1
Oxford Street, 136

Palm, 208
Pareus, David, 148–9, 285–8
Paris, 174, 264
Parousia, 231
Parris, Leslie, 184
Pathos, 57–61, 66–9, 172, 263
Paul, 136, 178, 204, 254
Paulson, Ronald, 238
Peak, the, 182–3, 198
Pearson, John, 9
Pelfrey, Patricia, 242
Pemaenmawr, 198
Perceval, Milton O., 25
Persephone, 109–10
Persepolis, 109
Peter, 195
Petrarchan tradition, 102, 109–10

Philadelphian period, 126
Philadelphian Society, 126
Philistines, 292
Phillips, Michael, 12
Piers Plowman, 123
Pinto, V. de Sola, 281
Plato, 35, 98, 106, 170, 256
Plinlimmon, 197
Plow, 211
Pluto, 109-10
Poe, Edgar Allen, 252
Polypus, 211, 214-15
Poole, River, 196
Poplar, 76
Poussin, Nicolas, 102-3
Pradus, 144, 146, 158-9
Predestination, 249-50
Prid, W., 73
Priestley, Joseph, 124, 132
Primrose Hill, 75
Prophets of Avignon, 128-30, 162
Proserpine, 109
Prospero, 252
Psychomachia, 173, 235
Pugh, Owen, 54-7, 241-2

Quakers, 271
Quaternary, 158
Quennell, Peter, 271
Quinlan, Maurice J., 248
Quintilian, 58

Ragan, 221
Rahab, 40-1, 68, 82, 100, 102, 190-1, 194, 224, 306
  sons and daughters of, 168
Raine, Kathleen, 30
Ranters, 123, 125, 147
Raphael, 84, 86, 89
Reason, 199, 202, 215, 245, 275
Reece, Richard, M. D., 133-4
Reeves, Marjorie, 121-3
Regan, 221
Regent's Park, 75
Reid, Thomas, 252
Rembrandt, 116
Resurrection, 211, 264, 292-3
Reuben, 104, 217, 219, 270-2, 298-9, 304-5
Reynolds, Sir Joshua, 85, 102
Rhine, River, 76
Richmond, Hugh, 106
Rintrah, 305
Ripa, Cesare, 111
Roach, Richard, 126
Robetta, 105-6
Robinson, Henry Crabb, 52, 75, 98, 99, 134
Roe, Albert S., 178
Rogers, Thomas, 73, 145
Romano, Giulio, 14, 84
Romney, George, 58-9, 85, 246, 275-6
Rosamund, 184-5, 188
  Rosamund's Bower, 182, 187
Roscoe, Thomas, 105
Rose, 180, 188
Rose, E. J., 83, 252, 282-3
Rosenblum, Robert, 84-5
Rossetti, Dante Gabriel, 16-17, 19
Rossetti, William Michael, 16, 19, 100, 151
Rosso (Il Rosso Fiorentino), 101
Rousseau, Jean-Jacques, 71
Rubens, Peter Paul, 83, 85, 115
Ruskin, John, 293
Russell, A. G. B., 114
Russell, Norma, 247

Sabrina, 222, 227
Sade, Marquis de, 226
Sadeler, Jean, 87
St. Erasmus, 102-3
St. Gregory, 144
St. Jerome, 144
St. John's Wood, 75-6
St. Pancras, 76
St. Paul's Cathedral, 112, 181
St. Victor, Richard of, 144
Saintsbury, George, 45
Salisbury Plain, 216
Salmon, Joseph, 130
Samson, 292
Sarah, 178
Satan, 4, 71-2, 76-7, 115, 186, 190, 193, 203, 208, 218, 231, 239-40, 262, 304
Saviour, 42
Schiff, Gert, 105
Scholfield, John, 217
Schorer, Mark, 27, 188
Scotland, 204, 229
Second Coming, 129
Seekers, 147
Selden, George, 196
Selfhood, 118, 211, 215, 232, 272, 305

Selsey, 205
Serpent, 107–10
Serpent Temples, 197, 276–7
Sexual division, 106–7
Shaddai, 108, 267
Shadow of Jerusalem, 192
Shakespeare, William, 33, 42, 70, 75, 176, 221–2, 227, 252, 254, 259
Sharp, William, 86, 130–1, 134
Shechem, 186
Shelley, Percy Bysshe, 63, 232, 254
Shiloh, 133, 141, 181, 272
Sihon, 185
Simon Magus, 254
Sirens, 190, 255
Skiddaw, 219
Skofield, 29, 41, 217, 276
Slavery, 127–8, 130, 186, 198, 207, 294
Sloss, D. J. and Wallis, J. P. R., 10–11, 21–3, 25, 28, 34, 104, 194, 231, 254, 279–80
Smaragdine Tablets, 254
Smart, Christopher, 47–9, 284, 290–1
Smollett, Tobias, 207
Snowdon, 197
Socrates, 219
Solomon, 136, 142, 150–2, 158, 160–2
Sons of Albion, 18, 23, 27, 41, 65, 68, 118, 167, 180, 193, 197, 208, 211–17, 221, 223, 228–9, 235, 239, 261, 269, 283, 292, 294, 305–6
Sons of Jerusalem, 184
Sons of Los, 262, 266–7, 294
Sophocles, 213
Southcott, Joanna, 131, 133–5, 227–8, 272
Southey, Robert, 2, 54–5, 131, 241
Spaces of Erin, 185, 253, 266
Spectre, 18, 63, 65, 68, 80, 102, 141, 183, 190, 208, 224, 251–2, 268–9, 275
Spectre of Albion, 66, 76–7, 173, 175, 199–200, 210, 233, 245, 258, 264, 298
Spectre of Los, 66, 79, 173, 175, 215, 234, 244–5, 249, 251–5, 259–61, 264–6, 273, 275, 282–3, 289, 294, 300
Spectre of Urthona, 240, 253, 261, 273
Spectre Sons, 193, 211, 217, 294
Spectrous Chaos, 298
Speed, John, 100
Spenser, Edmund, 172, 198, 303
Spiller, Robert E., 248
Spindle, 111, 182, 294
Spinning, 275–6
Spinning Aphrodite, 275
Spiritual Franciscans, 123
Spurzheim, Dr. J. G., 246
Stanhope, George, 145
Star of Bethlehem, 183
Star of David, 211
Stars, 203
States, 24, 46, 189, 197, 272, 283, 298, 312
Stead, William Force, 47, 49
Stedman, John Gabriel, 251
Sterne, Laurence, 290
Stevenson, W. H., 12, 29, 59, 140, 171, 183, 204, 207, 211, 213, 221, 226, 283
Stonehenge, 160, 216
Stothard, Thomas, 86, 142, 187
Story, A. T., 43
Stukeley, William, 276–7
Sublime, the, 57–60, 61–3, 65–9, 172, 274
Suhr, Elmer G., 275
Sumeria, 208
Summerson, John, 75, 164
Sun, 116, 191, 231, 269, 274, 301
Sunflower, 190–1
Surrey, 272
Sussex, 205, 248, 260–1, 294
Swedenborg, Emanuel, 77, 114–15, 125, 127, 129, 131, 161–3, 187, 190, 210, 221, 231, 250, 286
  Swedenborgians, 13, 20, 77, 115, 127–31, 207, 210
Swift, Jonathan, 290
Swinburne, Algernon Charles, 17–18, 34, 283
Sybilline Prophecies, 122
Synagogue of Satan, 129–30

Tabernacle, 145, 149, 154–5, 159–60, 223
Taliesin, 55
Talmud, 124
Tannenbaum, Leslie, 45
Tany, Thomas, 147
Tassie's Gems, 87
Tasso, Torquato, 123, 216

Tatham, Frederick, 3, 8, 14–15, 60, 176
Tayler, Irene, 65, 177, 225
Taylor, Edward, 274
Taylor, Thomas, 98–9
Temple, 136–7, 140–6, 149, 151–5, 157–62, 192, 194, 201
Thames, River, 198
Tharmas, 35, 79–80, 122, 174, 192, 201, 213, 254, 282, 287
Tertullian, 121–2, 127
Theosophical Society, 127–9, 131
Thomas, Dylan, 75
Thomas, Revd. Joseph, 184
Thompson, E. P., 125, 133, 224
Thrupp, Sylvia L., 121
Thune, Nils, 126, 147
Thurston, John, 184
Time, 185, 234, 267
  and Space, 183, 269, 307
Tintoretto, 106–7
Tirzah, 40–1, 69, 100, 102–3, 190, 193, 217, 224, 226, 306
Titian, 83–5, 200
Titus, 71
Todd, Ruthven, 6, 16, 34, 73, 83, 87, 94, 180–1, 205, 241, 276
Toland, John, 160
Tolstoy, Count Leo, 283
Tomb of Albion, 185, 209–10
Tongs, 238, 253, 274–5
Toomey, Deirdre, 100–1
Topographical symbolism, 18, 23, 76–7, 197–8, 218, 269–70
Transfiguration, the, 181
Treaties of Paris, 264
Tree, Albion's, 211, 261
Tree of Life, 207, 301
Tree of Mystery, 199
Tribes of Israel, 269
Trollope, Anthony, 194
Truchsessian Gallery, 84
Tulk, Charles Augustus, 13
Turner, Dawson, 2, 90
Tuveson, Ernest Lee, 120
Tyburns Brook, 198
Typho the Jew, 124

Uccello, Paolo, 202
Ulro, 81, 215, 271, 279, 283, 305
United Irishmen, 266
Universities, 229
Urania, 42
Urizen, 24, 52, 79, 82, 108, 173–5, 198–200, 234, 254, 260, 269
Urthona, 80, 82, 122, 235, 244, 254, 256, 260, 272–5

Vala, 18, 20, 25, 35–6, 68, 79, 93, 99–103, 108–12, 134, 153, 167–73, 175, 178–83, 186–96, 200, 216, 219, 224, 228, 232, 235, 255, 261, 264–5, 268, 276, 278, 292–4, 298, 300, 306
Valkyrie, 193, 225
Van Heemskeerck, Martin, 158
Van Leyden, Lucas, 87
Vasari, Giorgio, 237
Veil, 20, 111, 143, 149–50, 153, 155, 168–9, 175, 181, 194–6, 222–4, 228
Velázquez, Diego, 225
Venetian painting, 17, 107
Venus, 229, 275
Verulam, 204, 214
Vikings, 198
Villalpandus, 144, 146, 152, 154, 158–9
Visionary theatre, 285–7, 288
Vogler, Thomas A., 1
Voltaire, 71–2, 199
Vos, Martin de, 183
Vulcan, 234, 237

Wadström, Carl Bernhard, 128, 207
Wainewright, Thomas Griffiths, 3
Wales, 206, 241–2
Wandering Jew, 272
Wardle, Ralph M., 188
Warner, Janet A., 114, 182–3
Warner, Nicholas O., 181, 269
Warner, Revd. Richard, 205–7
Warton, Thomas, 60
Wasser, Henry H., 188
Watchman, 234, 238–9
Watts, Isaac, 74
Weaving, 101–2, 182, 224–5, 256, 275–6
Welsh poetry, 54–7, 241
Westminster, 39
Westminster Abbey, 112, 181
Wheat, 211
Wheel(s), 140, 156–7, 214–16, 304
White line etching and engraving, 5, 94, 99, 110, 116, 208, 275, 298–9
Whitman, Walt, 44
Whore of Babylon, 187, 190

Wicksteed, Joseph, 28, 98, 100, 102, 107, 113, 116, 169, 180–1, 183, 191, 222, 274, 276–7, 281
Wilkie, Brian, 257, 281
Willan's Farm, 75
William I, 76
William Blake Trust, 10, 90
Wilson, Mona, 94
Winchester, 229
Winchester, Elhanan, 132
Wine-press of Luvah, 229
Winstanley, Gerrard, 125
Witke, Joanne, 284–5
Wittkower, Rudolf, 145, 159
Wittreich, Joseph A., Jr., 124, 284–5, 291, 303
Woad, 204
Wolds, the, 197
Wöfflin, Heinrich, 31
Wollstonecraft, Mary, 188
Woman, 24, 312
Wood (of Bath), John, 152, 158–9
Wood, Polly, 176–7
Woodstock, 187
Worcestershire, 197
Wordsworth, William, 29, 52, 57, 62–3, 303
World week, 121–5
Worm, 77, 219, 221, 229, 272
Worrall, David, 100, 183, 198
Wright, John, 130–1
Wright of Derby, Joseph, 238
Wright, Thomas, 166, 249
Wyatt, David, 180
Wykeham, William of, 229

Yeats, William Butler, 23, 70, 136, 169, 186, 202, 260, 267; *see also* Ellis and Yeats
York, 204
Youngson, A. J., 164

Zelophehad, 190, 203
Zerubabel, 136
Zeus, 213
Zoas, 80, 153, 178, 183, 197, 201, 211, 231, 235, 254, 273, 282–3